The Wrong of Injustice

Studies in Feminist Philosophy is designed to showcase cutting-edge monographs and collections that display the full range of feminist approaches to philosophy, that push feminist thought in important new directions, and that display the outstanding quality of feminist philosophical thought.

The Wrong of Injustice

DEHUMANIZATION AND ITS ROLE IN FEMINIST PHILOSOPHY

Mari Mikkola

OXFORD
UNIVERSITY PRESS

OXFORD
UNIVERSITY PRESS

Oxford University Press is a department of the University of Oxford. It furthers
the University's objective of excellence in research, scholarship, and education
by publishing worldwide. Oxford is a registered trade mark of Oxford University
Press in the UK and certain other countries.

Published in the United States of America by Oxford University Press
198 Madison Avenue, New York, NY 10016, United States of America.

Library of Congress Cataloging-in-Publication Data
Names: Mikkola, Mari, author.
Title: The wrong of injustice : dehumanization and its role in feminist philosophy /
Mari Mikkola.
Description: New York : Oxford University Press, 2016. |
Series: Studies in feminist philosophy | Includes bibliographical references and index.
Identifiers: LCCN 2015049044 | ISBN 9780190601072 (hardcover : alk. paper) |
ISBN 9780190601089 (pbk. : alk. paper) | ISBN 9780190601096 (ebook (updf)) |
ISBN 9780190601102 (ebook (epub))
Subjects: LCSH: Humanism. | Feminist theory. | Social justice.
Classification: LCC B821 .M56 2016 | DDC 305.4201—dc23
LC record available at https://lccn.loc.gov/2015049044

1 3 5 7 9 8 6 4 2
Paperback printed by WebCom, Inc., Canada
Hardback printed by Bridgeport National Bindery, Inc., United States of America

{ CONTENTS }

{ ACKNOWLEDGMENTS }

This book is a culmination of many years of thinking and writing about gender, feminist philosophy, and injustice. Numerous people have helped me along the way by providing much-needed constructive critique as well as (both philosophical and professional) inspiration and encouragement to continue working on feminist philosophy. Feminist readers will no doubt immediately notice that the book's title is inspired by Louise Antony's wonderful 1998 paper " 'Human Nature' and Its Role in Feminist Theory." This paper has also inspired many of the questions that I address in the pages to come. Some parts of the book have previously been published, and I acknowledge permission to reprint in revised and abridged form the following earlier works: "Ontological Commitments, Sex, and Gender," published in Charlotte Witt, ed., *Feminist Metaphysics*, (Springer, 2011), 67–83; "Dehumanization," published in Thom Brooks, ed., *New Waves in Ethics* (Palgrave Macmillan, 2011), 128–149; "Gender Concepts and Intuitions," *Canadian Journal of Philosophy* (December 2009), available online: http://wwww.tandfonline.com/10.1353/cjp.0.0060; "Feminist Perspectives on Sex and Gender," in *Stanford Encyclopedia of Philosophy*, Summer 2008 / Fall 2012, available online: http://plato.stanford.edu/entries/feminism-gender/; and "Elizabeth Spelman, Gender Realism, and Women," *Hypatia* 21 (2006): 77–96.

I have presented draft versions of this book's materials at numerous conferences, workshops, and reading groups over the past few years—in fact, too many to name individually. My greatest debt is thus to the fantastic philosophers and feminists with whom I have discussed my work on these occasions—some discussions that took place many, many years ago now (and I apologize to those I may forget to mention): Dave Archard, Tuukka Asplund, Albert Atkin, Thom Brooks, Robin Celikates, Esa Díaz-León, Frank Hindriks, Miguel Hoeltje, Jules Holroyd, Rebekka Hufendiek, Rahel Jaeggi, Daniel James, Rosanna Keefe, Tine Kley, Heiner Koch, Kathleen Lennon, Dan López de Sa, Steve Makin, Alan Millar, Simone Miller, Johanna Müller, Lina Papadaki, Clea Rees, Beate Roessler, Komarine Romdenh-Romluc, Friederike Schmitz, Mark Sinclair, Michael Smith, Bob Stern, Natalie Stoljar, Alison Stone, Alessandra Tanesini, Nancy Tuana, Raphael van Riel, Eva von Redecker, Jay Wallace, Jon Webber, Garrath Williams, Charlotte Witt, and Julia Zakkou. I am especially indebted to two stellar feminist philosophers: first, to Jenny Saul for her challenging philosophical reflections on my work and for her continued support that goes much beyond her past role as my *Doktormutter* (as she would be called in Germany); second, to Sally Haslanger for her tremendous philosophical and personal support while working on this project (and others).

I am also grateful to the participants in my research colloquium at the Humboldt-Universität zu Berlin for having read the entire manuscript and for having provided painstakingly detailed, difficult, and challenging comments and questions: Sophia Ansorena, Lisa Baurmann, Max Bohnet, Melanie Brazzell, Francesca Bunkenborg, Hilkje Hänel, Cathrin Höfs, Sandra Köhrich, and Resa-Philip Lunau. Francesca also helped me with the preparation of the final manuscript. A debt of gratitude goes to my editors at Oxford University Press: Cheshire Calhoun and Lucy Randall. Working with them has been a joy, and their professionalism is unparalleled. The two anonymous referees for this book provided further significant challenges that greatly improved my thinking along the way.

Finally, my partner Bas is due special praise and thanks for having put up with me over the past few years with all the growing pains and Finnish "Angry Bird" moments that completing this book has brought along.

The Wrong of Injustice

Dehumanization as the Wrong of Social Injustice

1.1. Introduction

The definition of *social injustice* is somewhat like the definition of *pornography* according to Justice Stewart: we know it when we encounter it. But, of course, people disagree on whether what we have encountered is an instance of injustice or not. Here are some putative cases of contemporary structural social injustices.

- Constraints that female primary caretakers of small children face in their career options due to the lack of affordable child care and flexible working conditions.
- Restricting women's access to abortions in some US states by limiting the number of family-planning clinics or cutting their funding.
- Disadvantages and persecution that members of certain ethno-racialized groups face due to prejudicial and arbitrary stop-and-search policies.
- The differential and detrimental treatment faced by same-sex couples and trans* people on the housing market relative to heterosexuals and nontrans* individuals.
- Patronizing and demeaning ways in which people with mobility restrictions are viewed and treated due to false stereotypical beliefs about their supposed "defective" cognitive abilities.

These are exemplary of structural and sometimes hard-to-detect oppression, domination, and discrimination that are based on socially salient identifications—for me, the core forms of contemporary social injustice. With such examples in mind, this book asks: what makes these three forms of social injustice wrongful? Is there a single wrongness-making feature of oppression, domination, and discrimination due to social kind membership? If so, what is it? I will approach these questions from a distinctly feminist perspective. Thus, the book asks further related and more specific questions: why is sexist oppression of women wrongful? What are the wrongness-making features of patriarchal damage done to women? What does the wrongfulness of gender injustice consist in? In thinking about what normatively grounds contemporary social injustices, the book puts forward two substantive and related conclusions. To begin with, it argues for a paradigm shift in focus away from feminist philosophy that is organized around the gender concept *woman*, and toward feminist philosophy that is humanist. Politically effective feminist theory requires ways to elucidate how and why patriarchy damages women, and to articulate and defend feminism's critical claims in order to justify "its positive vision of equitable and sustaining human relationships" (Antony 1998, 67). In order to meet these normative demands, I argue, an influential theoretical outlook has emerged: most basically, that for emancipatory purposes, feminist philosophers should articulate a thick conception of the concept *woman*. However, I contend, we should resist this move. Part I of the book thus advances the view that we should stop taking *woman* as the organizing notion of feminist philosophy and reframe our analyses of injustice in humanist terms.

The book's second substantive argument continues on from this and spells out my humanist alternative to the more prevalent gender focus in feminist philosophy. I argue for a vision of humanist feminism that is normatively grounded in a particular notion of *dehumanization*, which I develop in the pages to come. With this notion, I go on to explicate the wrongness-making feature of social injustices, both in general and of those due to patriarchy. Part II then provides a regimentation of social injustice from a feminist perspective in order to spell out the specifics of the proposed humanist feminism and to demonstrate how it improves some nonfeminist analyses of injustice too. For me, dehumanization undergirds the wrongfulness of different forms of injustice (oppression, discrimination, domination) in their various contours (sexist, racist, heteronormative, trans*phobic, ableist, and classist injustices). Dehumanization is not another form of injustice—rather, it is that which makes forms of social injustice *unjust*. Since dehumanization not only normatively underpins feminist philosophy but also elucidates the wrong of social injustice per se, the current work is about first-order moral theory, feminist philosophy as well as social and political philosophy. Let me briefly introduce next in more detail the book's two main arguments.

1.2. Against the Gender Controversy

A major theoretical presumption constituting common ground among different feminist positions is that feminist philosophical work should orient itself around gender concepts. Feminism is said to be the movement to end the sexist oppression of women (hooks 2000, 26). We can understand the term 'woman' in this claim as a sex term: it picks out human females and being a human female depends on various biological and anatomical features (like chromosomes, or genitalia). However, in response to biologically deterministic accounts that took bodily anatomy to determine all behavioral, psychological, and sociopolitical features of women, feminists in the 1960s and 1970s began using 'woman' differently: not as a sex term, but as a gender term. Being a woman or a man was no longer considered to depend on the kind of anatomy one has but on particular social and cultural factors, like one's social position, or the amount of masculinity and femininity one exhibits. In so doing, feminists distinguished sex (being female/male) from gender (being a woman/a man).

This distinction originally enabled feminist theorists to do much-needed emancipatory and explanatory work. It showed vividly how behavioral traits and social roles are socially founded. However, over the past few decades, the idea of gender has taken a life of its own, and (I contend) one that very much goes beyond the theoretical role that it originally played. I refer to this as "the gender controversy." The story goes as follows: since genders and gender roles were taken to depend on social factors (broadly conceived), and it is the social realm that feminism aims to alter, the gender concept *woman* became feminism's defining concept both theoretically and politically. It became commonplace to treat *woman* as *the* concept around which feminist politics is organized and the term 'woman' as that which picks out the category that makes up feminism's subject matter. During the past few decades of feminist theorizing, though, the focus on the concept *woman* has generated two clusters of puzzles: one semantic, the other ontological. Both puzzles have their historical and conceptual roots in (what I term) 'gender skeptic' views. First, according to some, *woman* is ultimately meaningless and necessarily open-ended, which renders any attempt to define it futile and even politically counterproductive (Butler 1999 [original 1990]). Second, the social kind of women does not exist in any meaningful sense: either its existence is illusory (Butler 1999) or the kind is so hopelessly fragmented that any talk of women in plural is meaningless (Spelman 1990 [original 1988]). These influential gender skeptical views, and various other critiques of the sex/gender distinction, have generated the following clusters of puzzles.

- *Semantic puzzle*: Given that ordinary language users tend not to distinguish sex and gender (treating 'woman' largely as a sex term, or a mixture of social and biological features), what precisely are feminists talking about when they talk about women? What are the necessary and sufficient conditions that the concept *woman* encodes, if any such conditions exist to begin with?
- *Ontological puzzle*: How should we understand the category of women that is meant to undergird feminist political solidarity, if there are no necessary and sufficient conceptual conditions

underlying our gender talk? Do women make up a genuine kind, or simply a gerrymandered and random collection of individuals? What kinds of entities are gender and sex anyway? Are there *really* women and men, if gender is (in some substantial sense) socially constructed?

Feminist philosophers have provided numerous answers to these questions over the past few decades (e.g., Alcoff 2006; Benhabib 1992; Frye 1996; Haslanger 2000; 2003a; 2003b; 2005; Heyes 2000; Martin 1994; Mikkola 2007; Saul 2012a; Stoljar 1995; 2011; Stone 2004; Tanesini 1996; Witt 2011a; 2011b; Young 1997; Zack 2005). Nonetheless, there is precious little agreement on these semantic and ontological issues. In response to the former, some have argued that the concept *woman* is a cluster concept (Hale 1996; Stoljar 1995; 2000) and that the term 'woman' is a family resemblance term akin to 'game' (Heyes 2000). Others have claimed that, although the concept cannot be defined by appealing to our muddled and varied everyday intuitions and use, it can be defined pragmatically given feminist political goals (Haslanger 2000). It has further been proposed that the term 'woman' might be contextually shifty, sometimes picking out individuals on the basis of sex features, other times on the basis of gender features (Saul 2012a; for an opposing view, see Bettcher 2013). Whatever way the semantic questions are answered, all parties to the debate agree on one thing: that gender is not innate, but socially constructed or constituted. They also (if not explicitly, then implicitly) hold that the answer to the semantic puzzle tells us something about women's social kind that can help us resolve the ontological puzzle. But, given the variety of responses to the semantic issue, feminist views on the nature of gendered kinds vary as well. Some argue for gender nominalist positions that deny there to be something women qua women share; rather, they seek to unify women's social kind by appealing to a variety of external relations (e.g., Frye 1996; Stoljar 1995; 2011; Young 1997). Others have argued for gender realist positions that take there to be something women qua women share (e.g., Alcoff 2006; Haslanger 2000; Witt 2011a; Zack 2005). But the way in which we should understand that "something" differs from one feminist philosopher to the next.[1]

The semantic and ontological puzzles are alive and well—the contemporary philosophical discourse on gender, then, is a controversy. This controversy is not considered to be just an intellectual exercise in philosophy of

---

[1] Gender realism and more standard metaphysical realism are committed to slightly different views. For instance, contemporary gender realists do not hold that there exists some universal (strictly speaking identical and repeatable) property of *being a woman*. Nevertheless, they hold that women as women share some—usually a multiply realizable and complex—feature. I will have more to say about the specifics of gender realism in the chapters to come.

language and metaphysics, though. Rather, it is said to generate serious political concerns. Many have found the inability to pick out women's social kind (feminism's purported subject matter) and the kind's subsequent fragmentation problematic for political reasons (e.g., Alcoff 2006; Benhabib 1992; Frye 1996; Haslanger 2000; Heyes 2000; Martin 1994; Mikkola 2007; Stoljar 1995; Stone 2004; Tanesini 1996; Young 1997; Zack 2005). The possibility that—strictly speaking—this kind might be an ontological illusion appears to pull the rug out from under feminist politics. As Iris Marion Young puts it, unless there is "some sense in which 'woman' is the name of a social collective [feminism represents], there is nothing specific to feminist politics" (1997, 13). Over the past two decades, feminist philosophers have tackled the semantic and ontological puzzles precisely to avoid such politically paralyzing consequences. Some then take articulating a sufficiently thick notion of *woman*, and elucidating an inclusive category of women, to be prerequisites for effective feminist politics. In recent years, a rich literature has emerged that aims to conceptualize gender (e.g., Alcoff 2006; Frye 1996; 2011; Haslanger 2000; Heyes 2000; Stoljar 1995; 2011; Sveinsdóttir 2011; Young 1997; Zack 2005). This literature (among others) aims to respond to the two puzzles in order to make good conceptions of *woman* and women's social kind membership that support and ground normative demands of emancipatory feminism (for example, justifying feminist action on behalf of women as a group).

It is against this backdrop that (I contend) contemporary gender theorizing has taken a life of its own, and one that very much goes beyond the original role that gender played in feminist theory. Articulating a thick notion of *woman* has become a desideratum and a pivotal first step of an acceptable theory of gender. As Linda Alcoff puts it, the concept *woman* is "the central concept of feminist theory" in being "the necessary point of departure for any feminist theory and feminist politics, predicated as these are on the transformation of women's lived experience in contemporary culture and the reevaluation of social theory and practice from a woman's point of view" (2006, 133). A conception of *woman* should be thick enough to support specific normative demands, which include being able to elucidate how and why patriarchy damages women, to justify feminist critical claims about extant states of affairs, and to ground a vision of a feminist future. An account of what it is to be a woman ought to enable theorists to conceive of feminism's subject matter by providing a way to conceptualize women's social kind or category—perhaps even enabling us to articulate the grounds for feminist political solidarity. So the theoretical outlook that I am highlighting trades on certain prescriptive, pragmatic, and political considerations. First, in order to support normative emancipatory feminist claims, we ought to answer the question "What is it to be a woman?" in some sufficiently substantive sense. For instance, explicating womanhood negatively as nonmanhood will not do precisely because such an explication is empty: in knowing that women are not-men, we are none the wiser about those social conditions that render females *women*. Second, in order to provide an adequate theory of gender, feminists are faced with a pragmatic issue: since gender concepts are not carved in nature's joints, how is it that we ought to define womanhood, so that the definition will be theoretically helpful? Third, settling this pragmatic issue usually hinges on some political considerations that pertain to explicating patriarchy's damage, justifying feminist critical claims, and providing future visions of gender justice. Since womanhood is not carved in nature's joints, it is up to us—feminist philosophers—to offer a theory of socially constructed gender that is thick enough to be politically helpful. But, as demonstrated above, there is precious little agreement on what would be the proper or most helpful conceptualization of *woman*.

Relative to this philosophical background, I argue for giving up the gender controversy. As I see it, this dispute is theoretically bankrupt and intractable: the semantic and ontological puzzles have generated an analytical impasse that looks unsurpassable. Given the common theoretical underpinnings of extant feminist accounts of gender, and the profound disagreements that exist over gender concepts, I see little reason to suppose that continuing the debate will generate the desired results. Clearly, the lack of consensus is not a reason to stop theorizing; but this lack has become distracting, and it is hampering progress in feminist thinking about effective responses to social injustice. Thus, I aim to motivate a refocusing of feminist work in the hope that this will yield more fruitful feminist political and social philosophy: in short, to argue for a paradigm shift from gender-focused to humanist feminism.

Now one might immediately wonder whether the gender controversy really is a pressing issue facing feminist philosophy. One might point out that feminist philosophers have offered theories of injustice that appear to have none of the above commitments, and not all feminist philosophers explicitly start their theorizing from an analysis of the concept *woman*. Such freestanding feminist accounts of injustice then appear to undermine my diagnosis of the state of the debate, and it seems mistaken to claim that feminist articulations of injustice necessarily start with an analysis of *woman*. Further, it may seem that worries about "the woman question" were more prominent a decade ago, and that feminist philosophers are no longer that concerned about elucidating the content of gender concepts. Have I not then misdiagnosed the problem? I think not. First, my claim is not that feminist articulations of injustice must start with an analysis of *woman*, or they will surely fail. In fact, one of my arguments in this book is that we can provide a theory of injustice from a feminist perspective without having to elucidate a thick social conception of *woman*. Still, as a matter of fact, numerous feminist philosophers over the past two decades have proceeded to articulate precisely such a thick conception for feminist political purposes, which is why the proper content of gender concepts has become a feminist philosophical controversy. Second, there has been a steady stream of work over the past couple of decades and over the past couple of years (e.g., Bach 2012; Frye 2011; Saul 2012a; Stoljar 2011; Sveinsdóttir 2011; Witt 2011a) that aims to elucidate what it is to be a woman in order to support feminist political claims. If the proper or most helpful understanding of gender is not a feminist philosophical point of contention, these recent analyses of *woman* look puzzling and unmotivated. Even those who no longer tackle this issue "head-on" do not consider the debate to be settled, or no longer in need of being resolved. The issue of how we should cash out a politically helpful conception of *woman* is still very much a live one, which recent feminist philosophical work attests to. Finally, as long as we take the social gender concept *woman* to be the central category framing feminist philosophical work, we will be pressed to provide an analysis of it. Subsequently, concerns about how to grasp *woman* are present and lurking in the background even of putatively freestanding accounts of gender injustice, and of feminist philosophical work that does not wear the above theoretical presumptions on its sleeve (sections 7.3.3 and 7.3.4 discuss this at more length). Thus, although the adherence to the above outlook is sometimes implicit, this does not undermine my claim. Part of my project is to make the influence of certain theoretical commitments explicit and to critically examine our adherence to them. These commitments linger on for as long as feminist philosophers accept (as Marilyn Frye puts it) that it is "a fundamental claim of feminism that women [as a group] are oppressed" (1983, 1). Since contemporary feminist philosophers clearly accept this, they will be pressed to provide an analysis of *woman* to figure in the theoretical building blocks of emancipatory feminism. The gender controversy is far from over (something I will say more about in subsequent chapters).

The take-home message of the book's first part, then, is this: feminist philosophers should surpass the gender controversy and give up certain theoretical commitments that perpetuate it. We should change the terms of our debate, so that the gender concept *woman* no longer fixes the theoretical focal point of emancipatory feminism. Rather, we should articulate feminism's normative basis anew and in a way that avoids the conceptual stalemate of the current debate. This is where dehumanization comes in.

1.3. Going Beyond Gender: Humanist Feminism

Part I aims to motivate the feminist philosophical paradigm shift briefly introduced above. Part II elucidates this shift and offers a vision of humanist feminism. My contention is that gender concepts should no longer be taken to support feminist normative claims and demands: in order to speak on behalf of women, to articulate patriarchy's damage, to criticize the status quo, and to frame theories of resistance, we need not settle the gender controversy, as presumed by those views examined in Part I. These tasks will be undertaken by a particular conception of *dehumanization*, which I develop in Part II. Let me briefly introduce the idea behind my proposed humanist feminism. It is made up of two interconnected parts: one normative, the other social theoretical. The normative part is comprised of the developed notion of *dehumanization* (of which I will shortly say more). The social theory part contains a regimentation of injustice: spelling out the forms and contours of injustice. Specifically with respect to feminist concerns, this regimentation hinges on my first substantive argument: that feminist philosophers surpass the gender controversy and give up certain theoretical commitments that perpetuate it. We should no longer take a thick conception of *woman* to be central to feminist philosophical work. And contra those positions examined in Part I, the work of supporting feminist normative claims and political demands in the name of women will be undertaken by my proposed conception of *dehumanization*.

What is my proposal, then? In short: an act or a treatment is dehumanizing if and only if it is an indefensible setback to some of our legitimate human interests, where this setback constitutes a moral injury. This understanding differs from more traditionally Kantian accounts. To begin with, dehumanization for me is not about an assault on "our" human dignity, or value as Kantian ends in ourselves. I will have more to say about this in the chapters to come, but roughly my reasons are as follows: first, there is no clear and obvious way to understand the notion of *human dignity*, and philosophers often appeal to dignity as a justificatory tool without further elucidating what this amounts to. Appeals to "our" value and dignity (as I see it) are often opaque and unclear, where the specifics of these notions simply come down to individual philosophers' prior nontransparent metaphilosophical commitments. But given my theoretical commitments (to be outlined shortly), I will avoid appeals to dignity and worth as grounding the wrong of injustice. Moreover, on my account, dehumanization is a characteristic of *acts* and ways of *treating* others; it is not about objectification or treating someone as a mere means in a Kantian sense that would render the individual *dehumanized*. I may be treated in dehumanizing ways that underpin the oppression that I face; but (as I see it) this does not turn on others taking me as something as opposed to someone. This is because instances of contemporary social injustices work via setbacks to *human* agency. Hence, in order for legitimate human interests to be violable, it is a necessary precondition to acknowledge these interests as being those of *someone* (not of something).[2] Thus, I hold that we should not

---

[2] In this sense, my view is very much put forward in the spirit of Kate Manne's (2014) recent discussion of the events in Ferguson, MO. In her view, these events involved "punishing humanity" that only works if we first affirm the humanity of the affected people of color. If you like, it is the affirmation of humanity that renders its subsequent punishing possible.

understand dehumanization as being about reducing someone to something. Thinking about dehumanization attaching to actions and ways of treating others can better explicate what goes wrong with social injustice.

My argumentative strategy also differs from existing feminist accounts, although I draw on some prior humanist ideas in feminist philosophy. Louise Antony (1998; 2000) argues that there is a need for humanism in feminism. Her basic thought is this: in order to say what is wrongful about patriarchy, feminists must affirm women's humanity by asserting that they are "essentially beings of a certain kind" (namely, humans) and that "there are modes of treatment that are appropriate, and others that are inappropriate, for beings of this kind" (Antony 2000, 11). Antony takes Martha Nussbaum's well-known capabilities approach to exhibit this sort of humanist thinking. Nussbaum explicitly seeks to define *human being* as a normative ethical concept in order to explicate treatments that are impermissible. Antony, however, takes issue with Nussbaum and argues that her conception of humanity cannot do the required normative work. In fact, there is no understanding of humanity that can be employed to single out how women are damaged under patriarchy and that can ground positive feminist ethical and political claims. Herein lies the problem. In order to define *human being* in a genuinely inclusive manner, we must appeal to some human universals. Antony calls this an "externalist" strategy. But the only traits that have a claim to being such universals are biological or genetic traits, which have no normative import in themselves. Then again, Nussbaum's "internalist" approach makes values and norms part of the definition of *human being*. This provides the required evaluative element and generates ethical conclusions. However, Antony argues, Nussbaum's internalist definition will persuade only those who antecedently agree about which values and norms should define humanity. (Related to what I said above, my contention is that the same is true of dignity talk.) So the prospects of cashing out *human being* in a way that can ground feminist ethical and political claims seem unpromising because the concept will either be too normative or not normative enough. And this allegedly undercuts the prospects of developing humanist feminism: we cannot make sense of dehumanization if we are unable to cash out a genuinely inclusive, ethically thick conception of *humanity*.

I think that Antony is right about the shortcomings of the internalist approach. Still, we can develop humanist feminism *without* relying on such an approach. Or so I will argue in the second part of this book. My strategy is the following. First, we should understand *human being* in broadly externalist terms as a concept that helps pick out the biological kind of human beings, as we commonly understand this kind in everyday speech. Members of such a kind are typically of the *Homo sapiens sapiens* species (anatomically modern humans), they are featherless bipeds with certain cognitive capacities (like language and reasoning skills), which develop given the appropriate

environmental conditions. Second, I take it as an incontrovertible and unfortunate fact of life that members of this kind can be and are treated in dehumanizing ways. In particular, I take it that rape, or nonconsensual sex, is
a paradigm case of such treatment. Taking these two claims as our starting
point, we can develop a theoretically useful notion of *dehumanization*. That
is: having accepted that rape is a paradigm instance of dehumanizing treatment, I will examine what are the key features that make it so. I will then
use the insights gained to develop a general account of dehumanization as a
property or feature of acts and ways of treating others. We need not cash out
human being as a thick ethical concept, and yet we have the tools with which
to do the required normative work: the notion of *dehumanization* proposed
can be used to single out treatments that are damaging to women as well as to
frame positive responses to such treatments.

Taking the notion of *dehumanization* to underpin political and normative
claims of emancipatory feminism affords various benefits. To begin with, my
proposed humanist feminism can offer a more nuanced analysis of gender
injustice by correcting some presumptions that the gender controversy harbors and that steer feminist philosophical debates in unhelpful ways. For
one thing, feminist philosophers often hold that gendered social injustices
damage women qua women. But this is ambiguous and affords two readings.
One is about causal social explanation: my being a woman is part of the explanation for why I suffer (say) systematic sexualized violence. The other is
more constitutive, and justificatory: patriarchy targets women because they
are women, and this crucially *renders* some instances of oppression sexist instances. I suffer due to patriarchy because instances of sexist oppression track
something about me (my gender); and so they damage me accordingly qua
woman. Qua man, patriarchy does not damage me (though, of course, some
other form of oppression—say, in virtue of my race—might). So the first is
more about what causes patriarchal damage; the second is about what (at least
partly) constitutes such damage. These two readings are often not carefully
distinguished. And my contention is that this inattention lends itself to potentially misleading descriptions of the damage done by patriarchy. If with
the statement "Women are oppressed as women" we have the first explanatory sense in mind, I have no objection to it. But the second reading is trickier.
Since patriarchy tracks something about me (my being a woman), its damage
seems also to be to me qua woman. After all, patriarchy does not damage men
qua men. So the constitutive reading of the locution "damage to women qua
women" suggests that patriarchy's damage turns on damaging women as particular kinds of *gendered* beings. And this bypasses what I take to be the main
issue: that when women are treated in disadvantaging and damaging ways,
they are (as Antony puts it) "treated in ways that prevent or impede the full
development of their *human* capacities" (1998, 85). The fundamental damage
done by patriarchy is not to women qua gendered beings, but to women qua

human beings. This is obscured by the ambiguity of the locution "damage to women as women." And so, taking patriarchy's damage to turn on damaging women as *gendered* beings gets the underpinnings of gender injustice wrong. The constitutive reading of the locution unhelpfully lends itself to this understanding, which is why I take issue with it. Clearly, feminist philosophers do not reject that women qua human beings are damaged by patriarchy. But (I hold) they are quick to talk about the damage done to women as women without sufficiently elucidating their thought. And thus the expression lends itself to unhelpful interpretations, which one can also find in the literature (cf. Burgess-Jackson 2000).

The two readings can, nevertheless, be disambiguated with a distinction that I take to be crucial when thinking about social injustice: that between damage as *harm* and as *wrong*. This distinction is not often clearly made in existing works. Not all harms we suffer are wrongful; a painful medical condition may generate various harms, but the condition does not wrong me. And just because some treatment is harmful, this does not yet elucidate its wrongfulness. So my view is that we have prima facie good reasons not to conflate harms and wrong. Now there are surely specific harms that women qua gendered beings suffer due to patriarchy, like patterns of sexualized violence. This is about the above explanatory reading of how patriarchy damages women as women. Nevertheless, I hold, these harms wrong women qua human (and not qua gendered) beings. This claim is about the constitutive reading: what patriarchal damage (understood as wrong) amounts to, which is not equivalent to the harms caused. Appreciating this point is helpful in our analyses of gendered social injustices because it enables us more clearly to articulate what exactly is wrongful, and not just harmful, about such injustices. Further, it helps us to disambiguate the locution "women are oppressed as women" in a way that allows us to device more focused, effective, and differentiated ways of combating the harms and the wrong of patriarchy. These nuances are not well captured by extant feminist accounts. But, I contend, it is vital to elucidate both the harms and the wrong of patriarchal injustice in that they both play central roles in hampering women's lives. And this is one key task of my humanist feminism. (I will say more about this issue in section 6.2.)

Second, and drawing on the above point, even though feminist philosophical work on oppression, domination, and discrimination is laudable in many ways, existing positions seldom carefully disclose what these forms of injustice amount to. Even more seldom do feminist philosophers spell out in detail what is wrongful about these phenomena, although they clearly take *injustice* and its cognates to be moralized notions (e.g., Cudd 2006; Haslanger 2004; Young 1990). That is, feminist philosophers have offered helpful elucidations of injustice's harms, but not of what normatively underpins these harms. Since the harms and the wrong of gender injustice come apart and we cannot elucidate the latter just by identifying the former, I contend that we need an additional normative theory that explicates the moralized senses of key terms like 'oppression'. The position developed in this book offers precisely that: it elucidates not only what makes gendered injustice harmful, but also what undergirds its wrongfulness. In fact, I take this to be a vital aspect of a general theory of injustice—a theory that I will develop here from a feminist perspective.

Third, I aim to facilitate social theory building by better understanding the wrongness-making feature of social injustice per se. With "social theory" I refer to theorizing that aims to explain the existence, maintenance, and resilience of our social practices and institutions. For instance, a feminist social theory aims to explain women's oppression (cf. Cudd 2006): how did gendered injustices begin? Which social institutions and structures enact, maintain, and perpetuate gender injustice? How are patriarchal discrimination and oppression sustained, and what would it take to overcome them? My view is that a normative theory cashing out the wrongfulness of social injustice allows us to answer these questions. That is, a theory of injustice requires both descriptive and normative components. Any attempt to formulate a good normative theory (say, of how women ought and ought not to be treated) cannot avoid a social theory. But I hold that all adequate social theories require, and cannot avoid, normative commitments that articulate *why* some ways of treating others are wrongful and thus illegitimate. This is what I take my humanist feminism to offer.

Now providing an elucidation of the wrong of social injustice may strike one as odd. If *injustice* and *oppression* are moralized notions, they seem to wear their moral wrongfulness on their sleeves. Treating people in oppressive and unjust ways would be ipso facto wrong. And, one might think, the treatment is wrong *because* it is oppressive and unjust. However, this response is unsatisfyingly circular, and I think that more needs to be said. Seeing more clearly what makes injustice wrongful can help us overcome terminological confusions about 'injustice' and its cognates. Although historically terms like 'oppression' clearly referred to political tyranny, contemporary usage is much less unequivocal. Putative forms of injustice involve (at least) deprivation of freedoms, rights, or deserved privileges, as well as differential treatment. In Ann Cudd's words, the post-twentieth-century usage of 'oppression' refers to "unjust violence, and economic, social, political, and psychological injustices suffered by a wide variety of social groups. These cases include: colonial natives, racial and ethnic minorities, religious minorities, gays and lesbians, and the disabled" (2006, 20). Conceptual clarity is important for emancipatory political movements; it is needed in order to specify which groups really are oppressed, and which resistance strategies can thus be effective. For example, I take such clarity to be imperative so that we can better conduct discussions with "oppression skeptics": people who deny (say) that women are disadvantaged by certain workplace arrangements. I take my normative analysis of injustice's wrongfulness to be an integral part of this conceptual task precisely in elucidating the moralized senses of *injustice* and its cognates. Moreover, and related to this, it is important to have a clear view about what (for instance) makes patriarchal treatment of women wrongful in order to ensure that calls for gender justice have the required force. I concur with John Stuart Mill (1974 [original 1859]) that in order to prevent our intellectual and political commitments stagnating and becoming "mere dead dogma," we must interrogate those commitments and their rational foundations. In this way, the justifications for our commitments are kept alive. In many existing feminist works, however, such justifications are largely presumed and not elucidated. This is how my position differs from those put forward by Cudd (2006), Haslanger (2004), and Young (1990): these feminist philosophers understand *injustice* and *oppression* as moralized notions; but they do not explicitly spell out what makes this so, even though they provide detailed and laudable elucidations of patriarchal harms. In this sense, I take them to lack a crucial normative component—an elucidation of the wrong of social injustice. This does not mean that the said positions lack normativity altogether. However, I will argue in the chapters to come that a satisfying feminist (or any emancipatory) social theory must include the *aforementioned* component, which for me will be elucidated with the proposed understanding of dehumanization.

1.4. Methodological Commitments

Before advancing my arguments against the gender controversy and for a version of humanist feminism in earnest, I want to make few brief notes about my methodological commitments. The approach of the current work is that of analytical feminist philosophy. This means that I combine the practical focus of feminism, here tentatively understood as a political movement to end sex-and/or gender-related injustices, with common analytical methods (e.g., conceptual analysis and systematic argumentation). Feminist philosophy aims both to critique patriarchal social structures by utilizing mainstream philosophical tools and to shape mainstream philosophy with the help of feminist political insights. It offers us a way to do politically informed philosophical investigation.

With this in mind, I reject the view of philosophy as value-free, neutral investigation upon which feminist insights neither can nor should bear. That is, I reject the view that the political *value* commitments of feminism are inconsistent with the supposed *valueless* theoretical commitments of philosophy (cf. Searle 1993). First, philosophy is already rife with value commitments of various kinds, which is often nontransparent to philosophers themselves. All philosophical analysis starts from some theory-framing background beliefs and methodological outlooks (or the attempt to eschew them, which is also a guiding theoretical belief). This includes philosophers' underlying metaphilosophical commitments and beliefs about how research should proceed that guides our selection of method and theory. For instance, contemporary analytic ontology (roughly, the study of what exists; what is the basic "furniture" of reality out of which all else is constructed) might seem to be a paradigmatic value-free philosophical endeavor. But I disagree: bluntly put, ontologists aim to provide unified, nondisjunctive, truth-tracking, explanatorily simple, parsimonious, non–ad hoc, consistent, and rigorous total theories of some subject matter (like the fundamental components of reality). This demonstrates that, contra first impressions, some values are part and parcel of method and theory choices even for philosophical areas that endorse a rather strict fact/value distinction. One can respond that epistemic or cognitive values are surely legitimate in our theory and method choices, but that moral, practical, or political values are not. This takes me to my second, more radical, point. I contend that we cannot, and should not, generally draw a clear distinction between allegedly *constitutive* theoretical and cognitive values and *contextual* social, practical, or ethical values (cf. Longino 1990). Relying on some moral, practical, and political values is legitimate when making theory choices even in areas like ontology. This claim draws on Elizabeth Anderson's reflections on feminist engagements with scientific theory choice. For her, significance and impartiality turn on "the background interests that drive inquiry through the way questions are framed," while our interests are formed relative to the social context of inquiry and thus have moral and political content (1995, 42). Roughly, the questions we take to be relevant and significant already reveal our practical values. Since the factual criteria of significance and impartiality are to be justified relative to our interests, such criteria also require moral and political justification. This gives contextual values a legitimate role in theory choice: determining significance, relevance, and the questions we ought to ask is not just about truth-trackingness, but must be done relative to a wider range of values, including practical ones.

To illustrate, consider briefly contemporary ontological inquiry. Such inquiry tends to separate pure and applied ontology. On the former view, ontology aims to elucidate the fundamental components (properties and relations) of reality. It is often taken to be continuous with science (cf. Quine 1953); and those involved in pure ontology standardly value parsimony (positing the fewest number of kinds of entities) and simplicity of explanations in order to achieve their theoretical goals. Against this backdrop, some deny the existence of tables, chairs, and other middle-sized goods: only fundamental particles arranged table- and chair-wise *exist*, since only they are needed for adequate explanations, and positing the existence of derivative entities would be unparsimonious (e.g., van Inwagen 1990; Merricks 2001). Others think that even though derivative phenomena exist, their investigation is second-ary to the proper object of ontological inquiry: what grounds what (Schaffer 2009). What is strikingly missing from such first-order ontology is the social realm, which either does not exist or is secondary to the proper business of ontology—and so much worse for the social realm! The messy stuff of social properties, objects, and relations is relegated to the realm of applied ontol-ogy, and this comes down to how the significant ontological questions are framed. However, one might legitimately wonder: why *these* significant questions? Hasn't something gone seriously wrong in our question framing when our chosen theory denies the existence of tables, chairs, social insti-tutions, and (putatively disadvantaged and privileged) social agents? Given one's practical concerns and interests, one might hold that such outlandish results should tell against some theory choice, and to demonstrate the need to revise what we hold to be relevant, and significant when examining what there is. As Anderson puts it, we must *do justice* to the subject matter of our investigation in order for our analysis to be (in some sense) accurate, and even truth tracking. This oftentimes requires that we, ethically speaking, do justice to the objects of our study in order to, epistemically speaking, also do our subject matter justice (Anderson 1995, 52). One might therefore hold that doing justice to the structure of reality requires more than a focus on "small" microparticles; we should also keep in mind the "big" macroworld of tables, chairs, and social institutions. Since doing justice to our subject matter is partly a function of contextual practical values, I contend, philosophical inquiry generally speaking ought not sharply to separate contextual and con-stitutive values of inquiry and to discard the former.

Much more should be said about the above reflections. Still, they ought to provide at least an initial motivation for the view that philosophy is not a value-free endeavor simpliciter. And this supports the view that bringing in feminist insights when doing philosophical investigation is not illegitimate simply because of the value judgments embodied therein. The important questions for feminist philosophers now become these: which contextual/ constitutive values, and for what ends? In order to provide a provisional methodological yardstick, my theory of injustice and my investigation of dehumanization are *nonideal* (Mills 2005). They are nonideal in reject-ing methodological tools that exclude or marginalize actual states of af-fairs. One such tool is idealization prominent in (for example) John Rawls's (1971) theory of justice.[3] Onora O'Neill (1987) has characterized this sort of

---

[3] This rejection of idealization as a helpful methodological tool once more underpins my rejec-tion of dignity talk and of appealing to "our" value as Kantian ends in ourselves in the service of theory justification. I wish to reject an idealized picture of humanity that hinges on notions like *dignity, autonomy,* or (Kantian) *worth*. Doing so tends to explain a difficult notion (e.g., *humanity*) in terms of other obscure and contested "big" philosophical notions. Given my commitment to noni-deal theorizing, I take such a move to be methodologically problematic.

idealization as follows (I have modified her characterization to fit Rawls).
The first step is to posit descriptions of just and well-functioning societies that are *idealized* and satisfied only by hypothetical human societies.
The problem here is not that something about actual societies is omitted
in our theory of justice, but rather that too much of something nonexistent
has been added to our conception of a just society. The second step takes
such an enhanced version and description of a just society as an *ideal* for all
human societies—it is posited as the (unachievable) standard against which
actual societies are measured.

Now I doubt the usefulness of such tools in endeavors that aim to advance
social justice. Feminist philosophers (among others) have already amply critiqued Rawls's position (e.g., Tessman 2009), and I will not rehearse these
critiques here. However, in rejecting idealization and in endorsing nonideal
theory I am making a methodological break to some prominent existing positions. This has significant theoretical consequences. Positions like Rawls's
(and Nussbaum's, to be discussed later) aim to elucidate an idealized just
society that can be used to measure actual social arrangements in order to
demonstrate their shortcomings. That is, let's first fix what justice amounts
to, and then see in which ways extant societies/social relations fall short of
justice. Those that do are characterized by social *in*justice. I am offering
something else: an explication of injustice that does *not* trade on a prior
theory of justice. In my view, we should not try to understand injustice
via the lens of justice. Instead, we need different theoretical tools. And so
(contra, e.g., Jaggar 1983a) I contend that elucidating justice and elucidating injustice are not two aspects of the same theoretical undertaking. What
is needed, and what I develop here, is an interim feminist theory of injustice that can subsequently be employed to develop a fully-fledged theory
of social justice (although this is a task for another time). So in a sense,
the ultimate goal of my undertaking and those of Rawls and Nussbaum is
broadly the same: to offer theoretical tools to advance social justice. With
my methodological focus, though, we go about doing so differently. We
start by examining what social injustice amounts to; the insights gained
will then figure in the building blocks of a theory of justice. Adopting a
nonideal approach enables us to examine social reality from a perspective
that yields more helpful results. This is because, as I see it, unless we first
understand the nonideal, we cannot even hope to get to the ideal. With
this in mind, the theory of injustice on offer here stays grounded in actual
states of affairs as much as possible. I start my theorizing from such intuitively nonideal states of affairs, rather than starting with an ideal account
of humanity. My investigation advances from cases that are deeply nonideal insofar as I start by looking at rape as paradigmatically dehumanizing. In short, I aim to undertake nonideal theorizing that stays as close as

possible to actual states of affairs, which are prima facie deeply worrying from the point of view of social justice.[4]

Two further specifications are needed. First, an appeal to humanity in the service of feminist aims is usually taken to be a distinctly liberal strategy. However, my proposal aims to be politically nonpartisan and *not* a liberal feminist analysis of injustice. What I am proposing here starts from a neutral standpoint relative to liberal, Marxist, radical, or socialist feminist strands in order to have broader appeal. Second, a particular limitation of my account is worth noting. My theorizing in this book starts from the social position that I as a white, Western, educated, cis woman inhabit. Nevertheless, I hope that it does not stay there. I will have little to say in the current work about global or transnational injustices in particular. Nonetheless, I take my approach to have wider applicability and to be useful in theories of international justice too. Spelling this out, again, falls under the scope of developing a fully-fledged theory of social justice—a task that I cannot undertake here and that must be reserved for future endeavors. Still, my optimistic hope remains.

1.5. Structure of the Book

Part I puts forward my negative argument against the prevalent gender focus in feminist philosophy. In chapter 2, I outline the history of the gender controversy, elucidate the semantic and ontological puzzles further, and demonstrate how these puzzles appear to threaten emancipatory feminism. Next I discuss recent feminist responses to the puzzles, which aim to make good a sufficiently thick conception of gender in order to support feminist normative claims. This will be done in two parts: in chapter 3, I consider nominalist responses; in chapter 4, realist ones. The purpose of these chapters is twofold: first, to do some philosophical excavating that demonstrates prevalent theoretical underpinnings of recent feminist positions (underpinnings that I ultimately find not worth preserving); second, to show that recent influential responses to the semantic and ontological puzzles fail, that the considered accounts of gender are in various ways unsatisfying by their own lights. (This further provides an opinionated introduction to contemporary feminist philosophical debates on gender for those unfamiliar with the debates.) In the

---

[4] It is worth noting further that since I do not take a theory of injustice just to be the reverse of a theory of justice, I will not here take issue with positions like Rawls's. I take myself to be engaging in a slightly different controversy, which is not about the content of justice. This follows from the above substantive methodological commitments about doing nonideal social and political philosophy. I take my approach to offer a useful alternative to more traditional theories of justice. But since my undertaking is a subtly different one, I will not consider here how my view fares in comparison to more traditional theories of justice.

course of chapters 3 and 4, I will assume for argument's sake that the semantic and ontological puzzles are worth responding to. That is, I will assume that instead of abandoning the gender controversy, the appropriate response is to engage in *more* theorizing about gender. Nevertheless, I go on to argue in chapter 5 that this is the wrong strategy: we can deflate the puzzles instead of looking for solutions to them. And so we can surpass the gender controversy, which motivates my proposed feminist paradigm shift toward humanist feminism. That surpassing having been done, Part II proposes a new way to ground feminist political and ethical claims with the help of dehumanization. To explicate this move, I offer a regimentation of social injustice. In chapter 6, I develop my notion of *dehumanization* as grounding the wrong of injustice. Here a trigger warning is in order: given my commitment to nonideal theorizing and my argumentative strategy that starts from thinking about rape as paradigmatically dehumanizing, this chapter contains examples that readers may find harrowing and disturbing. In chapter 7, I outline different forms of injustice (oppression, domination, discrimination) and spell out how dehumanization provides their wrongness-making feature. Chapter 8 continues on from this and outlines injustice's contours: it elucidates what it means for injustice to be characterized as sexist, racist, ableist, or homophobic. These three chapters (I contend) complete my theory of injustice as well as spell out the normative and social theoretical tenets of my proposed humanist feminism. The chapters offer theoretical resources not just for feminist philosophers, but for all social and political philosophers investigating injustice. What I take *social injustice* to consist in from a distinctly feminist perspective having been spelled out, the final chapter considers what overcoming dehumanization requires. Although I cannot provide a full discussion, my reflections in this final chapter point to what lies at the heart of social justice.

PART I

Against the Gender Controversy

{ 2 }

The Gender Controversy

Contemporary feminist philosophical discourse on gender (I contend) is a controversy whose resolution is taken to be important on feminist political grounds. In order to better understand this, let's start by sketching out why feminists appropriated gender talk, and why over the past few decades a philosophical analysis of the concept *woman* has become so important.

2.1. Biological Determinism and Gender Terminology

Speakers ordinarily seem to think that 'gender' and 'sex' are coextensive: women and men are human females and males, respectively, and the former is just the politically correct way to talk about the latter. Feminists typically disagree and many have historically endorsed a sex/gender distinction. Its standard formulation holds that 'sex' denotes human females and males, and depends on *biological* features (chromosomes, sex organs, hormones, other physical features). Then again, 'gender' denotes women and men and depends on *social* factors (social roles, positions, behavior, self-ascription). The main feminist motivation for making this distinction was to counter biological determinism: the view that one's sex determines one's social and cultural traits and roles. Many historical examples demonstrate that social, cultural, and psychological differences between men and women were taken to be manifestations of some underlying physiological differences between the sexes; and these physiological differences have been used to justify a range of oppressive social conditions. Toril Moi characterizes such views as being committed to a "pervasive view" of sex (1999, 11). Biological sex traits are thought to pervade every aspect of an individual, down to their social position and intellectual capacities, as well as to provide general frameworks for social and political arrangements along gendered lines.

A typical example of a biologically determinist view is that of Geddes and Thompson, who, in 1889, argued that social, psychological, and behavioral traits were caused by metabolic states. Women supposedly conserve energy (they are "anabolic"), which renders them passive, conservative, sluggish, stable, and uninterested in politics. Men expend their surplus energy (they are "katabolic"), being thus eager, energetic, passionate, variable, and interested in political and social matters. These supposed biological "facts" were used not only to explain behavioral differences between women and men, but also to inform our social and political arrangements. More specifically, they were used to argue for withholding from women political rights accorded to men because (according to Geddes and Thompson) "what was decided among the prehistoric Protozoa cannot be annulled by Act of Parliament" (quoted from Moi 1999, 18). It would be both inappropriate and futile to grant women political rights since they are unsuited to hold them and, due to their biology, women are simply uninterested in exercising those rights.

In response, feminists have argued that behavioral and psychological differences have social, rather than biological, origins. For instance, Simone de Beauvoir famously claimed that one is not born, but rather *becomes* a woman, and that "social discrimination produces in women moral and intellectual effects so profound that they appear to be caused by nature" (1972, 18). Anatomy or chromosomes, then, do not cause commonly observed behavioral traits associated with women and men. Rather, such traits are culturally learned or acquired.[1] In order to distinguish biological differences from social/psychological ones and to talk about the latter, feminists appropriated the term 'gender'. Psychological writings on transsexuality were the first to employ gender terminology in this sense. Until the 1950s and 1960s, the term 'gender' was used to refer to masculine and feminine words, like *le* and *la* in French (Nicholson 1994, 80; see also Nicholson 1998). However, in order to explain why some people felt that they were "trapped in wrong bodies," psychologists like John Money and Robert Stoller began using 'sex' to pick out biological traits and 'gender identity' to pick out the amount of femininity and masculinity a person exhibited. Although (by and large) a person's sex and gender complemented one another, separating them made theoretical sense, and seemingly explained transsexuality: transsexuals' sex and gender simply do not match.

A note about terminology is in order here. Nowadays, the term 'transsexual' is specifically used to refer to individuals who use medical means and technologies to alter their bodies, so that their bodily presentation conforms

---

[1] Although simplistic biological determinism of the older kind is nowadays less common, the idea that behavioral and psychological differences have biological causes has not disappeared. Brain differences have been used more recently to justify sex-segregated educational models, to explain how and why women and men make different kinds of business leaders, and to explain men's diminished emotional capacities. Cordelia Fine (2010) provides an excellent outline and critique of these contemporary views. For more historical examples, see my 2012, section 1.1.

to their gendered sense of self (Bettcher 2009). By contrast, it is more common to employ terms like 'transgender' to refer to

> people who "do not conform to prevailing expectations about gender" by presenting and living genders that were not assigned to them at birth or by presenting and living genders in ways that may not be readily intelligible in terms of more traditional conceptions of gender. Used as an umbrella term, it generally aims to group several different kinds of people such as trans-sexuals, drag queens and kings, some butch lesbians, and (heterosexual) male cross dressers. (Bettcher 2009)

In many activist circles, the denotation "trans*" has recently been used to refer to "transgender, transsexual, genderqueer, non-binary, genderfluid, genderfuck, intersex, third gender, transvestite, cross-dresser, bi-gender, trans man, trans women, agender."[2] Trans* is contrasted with "cis," which denotes (roughly) women born female and men born male, who have typical gender identities and presentations. "Trans*" is also considered to be more inclusive than "trans," which is taken to refer to medically or hormonally altered trans-sexual men and women. This shows that the talk of transsexuals alone would be inadequate and overly simplified. For the remainder of this book, then, I will follow the convention of using "trans*" as the inclusive umbrella expression, and "trans" to denote transsexuality in the narrower medical sense.

Second-wave feminists also found it useful to distinguish sex and gender. This enabled them to argue that many differences between women and men were socially produced and mutable. One of the first feminists to employ gender terminology, Gayle Rubin, uses the expression "sex/gender system" in order to describe "a set of arrangements by which the biological raw material of human sex and procreation is shaped by human, social intervention" (1975, 165). Rubin employed this system to articulate the part of our social lives that provides the locus of women's oppression—she thus described gender as a social division imposed on the sexes. Rubin's thought was that although biological differences are fixed, gender differences are the oppressive results of social interventions that dictate how women and men should behave. Women are oppressed *as women* and "by having to *be* women" (Rubin 1975, 204). However, this being the case, gender is thought to be alterable by political and social reform that would ultimately bring an end to women's subordination. Feminism should aim to create a "genderless (though not sexless) society" in which anatomy is irrelevant to one's abilities, identity, actions, and sexual preferences (1975, 204). In such earlier interpretations, sex and gender were thought to complement one another. The slogan "Gender is the social interpretation of sex" captures this view. Nicholson (1994) puts this in

---

[2] *You Know When You're Trans* When . . . Blog*, http://youknowyouretrans.tumblr.com/.

foundationalist terms: gender (masculinity and femininity) is superimposed upon the "foundation" of sex as each society projects onto sexed bodies its cultural conceptions of how males and females should behave. This socially constructs gender differences—or the amount of femininity/masculinity of a person—upon sexed bodies. According to this view, all humans are either male or female; their sex is fixed. But cultures interpret sexed bodies differently and project different norms onto those bodies, thereby creating feminine and masculine persons. Distinguishing sex and gender also enables the two to come apart: one can be sexed male and yet be gendered a woman, or a man who is sexed female (Haslanger 2000; Stoljar 1995).

2.2. Gender Construction

Feminist arguments against biological determinism suggested that gender differences result from cultural practices and social expectations. Nowadays it is more common to denote this by saying that gender is socially constructed. In its simplest formulation, this means that genders (women and men), and gendered traits (like being nurturing or ambitious) are the "intended or unintended product[s] of a social practice" (Haslanger 1995, 97). But which social practices construct gender, what social construction is, and what being of a certain gender amounts to are major feminist controversies. There is no consensus on these issues. By way of example, consider the following historical accounts that appeal to socialization, psychosocial ego development, and eroticized dominance and submission, respectively. (In chapters 3 and 4, I will consider more recent elucidations of gender construction.)

One way to interpret Beauvoir's claim that one is not born but rather becomes a woman is to take it as a claim about gender socialization: females become women through a process of acquiring feminine traits and behavior. Masculinity and femininity are thought to be products of nurture, or how individuals are brought up. They are causally constructed (Haslanger 1995, 98): social forces either have a causal role in bringing gendered individuals into existence, or they (to some substantial sense) shape the way we are qua women and men. The mechanism of construction is social learning. For instance, Kate Millett (1971) takes culturally based gender differences to result from differential treatment: gender is "the sum total of the parents', the peers', and the culture's notions of what is appropriate to each gender by way of temperament, character, interests, status, worth, gesture, and expression" (Millett 1971, 31). More generally, social learning theorists hold that a huge array of influences mold us into women and men. Some are overt: children are often dressed in gender stereotypical clothes and colors (boys are dressed in blue, girls in pink), and given gender stereotypical toys. Parents also (intentionally or not) tend to reinforce certain "appropriate" behaviors. While the precise form of gender socialization has changed since the onset of second-wave feminism, even today girls are discouraged from playing rough-and-tumble games or sports like football and are more likely than boys to be given dolls or cooking toys to play with. Boys are told not to "cry like a baby," and are more likely to be given masculine toys like trucks and guns (Kimmel 2000, 122–126).[3] Further, parents often unconsciously treat their female and male children differently. When asked to describe their twenty-four-*hour* old infants, parents did so using gender-stereotypic language: boys are describes as strong, alert, and coordinated; girls as tiny, soft, and delicate. Parents' treatment of their infants (for instance, how they are held) further reflects these descriptions (Renzetti and Curran 1992, 32). Such behaviors fit a kind of confirmation bias. Parents interpret their children's behaviors in ways that reflect their prior beliefs about gender differences. They then treat children accordingly, and in ways that foster the development of particular traits, which in turn can result in their children exhibiting the relevant gendered behaviors. And this appears to confirm the parents' initial gendered interpretations of their children's behavior. This suggests a more specific causal sense in which gender is socially constructed. It is discursively constructed: we are gendered the way we are, at least to a substantial extent, because of what is attributed to us by others (Haslanger 1995, 99). Socializing influences send implicit messages about how females and males are expected to behave, which shapes us into feminine and masculine persons. Feminine and masculine gender norms that mold individuals are problematic, however, in that the resulting behaviors reinforce women's subordination. Women are socialized into subordinate social roles by learning to be passive, ignorant, docile, emotional helpmates for men. But since these roles are simply learned, we can create more equal societies by "unlearning" them. And so feminists should aim to diminish the influence of oppressive socialization.

Nancy Chodorow (1978, 1995) has criticized social learning theory as too simplistic to explain gender differences (see also Deaux and Major 1990; Gatens 1996). Instead, she holds that gender is a matter of having feminine and masculine personalities that develop in early infancy as responses to prevalent parenting practices. In particular, gendered personalities develop because women tend to be the primary caretakers of small children. This provides a second way to understand gender construction. Chodorow holds that because mothers (or other prominent females) tend to care for infants, infant male and female psychic development differs. Crudely put: the mother-daughter relationship differs from the mother-son relationship because mothers are more likely to identify with their daughters than their sons.

---

[3] The era of gender-coded toys is far from over. For some recent examples, see the *Feminist Philosophers Blog* (http://feministphilosophers.wordpress.com), category "gendered products."

This unconsciously prompts the mother to encourage her son to individuate himself from her, thereby prompting him to develop well-defined and rigid ego boundaries. However, the mother unconsciously discourages the daughter from individuating herself, thereby prompting the daughter to develop flexible and blurry ego boundaries. Childhood gender socialization further reinforces these unconsciously developed ego boundaries, thus finally resulting in feminine and masculine persons (Chodorow 1995, 202–206). For instance, women are stereotypically more emotionally dependent upon others around them, supposedly finding it difficult to distinguish their own interests and well-being from those of their children and partners. This is said to be because of their blurry and confused ego boundaries: women find it hard to distinguish their own needs from the needs of those around them because they cannot sufficiently individuate themselves from those close to them. By contrast, men are stereotypically emotionally detached and distant. These traits are said to result from men's well-defined ego boundaries that enable them to prioritize their own needs and interests at the expense of others.

Chodorow thinks that these gender differences should and can be changed. Feminine and masculine personalities play a pivotal role in women's oppression since they make females overly attentive to the needs of others, and males emotionally detached and deficient. In order to correct the situation, males and females should be equally involved in parenting (Chodorow 1995, 214). This would help in ensuring that children develop sufficiently individuated senses of selves without becoming overly detached, which in turn should help to eradicate common gender stereotypical behaviors.

From a rather different perspective, Catharine MacKinnon has developed a theory of gender as a theory of sexuality. For her, the social meaning of sex (i.e., gender) is constituted and created by sexual objectification of women: women are viewed and treated as objects for the satisfaction of men's desires (MacKinnon 1989). Masculinity is defined as sexual dominance, femininity as sexual submissiveness; thus genders are "created through the eroticization of dominance and submission. The man/woman difference and the dominance/submission dynamic define each other. This is the social meaning of sex" (1989, 113). MacKinnon's position takes gender to be constitutively constructed (although she does not herself employ this terminology). This means that in defining genders (or masculinity and femininity) we must make reference to social factors (Haslanger 1995, 98). In particular, we must make reference to one's position in the sexualized dominance/submission dynamic: men occupy the sexually dominant position, women the sexually submissive one. As a result, genders are *by definition* hierarchical, and this hierarchy is fundamentally tied to sexualized power relations. Talk of "gender equality," then, makes no sense. If sexuality ceased to be a manifestation of dominance, hierarchical genders would simply cease to exist.

Gender difference for MacKinnon, then, is not a matter of having a particular psychological orientation or behavioral pattern; rather, in patriarchal societies it is a function of hierarchal sexuality. This is not to say that men are naturally disposed to sexually objectify women, or that women are naturally submissive. Instead, male and female sexualities are socially conditioned too: men have been conditioned to find women's subordination sexy, and women have been conditioned to find a particular male version of female sexuality as erotic—one in which it is erotic to be sexually submissive. For MacKinnon, both female and male sexual desires are defined from a male point of view that is conditioned by pornography (MacKinnon 1989, chap. 7). Pornography portrays a false picture of "what women want," suggesting that women in actual fact are and want to be submissive. This conditions men's sexuality so that they view women's submission as sexy. Male dominance then projects this vision of sexuality onto women, sometimes by force. MacKinnon's thought is not that male dominance is a result of social learning; rather, socialization is an expression of power. Socialized differences in masculine and feminine traits, behavior, and roles are not responsible for power inequalities. Instead, females and males are socialized differently *because* there are underlying power inequalities: dominance (power) is prior to difference (gendered traits, behaviors, roles) (MacKinnon 1987). MacKinnon thus sees legal restrictions on pornography and on other mechanisms of male power as paramount to ending women's subordination and to doing away with gender.

These three ways of understanding gender construction show how particular thick conceptions of womanhood were taken to direct feminist political efforts: if we accept social learning theory, the appropriate political response is to seek to undermine gender socialization. But if Chodorow is right, feminists should work toward undermining the male-breadwinner/female-carer family dynamic. Then again, following MacKinnon, feminist efforts should go (among other things) to fighting pornography. In each case, the presumption is that our analysis of gender supports feminist normative claims: it tells us something insightful about women (and their oppression) that guides feminist politics and strategies of resistance. A sufficiently thick account of what it is to be a woman presumably helps us to articulate the damage done by patriarchy, which ought to be useful in feminist emancipatory efforts. Now, although the above positions afforded important explanatory advances in demonstrating that gender is constructed rather than found in nature's joints, the early feminist theories of gender paved the way for the gender controversy. Certain influential critiques of positions like those above generated the semantic and ontological puzzles.

- *Semantic puzzle*: Given that ordinary language users tend not to distinguish sex and gender (treating 'woman' largely as a sex term, or a mixture of social and biological features), what precisely are

feminists talking about when they talk about 'women'? What are the
necessary and sufficient conditions that the concept *woman* encodes,
if any such conditions exist to begin with?

- *Ontological puzzle*: How should we understand the category of
women that is meant to undergird feminist political solidarity, if
there are no necessary and sufficient conceptual conditions underlying our gender talk? Do women make up a genuine kind, or simply
a gerrymandered and random collection of individuals? What kinds
of entities are gender and sex anyway? Are there *really* women and
men, if gender is (in some substantial sense) socially constructed?

I will consider next three important and influential concerns with the sex/
gender distinction that have been raised over the past twenty years. As I see it,
the distinction theoretically underpins the gender controversy, and the problems discussed next are responsible for the semantic and ontological puzzles.
The following critiques have been pivotal in the emergence of more recent
feminist literature on gender, which attempts to resolve the puzzles in order
to salvage the normative basis of feminism by articulating a thick enough
conception of womanhood without falling prey to the following critiques.
(This newer literature will be discussed in chapters 3 and 4.)

2.3. Uniformity of Gender

The positions outlined above share an underlying metaphysical perspective
of *gender realism*. On this view, women as a group are assumed to share some
characteristic feature, experience, common condition, or criterion that defines
their gender and makes them women (as opposed to, say, men). For example,
MacKinnon thought that sexual objectification is the common condition that
defines women's gender and is what women as women share. Further, pointing out females who are not sexually objectified does not provide a counterexample to MacKinnon's view. Being sexually objectified is constitutive
of being a woman; a female who escapes such treatment simply would not
count as a woman. A note about terminology is in order here. Positions like
MacKinnon's are more commonly said to be gender *essentialist*. However, I
will largely avoid this common terminology since feminist usage of the term
'essentialism' varies tremendously. As Cressida Heyes nicely puts this point,
"If Wittgenstein is correct that the meaning of a word lies in its use, then
feminists will find it hard to know what 'essentialism' means" (2000, 11).
First, classificatory essentialism is about kind membership: if some feature or
property is necessary for membership in type F, that feature is essential to *F*s
qua *F*s. There is considerable confusion, though, about what kinds of properties are essential in this sense. Some feminist discussions equate essentialism

with biologism. But clearly social features can also be essential in the sense of fixing type membership. (Just think of the type of politicians.) Second, individual essentialism is about individuation. On this view, having some feature or property that makes one a member of the kind F is essential to Fs qua individuals: if one were to lose this feature, one would cease to be that very same individual. For instance, if being a member of the kind dog is individually essential to Lassie, were Lassie to lose this feature, he would cease to be *Lassie*. The two kinds of essentialisms are sometimes treated as codependent in feminist discussions (cf. Stoljar 1995): if some feature is essential for membership in women's kind, then this feature must also be essential to individual women qua individuals. But this does not necessarily follow. Being red is necessary for membership in the type red entities, but being so colored is not necessarily essential to red entities qua individuals. If a red car were painted blue, it would no longer be a member of the class of red entities, but the car would not cease to be the very same car that it is. (For more on gender essentialism and for helpful discussions, see Heyes 2000; Mikkola 2016; Stone 2004; 2007; Witt 1995.) In order to disambiguate and clarify the present discussion, I will use "gender realism" to capture the position of classificatory essentialism. Furthermore, by avoiding the talk of essences, gender realism remains neutral on whether the shared, type-defining feature is biologically fixed or socially constructed.[4]

One may wish to critique the three accounts outlined above by rejecting the particular details of each account. For instance, Harris (1993) and Stone (2007) criticize MacKinnon's view that sexual objectification is the common condition definitive of women's gender in that it fails to take into account differences in women's backgrounds and how that variation shapes sexuality. For instance, during the era of American slavery black women were hypersexualized and thought to be always sexually available; white women were thought to be pure and sexually virtuous. In fact, the rape of a black woman was thought to be impossible (Harris 1993). This does not, of course, imply that only black women were women—MacKinnon presumably would hold that white women were also sexually objectified, which is the constitutive condition of womanhood. MacKinnon's opponents, then, argue that sexual objectification cannot serve as the basis of womanhood: it varies too much depending on one's race and class to capture anything genuinely shared by all women. (See Spelman 1990, chap. 4, for a critique of Chodorow's view.) In MacKinnon's defense, Rapaport (2002) has argued that sexual objectification can be viewed as the common condition that defines women's gender, if we take it to be multiply realizable. So, even though women in general are all sexually objectified, this experience need not be uniform—black and white

---

[4] For a novel recent elucidation of individual gender essentialism, see Witt 2011a.

women are simply sexually objectified in different ways. Still, this sort of defense does not persuade those who have leveled a more thoroughgoing critique at the metaphysical perspective of gender realism per se. It has come under sustained attack on two grounds: first, that it fails to take into account how racial, cultural, and class differences construct women differently (particularity argument); second, that it posits an exclusionary normative ideal of womanhood (normativity argument). The positions that advance these arguments are ones that I call "gender skeptical" because they hold that no genuine type or kind of women exists.

Both the particularity and the normativity arguments are closely related to *intersectional* analyses of gender and oppression (cf. Crenshaw 1989). This feminist and antiracist analytical tool aims to make our accounts of gender and oppression more nuanced and so empirically more accurate. It emphasizes our situatedness in the intersections of many social categories. Not appreciating this prevents an adequate analysis of (say) the situation of black women. A focus just on their gender leaves out their race, and a focus just on their race leaves out their gender. An analysis that disregards intersectionality is unsatisfying because it fails to note that black women's situation is different from the situation of *both* women in general *and* blacks in general. Rather, critical race theorists have argued that many of the disadvantages black women suffer are due to the intersections of their race and gender (Grillo 2006). In a similar vein, Elizabeth Spelman has famously argued that women's individuality and their diverse and dissimilar experiences as women count against gender realism. Spelman rejects the view that there is a *single* class of women; by contrast, she argues that there are multiple gender classes that are culturally and socially specific. In her *Inessential Woman*, Spelman sets out to refute gender realism, or the view that "underneath or beyond the differences among women there must be some shared identity—as if commonality were a metaphysical given" (1990, 13). Instead, she argues that the features women are presumed to share (qua women) are in fact features that only some women share because *being a woman* is inseparable from other aspects of one's identity, such as race and class. Since gender is socially constructed and social construction differs from one society to the next, womanhood is a culturally specific feature: only women with similar racial, cultural, and social backgrounds can share a *particular* gender. Let me spell out Spelman's view in somewhat more detail.

Very roughly, metaphysical realists about properties hold that individual entities of a certain sort share a universal feature that makes them entities of that sort. For instance, Bertrand Russell writes that all just acts must "partake of a common nature, which will be found in whatever is just and in nothing else. This common nature, in virtue of which they are all just, will be justice itself, the pure essence the admixture of which with facts of ordinary life produces the multiplicity of just acts" (1967, 52). In order to denote such a shared nature, he uses the term 'universal', where "*a universal* will be anything which may be shared by many particulars" (Russell 1967, 53).[5] Spelman holds that much of feminist theory shares a philosophical outlook with this kind of metaphysical realism (1990, 1–2). Gender realists supposedly hold that individual women share the very same gender-defining universal feature, which binds the category of women together and so forms the basis of feminist political solidarity. For Spelman, though, no such universal feature exists—thus gender realism is false. First, the feminist gender realist view results from white, middle-class, Western feminists falsely theorizing gender and women's oppression from the perspective of "white solipsism": the tendency to "think, imagine, and speak as if whiteness describes the world" (Adrienne Rich, quoted in Harris 1993, 356). The presumption is that the "womanness" underneath women of color is "colorless"—that of white women (Spelman 1990, 13). Earlier feminists assumed that women all share some single identical feature and theorized this feature as the one *they* possess. In so doing, they failed to understand the importance of race and class, and inadvertently created a conception of womanhood where the common nature underneath the supposedly distorting cultural conditions was of white, middle-class, heterosexual, Christian, and able-bodied women. Furthermore, this false conception is "being passed off as a metaphysical truth" that privileges some women, and marginalizes others (1990, 186). Betty Friedan's (1963) well-known work is a case in point of white solipsism.[6] Friedan saw domesticity as the main vehicle of gender oppression and called upon women in general to find jobs outside the home. But she failed to realize that women from less privileged and poor backgrounds, who were often people of color, already worked outside the home. Friedan's suggestion, then, was applicable only to a particular subgroup of women (white, middle-class, American housewives), but was mistakenly taken to apply to all women's lives.

Spelman's discussion of white solipsism points to a further mistaken feminist assumption: what makes x a woman is the same as what makes y a woman. By contrast, "gender is constructed and defined in conjunction with elements of identity such as race, class, ethnicity, and nationality" (1990, 175). As individuals, we stand in the intersections of many different social categories. Thus, what makes it true that x and y are women is not some common shared nature that we can separate from other aspects of women's identities and that is interchangeable between them (1990, 158). Those committed to

---

[5] A number of different metaphysical positions may be characterized as property realist. These positions differ in the ways they understand the *natures* of universals: whether they are abstract or concrete, whether there is a distinct realm in which they exist or not, etc. (cf. Armstrong 1989). Providing a full characterization of all realist positions is a task that I cannot undertake here. For my purposes, the above rough-and-ready characterization suffices—it captures the common thread running through different realist positions.

[6] Note that this does not mean Friedan's view is gender realist in the sense discussed here.

gender realism (Spelman critiques) falsely assume that a woman's womanness is a neatly distinguishable part of her identity. Were gender separable from race and class in this manner, all women would experience their gender in the same way. This clearly does not hold, as Spelman rightly points out. She puts forward a thought experiment to illustrate:

> If it were possible to isolate a woman's "womanness" from her racial identity, then we should have no trouble imagining that had I been Black I could have had just the same understanding of myself as a woman as I in fact do. . . . To rehearse this imaginary situation is to expose its utter bizarreness. (1990, 135)

If it were possible to separate one's gender from one's racial identity, then it should be possible—even easy—to imagine that had I been of a different race, as a woman I would have been the same. Nevertheless, it seems to be very difficult (if not impossible) to imagine this, which suggests to Spelman that gender realism is false. Following from this, she suggests that women (qua women) do not share a single gender since their gender identity is shaped by specific cultural and social backgrounds—females learn to be women differently. And so, if females are made into women via social conditioning, and such conditioning differs depending on one's society, there is a variety of genders among women (Spelman 1990, 175). Subsequently, women who come from similar social and cultural backgrounds come to have a *particular* gender in common. Females become particular kinds of women (1990, 113): they become Jewish working-class women, black middle-class women, poor white women, wealthy aristocratic European women, and so on.

This line of thought has been extremely influential in feminist philosophy. For instance, Iris Marion Young holds that Spelman has *definitively* shown that gender realism is untenable (1997, 13). Nevertheless, Young does not take Spelman's position to be unproblematic. This is because Spelman seems to assume that the categories of race, class, religion, and ethnicity are stable and unified (Young 1997, 20). Independently of Young, Uma Narayan has argued in a similar vein. To assume a commonality among all Western women or all Jewish women (for instance) is just as misguided as the assumption that all women qua women have something in common. After all, particular racial, cultural, and religious groups are themselves internally diverse. This way of attending to women's differences then "endorses and replicates problematic and colonialist assumptions. . . . Seemingly universal essentialist generalizations about 'all women' are replaced by *culture-specific* essentialist generalizations" (Narayan 1998, 87). If Spelman's strategy is to avoid these charges, it must be committed to dissolving groups into individuals. In this case, we can legitimately address only *individual* women, and talk about their experiences. In this sense, Spelman's view is (in my terms) gender skeptical: in rejecting the existence of a single unified social kind of women, her view ends up being committed to women making up a merely unbound and gerrymandered collection of individuals.

Along with Spelman's particularity argument, Judith Butler's *normativity argument* is probably one of the most well-known critiques of gender realism. Butler critiques the sex/gender distinction on two grounds. First, she rejects gender realism with her normativity argument; second, she holds that the sex/gender distinction is unintelligible (this will be discussed in section 2.4.). Butler's normativity argument is not straightforwardly directed at the metaphysical perspective of gender realism, but rather at its *political* counterpart: identity politics. This is a form of political mobilization based on membership in some (racial, ethnic, cultural, gender) group, and group membership is delimited by some common experiences, conditions, or features (Heyes 2000, 58; see also Heyes 2012). Subsequently, feminist identity politics seemingly presupposes gender realism in that political representation is mobilized around women as a group, where group membership is delimited by some supposedly shared condition, experience, or feature definitive of women's gender. Butler's critique of identity politics in her *Gender Trouble* also begins with antiessentialism: her work aims to "trace the way in which gender fables establish and circulate the misnomer of natural facts" (1999, xxxi). According to Butler, it appears as if the term 'woman' has some unitary cross-cultural and transhistorical meaning, and as if the term picks out some determinate group of people who have a feature in common qua members of that group. Unitary gender concepts (for Butler) falsely suggest that women form a group of some kind that functions as the foundation for feminist theory and captures a feminist "sisterhood." Contra such a mistaken picture, Butler calls into question the content of the concept *woman*. She argues that the concept has no stable meaning across different cultures and societies (or even within a given society). Rather, "*woman* itself is a term in process, a becoming, a constructing that cannot rightfully be said to originate or end. As an ongoing discursive practice, it is open to intervention and resignification" (Butler 1999, 43). She further claims that to assume women share something that makes them women is seriously misguided; in fact, there is no shared "gender identity behind the expressions of gender" (1999, 33).

The feminist picture of gender (for Butler) in no meaningful sense describes the way the world is; there are no "facts of the matter" about how to be a woman, identify as a woman, or think of one's gender. Rather, the picture is an unwitting *product* of feminist politics in its efforts to represent the interests of certain political subjects—namely, of women. On Butler's view, in aiming to aid women by representing their interests, feminism "constitutes the subject for whom political representation is pursued" (1999, 3). This being the case, any notion of womanhood that is used to explicate the class of women as feminism's subject matter unhelpfully masks rather than discloses what women are like. Holding on to a unitary sense of womanhood does not yield political gains for feminists, but rather generates numerous problems:

> I would argue that any effort to give universal or specific content to the category of women, presuming that that guarantee of solidarity is required *in advance* [as the foundation of feminist politics], will necessarily produce factionalization ... "identity" as a point of departure can never hold as the solidifying ground of a feminist political movement. Identity categories are never merely descriptive, but always normative, and as such, exclusionary. (Butler 1991, 160)

Gender concepts articulated by feminist theorists turn out to articulate a set of conditions that those hoping to gain feminist political representation *should* satisfy; thus, they prescribe a supposedly correct picture of how to be, live, and behave as a woman (Butler 1999, 4). In fact, Butler's view is that *woman* can never be defined in a way that does not prescribe some "unspoken normative requirements" that women should conform to (1999, 9). She takes this to be a feature of terms like 'woman' that purport to pick out social identity categories. The underlying presumption appears to be that such terms can never be used in a nonideological way (Moi 1999, 43) and that they will always prescribe some conditions that ought to be satisfied. This is explained by Butler's view that all processes of drawing categorical distinctions involve evaluative and normative commitments, which in turn involve the exercise of social power (Witt 1995).[7]

Butler acknowledges that feminist theorists did not intentionally set out to prescribe exclusionary normative gender notions. They undertook the task of elucidating the concept of *woman* in good faith and aimed to do so in a manner conducive to feminist political goals. Nevertheless, and as Spelman also argued, they failed to take into account women's diverse, concrete, and dissimilar experiences and traits *as women* (Butler 1999, 19–20). By assuming that all women identify with one another and that women (qua women) share something that makes them women, feminist theorists in effect distorted rather than clarified gender notions. In fact, feminist theorists failed to pay sufficient attention to "the concrete array" of women because feminist theory *itself* was guided by certain normative ideological views that unwittingly reflected mainstream society and politics: those of white solipsism and heterosexism. As already outlined, the former is the tendency to treat whiteness as the normative standard, thereby failing to consider ways in which racial and ethnic differences affect individual women.[8] Heterosexism is the

---

[7] Butler is not alone in holding such a view: Hale (1996) also takes *woman* to be an "essentially" normative concept.

[8] Another good illustration of white solipsism comes from bell hooks, who rightly pointed out that many women from racially, culturally, and economically oppressed groups find the feminist ideal of gender equality foreign:

tendency to treat heterosexuality as a normative standard and to naturalize heterosexual sexual practices. That is, heterosexist norms, ideals, and traditions encourage (if not coerce) heterosexual behavior (Salih 2002, 49); and heterosexism creates a worldview where sexual practices between cis men and cis women are "natural" and normal. Homosexual behavior is considered to be deviant, marginal, "unnatural" (whatever that means) and something that should be prohibited. According to this kind of queer feminist critique, traditional feminist theory not only failed to take into account racial and class differences, but also maintained a heteronormative and heterosexist view of gender. Those who do not conform to the picture of womanhood informed by white solipsism and heterosexism risk being alienated or, worse still, excluded from feminist politics altogether. Nicholson captures this thought nicely: "the idea of 'woman' as unitary operates as a policing force which generates and legitimises certain practices, experiences, etc., and curtails and delegitimizes others" (1998, 293). For Butler, the practices deemed illegitimate are usually those of minority races, cultures, ethnicities, and sexualities, with the result that much of feminist politics privileges white, heterosexual, and Western women's experiences.

Butler's aim is not, however, merely to critique prevalent feminist conceptions of *woman* and to show that they leave something to be desired. Her argument is stronger than this: every definition of *woman* will have such normative results, and this makes all such definitions politically insidious. So the mistake is not that feminists provided the incorrect elucidation of *woman*. Rather, their mistake was to attempt to define womanhood at all. In order to avoid excluding and marginalizing some women, we must give up the view that *woman* can be defined in a unitary manner. Connected to this is Butler's view of gender performativity. Butler claims that people are usually assumed to have certain essential gender "cores" by virtue of which they are either men or women: women are females with feminine behavioral traits and heterosexual desire toward men; men are males with masculine behavioral traits and heterosexual desire toward women. Individuals have "intelligible genders" when they exhibit this sequence of traits in a coherent manner—when sexual desire follows from sexual orientation that in turn follows from feminine/masculine behaviors thought to follow from biological sex (Butler 1999, 23). Those who exhibit *incoherent* sequences (like lesbians) are thought to be doing their gender "wrong," and such sequencing of traits is not socially sanctioned (just think of homophobic discrimination). This picture of gender, however,

---

Since men are not equals in white supremacist, capitalist, patriarchal class structure, which men do women want to be equal to? Do women share a common vision of what equality means? . . . [W]omen in lower class and poor groups, particularly those who are non-white, would not have defined women's liberation as women gaining social equality with men. . . . Knowing that men in their groups do not have social, political, and economic power, they would not deem it liberatory to share their social status. (hooks 2000, 19)

mirrors the conditions of the socially powerful and functions to marginalize and police those who fail to conform. Gender cores are nothing more than illusions created by norms and practices that seek to render gender uniform, dimorphic, and somehow natural (Butler 1999, 42). Such gender dimorphism serves a heterosexist ideology by implying that it is natural to sexually desire the opposite sex/gender. Subsequently, being feminine and desiring men are assumed to be expressions of one's gender as a woman.

Butler denies this and holds that gender is performative. It is not "a stable identity or locus of agency from which various acts follow"; rather, gender comes into being through "a *stylized repetition of* [habitual] *acts*" (1999, 179). Gender is not something that one is; it is something that one does in wearing certain gender-coded clothing, in walking and sitting in gender-coded ways, in styling one's hair in gender-coded manner, and in desiring sexually the opposite sex/gender. Gender is a sequence of acts, a doing rather than a being. And repeatedly engaging in "feminizing" and "masculinizing" acts congeals gender, thereby making people falsely think of gender as something they naturally are. By contrast, gender only comes into being through these gendering acts. A female who has sex with males does not thereby express her gender as a woman; this activity (among others) *makes* her a woman. The constitutive acts that gender individuals create gender as a "compelling illusion" (Butler 1990, 271). Our gendered classification scheme is a strong pragmatic construction: Social factors wholly determine our use of the scheme, and the scheme fails to represent accurately any "facts of the matter" (Haslanger 1995, 100). Genders are true and real only to the extent that they are performed (Butler 1990, 278–279). It makes no sense, then, to say of a male-to-female trans* person that she is really a man who only appears to be a woman. A trans* person's gender is just as real or true as stereotypical cis person's (1990, 278).[9] Without heterosexism that compels people to engage in certain gendering acts, there would be no gender. And ultimately the aim is to abolish norms that compel people to act in these gendering ways.

With this in mind, Butler suggests that feminist theorists should actively resist defining the concept *woman*: they should deconstruct it, thereby releasing the notion "into a future of multiple significations, to emancipate it from the [oppressive and exclusionary] ontologies to which it has been restricted, and to give it play as a site where unanticipated meanings might come to bear" (Butler 1991, 160). She claims that *woman* should always be open to a

---

[9] Confusingly, Butler writes elsewhere: "In no sense can it be concluded that the part of gender that is performed is therefore the 'truth' of gender" (1997, 20)—something that appears to contradict the claim considered here. The source of the confusion stems from Butler's equivocation on "true." In this quote, she uses the term to denote "independently existing" rather than "real." So: genders are real only to the extent that they are performed because gender does not exist independently of the gendering activities.

multiplicity of different and noncompeting definitions, and so the idea that women have something in common that makes them women "ought not to be the foundation of feminist politics" (Butler 1999, 9). On Butler's view, the term 'woman' has no definite meaning, and, given the normativity of identity categories, it would be politically dangerous to try to definite the term in a way that picks out the class of women for feminist political representation. In this sense, her view is strongly gender skeptical: it is not only empirically misguided to think that a unified class of women could capture the multiplicity of women; holding that a unified class is politically worth seeking is also a dangerous illusion and an ideological tool of exclusion and marginalization.

2.4. Sex Classification

The previously discussed critiques of the sex/gender distinction focused on the gender side of the divide. However, feminists have also discussed the sex side. Many people, including many feminists, have taken sex ascriptions to be solely a matter of biology with no social or cultural dimension. It is commonplace to think that there are only two sexes and that biological sex classifications are utterly unproblematic. By contrast, feminist philosophers and biologists have disputed this and argued that sex classification is not a thoroughly nonevaluative matter. In order to make sense of this, it helps to distinguish object construction from idea construction (Haslanger 2003b): ideological forces and material social conditions can be said to construct certain kinds of objects (e.g., sexed bodies or gendered individuals) and certain kinds of ideas (e.g., sex/gender concepts). It is worth briefly noting what is meant by ideology here. I will follow Haslanger's definition of ideologies as "representations of social life that serve in some way to undergird social practices" (2011, 180). An ideology provides the "background cognitive and affective frame that gives actions and reactions *meaning* within a social system and contributes to its survival" (2011, 181; italics mine). Now consider the object construction of sexed bodies. Secondary sex characteristics, or the physiological and biological markers commonly associated with males and females, are affected by material social practices. In some societies, females' lower social status has resulted in them receiving less to eat, and the lack of nutrition (among other factors) has had the effect of making women smaller in size (Jaggar 1983b, 37). Uniformity in muscular shape, size, and strength within sex categories is not straightforwardly caused by genes and hormones but depends heavily on exercise opportunities. If males and females were equally encouraged to exercise, it is thought that bodily dimorphism would diminish (Fausto-Sterling 1993a, 218). A number of medical phenomena involving bones (like osteoporosis) have social causes directly related to expectations about gender, like women's diet and exercise patterns (Fausto-Sterling 2005). These examples suggest that physiological features thought to be sex-specific and not affected by social and cultural factors are, in fact, to some extent products of social and ideological forces. Our social practices having to do with exercise and food take place within broader social frameworks that render those practices, relative to a context, socially meaningful. Such ideology-laden practices shape our biology, and in this sense we can say that sexed bodies are also socially constructed.

Next, consider the idea construction of sex concepts. Our concept of *sex* is said to be a product of ideological forces in the sense that what counts as sex is shaped by social practices and what we take to be socially meaningful. Standardly, those with XX chromosomes, ovaries that produce large egg cells, female genitalia, a relatively high proportion of "female" hormones, and other secondary sex characteristics (relatively small body size, less body hair) count as biologically female. Those with XY chromosomes, testes that produce small sperm cells, male genitalia, a relatively high proportion of "male" hormones, and other secondary sex traits (relatively large body size, significant amounts of body hair) count as male. Some argue that this understanding is (surprisingly) fairly recent (Laqueur 1990). The prevalent scientific view from ancient Greeks until the late eighteenth century did not consider female and male sexes to be distinct categories with specific traits. Instead, in this "one sex" model, males and females were thought to be members of the same sex category; females' genitals were thought to be the same as males' but simply directed inside the body. Ovaries and testes (for instance) were referred to by the same term, and whether the term referred to the former or the latter was made clear by the context (1990, 4). It was not until the late 1700s that scientists began to think of female and male anatomies as radically different, moving away from the one-sex model of a single sex spectrum to the (nowadays prevalent) two-sex model of sexual dimorphism.

Anne Fausto-Sterling (1993b; 2000a; 2000b) has argued that this two-sex model isn't straightforward either. A meta-analysis of medical literature from 1955 onward shows that an estimated 1.7 percent of all live births fail to conform to a "Platonic ideal of absolute sex chromosome, gonadal, genital, and hormonal dimorphism" (Blackless et al. 2000, 161). Recognition of intersexes suggests that feminists (and people more generally) are wrong to think that humans are exclusively *either* female *or* male. The case of the athlete Maria Martínez-Patiño illustrates the idea construction of sex further. Martínez-Patiño has female genitalia, considered herself to be female, and was considered so by others. However, she was discovered to have XY chromosomes and was barred from competing in women's sports (Fausto-Sterling 2000b, 1–3). Martínez-Patiño's genitalia were at odds with her chromosomes, and the latter were taken to determine her sex. However, she successfully fought to be recognized as a female athlete, arguing that her chromosomes alone were not sufficient *not* to make her female. (In fact, sex verification in elite sports based on chromosomes was abandoned in response to Martínez-Patiño's case.) Cases like this illustrate that our conceptions of sex vary relative to what we think of as significant and socially salient, which suggests that there is no obvious nonevaluative biological way to settle what sex amounts to. Deciding what we mean by *sex* involves evaluative judgments that are influenced by social and ideological factors.[10]

The above considerations raise questions about the value neutrality of fixing sex classes. In addition to arguing against identity politics and for gender performativity, Butler has further questioned biology's supposed nonconstructedness. She holds that distinguishing biological sex from social gender is unintelligible. For her, both are socially constructed: "If the immutable character of sex is contested, perhaps this construct called 'sex' is as culturally constructed as gender" (1999, 10).[11] The idea that sex is a social construct boils down to the view that our sexed bodies are also performative, and so they have "no ontological status apart from the various acts which constitute [their] reality" (Butler 1999, 173). Prima facie this implausibly suggests that female and male bodies do not have independent existence, and that if gendering activities ceased, so would physical bodies. This is not Butler's claim; rather, her point is that bodies viewed as the material foundations on which gender is constructed are themselves constructed *as if* they provide such material foundations (Butler 1993). Gendered cultural conceptions about bodies figure in "the very apparatus of production whereby sexes themselves are established" (Butler 1999, 11). For Butler, sexed bodies are not empty matter outside of social meanings on which gender is subsequently constructed; rather, how we understand gender shapes how we understand sex (1999, 139). Sexed bodies are discursively constructed in virtue of what is attributed to them and how they are classified. When doctors call a newly born infant a girl or a boy, they are not making a descriptive claim; in fact, the doctor is performing an illocutionary speech act that makes infants into girls or boys. Thus, calling someone "female" or "male" is a normative matter (Butler 1993, 1), but we engage in activities that make it seem as if sexes naturally come in two, and that being female or male is an objective (nonsocial and agent independent) feature of the world. This is what Butler means when

---

[10] In 2012, the International Olympic Committee issued a new policy to determine who is eligible to compete in women's sports. They abandoned "sex testing" almost a decade earlier in order to avoid difficult questions about what really makes one female or male. However, the new policy advocates a check on androgens levels, like the level of testosterone. If athletes' levels are too high, they are deemed to be "too masculine" and barred from competing in women's sports (Karkazis et al. 2012, 3). Critics might say that in this decision too we can see ideologies and social meanings at work.

[11] Butler is not alone in questioning tenable distinctions between nature/culture, biology/construction, and sex/gender. See also Antony 1998; Gatens 1996; Grosz 1994; Prokhovnik 1999; Sveinsdóttir 2011.

she says that physical bodies never exist outside of cultural and social meanings. She does not hold that material bodies are made out of immaterial discursive practices (contra Nagl-Docekal 1999, chap. 1). Social construction via discursive practices (among others) makes the existence, nature, and significance of physical bodies *intelligible* to us.

2.5. Usefulness of the Sex/Gender Distinction

Some feminists hold that distinguishing sex and gender is (no longer) useful.[12] For a start, it is thought to reflect politically problematic dualistic thinking that undercuts feminist aims: the distinction is said to reflect and replicate androcentric oppositions that have been used to justify women's oppression, such as mind/body, culture/nature, and reason/emotion (e.g., Grosz 1994; Prokhovnik 1999). In oppositions like these, the argument goes, one term is always superior to the other, and the devalued term is usually associated with women (Lloyd 1993). For instance, human subjectivity and agency are identified with the mind; but since women are usually identified with their bodies, they are devalued as human subjects and agents. The opposition between the mind and the body is said to map onto other distinctions too, like those of reason/emotion, culture/nature, and rational/irrational, where the right-hand side of each distinction is devalued and associated with women.

The mind/body dualism is also said to map onto the sex/gender distinction (Grosz 1994; Prokhovnik 1999). The idea is that gender maps onto mind, sex onto body. The basic idea can be summed up by the slogan "Gender is between the ears, sex is between the legs." The implication is that, while sex is immutable, gender is something individuals have control over. It is something we can modify through individual choices. However, since women are said to be more closely associated with biological features, while men are treated as gender-neutral persons, this implies that "man equals gender, which is associated with mind and choice, freedom from body, autonomy, and with the public realm; while woman equals sex, associated with the body, reproduction, 'natural' rhythms and the private realm" (Prokhovnik 1999, 103). This conceptual contamination supposedly renders the sex/gender distinction inherently repressive and drains it of any emancipatory potential: rather than facilitating gender role choices for women, it reinforces their association with "natural" bodily functioning (1999, 103). Contra views like Rubin's, the sex/gender distinction fails to offer a theoretical tool that dissociates conceptions of womanhood from biology and reproduction.

---

[12] I am very sympathetic to this view, although for reasons other than those outlined here. I will return to this issue in chapter 5, where I put forward my own case for giving up the sex/gender distinction.

Toril Moi has further argued that the distinction is useless given certain theoretical goals (1999, chap. 1). It worked well to show that the historically prevalent biological determinism was false. However, Moi holds, the sex/gender distinction is "simply irrelevant to the task of producing a concrete, historical understanding of what it means to be a woman (or a man) in a given society" (1999, 4–5). If we want to know what it is to be a woman, the distinction traditionally understood does no useful work because neither sex nor gender is fully constitutive of womanhood. Gendered social norms play a significant part in making us into women and men. But gender alone cannot do the job. The standard distinction has turned sex, or sexual difference, into a biological essence that supposedly has no cultural or historical dimension. With this conception of sex, and the desire to avoid biological determinism, feminists have devalued sexual difference and focused on the allegedly constructed side of gender. For Moi, this is blinkered: the move assumes that there are no facts about sexual difference that are relevant for being a woman or a man. We should not treat sexual difference as being outside of evaluative judgments, and we should reject the claim that biology determines gender norms. But feminists should not ignore sexual difference altogether because "The woman I have become is more than just gender, she is a fully embodied human being whose being [nevertheless] cannot be reduced to her sexual difference, be it natural or cultural" (Moi 1999, 78). What it is to be a woman cannot be explicated in terms of gender or in terms of sex alone. In order to produce a good feminist theory of embodied and gendered subjectivity, Moi claims, we must rely on something other than the traditional sex/gender distinction.

2.6. Women as a Social Kind

The above critiques give rise to the semantic and ontological puzzles. Feminism is thought to represent particular political subjects, who satisfy the gender concept *woman*, and this binds them together. If this way of singling out feminism's subject matter is correct, the term 'woman' should pick out all and only women. But, as various feminist philosophers have compellingly argued, attempts to conceptualize a unified women's social kind exclude many minority women. The concept forming the basis of feminist politics, which was assumed to have cross-cultural and transhistorical content, actually encodes conditions satisfied by only some white, cis, middle-class, Western, heterosexual women. Further, framing *woman* as a social gender notion falsely theorizes *female* as an immutable biological concept; and this generates an unhelpful and untenable sex/gender dichotomy. The supposedly shared conditions of womanhood are clearly partial at best. And gender skeptics like Butler hold that feminists cannot discover any nonproblematic conditions for satisfying *woman* since they themselves are implicated in exclusionary ways of grasping the concept. Thus, she proposes that *woman* should be understood as an open-ended concept without any discernible content. Views like these give rise to the semantic puzzle: What are the conditions that the concept *woman* encodes, which would make feminism genuinely inclusive? How should we conceive of the term 'woman' so that it properly picks out feminism's subject matter? The ontological puzzle emerges out of its semantic counterpart. In this sense, the feminist gender controversy is analogous to (what Joshua Glasgow [2009] calls) the "race debate": the semantics of racial concepts will settle ontological issues about racial classification—namely, which social kinds do our racial terms track. For instance, if our race talk turns out to be empty and meaningless, there are no (social or natural) kinds for our racial terms to track. In a similar vein, semantic confusion over *woman* is thought to result in ontological confusion about women's social kind. If (as Butler claims) the definition of *woman* is "incomplete," "permanently moot," and "permanently deferred" (1990, 21–22), we cannot articulate the concept's application conditions. And not knowing these conditions makes it unclear which individuals are within the extension of 'woman'—we cannot delimit women's social kind. This threatens a basic tenet of feminism: if *woman* is an open-ended concept, so that the conditions for satisfying it cannot be discerned, it seems impossible to maintain that 'woman' marks off the class of individuals feminism ought to be organized around. Insofar as feminists accept that (as Marilyn Frye puts it) it is "a fundamental claim of feminism that women [as a group] are oppressed" (1983, 1), how can we fight against injustices experienced by women as a group, if, strictly speaking, no such group exists? How can feminist work proceed if we accept that the "rifts between and amongst women over the content of the term ['woman'] ought to be safeguarded and prized, indeed, that this constant rifting ought to be affirmed as the ungrounded ground of feminist theory" (Butler 1991, 160)?

If the aforementioned critiques and gender skepticism are accepted, there is no principled way to bind women as women together, and they fail to make up a genuine kind. Women make up a merely gerrymandered—random and arbitrary—collection of individuals. The subsequent situation would be one where feminist theorists aim to speak and make political demands in the name of women as a group, at the same time rejecting the idea that 'woman' names such a group (Alcoff 2006, 152). However, many have found the fragmentation of women's kind problematic for political reasons and have subsequently held that the semantic and ontological puzzles must be resolved (e.g., Alcoff 2006; Benhabib 1992; Frye 1996; Haslanger 2000; Heyes 2000; Martin 1994; Mikkola 2007; Stoljar 1995; Stone 2004; Tanesini 1996; Witt 2011a; Young 1997; Zack 2005). Here are some representative examples. Cressida Heyes writes that the confusion over the extension of the term 'woman' generates a number of feminist concerns:

> To whom does the word "women" refer? Can we offer a set of necessary and sufficient conditions for being a woman? How can we make decisions about which similarities between women count as such conditions and which differences are irrelevant to uses of the term? . . . Should part of the task of feminist theory be to define the parameters of the concept "women" or to "get it right" about who women are? (2000, 37)

Heyes claims that if these concerns are not satisfyingly responded to, and if feminism's scope is not fixed, "there can be no basis to feminist mobilizing, i.e., that if the very category 'women' is ungrounded, then feminist activism cannot proceed" (2000, 39). Similarly, Natalie Stoljar holds that unless the semantic and ontological puzzles are settled, there will be no "justification for feminist action on behalf of women" (1995, 282). Louise Antony notes that the fragmentation of women's kind (and the inability to articulate a theory of gender) has "generated enormous controversy among feminists," many of whom "feel that the availability of gender as an analytical category is vital to progress towards feminist goals" (1998, 75). Young takes gender skeptical positions like Butler's to be politically paralyzing:

> Do these arguments imply that it makes no sense and is morally wrong ever to talk about women as a group, or in fact to talk about social groups at all? . . . If not, then what can it mean to use the term 'woman'? More importantly, in the light of these critiques, what sort of positive claims can feminists make about the way social life is or ought to be? (1997, 16)

She further claims that unless there is "some sense in which 'woman' is the name of a social collective [that feminism represents], there is nothing specific to feminist politics" (1997, 13). Any attempt effectively to respond to women's oppression requires that feminism be organized around the category of women. And this requires that feminists can identify such a category: "Without conceptualizing women as a group in some sense, it is not possible to conceptualize oppression as a systematic, structured, institutional process" (1997, 17). After all, if there is no discernible group of women disadvantaged by patriarchy, instances of oppression that women face turn out to be accidental and random as opposed to reflecting systematic institutionalized injustices.

To illustrate what is at stake, consider sexual violence. Women as a social kind or group prima facie suffer more sexual violence than men, and ending this kind of violence is an important feminist task. But if gender skeptics are right, how can feminism effectively respond to systematic violence women face, if the kind apparently subject to such violence is not (and cannot be) marked off? In this case, not being able to articulate the category of women seems to have precisely the kind of paralyzing effect Young notes: feminists would simply be unable to act against structural and systematic injustices women as a group face in the absence of an identifiable group experiencing such injustices. Or, to put the point differently: systematic oppression cannot but target some particular social kind; so if systematic oppression targets women as women, their social kind *must* exist in some sense. The challenge for feminist philosophers is to articulate the sense in which it does. Doing so (the argument goes) is a prerequisite for effective emancipatory feminism. And if discerning the conditions for satisfying the concept *woman* enables feminists to articulate women's social kind, which on the face of it seems plausible, an analysis of *woman* would be the natural first step (cf. Haslanger 2000). If our analysis is fruitless and we cannot elucidate how women make up a genuine kind, the rug is pulled under feminist politics.

As a result, some feminist philosophers take the articulation of a genuine social kind of women that is inclusive in accommodating intersectionality to be the prerequisite for effective feminist politics. In recent years, a rich literature has emerged that aims to conceptualize women's kind in order to prevent it from disintegrating into a gerrymandered collection of individuals. The prevalent strategy has been to respond to the semantic and ontological puzzles and to do so in a particular manner: by providing a thick enough conception of womanhood that can support feminist normative demands, for example, enabling feminists to speak against the status quo on behalf of women, while avoiding the charge of being exclusionary. In subsequent chapters, I will consider feminist positions that aim to do just that. Of course, feminists could have argued for thin conceptions of *woman*. But this move as a matter of fact has not been popular, which illustrates the pull of certain—in my view, unhelpful—theoretical presumptions in feminist philosophizing. Ultimately, I will argue that responding to the semantic and ontological puzzles is the wrong strategy, and I hold that these puzzles can be deflated (cf. chapter 5). Thus, we can give up the view that articulating a thick notion of *woman* is a desideratum of an acceptable theory of gender, and that such a notion is needed to support feminist political demands. This will motivate my proposed paradigm shift to humanist feminism (cf. Part II). But first let's examine how and why the prevalent strategy is unsatisfying.

Nominalist Responses to the Semantic and Ontological Puzzles

How best to cash out under which social conditions someone counts as a woman has concerned a number of contemporary feminist philosophers, and it is a major feminist controversy. For one thing, social and cultural diversity imply that no shared social conditions for satisfying the concept *woman* exist to begin with. How best to define the notion is not simply a matter of disagreement; cultural difference undermines the whole project and creates apparently insurmountable difficulties for elucidating *woman*—difficulties that are not merely semantic, but are also said to generate ontological worries that in turn give rise to political problems. Eradicating women's oppression (feminism's supposed political goal) is thought to require that feminist politics orient itself around those who fall under *woman*. But not knowing the social conditions constitutive of womanhood makes it unclear which individuals feminism ought to be organized around. And not being able to articulate a genuine women's social kind appears to stifle feminism politically. Linda Alcoff captures the worry as follows:

> What can we demand in the name of women if "women" do not exist and demands in their name simply reenforce the myth that they do? How can we speak out against sexism as detrimental to the interests of women if the category is a fiction? How can we demand legal abortions, adequate child care, or wages based on comparable worth without invoking the concept of "women"? (2006, 143)

Given the apparently looming political worries, many have claimed that articulating a thick social notion of *woman* is a desideratum and the vital first step of an acceptable theory of gender (e.g., Frye 1996; Haslanger 2000; Heyes 2000; Stoljar 1995; Stone 2004; Tanesini 1996; Young 1997). An account of gender ought to enable us to conceive of feminism's subject matter—perhaps even of feminist political solidarity—by providing a way to conceptualize

women's social kind. Further, this conception should be thick enough to support feminist normative claims: to elucidate how and why patriarchy damages
women, to justify feminist critical claims about extant states of affairs, and to
ground a vision of a feminist future—all in the name of women. And finally,
in response to various gender skeptic and intersectional critiques, feminist
philosophers hold that such a conception should be inclusive and recognize
women's diversity. So the desiderata of an adequate theory of gender are (1) to
articulate *woman* in a thick enough manner so that it marks off a politically
helpful social kind and supports feminist normative demands; (2) to do so in
a nonexclusionary manner.

Recent accounts of gender that aim to respond to the semantic and ontological worries are aiming to satisfy these desiderata. All of those opposing gender skepticism argue that we can make sense of women as a genuine
kind, contra the view that women make up a merely gerrymandered set of
individuals. We can understand genuine kinds as either natural or social.
With respect to gender, it is not usual to argue that women make up a natural
kind (for a notable exception, see Bach 2012. This view will be discussed in
chapter 4). Instead, women are thought to make up a genuine *social* kind,
and this view is explicitly or implicitly based on some configuration of the
sex/gender distinction. Nevertheless, feminist philosophers do not agree on
which theory of gender provides the best articulation of womanhood. In fact,
there are almost as many theories as there are feminist philosophers working
on the topic. Still, we can divide recent responses roughly into two:

a. *Gender nominalism* denies that there is some normatively and ethically significant feature that women qua women share; still, it holds
   that there is *something* that unifies women's social kind, which is
   normatively significant (e.g., some relations in which women stand).
b. *Gender realism* takes there to be some (normatively) important feature that women qua women share, which unifies their social kind.
   Such a feature is usually thought to be socially constructed and individually nonessential.[1]

In this chapter, I will focus on recent gender nominalist positions. In chapter 4,
I will consider gender realist accounts and the view that women make up a
natural kind. This and the next chapter intend to accomplish the following.

---

[1] It is worth noting that different feminist philosophers' typology of these positions differs. For
instance, gender nominalism is at times taken to be the position that there are no women, or that
their social kind is a "fiction" (Alcoff 2006). However, the view that women's social kind simply does
not exist is one that I term gender skepticism, not nominalism. So on my typology nominalists do
not reject the existence of women's genuine social kind. They merely reject the view that there is
something women as women *share*, which unifies this kind. In a sense, gender skeptics are radical
gender nominalists. But in order to clarify the various feminist positions, I find it helpful to avoid
calling the radical version "gender nominalist."

First, to demonstrate the pull of certain theoretical presumptions in feminist accounts of gender that (I hold) we need not preserve. Second, to show that the considered theories of gender do not succeed: in various ways, they are unsatisfying by their own lights. So for now I will assume (for argument's sake) that the semantic and ontological puzzles are worth responding to; however, my argument goes, the views discussed have individual weaknesses that render them untenable as satisfying responses to the puzzles. Later on, I will argue for a more radical conclusion (cf. chapter 5): articulating a thick conception of *woman* is unnecessary because we can deflate the semantic and ontological worries.

3.1. The "Positive" Category of Women

Marilyn Frye (1996) aims to articulate a unified women's social kind, at the same time rejecting that women share some feature(s) as women. For her, classificatory efforts need not rely on some set of shared features necessary and sufficient for being a woman, nor can we identify any intrinsically or inherently important factor about women that has normative significance. Rather, particular *relations* in which women stand relative to one another ground classification and tell us what it is to be a woman in some politically significant sense. Frye takes these relations to be understood in terms of certain practices that women engage in. Conceiving of womanhood in this manner constitutes (what Frye calls) a "positive category" of women: women make up a social kind that is "self-supporting rather than dependent on nega-tion" (1996, 998). Such a kind should be understood in a way that relies solely on aspects relevant for women's lives, experiences, and conditions *as women*. And constructing such a "positive" category of women "is a vital political function of feminist community and politics" (Frye 1996, 998).

According to Frye, de Beauvoir (1972) and Irigaray (1985) are paradigm feminists who have understood gender classes incorrectly and against whom she develops her own position. She takes both de Beauvoir's existentialist and Irigaray's psychoanalytic theories of gender to rely on a notion of *woman* that is merely a negation of *man*. Both claim that under certain oppressive social conditions "subjectivity" is coextensive with "'masculinity.'" As this is the case, women turn out to lack subjectivity, and it is this *lack* that is definitive of their gender. For de Beauvoir, subjectivity requires living a life of "tran-scendence": one must be autonomous, free to decide one's own destiny and to freely pursue one's self-chosen goals and aims. But only men are currently capable of such a life. Women's actions are constrained by their biology and childbearing ability, which confine them to a life of "immanence": to a life of stagnation and repetition of mundane tasks, where one's potential as an active human subject cannot develop. For Irigaray, subjectivity requires that one be a signifier: a source and creator of meanings, someone with the power and authority to signify, to be meaningful and significant, and to speak authoritatively. But only men have the power and authority to signify because their bodies are endowed with certain required symbolic meanings, which women's bodies lack.

For Frye, articulating "what it is to be a woman" is crucial for feminist philosophy and politics (1996, 998), but defining womanhood as lacking masculine qualities is highly problematic. Doing so constructs "the social/ontological category of men as the A side of a universal exclusive dichotomy: A/not-A" (Frye 1996, 994). Instead of understanding gender via negation, gendered kinds should be understood as self-standing: A (men) and B (women), respectively. The unsatisfying "negative" picture of womanhood stems from feminist theorists' alleged reliance on set theory, which determines class membership in terms of certain necessary and sufficient conditions. More recently, Frye has elaborated on what is problematic about this set theoretic approach. We talk about membership *in* some social kind just as we talk about peas being *in* the can. And this metaphorically suggests that social kinds are like containers, where some features are necessary and sufficient for being in the kind (Frye 2011, 86). All and only those particulars that possess these features get in, while others stay out. Furthermore, this approach defines one side of the dichotomy as a distinguishable something, whereas the other side encompasses everything else. So, in order for certain entities to constitute a genuine type (as opposed to a merely gerrymandered set of things) they must possess certain features required for type membership. The collection of entities that lacks these features will include every other entity, which makes it a thoroughly gerrymandered and miscellaneous collection of things. The set theoretical approach attributed to de Beauvoir and Irigaray consequently defines *being a woman* as that which does not satisfy the conditions for *being a man*. And this renders our conception of womanhood vacuous and nonsubstantive. Subsequently: "The man/not-man dichotomy makes no distinctions on the not-man side. . . . Undifferentiated from the rest of not-man, woman is not a category. There are no categories in not-man; it is a buzzing blooming confusion. Everything is similar to everything" (Frye 1996, 1000). Instead, feminist theorists need to understand women's kind in a self-sustaining manner, and not rely on features that women *fail* to possess.

However, doing so should not appeal to any form of realism about gender—a position Frye rejects given women's particularity and diversity. Rather, women's social kind should be cashed out in terms of women's differences, and Frye's alternative method for category building has three analytically required criteria. First, members of a category must be related to one another in some way. Second, these relations must be structured. Third, the structure must be internally complex. Frye elaborates the second criteria with an example of a club for people with red hair:

> What makes the Redheads' Club a club is not that all the individuals who are members of it have red hair, or that they have identical experience, though hair color and experience are salient; it is that individuals are involved, in various ways, in a structure. (1996, 1001)

She further justifies the internal complexity of such a structure by claiming that any viable and useful structure must be internally diverse. Minimally, members of internally complex structures "differ in their relations to each other (e.g., one is to the left of another, but the second is to the right of the first); but organic and social entities require differentiation on many vectors" (1996, 1001). If all the members of the redheads' club had exactly the same attributes, experiences, and features, they would not form a genuine club because internal complexity would be missing. The three criteria mentioned (relations, structure, diversity) then provide a way to conceive of women's self-standing social kind in a manner that is supposedly inclusive and responsive to intersectional worries.

How such a social kind of women is actually constructed is not entirely clear. Frye claims that such a category-building method suggests a political strategy of "deliberately, creatively elaborating and articulating the differences among women in, by, and as a means to constructing a sociality" (1996, 1002). She goes on to claim that this manner of formulating women's social kind is not new. Rather, it has taken place unwittingly through certain practices women have engaged in. For Frye, places where such practices occur include women's music and arts festivals; the US National Women's Studies Association; creative writing groups for women; communities of authors, editors, and audiences of feminist publications; collectives of women producing and circulating such publications; women's bookstores and international women's book fairs; women's caucuses, collectives, projects, conferences, and gatherings that "share certain distinctions of race, ability, sexuality, religion, ethnicity, nationality, politics, citizenship status, and/or interests in arts, sport, adventure, entertainment, scholarship, technology, and so on" (1996, 1006). If such practices are engaged in for any length of time, women will become profoundly involved in

> articulating, elaborating, appreciating, defining, exploring, recognizing, negotiating, consolidating, and travelling differences among women. . . . If women were going to be together in women-focused, women-defined, and women-defining spaces and enterprises, women were going to engage in many varieties of what might be called "the practice of differences." (Frye 1996, 1007)

That said, it is unclear why individuals get involved in the kinds of practices Frye outlines, and she does not elaborate on this point. The most obvious answer is they have some shared identity, interests, affinities, or goals. But this cannot be what brings individual women together; in fact, Frye takes shared affinities and experiences to *follow* from being a member of women's social kind, which is characterized by certain structured relations of diversity resulting from participation in women-focused practices.

We can see the theoretical outlook that I wish to resist at work in Frye's position. Feminists must be able to articulate a conception of *woman* in some determinate and thick enough manner, and being able to do so is a vital task of feminist theory and politics. As long as womanhood is defined "negatively," feminist theory will not be able to delimit women's social kind (feminism's subject matter), or say anything politically helpful about what it is to be a woman—in fact, we cannot say anything about women since women will be akin to everything that is "not-man." In order to respond to gender injustice, feminists need to understand women's social kind in the self-sustaining manner as a category characterized by structured relations of differences amongst women. I will have more to say about Frye's position shortly (cf. section 3.3.) But first, consider Iris Marion Young's prominent alternative version of gender nominalism.

3.2. Women as a Social Series

Young suggests that a pragmatic orientation to classification answers the ontological puzzle. By this she means "categorizing, explaining, developing accounts and arguments that are tied to specific practical and political problems, where the purpose of this theoretical activity is clearly related to those problems" (1997, 16–17). The specific political and practical problem Young has in mind is to prevent feminist theory from evaporating and becoming politically ineffective by means of offering a way to articulate women's social kind. In order to do so, Young conceives of gender with the help of Jean-Paul Sartre's (1976) notion of *seriality*. This bypasses gender realism and the view that women as women share some attributes or experiences. Simultaneously, it avoids the gender-skeptical view that there is no genuine women's social kind, it can deal with intersectional worries, and the position allegedly respects women's particularity.

A crucial aspect of Sartre's (and Young's) position is the distinction between groups and series. Sartrean groups have four features: (1) they are collections of people who recognize themselves and others as being in some unified relation; (2) group members mutually acknowledge that they undertake some common project together; (3) they are united and bound together by *action* that is jointly undertaken; and (4) in acknowledging their group membership, individuals acknowledge that they are working toward shared goals with other group members. In short, group membership requires that individual members share some experiences, traits, or features and thus have a particular identity or self-ascription as group members in common (Young 1997, 33). Prior feminist efforts to classify women have been problematic precisely because they attempted to make sense of women's social kind as a group in this sense—as a collection of individuals with common experiences that gives rise to a shared identity as women. Since no such identity exists, such efforts to conceptualize women as a group are bound to fail. By contrast, a series for Sartre lacks the feature of being unified by common goals, pursuits, or identity. So if women form a series, we can avoid the earlier problems because series membership does not require any shared attributes or experiences that support a common identity. A series is

> a social collective whose members are unified passively by the objects their actions are oriented around and/or by the objectified results of the material effects of the actions of the others, . . . The unity of the series derives from the way that individuals pursue their own individual ends in respect to the same objects conditioned by a continuous material environment, in response to structures that have been created by the unintended collective result of past actions. *(Young 1997, 23–24)*

Individual series' members do not aim to accomplish any shared goals, and rather pursue their own individual aims. In so doing, they unwittingly constitute a series, as the objects and practices with which they pursue their individual goals are (in a sense) similar. Applying seriality to gender then "makes theoretical sense out of saying that 'women' is a reasonable social category, expressing a certain kind of social unity" without relying on shared features or experiences (1997, 27).

Why does an appeal to certain *objects* around which individual action is oriented provide a plausible way to understand social kinds like gender? Sartre's existentialist philosophy may provide an explanation. As Young puts it, Sartre's notion of human freedom takes social relations to be understood in relation to the production of actions (1997, 23). Recall de Beauvoir's feminist existentialism discussed above. She claimed that women are not fully-fledged human subjects because they are confined to repeating mundane tasks through which they cannot realize their human potential, whereas (white, affluent) men are free to set and pursue their own individual goals and be the authors of their own destinies. Human action is a prerequisite for human freedom, but clearly different kinds of action exist; for example, there is action that is organized around shared goals and aims (like the storming of the Bastille), and there is action that is organized around everyday life, habit, and routine (like doing one's weekly shopping in a particular supermarket). In both cases, certain objects organize these actions (the Bastille or the supermarket). The subsequent collections of people differ because the objects around which their actions are organized differ. Further, the natures of collectives differ relative to the organizing objects. Some objects (like the Bastille) afford straightforwardly shared goals, while other objects (like the supermarket) for the most part provide no impetus to develop clearly defined shared goals. They merely regulate our habitual actions. It is precisely in such a manner that social kinds like the working class and women are organized. We can say that they are social collectives in *some* sense. And so women's lives are unified at the level of similar everyday habits and routines, not at the level of shared goals and action. They form a series, and this provides a way for feminist philosophers to understand a unified women's social kind.

Series form in response to individuals' practico-inert realities: material objects and actions of other people. Those who are faced with the same or similar realities constitute a particular series. Being a member of a series in a sense defines an individual: one "is" a woman together with other series members in that the two persons are similarly positioned. But this identification does not describe one's identity as a woman, which one shares with other women. Rather, it tells us something about women's lived material conditions. What, then, are the practico-inert objects and realities that serialize women? First and foremost, these include physical facts about female bodies as well as social practices, rules, and meanings bodies are endowed with (e.g., the social rules of menstruation, material objects associated with menstrual practices, biological events like pregnancy, childbirth, and lactation) (Young 1997, 28). Further, female bodies along with objects and events associated with them are rendered practico-inert by (the ideology of) enforced heterosexuality, which defines the meaning of bodies "not as mere physical objects but as practico-inert" (1997, 28). Unfortunately, Young does not elaborate much on this thought. Her view seems to be that female bodies are endowed with certain kinds of meanings since we live within the remits of compulsory and enforced heterosexism (cf. Butler's normativity argument in section 2.3.). Women do not create these meanings; rather, oppressive patriarchal social arrangements enable men to create and impose them on women, which constrains women's independent action. This apparently renders female bodies practico-inert on Young's view. However, women are serialized in other ways too, and a huge array of other objects also determine our gendered experiences. These include gendered pronouns; verbal and visual representations that create and reproduce gendered meanings; artifacts and social spaces that are gender coded, like clothes, cosmetics, tools, furniture, and spaces that materially inscribe gender norms (Young 1997, 29). These practico-inert objects are not ideologically governed by enforced heterosexuality, but rather by the sexual division of labor. It renders (say) the use of certain kind of language, clothing, and work "natural" to women (like women working in offices wearing skirts and makeup).

This way of thinking, Young holds, meets the desiderata of a satisfying theory of gender. Seriality supposedly avoids the pitfalls of gender skepticism, on the one hand, and gender realism, on the other. It deals with intersectional worries about homogenizing women's experiences as women, since each woman will have her own particular way of responding to the practico-inert structures that genders her. Further, Young aims to articulate a (passively) unified women's social kind in a politically thick enough manner. Her elucidation of the kind is meant to enable us to "conceptualize oppression as a systematic, structured, institutional process" (Young 1997, 17). Without doing so, and without articulating women's social kind, feminism will be undermined, since there will be "nothing specific to feminist politics" (1997, 13). Again, a conception of *woman* ought to be articulated in a thick enough manner to satisfy feminist political demands and to enable us to analyze oppressive social relations.

3.3. Unity, Normativity, and Oppression

Both Frye and Young aim to respond to the ontological puzzle in order to save feminism's normative grounding. Frye claims that engaging in certain woman-centered practices of difference makes women structurally related to one another in an internally diverse manner. This allows us to understand women's social kind as a self-standing positive category, which makes the category substantive and prevents it from being vacuous. Young claims that women are passively unified into a social series. They do not self-consciously share any attributes, features, or experiences qua women. Instead, the unity of the kind derives from women pursuing individual goals and aims, where this is organized around practico-inert realities regulated by compulsory heterosexuality and the sexual division of labor. However, I contend that neither provides a good response to the ontological puzzle (accepting, for now, that this is a worthwhile goal). Moreover, the positions fail on the same grounds: neither provides a unified account of women's social kind, and thus both fail to support feminist normative claims and demands.

Consider the unity of women's social kind first. Both proposals are rather vague with respect to this issue, and it is unclear whether the grounds given are enough to unify women. Neither position can appeal to shared features since they reject gender realism. But my view is that doing so renders the positions implausible. Frye claims that women's diversity does not undermine the idea that women constitute a single social kind (1996, 1005). Further, as the structure by virtue of which women as a group are supposedly unified requires that individuals so classified differ from one another, feminists have no reason to demand that the members of this class have something in common qua class members. And in being unified by structured relations of diversity, women will supposedly be constantly faced with and reminded of the differences between them, which is politically valuable. Now, women do differ from one another, but this may be just a trivial point about each individual qua individual differing from others. On a more substantive reading, the claim is that women qua woman differ—that is, diversity is in the nature of womanhood. But I do not see how this gives women's kind the sort of unity that Frye is after. What Frye needs is some account of how, despite individual differences, there is *something* that motivates women to engage in woman-focused practices and that binds them together.

Take Frye's discussion of the redheads' club: she claims that what makes this club *a club* is that the individual members become involved with one another despite their particular differences. They may come from different religions, cultures, or parts of town, which makes the group of redheads internally complex and diverse. Now, this may qualify for being *a club*, but being a *redheads'* club is going to require something else. In order to say why this club is a redheads' club, the most obvious answer is that the individual members share some salient feature: they all have red hair, and *this* has brought them together. Although Frye dismisses this as grounding the unity of the redheads' club, she admits that hair color is not irrelevant to membership. However, in her discussion of women this point is rejected. In fact, Frye seems to think that attributions of womanness *result from* belonging to a structured internally diverse collection of individuals. Only after women engage and partake in certain practices do they make up a positive self-standing category, and a genuine social kind. But this renders the account wrongheaded. Consider the redheads' club, which Frye maintains is structurally analogous to women's social kind. If our gender attributions result from partaking in common woman-focused practices, we would have to say that because individual members of the redheads' club have come together and constitute a club, they come to have red hair. But this is clearly false; the situation is precisely the opposite. So, Frye's position either fails to achieve its goal (it does not give us grounds for thinking that women make up a *unified* social kind) or ends up being deeply implausible (being a member of the redheads' club makes the members redheaded).

Young's position faces similar problems. For her, the unity of women's social kind derives from individual women pursuing their own goals and aims, where their pursuit is organized around similar practico-inert realities. But how do the above-mentioned realities constitute a *single* series of women, who vary so considerably from one another? This question is particularly pressing since Young claims that women's series includes *all* females who currently exist, and many who existed in the past (1997, 36). To illustrate problems with her position, consider just one example of practico-inert realities that serialize women: "the social rules of menstruation, along with the material objects associated with menstrual practices" (Young 1997, 28). The relevant rules and material objects differ greatly across human populations and times. Prior to the invention of modern sanitary towels (in the 1920s), females wore garments similar to babies' diapers that they washed and reused (Delaney et al. 1988, 58). Many extant females still do out of necessity, or by way of protest against capitalist consumerism's "throwaway culture." Others make use of disposable sanitary towels and have a staggering choice of products from a range of manufacturers, sizes, and shapes. All of this demonstrates the complexity of the material objects around which menstrual practices are oriented. Bearing in mind many cultural taboos and menstruation rites, the social rules of menstruation become more diverse still. A relatively moderate practice followed by Orthodox Jewish women is to refrain from sexual intercourse until seven days after their menstruation has ended, and only after they have immersed themselves in a ritual bath or *mikveh* (Delaney et al. 1988, 39). Historically, other more extreme cultural practices and menstruation rules have been observed. For example, "The Kolosh Indians of Alaska confined pubescent girls in a tiny hut, completely blocked except for one small airhole, for one year, during which time they were allowed no fire, no exercise, no company" (1988, 29). This rite marks the passage from childhood to adulthood, after which females were usually considered to be marriageable. A Brazilian ethnic group, the Uaupés, have exercised even more extreme menstrual rites to make their daughters marriageable:

> At her menarche, a girl is confined to her house for a month, with only a little bread and water for nourishment. When her seclusion is complete, she is brought out naked to be beaten with sticks by her relatives and friends of her parents until she falls senseless or dead ... [If she recovers] "the flagellation is repeated four times, at intervals of six hours, and it is considered an offense to the parents not to strike hard. Finally the sticks are dipped into pots of meat and fat and given to the girl to lick. She is now considered a marriageable woman." (Delaney et al. 1988, 32; Quoting Webster 1942, 90–91)

By contrast, in some cultures menarche is celebrated: in Japan a special dish of *sekihan* (glutinous rice colored red by beans) is prepared to mark the occasion. Now, the practico-inert objects and realities described in these examples differ hugely from one another. In thinking about these different cases, it is not immediately obvious to me why the women mentioned are members of the *same* series, and apparently so on the *same* grounds given how radically (for instance) menstrual practices differ. Young does have a way out: to claim that those serialized as women do have some feature in common—they are biologically female (because of which they typically menstruate). But this is not an option for Young because she rejects the gender-realist view that women share something as women. Doing so, however, prevents her from plausibly articulating what unifies women.[2]

In response, Young might claim that the above considerations are non-problematic because she aims to provide a pragmatic response to the problem of gender classification, not a full social theory. Being pragmatic means "categorizing, explaining, developing accounts and arguments that are tied to specific practical and political problems" (Young 1997, 17). She contrasts this approach with a theoretical stance, which aims to provide comprehensive and systematic explanations of social relations once and for all. From such a stance, "one can derive particular instances, or at least one can apply the theoretical propositions to particular facts, which the theory's generalities are supposed to 'cover'" (1997, 16). Had Young aimed to provide a theory in this sense, the lack of unity would be problematic. But since she is only providing a pragmatic account of gender, one might claim, the problems I have raised are not relevant: Young's proposal is not designed to answer my worries because it does not aim to provide a theory of gender once and for all. However, there are two issues here: how we should formulate our *goal* given some pressing problems; and what sort of a *response* yields the best result(s) given our goal. Young's view is pragmatic relative to its goal formulation: feminists must be able to articulate a theory of gender that unifies women's social kind because otherwise feminist politics will evaporate. Her response relative to this goal must be theoretical in her sense, though. In order to make good a unified conception of women's social kind, Young must provide a general theory of the kind—a theory that "covers" the relevant individual instances. Otherwise her appeal to social series yields a merely gerrymandered collection of individuals, who are randomly and arbitrarily connected via hugely divergent practico-inert realities. And such a random collection of individuals cannot be subject to nonaccidental, systematic forces of oppression. So, given that Young aims to make good women's social kind, which enables us to identify and examine systematic gender injustices, in lacking a principled way to collect women together, Young's articulation of gender (like Frye's) does not meet her self-set desiderata of a satisfying theory of gender.

---

[2] Whether Young can maintain her rejection of gender realism is questionable. Her proposal purports to be a response to Spelman's worries about diversity, and Young thinks that she has successfully avoided these worries. However, Alison Stone (2004) has questioned this: ultimately, on Young's view, something women as women share binds them together—common practico-inert realities. Of course, these realities are made up of diverse sets of more specific features. Nevertheless, women on Young's view share something, albeit something highly disparate.

These qualms about unity point to a deeper worry: how are feminist normative demands and claims to be supported with the proposed accounts of gender? Both Frye and Young accept that a desideratum of an adequate theory of gender is to articulate womanhood in a thick enough manner that it marks off a politically helpful women's social kind, which acknowledges and respects diversity. But since their positions are unsuccessful in responding to the ontological puzzle, they fail to provide tools with which feminists can fight patriarchy or explicate systematic gendered injustices. Now, one might point out in response that both Frye (1983) and Young (1990) have provided freestanding theories of oppression elsewhere that perhaps do the required normative work. And (the objection goes) their theories of gender aim to do something quite different, which is why it is no wonder that they do not help feminists articulate the damage done by patriarchy or support feminist critiques of the status quo.

This is a powerful rejoinder, but ultimately unsuccessful. Both Young and Frye *explicitly* maintain that responding to the ontological puzzle is pivotal for feminist politics (Frye 1996, 998; Young 1997, 16). And both maintain that their positions tell us something about what it is to be a woman, which is politically significant and worth knowing. For instance, Young takes the articulation of women's social series to be a prerequisite for conceptualizing systematic gendered oppression. And Frye rejected the A/not-A classificatory method because it tells us nothing substantive about women—all it tells us is that women lack the features definitive of men, which is unhelpful in being vacuous. The whole point of her alternative, "'positive" account is to *learn* something about women, which feminist politics apparently needs to know. So if their theories of oppression are meant to be freestanding and utterly distinct from their theories of gender, why do Frye and Young explicitly note such normative considerations as desiderata of their articulations of gender? Why take up an analysis of gender at all, if not for political reasons: to help elucidate how and why patriarchy damages women, to justify feminist critical claims, and to ground a vision of a feminist future? Frye and Young certainly do not take the ontological puzzle to be just a metaphysical matter with no political significance. And so, to maintain that their theories of oppression are about feminist politics but that their theories of gender are not strikes me as unfounded. Actually, I am not convinced that the accounts of oppression Young and Frye provide elsewhere are freestanding from gender or the analysis of *woman*. I wish to postpone discussing this until chapter 7. However, I should already stress that seeking a theory of injustice that is not dependent on a thick articulation of gender is on the right track and going into the right direction—nonetheless, I think that Young's and Frye's articulations of injustice that are putatively freestanding of gender simply do not go far enough, despite being in other ways insightful.

3.4. Women as a Resemblance Class

A major stumbling block for Frye and Young is the lack of sufficient unity to make good women's social kind membership. Natalie Stoljar (1995, 2011) offers a more sophisticated gender nominalist account and argues that *resemblance nominalism* provides a way to respond to the ontological puzzle. Resemblance nominalism is (roughly) the view that individual entities can be classified into a genuine type on the basis of certain resemblance relations holding (Armstrong 1989, chap. 3). Stoljar too rejects gender realism, and holds that "women are *particular*, not the same" (1995, 262). Still, women are members of the same resemblance structure, and this enables feminists to articulate their genuine social kind. This strategy is needed in order to satisfy a key feminist political desideratum: to provide a "justification for feminist action on behalf of women" (Stoljar 1995, 282). Stoljar starts by carefully elucidating why gender realism is untenable, which motivates her nominalist approach. Let's start by considering her rejection of gender realism.[3]

3.4.1. TENABILITY OF GENDER REALISM

Stoljar outlines three ways to characterize gender realism (although she employs the language of essentialism). First, Aristotelian kind essentialism takes kind membership to be delimited by the possession of some feature definitive of a species-essence. All kind members share this feature, *and* it is essential to the members qua individuals (Stoljar 1995, 267). In a gendered version of Aristotelian essentialism, women would constitute a species and have a biological species essence. This essence would be necessary and sufficient for membership in women's social kind; and were an individual woman to lose this feature, she would cease to be the very same individual. As the Aristotelian view considers species essences to be biological, the only plausible candidate for women's species essence would be femaleness—it is the only biological feature that individual women could not sustain the loss of. Stoljar goes on to claim (and rightly so) that such an Aristotelian account is implausible. This is because females/women simply do not constitute a distinct species. For one thing, this violates our modal intuitions:

> If women constitute a species, it would be logically impossible for particular men to be women in the same way that it is logically impossible for particular men to be insects or eagles. Yet there is a qualitative difference between the claim that, for example, Michelangelo could have been an insect and the claim that he could have been a woman. (Stoljar 1995, 269–270)

---

[3] It is worth noting that the positions Stoljar characterizes as gender realist differ substantially from those gender-realist positions that I will discuss in chapter 4.

We cannot conceive of Michelangelo's mother giving birth to an insect, but we can conceive of her giving birth to a baby girl. Nevertheless, if females were a distinct species, our intuitions should be on a par: whether we are talking about insects or baby girls should make no difference. Thus, the Aristotelian picture is implausible.[4]

Stoljar's second—women's kind-defining—feature is also biological, but nonnecessary: womanhood would be about having "an intrinsic, natural, [and] yet accidental property" (Stoljar 1995, 272). Stoljar's terminology here is potentially confusing. For her, nonnecessary features are not essential to individuals qua individuals, and in this sense they are accidental. Nonetheless, nonnecessary properties *are* essential for type membership, and in being natural they cannot be socially revised. For example, those who have the same facial structure or skin color have such an intrinsic, individually accidental, natural feature in common (1995, 272). The idea is that having a tall forehead, for example, is not an essential feature of individuals with tall foreheads. If they were to undergo forehead reduction surgery, they would not cease to be the same individuals. Still *having a tall forehead* is a biological feature that all tall-foreheaded individuals share, and it is necessary for membership in the kind of tall-foreheaded people. On this view, *being a woman* would be an analogous property: it would be a natural feature all women (qua women) share, but it would be accidental to individual women. Again, the most plausible view would be to hold that *being a woman* is equivalent to *being a human female* (Stoljar 1995, 273)—the latter would simply be individually nonnecessary. However, our language use supposedly counts against this second gender-realist view: the concept of *woman* fails to capture all and only female humans because 'woman' also picks out nonfemales, like male-to-female trans* people and intersexes (1995, 273). MTF trans* individuals have many social features associated with women, which explains why the term picks them out. Still, some will be biologically male. This suggests to Stoljar that 'woman' does not pick out individuals on the basis of their sex features alone, but rather on the basis of something else.

Finally, Stoljar considers whether a plausible gender realist position could be cashed out in terms of shared social features. Feminists inspired by Lockean nominal essentialism apparently hold such a position. Nominal

---

[4] Stoljar claims that feminist philosophers commonly think arguments like Spelman's count against the Aristotelian view. Contrary to this allegedly common belief, Stoljar holds "the Aristotelian essentialist position that all women have the same essential womanness—a position which has been the target of so much feminist criticism—will fail for reasons which are quite independent of the feminist arguments," like those of Spelman (1995, 272). However, I disagree with Stoljar that Spelman's arguments are aimed against the Aristotelian picture. Spelman is quite clearly not arguing against the view that women constitute a species, or that women share some essential species-defining *biological* feature. This being the case, it is not surprising that Spelman's appeal to social diversity does not count against an Aristotelian conception of gender.

essences are sets of manifest properties that help us to navigate and classify our vague natural world. For example, on the Lockean view, we would classify entities as gold on the basis of some overtly perceived superficial features (yellowness, shining color, malleability), and not on the basis of internal constitution (atomic structure). A feminist nominal essentialism, then, would take women to be unified on the basis of some perceivable superficial features, like social subordination. [5] Stoljar, however, rejects this proposal too. If we define *woman* in terms of a certain social relation, being in that relation becomes necessary and sufficient for counting as a woman. But this warrants the rejection of all Lockean-inspired feminist positions: they rely on some definitive property (or properties) constitutive of womanhood and thus cannot cope with Spelman's particularity argument (Stoljar 1995, 275). Stoljar takes MacKinnon's position as a putative example of nominal essentialism. For MacKinnon, gender is constituted by the position one inhabits in eroticized dominance and submission relations (MacKinnon 1989; cf. section 2.2.). Roughly, one's gender depends on whether one is positioned as sexually subordinate (women) or dominant (men). This makes *being sexually subordinate* women's nominal essence, which is "literally the same relation or experience in all individuals who are women—that is, it is a universal" (Stoljar 1995, 279). Such a position supposedly goes against the particularity argument because in defining what it means to be a woman by using a single feature, MacKinnon fails to take social diversity into account.[6]

One might wonder whether the above three arguments refute gender realism altogether, and provide a prima facie motivation for resemblance nominalism. After all, showing that the above three features are implausible candidates for a shared feature does not yet show that there are *no* plausible candidates for such a feature. I have previously argued (2006) that Spelman's case against gender realism is unsuccessful precisely because Spelman merely rules out some specific gender realist positions, but not gender realism per se. If this is right, Stoljar's arguments against gender realism and her motivation

---

[5] Although this position is called "nominal essentialism" it is important to bear in mind that the feminist views inspired by Locke are not gender-nominalist positions in my sense. On the Lockean view, women do share some single feature (or set of features) that makes them women, albeit a superficial one. So nominal gender essentialism is a gender-realist position.

[6] Stoljar concedes that MacKinnon's position might be rescued if the single relation MacKinnon posits were realizable in multiple ways (it takes many forms and is experienced in contextually specific ways). In fact, MacKinnon does hold that subordination can be sexualized in diverse ways and that sexual subordination of women takes various forms: "Pressure, gender socialization, withholding benefits, extending indulgences, the how-to books, the sex therapy are the soft ends; the fuck, the fist, the street, the chains, the poverty are the hard end" (1989, 136). Still, Stoljar holds that this way of rescuing MacKinnon's position would ultimately be unconvincing: "The greater the difference in manifestation, the less plausible will be the claim that those manifestations are of a *single* role or experience" (1995, 280).

for nominalism may also be undermined. Stoljar has more recently taken issue with my earlier argument, and it is worth pausing here to discuss this in order to illustrate further why she takes gender realism per se to be untenable. My contention is that gender realism is not undermined by common feminist appeals to the diversity and particularity of women. Rather, these are compatible with some gender realisms, and I have previously developed one such conception (2006). I am no longer committed to that position. This is not because I view it as implausible. The reason for distancing myself from my earlier view boils down to the first substantive argument of this book: I no longer see the need to formulate responses to the ontological puzzle. Be that as it may, I am nevertheless still convinced that Spelman's arguments do not undermine gender realism in general. I further hold that Stoljar's critique of my earlier view is unsuccessful.

Stoljar (2011) outlines five arguments against gender realism: those from social construction, diversity, nonseparability, particularity, and complexity. The final of these argues for resemblance nominalism on explanatory grounds: although women's diversity may be *compatible* with them having some feature in common, women's diversity is better explained by nominalism than realism. I will briefly discuss this in the following section. I will also leave aside the argument from nonseparability since Stoljar herself thinks it does not establish gender nominalism. Let us then focus on the three remaining arguments, which allegedly count against gender realism (and for resemblance nominalism about gender).[7] Start with the arguments from social construction and diversity. Stoljar considers my example of *being a wife*, which I claim to be analogous to *being a woman*:

> The feature of being a wife is extrinsic as it depends on numerous external factors; in order for x to have this feature x must be a woman, the institution of marriage (broadly construed) must exist and x must be married to some other individual (or individuals). The feature is also socially constructed: it is a product of certain social practices that differ enormously from one society to the next. For example, many African tribes have traditionally engaged in the practice of polygyny (having multiple wives) in two ways: males can take multiple (female) wives or females can take multiple (female) wives. This latter practice, woman-marriage ... was documented in around forty precolonial African societies and has endured in some societies. It seems fair to claim that this practice of woman-marriage differs hugely from a traditional Christian practice of monogamous-marriage

---

[7] In fact, Stoljar take the case for resemblance nominalism also to hinge on the rejection of trope theory with respect to gender (2011, 43). However, I won't consider Stoljar's arguments against gender tropes here since I am in full agreement with her. For more on trope theory in general, see Armstrong 1989.

between a (male) husband and a (female) wife. The feature of being a wife
in these two practices, as a result, seems also to differ greatly. (Mikkola
2006, 89)

This example was intended to undermine Spelman's view that *because* gender
is socially constructed (societies make women out of females) the feature of
being a woman must be diverse. My intention was to show that social construction per se does not undermine gender realism understood as the thesis
that women as women share something. After all, being a wife is also a socially constructed and contextually variable feature. Nevertheless, there is
something wives as wives (generally speaking) share: they are women in contexts where the institution of marriage (broadly construed) exists, and they
have entered a marriage contract with some other individual(s) in line with
their social, cultural, or religious conventions. Stoljar acknowledges that I am
right to say that gender nominalism is not entailed by social constructionism
(2011, 31). Still (according to her) I fail to distinguish that there is a further
argument from diversity against gender realism. So, social construction is not
really doing the work; what is doing the work is that different societies create
women out of females *differently*.

In a sense, Stoljar is right: I do not distinguish the arguments from social
construction and diversity. This is because I am discussing Spelman's view,
and she runs the two together: gender is socially constructed; thus, women
are diverse; thus, gender realism is false. My argument against Spelman runs
thus: gender is socially constructed; thus, women are diverse; but this is compatible with gender realism. After all, *being a woman* could be a multiply realizable socially constructed feature that women as women share, and so akin
to *being a wife*. However, Stoljar disagrees, and takes the parallel to be unsuccessful. First, she claims that my example posits *being a wife* as a social universal, so that "being a wife is *exactly* the same relation for everyone standing
in it" (2011, 32). I cannot establish that diversity is compatible with gender
realism using the analogy between women and wives, if on my account wives
are in *exactly* the same relation qua wives. Second, I have purportedly made
the mistake of trying to reduce "the social reality of being a wife . . . to a single
relation 'being married' that all wives share" (Stoljar 2011, 33). In so doing, my
account does not capture the complex social reality of being a wife.

My contention is, however, that Stoljar's objections understand "having
the same feature" differently than my original argument. Her claims hold
only if on my view "having the same feature" is about numerical identity: if
being a wife is literally and strictly speaking the same property for all wives,
and "sameness" is understood as (for instance) two people having the very
same biological progenitor. But my remarks about the social construct-
edness and contextual variability of *being a wife* (i.e., it being an extrinsic, socially constructed, and multiply realizable feature) show that for me

"sameness" is not about numerical identity. It is like noting that you and I are wearing the same shirt (we are wearing two shirts of the same make). Further, Stoljar's complaint that my account reduces the reality of being a wife to a single identical relation of *being married* can be deflated. After all, I do not claim that this relation is numerically identical for all married individuals. In fact, Stoljar offers the following as evidence for why I am wrong: "In Western societies, a common law (i.e. unmarried) wife is a wife; in other societies, close female relatives such as sisters or cousins fall into the class of 'wife'" (2011, 33). But I fail to see how this counts against my view, and Stoljar's example rather precisely illustrates my point (that being a wife is a socially constructed feature, which is a product of contextually specific and variable social practices). After all, being a common-law wife hinges on one's jurisdiction taking the couple to have entered a marriage contract of *some* kind. The institutions regulating the practice of marriage differ, which is why being a wife is realizable in multiple ways. With the benefit of hindsight, I should have originally framed the issue in terms of the concept-conception distinction: even though all wives fall under the concept *wife*, there are many culturally specific and localized conceptions of the concept. Nonetheless, we can articulate "core" wife-making features, which are multiply realizable because of social variance.

The argument that Stoljar takes decisively to count against gender realism (and for gender nominalism) is that from particularity. This is the view that "identity properties such as gender or race are *particular*: their *natures* differ according to the unique constellation of identity properties instantiated by each individual" (Stoljar 2011, 38). Because of this, members of women's social kind cannot exemplify the same universal, and each woman's gender is uniquely particular to her. According to Stoljar, I take this "premise of particularity" to be implausible because Spelman's arguments in support of it are suspect: in short, because Spelman arrives at the premise by appealing to women's divergent *experiences*. On my view, Spelman's premise of particularly undermines only those gender realist positions that are made in experiential terms: if we take gender to be an identity of individuals that designates something about their psychologies or senses of self, then differential experiences count against gender realism. But imagine we understand gender differently, for instance, as designating occupancy of a structurally subordinate social position. In this case, how one experiences one's womanhood is neither here nor there—what matters for unified type membership is one's social position occupancy. And so, I claim, any realist theory that avoids defining *gender* as an identity of individuals can deal with Spelman's particularity argument. Stoljar finds this unconvincing, though. She asks us to suppose that gender *is* a subordinated position in a social hierarchy. Facts about structural intersectionality, however, suggest that such a social position is likely to be constituted by numerous intersecting relations of subordination that come together in particular ways. Stoljar cites Kimberlé Crenshaw's description of battered minority women, who are not only disadvantaged by their attackers but also by poverty, lack of education, and by child-rearing tasks, where these burdens are the consequence of their intersecting gender, class, and racial oppression. So actual women are "in a particular kind of socially subordinated position, one in which multiple structures of oppression coincide" (Stoljar 2011, 40).

I agree with Stoljar about the structural intersectionality of oppression. But in her discussion, Stoljar oscillates between womanhood *being* a subordinated social position, and individual women being *in* subordinated social positions. And although the latter is surely accurately captured by intersectional analyses, this does not count against my critique of Spelman. The key issue is still what constitutes womanhood. Part of Spelman's case against gender realism is that, if the constitutive conditions of gender are shared, women will have identical experiences of gender. Since their experiences differ, this entails that the constitutive conditions are particular too. My point is to undermine this move: even if women experience their gender or subordinated social positions differently since they are in different positions, this does not show that the underlying constitutive conditions of gender also differ. One may be a woman due to occupying a subordinate position in a sexualized power dynamic (as MacKinnon claims), but precisely because of intersectionality, women are *in* distinct subordinated situations, thus experiencing their sexualized subordination differently. This does not, however, entail that the constitutive conditions are particular.

Consider an analogy with being an artist. Conceivably, what it is to be an artist is to be positioned in a particular way relative to an art world. (Whether this is widely accepted does not matter. I am making a merely logical point.) It seems to be trivially true that every artist experiences "being an artist" differently—some are smug, some desperate, some overly convinced of their creative abilities, some quietly confident, and so on. It seems also true that each artist's relationship to and experience of the art world differs: because of the intersections of various identity categories, individual artists are likely to have different experiences of the art world (for instance, white Westerners perhaps have easier access to galleries and buyers, are more likely to attend art schools, and so on). Nevertheless, neither the individuals' differential experiences nor their intersecting identities make a difference if the constitutive conditions of *being an artist* are indexed to an art world, where this indexing is multiply realizable. The same (I submit) is true relative to oppression being constitutive of gender: if womanhood is constituted by occupying a subordinate social position that is realizable in multiple ways, intersectionality of oppression does not make this constitutive condition particular in the manner Stoljar suggests. Intersectionality makes a difference to which social positions we in fact end up occupying (and what material resources, say, are subsequently available to us), but it does not change the underlying constitutive condition (social position occupancy). Individual experiences alter the constitutive conditions of being a woman or an artist only if experiential considerations are part and parcel of those conditions. Insofar as some gender realist positions do not turn on experiential considerations, *these* gender realist positions are not undermined by Spelman's particularity argument.

3.4.2. PLAUSIBILITY OF RESEMBLANCE NOMINALISM

As I see it, neither Stoljar nor Spelman makes good the premise of particularity. Stoljar herself at times alludes to explanatory benefits: gender nominalism better explains observed variation than does gender realism. This is a stronger defense of the premise than that offered by Spelman. Nevertheless, my contention is that Stoljar also fails to make a convincing case that gender nominalism offers a better account of women's heterogeneity. She holds that my example of being a wife can allegedly "be turned on its head" (2011, 33): the example shows that the class of wives is actually rather heterogeneous, and prima facie nominalism is a compelling explanation of this. She then asks us to entertain the following options:

> which of the following alternatives is a better explanation of the heterogeneous nature of the class [of women]: are there many different relations of subordination, and hence many different kinds of womanness, or is there a single relation that is perceived by us in different ways? (2011, 36)

Apparently we will intuitively assent to the former view, and thereby gender nominalism has an explanatory advantage. But this does not offer a principled reason to favor gender nominalism on explanatory grounds; rather it turns on trading intuitions. Furthermore, observed variation among women is not the only thing in need of explanation—women's *similarities* are also in need of explanation. Stoljar even accepts this, which is why she argues for resemblance nominalism. After all, resemblance nominalism is precisely meant to make good women's similarity and difference. Subsequently, as I see it, our judgment of which metaphysical position is explanatorily superior depends on what we are aiming to explain: similarity or difference (or both). Thus, more needs to be said about explanatory advance in support of gender nominalism, and Stoljar has not yet sufficiently motivated resemblance nominalism in appealing to our pretheoretical intuitions about the matter.

Be that as it may, consider next her preferred metaphysical position. Let's assume for argument's sake that Stoljar is right about gender being particular. For her, this shows that we should be nominalists, and particularly that we should to endorse resemblance nominalism. Resemblance nominalism holds that if some entities resemble one another in appropriate ways, they will be members of the same type (Stoljar 1995, 263). Certain semantic considerations support such a view about gender. Take any two women who have no single feature in common, but to whom we nevertheless attribute womanness. As there is nothing shared on the basis of which we do so, the term 'woman' is applied on the basis of some features that the women individually possess. This suggests to Stoljar that attributions of womanhood turn on a complex cluster-concept (2000, 27). The term 'woman' is like the term 'game': if we look at all the various entities called games, we "will not see something that is common to *all*, but similarities, relationships, and a whole series of them" (Wittgenstein 1997, 31e).[8] The term 'woman' does not pick out entities that share some single feature. Rather, different uses of the term capture features from some (or all) of the following clusters of features that are commonly associated with women (though Stoljar admits that this list is not exhaustive).

a. Female sex: XX chromosome, secondary sex characteristics, general morphology, bodily characteristics like gait or voice quality.
b. Phenomenological features or "what it feels like to be a woman": "having menstrual cramps, and female sexual experience, and the 'lived experience' of child-birth, breast-feeding, or at least the potential to have such lived experience . . . feelings which are the product of social factors, like fear of walking on the streets at night or fear of rape."
c. Certain roles: wearing typically female clothing, being oppressed on the basis of one's sex, or undertaking "private" child-care responsibilities, rather than having "public" responsibilities.
d. Self-attribution and the attribution of womanness by others: "calling oneself a woman, being called a woman." (Stoljar 1995, 283–284)[9]

This explains why the term 'woman' applies in the absence of some single shared feature: it applies due to a cluster of features that are particular to individual women. And Stoljar takes this to *entail* that gender resemblance nominalism should be endorsed (2000, 28).

Resemblance nominalists commonly hold that entities are classified together on the basis of a resemblance relation that holds between these entities. Some claim that this relation is egalitarian, where x is a member of some type F by virtue of resembling *all other* entities that are F (Rodriguez-Pereyra 2002). Others claim the relation is aristocratic, where x is a member of F by virtue of resembling some *paradigm* or *exemplar* of F (Price 1953). On this latter view, paradigms are necessary for cashing out resemblance classes, and these standard objects or exemplars hold a resemblance class together. Stoljar is committed to the aristocratic view. For her, entities count as women by

---

[8] Stoljar is not alone in suggesting that *woman* is a cluster concept and that the class of women can be made sense of with Wittgensteinian family resemblances. See also Heyes 2000; Nicholson 1994.

[9] For an alternative list of features, see Hale 1996. He proposes thirteen different features involved in our everyday gender talk, which largely fit Stoljar's proposed list of features.

virtue of resembling sufficiently closely an exemplar of the type, a woman paradigm. Woman paradigms are picked out using the different features associated with women (sex, phenomenology, roles, gender attribution), which are elucidated by different uses of the term 'woman'. Woman paradigms must possess features from at least three of the four clusters of features mentioned (although Stoljar admits that this is not uncontroversial) (1995, 284). She goes on to outline four woman paradigms, though these are clearly not the only ones.

(i)   An Afro-American who has an XX chromosome and female sex characteristics, a characteristic female gait, attributes womanness to herself, and is oppressed on the basis of sex.

(ii) An Asian-American transsexual who attributes womanness to herself and dresses as a female, has female secondary sex characteristics, and has many of the elements of female phenomenology though she lacks an XX chromosome.

(iii) A white European hermaphrodite who has been brought up "as a girl" and as a result satisfies typical female roles, has many aspects of female phenomenology, and dresses and lives as a female though she lacks female sex characteristics.

(iv) A Papua New Guinean with an XX chromosome and female sex characteristics who calls herself and is called a woman, and has responsibility for child-rearing and other family oriented tasks (Stoljar 1995, 284).

For Stoljar, then, "Any individual resembling any of the paradigms sufficiently closely (on Price's account, as closely as they resemble each other) will be a member of the resemblance class 'woman'" (1995, 284).[10] This way of conceptualizing women's kind is meant to provide a way for feminists to act politically on behalf of women, insofar as it provides a way to unify women (Stoljar 2011, 44). The kind will be genuine, not gerrymandered, since resemblance nominalism "carves *social* reality in a way that is significant in explaining our causal interactions with the world" (2011, 44). Here we can see how the prevalent theoretical outlook that is gender-focused frames Stoljar's explication: we should (in pragmatic and political senses) articulate women's social kind in some sufficiently thick way that enables feminists to speak on behalf

---

[10] One might be tempted to think that typical cases of women should function as woman paradigms precisely because they *are* typical cases. In general, resemblance nominalists think so: for instance, red-paradigms usually include objects like tomatoes, British postboxes, and certain bricks that are chosen precisely because they are typical red-exemplars (Price 1953, 20). But Stoljar does not appeal to typical cases when picking out woman paradigms. This is because the aim is to elucidate an inclusive and nonmarginalizing kind of women that also includes "atypical" women (like those Stoljar outlines).

of women in order to fight patriarchy. Further, Stoljar aims to articulate the kind in an inclusive manner so that it will be sensitive to intersectionality. But, I will argue next, Stoljar's nominalism does not delimit women's social kind. So even if we accept that this is a worthwhile goal, Stoljar does not provide an acceptable way to do so.

Type membership trades on sufficient resemblance to a woman paradigm. Stoljar's notion of *sufficient resemblance* is meant to be equivalent to Price's, for whom it means one should resemble a paradigm as closely as the paradigms resemble each other (1953, 22). On this view, the degree to which x must resemble the F paradigms (in order to count as F) should be the same degree to which the F paradigms *themselves* resemble one another. But it turns out that Stoljar's notion of *sufficient resemblance* is not so clear after all. This is because the woman paradigms do not resemble one another to any single degree. Recall Stoljar's woman paradigms (for quick reference, they are expressed in table 3.1).

The woman paradigms resemble one another in either two or three respects. Therefore, it is unclear whether some particular should resemble a woman paradigm in two or three respects in order to count as a woman. Imagine a male-to-female trans* person, who was brought up "as a boy" and has male anatomy. She embraces many roles typically associated with women (like wearing female-coded clothing) and attributes womanness to herself (thus possessing features R and A). Whether she should resemble a woman paradigm in two or three respects in order to count as a woman is pivotal. If it is the former, the individual is in (she resembles the woman paradigms in two respects). But if the degree sufficient for classification is the latter, she will not be—a result that (I suspect) Stoljar would be unhappy with.

Gonzalo Rodriguez-Pereyra has argued that when faced with such problems a Pricean resemblance nominalist should posit that "particulars resemble each paradigm at least as closely as the least resembling of the paradigms resemble each other" (2002, 129). As Stoljar is committed to a Pricean resemblance relation, perhaps Rodriguez-Pereyra's modification can be applied to her woman paradigms in order to clarify the notion of *sufficient resemblance*. Thus, on the modified understanding any individual who resembles a woman paradigm to (at least) the same degree as the least resembling woman paradigms resemble one another will count as a woman. The least resembling pairs of woman paradigms—(i) and (iii), (iii) and (iv)—resemble one another in two respects

TABLE 3.1 Stoljar's Woman Paradigms

Paradigm	S (female sex)	P (phenomenology)	R (roles)	A (attribution)
(i)	S	(unclear)	R	A
(ii)	S	P	R	A
(iii)	Not-S	P	R	A
(iv)	S	(unclear)	R	A

(R and A). So, in order to count as a woman, one would need to resemble a woman paradigm in (at least) two respects, regardless of what those respects are. With this in mind, consider the trans* person mentioned above. On the modified understanding of *sufficient resemblance*, she does count as a woman, as she resembles all of the woman paradigms in two respects, R and A. At least in this case, Rodriguez-Pereyra's modification clarifies Stoljar's notion of *sufficient resemblance* in the desired manner and yields the right results.

This clarification does not, however, render Stoljar's position unproblematic. Unlike Price, who maintained that an entity must resemble *all F* paradigms in order to count as *F*, Stoljar maintains that resembling only *one* paradigm is sufficient for classification (1995, 284). For her, in order to count as a woman an individual only needs to resemble one woman paradigm sufficiently closely (as closely as the least resembling woman paradigms resemble one another). But now the criterion for social kind membership becomes too loose. Here are just two examples that prima facie should not qualify, but do. (1) An elderly male who stays home caring for his sick wife and fears walking in the streets at night dreading that he might be attacked. On Stoljar's criterion, he will resemble paradigms (ii) and (iii) sufficiently (in two respects): he shares certain phenomenological features associated with women, and he engages in typically female roles. And so the elderly male will count as a woman because he sufficiently resembles an Asian-American transsexual and a white European hermaphrodite. (2) An incarcerated American cis man, who fears rape because of its prevalence in US prisons. Applying Stoljar's model, he would also count as a woman since he resembles paradigm (iii), a white European hermaphrodite, in (at least) two respects: in the respect of lacking female sex characteristics, and in the respect of having aspects of female phenomenology. But if this is the upshot of Stoljar's view, the conditions for womanhood seem too loose, and they yield the wrong results.

Perhaps Stoljar has an easy way out, though. Following Price, she could insist that individuals should resemble *all* woman paradigms in order to count as women. But it is unlikely that she could commit herself to this view. In order to count as a woman paradigm, an individual must exhibit features from (at least) three of the four clusters of features that pick out paradigms (female sex, phenomenology, roles, gender attribution). Given how loosely these features are spelled out, though, Stoljar's class of woman paradigms will turn out to be huge. And to insist that one must sufficiently resemble all paradigms no longer seems sensible; for one thing, the epistemic problems with insisting that one must resemble all woman paradigms seem insurmountable. Further, it looks quite improbable that any individual could resemble all of the paradigms; even Stoljar herself appears to think so. Time and again she stresses the numerous ways in which women differ, and it is precisely for this reason that she argues for resemblance to only one paradigm as being sufficient.

One might in response claim that the incarcerated cis man does not resemble paradigm (iii) *in such a way* that he would count as a woman. This is because one of the two respects in which he resembles the woman paradigm is not relevant for being a woman (in *not* having female sex characteristics). As this is something that people commonly think of as relevant for womanhood, the incarcerated cis man does not count as a woman. However, this response does not succeed. On Stoljar's position, all that is needed for the cis man to count as a woman is that he resembles a woman paradigm sufficiently closely *regardless* of which features are responsible for this resemblance. After all, on Stoljar's nominalist account there are no features that must be had for membership in women's social kind. Of course, in order for someone to be a woman paradigm, possession of some particular features is relevant, and when constructing the class of woman paradigms, possessing female sex characteristics is a relevant feature. But in order to be classified as a woman, there are no relevant features that must be had apart from the feature of *sufficiently resembling a woman paradigm*. Being classified as a woman does not depend on sufficient resemblance in some relevant respect(s)—it depends on sufficiently resembling a woman paradigm regardless of which respects are responsible for this resemblance. Moreover, resemblance to a paradigm is crucial for Stoljar. If women's kind membership were merely a matter of possessing some relevant features, woman paradigms would be unnecessary; individuals would count as women simply by virtue of possessing those relevant features. But this is something Stoljar explicitly rejects (1995, 283), and it would collapse her account into a gender realist one.

The upshot of the discussion is this: even if one is convinced of the urgency of responding to the problems raised by the ontological and semantic puzzles, and one holds that salvaging feminist politics requires accounting for women's social kind membership, resemblance nominalism does not provide a satisfactory way to do so. As it stands, the membership criteria are too loose, and it is far too easy to sufficiently resemble Stoljar's woman paradigms. Unless the criteria are made stricter, I cannot see how Stoljar can draw principled boundaries between different gendered social kinds. That said, if Stoljar makes the criteria stricter, it is unclear what is left of her resemblance nominalist approach. If it becomes necessary to resemble paradigms in some particular way or relative to some particular traits, her position starts looking less like gender nominalism and more like gender realism: there will be some determinate feature or set of features that must be had in order for one to count as a woman. This undermines Stoljar's self-set commitment to the truth of the premise of particularly, which is crucial for her elucidation of what justifies feminist action on behalf of women.

Realist Responses to the Semantic
and Ontological Puzzles

The previous chapter examined nominalist responses to the semantic and ontological puzzles and argued that these responses fail to provide plausible accounts of women's unified social kind. This chapter considers recent gender realist positions, which take there to be something prescriptively important that women (*as* women) share and that unifies their kind. Each position endeavors to do justice to the particularity and diversity of women, and so not to fall prey to gender-skeptical critiques of Spelman and Butler. At the same time, they aim to articulate a conception of womanhood that is thick enough to support feminist political claims. Before proceeding, it is helpful to pause for a moment in order to clarify some of the metaphysical underpinnings of these views. The metaphysics of properties is too extensive to review here (for a helpful introduction, see Swoyer and Orilia 2011). However, some clarificatory remarks should help us understand the subsequent gender realist positions better.

Gender realists hold that there is something women as women share, and this "something" unifies their social kind. My formulation is intentionally vague since there are many ways to cash this out in detail. Relevant for the discussion at hand, however, are three distinctions pertaining to the nature of properties. First the distinction between *monadic/polyadic* properties. Monadic properties are usually captured by one-place predicates like "is *F*." Polyadic properties are captured by n-place predicates that are expressive of relations like *a*, relation *R*, *b*. The property of *being red* is conceivably of the former kind; the property of *being to the north of* is of the latter. For instance, it makes no sense to say "London is to the north of"—in order for this expression to make sense, we must know the subject and the object of "is to the north of." Now, the gender nominalist positions considered in the previous chapter take women's social kind to be unified via some polyadic property; for example, the relation of *sufficient resemblance to* (a woman paradigm) does the work for Stoljar. Gender realists considered in this chapter by and large appeal to some complex monadic property that unifies women's social kind. To clarify: both gender nominalists and realists make use of the one-place predicate "'is a woman." But nominalists typically take there to be a poly-adic property underlying such talk. So, "x is a woman" is merely shorthand for saying (as for Stoljar) "x sufficiently resembles a woman paradigm y." For feminist philosophers of the realist persuasion, the properties underlying our gender talk are not strictly speaking relations but complex monadic proper-ties that nonetheless ontologically depend on a social context.

The distinction between *intrinsic/extrinsic* properties elucidates this. The former denotes properties that a particular has merely by virtue of itself; the latter denotes properties that a particular has by virtue of something exter-nal to it (like particular social relations). That I am 156 cm tall is an intrin-sic property of me; my height does not ontologically depend on how tall or short others around me are. That Sandy is a landlord is an extrinsic prop-erty of them, and this ontologically depends on something other than Sandy alone: most obviously, that they own a piece of property rented to someone else. We can discover the fact about my height simply by examining me; but we cannot discover that Sandy owns a piece property that is rented out by examining Sandy alone. With the intrinsic/extrinsic distinction in mind, we can understand how a property can ontologically depend on social relations, but not be a relation. Take the property of *being a landlord*. This property is not a relation between two particulars in the sense that *being to the north of* is. However, being a landlord does ontologically depend on wider social and cultural conditions: for one, it depends on there being the institution of pri-vate property. So, it is relation*al*, but not a *relation*. The idea of gender being a monadic extrinsic property is akin to this.

Saying that, it is important to keep in the mind the final relevant distinc-tion between individually *essential/nonessential* properties. If some property is individually essential to me, I cannot survive the loss of this property. Were I to lose it, I would cease to exist.[1] Conceivably, psychological continuity is a good candidate for being an individually essential property: were I to lose all of my memories, it would not seem unwarranted to say that one person has ceased to exist, and a new one has emerged. Qua human organism, I would remain the same; but qua person, I would not have survived this psychologi-cal rupture. Then again, having hair is a good candidate for being individually nonessential: I lose bits of my hair all the time without ceasing to be me. Now, the monadic extrinsic property of *being a woman* can be either individually essential or nonessential: if the former, individuals cannot survive the loss

---

[1] I am being intentionally vague here about how properties can be nonessential, and not making the (somewhat controversial) distinction between essential and accidental properties. However, for my purposes here nothing hangs on elucidating the essential/accidental distinction.

of their womanhood; if the latter, they can. The gender realist accounts considered shortly generally take *being a woman* to be individually nonessential. This makes sense of sex/gender transitioning because, qua human organism and person (understood via psychological continuity), I can survive the loss of my gender. This is particularly so for accounts like Sally Haslanger's (considered shortly) where gender is defined in terms of social position occupancy.

Being committed to extrinsic and individually nonessential conceptions of womanhood, newer gender realist positions differ significantly from the earlier realist positions that generated skepticism about gender. Earlier gender realisms took *being a woman* to be an essential property definitive of female gender in a way that left them vulnerable to the problems considered in chapter 2. And even though they rejected the idea that womanhood is an innate biological property in endorsing the sex/gender distinction, the older realist positions came close to saying that gender is intrinsically founded. After all, on those views, being a woman is not perfectly analogous to (say) being a landlord: if gender is the social interpretation of sex, an investigation of my sex alone will give us fairly strong evidence of my gender. Contra these commonly termed "essentialist" positions, the neorealist positions aim to conceptualize gender in a way that makes *being a woman* more akin to social kinds like landlords and politicians. They aim to make sense of the claim that there is *something* that women by virtue of being women share, which is not intrinsic, innate, or essential to women qua individuals. And they aim to make sense of the idea that women have in common some socially constructed extrinsic feature or set of features qua women. Given these metaphysical commitments, neo-gender-realist views are meant to avoid common critiques that appeal to women's diversity and particularity, while making good a conception of women's unified social kind. Further, all of the positions examined next are motivated by explicit self-proclaimed feminist political goals. I will, nevertheless, argue that these realist theories face problems in satisfying the self-set political goals. So, again, even if one takes the semantic and ontological worries seriously, these worries are not satisfyingly responded to by recent gender realisms.[2]

---

[2] There is a notable omission in the views that I will next discuss. I will not consider Charlotte Witt's (2011a) recent argument for a particular sort of gender essentialism—one that she terms "gender uniessentialism." Her starting point is the question: would you be the same individual if you were gendered differently? According to Witt, most ordinary social agents take the answer to be an obvious no, and they have no difficulty providing the answer. By contrast, most academic feminists find the answer neither obvious nor easy. What generates such divergent views, and why are ordinary agents so secure in their gender ascriptions? Witt aims to articulate and make good ordinary social agents' gender-essentialist intuitions by arguing that gender is uniessential to them qua social individuals. Social individuals are possessors of social roles and distinct from persons and human organisms. These three aspects of our selves are bound together via a constitution relation. So were a biologically human person to lose or alter their gender, the individual would persist

4.1. Women as FMP Category

Naomi Zack argues for a version of inclusive feminist social theory, which should satisfy the following five requirements:

1. It should be "unapologetically normative" insofar as feminism's goal is to better the lives of women.
2. Such a theory should be grounded in "facts about the existence of real women," where *being a woman* is a relational property that is common to all women (and thus fixes their social kind).
3. Feminist social theory should explain women's oppression.
4. It should be "comprehensive and address oppressions of women that are apparently distinct from gender, such as racism and classism."
5. Feminist social theory should be "methodologically distinct from feminist psychological theory so that political action is possible." (2005, 63)

Let's unpack these requirements. The first and the third requirements are fairly straightforward. Feminism is about ending women's oppression, which requires a satisfying explanation of their oppression (cf. [3]). Further, emancipatory feminism ought to satisfy certain normative demands (as I put it): to elucidate how and why patriarchy damages women, to justify feminist critical claims about extant states of affairs, and to ground a vision of a feminist future (cf. [1] and [3]). Zack's social theory is aiming to respond to both explanatory and normative political issues, and she aims to articulate a conception of womanhood that can do the required political and social theoretic work. The rest of the requirements are somewhat more opaque. The main gist of the fifth requirement is that feminist politics should first and foremost focus on altering the structural and material conditions that oppress women, rather than on altering people's individual psychologies. The fourth requirement aims to capture intersectionality.

This leaves the second requirement, which is significant for my purposes. Antiessentialist and intersectional critiques demonstrate that there is no substantive gender essence of the kind supposedly posited by earlier gender realists (like MacKinnon). Nevertheless, Zack argues that we can conceive of women having an essence understood as a particular disjunctive relation:

> Women are those human beings who are related to the historical category of individuals who are designated female from birth or biological mothers

---

as the same human organism and person, but they would not persist as the same gendered social individual. Thinking of gender as an aspect of social individuals (rather than of persons or human organisms) explains ordinary agents' gender-essentialist intuitions. As interesting as I find Witt's view, I will not discuss it in detail here. This is because Witt aims to elucidate individual, rather than kind, essentialism (or realism). Although I think that her view is a response to the ontological puzzle or primary sexual choice of men. Call this category FMP . . . This relation of assignment to, or identification with, the FMP category is a necessary and sufficient condition for being a woman, and there is every reason to view it as an essence shared by all women. (2005, 8)

Although women share the FMP designation as their social kind essence, this gender essence is not a causal one. Were it of this latter kind, women's commonality would *cause* common experiences (Zack 2005, 14). But (Zack claims) women need not share some unitary, common experience as women in order to have, nonetheless, something qua women in common. Actually, "The relational nature of women's identity as women *entails* that the womanhood of all women is located somewhere outside each woman" (2005, 23; italics mine). Further, insofar as women share the FMP designation, it is essential for social kind membership. But none of the disjuncts are individually necessary for being a woman, though satisfying any is sufficient (2005, 8–9). In fact, one need not even *be* a mother or female or heterosexual—one can be assigned these features by others, who imagine them accurately to describe one's social existence given the prevalent heterosexist dual-gender system. Finally, being designated as female is not purely a matter of biology. The example of intersexes, and the quickness with which parents position their children into the accepted male-female binary, show that many social norms and descriptions go into "sexing" individuals. Thus, being designated as female neither takes place from some agent-independent biological perspective nor relies on some purely nonsocial facts. Rather, Zack's view is that our sex concepts have also been socially constructed (cf. section 2.4.).

Zack's position offers novel ways to answer the semantic and ontological puzzles. She holds that the "right" definition of *woman* and the assignment to the FMP category must be open for alterations (2005, 28). Nevertheless, insofar as womanhood is fixed relative to the category of individuals designated F or M or P, we are meant to have an inclusive account of women's social kind membership. This way of conceptualizing gender is meant to be nonessential but thick enough to be politically beneficial. Zack herself summarizes these benefits as follows:

What good can such an identity [of women as FMP] do for anyone interested in changing the world or understanding and empowering herself? The answer is that the relation of being a woman is sufficient for social existence in a dual woman-man (or man-woman) system. It is not necessary for existence [in this dual system] because one could be a man. But it is necessary for social existence in such a system that one be either a man or a woman. Thus the relation of being a woman is a social identity.

---

in disguise, I will focus here on realist positions that seek more explicitly to fix women's social kind by responding to the puzzles.

Assignment to the FMP category constitutes the external identification of human beings as women, and their identification with the category constitutes their subjectivity as women. (2005, 23)

Zack is explicitly aiming to conceptualize women's social kind in a way that does some helpful political work and does not fall prey to the pitfalls of gender skepticism and intersectional critiques—thus, her aim to articulate an *inclusive* social kind of women. All of this shows that the normative outlook I outlined earlier (cf. chapter 1) is at work in Zack's articulation of gender.

One of the main problems with Zack's position, however, is that her metaphysics is hard to comprehend. She claims that women are (1) a subgroup of human beings, (2) who are related to the historical category of individuals (3) designated F or M or P. And it is the *relation to* (understood as assignment to or identification with) the FMP category that is necessary and sufficient for being a woman. So what appears to be doing the work is the assignment to by others, or thinking of oneself as a member of, the category—this is what makes one a woman. In this sense, Zack seems to depart from the other neorealist positions considered here: she is putting forward a polyadic property of *being a woman* (x, relation R, FMP). This is akin to Stoljar's positions, although Zack and Stoljar explicitly characterize their positions as gender realist and nominalist, respectively.[3] That said, there is nothing necessary about the FMP *disjunction*, and this side of the relation could be made up of any constellation of features associated with women. After all, what matters is the right kind of relation to the typical features, not the features themselves, as these are nonessential to womanhood and open to revision. Presumably the idea is that the features of F, M, and P capture the general, pretheoretic folk understanding of womanhood. This is what the folk think womanhood amounts to, and gendered character traits literally develop out of being assigned membership in this category and by being treated accordingly. Further, since the FMP disjunction is contingent, we can envision changes in our conceptions of womanhood—precisely what Zack thinks the "right" definition of *woman* should be able to accommodate. Nevertheless, we must keep constant the relation R: being assigned to or identifying with whatever the disjunction of typical "womanly" features is. Here Zack's metaphysics runs into trouble though. Trying to fix women's social kind membership on the basis of such bare relations does not provide us with a genuine and unified kind. Doing so makes no principled differentiations between different social kinds, and we could be talking about almost any identity dimension (gender, race, class). Zack's position cannot even differentiate between the social kinds of women,

---

[3] In fact, this raises questions about whether Stoljar can maintain her gender nominalism. After all, one could claim that there is something women qua women on her account share: the resemblance relation to a woman paradigm. This would make Stoljar's position gender realist, not nominalist.

men, and trans*, if we merely appeal to the bare relations of *assignment to* and *identification with*. These relations must be more substantive in order to pick out specifically *women's* social kind. Zack intends to define womanhood in thick enough way to support feminist political claims; but she fails to do so by relying on merely bare relations.

One way to render the relevant relations more substantive and make good a unified women's kind would be to view the FMP disjunction as an integral part of the gender-defining relations. So it is not enough that women stand in certain relations to typical gender features: it is crucial that they stand in appropriate relations precisely to these—F, M, and P—features. Now the FMP disjunction is no longer as contingent as it first seemed. After all, it is assignment to and identification with *this* property cluster that matters. This raises another set of worries though about how politically helpful the proposal is.[4] Zack thinks that transformative, politically effective, and inclusive feminist social theory should be "grounded in" facts about women "who can all be defined by their common relation to the FMP category" (2005, 63). But it is unclear to me what we gain from this. How does knowing that women are by definition designated female or biological mothers or men's primary sexual choice help us in articulating what is wrongful about patriarchy and how women should be treated? Zack herself even notes that although the denotation of *woman* is easy and refers "unproblematically" to a certain subgroup of human beings, feminists have struggled with the connotation or meaning of *woman* (2005, 27). And part of the project of inclusive feminism is to articulate the latter in a way that enables feminist politics to be organized around women's inclusive social kind. But I cannot see what the FMP designation brings to our political endeavors or how it contributes to a politically helpful articulation of (the content of) *woman*. In fact, it is unclear to me why the political desiderata of Zack's feminist social theory could not be achieved by relying on the unproblematic denotation of *woman* (actually I will argue for something similar in chapter 5). For instance, Zack writes:

> Feminist social theorists should be able to explain why a given social practice or structure is oppressive to women and what keeps it in place. To do this they need accounts of women's autonomy and flourishing, against which something can be seen to be oppressive; of women's motives, goals, and intentions, to explain what situations of oppression mean to them; of how their culture assigns women to institutions and otherwise trains them in ways that perpetuate oppression. (2005, 71)

---

[4] We could also reject Zack's metaphysics by rejecting the view that disjunctive properties are genuine properties. However, for my purposes nothing hangs on accepting or rejecting disjunctive properties. So I will accept for argument's sake that such properties exist.

But in order to accomplish these tasks, I need not be familiar with Zack's conception of *woman*, and I do not see how an appeal to the FMP disjunction helps—knowing Zack's formulation of womanhood tells me nothing about what oppresses women, about their goals and intentions, or about cultural institutions that perpetuate oppression. Or perhaps Zack's view is that the F, M, and P designations *are* precisely those aspects of women's gendered realities that oppress them. So her theory of gender does in fact tell us the source of women's oppression, which is normatively important (the source is to be or imagined to be female, a mother, or men's sexual choice). However, this is not unproblematic. To be designated F, M, or P is not taken to be something wholly negative, and (as Zack herself holds) many women identify with these designations. Claiming that these features are at the core of women's oppression is not uncontroversial, and Zack would have to spell this out more carefully in order to justify her view (if this indeed is her view). Then again, that the F, M, and P disjuncts are meant to be contingent and open to revision counts against the view that they constitute the core features responsible for women's oppression. Presumably, if these features are open to revision, we can conceive of the typical women's features changing over time without this necessarily doing away with oppression. If the FMP disjunction is nevertheless integrally tied to women's oppression, it (again) cannot be as contingent and open to revision as Zack claims. I agree with Zack about the feminist political desiderata; but I fail to see how her theory of gender provides the tools with which to do the required political work.

4.2. Social Subordination and Privilege as Marks of Gender

4.2.1. AMELIORATIVE ANALYSIS OF *WOMAN*

In a series of impressive articles, Sally Haslanger provides an analysis of the concept *woman*, which she calls "ameliorative." Her account is explicitly put forward as a response to the semantic and ontological puzzles, and Haslanger aims (among other things) to elucidate how women make up a genuine type rather than a merely gerrymandered collection of individuals. Doing so is meant to provide the basis for feminist political organizing and to enable feminists to achieve certain political goals. In some articles, Haslanger takes this analysis to be revisionary (2000; 2003a; 2003b); in others, she takes her analysis to be less so (2005; 2006). Consider the former view first. Haslanger contrasts her ameliorative analysis with two more standard analyses: conceptual, and descriptive. The former aims to articulate our ordinary concepts by consulting native speakers' intuitions. These are the concepts that we take our language use to express, and are (what Haslanger calls) our manifest concepts.[5]A conceptual analysis of *woman*, then, would aim to elucidate the conditions under which native English speakers think someone satisfies *woman*, and such an analysis probably reveals that the content of our manifest *woman* concept is that women are human females. A descriptive analysis focuses on our terms' extensions and investigates whether our language use tracks some natural or social kinds. It is concerned with everyday language use, and Haslanger terms concepts analyzed in this manner our "operative concepts." So a descriptive analysis of *woman* would examine applications of 'woman' that are expressive of our operative *woman* concept, in order to identify the social kind that the term tracks. Now, Haslanger argues for an ameliorative analysis that aims to "elucidate 'our' legitimate purposes and what concept of *F*-ness (if any) would serve them best" (2005, 20). On this approach,

> we begin by considering more fully the pragmatics of our talk employing the terms in question. What is the point of having these concepts? What cognitive or practical task do they (or should they) enable us to accomplish? Are they effective tools to accomplish our (legitimate) purposes; if not, what concepts would serve these purposes better? (Haslanger 2000, 33)

Ameliorative analyses aim to elucidate those concepts we *should* be using—our target concepts. Such an analysis of *woman* defines the concept for feminist purposes: given feminists' legitimate goals, the target concept *woman* ought to be defined in a way that best serves those goals. This project is not entirely distinct from a descriptive one. An ameliorative analysis of *woman* offers an analysis of the concept that we usually think tracks women's social kind but that does so in a way that "usefully revise[s] what we mean [by *woman*] for certain theoretical and political purposes" (Haslanger 2000, 34).

Haslanger holds that straightforward conceptual and descriptive analyses of *woman* are insufficient for two reasons. First, they are theoretically unhelpful. Both analyses aim to explain, articulate, and refine our ordinary *woman* concept. But, she claims, everyday gender vocabulary is simply not specific enough to do the necessary theoretical work: ordinary gender concepts are too vague, their uses are idiosyncratic, and there are too many different ways to understand them (Haslanger 2000, 34). This requires some clarifying: Haslanger seems to hold both that the ordinary *woman* concept is the same as *female* (2000, 31) and that it is not, because 'woman' is applied on various idiosyncratic grounds (2000, 34). Prima facie these views are in tension with one another. In fact, they are not. Haslanger's view is that our

---

[5] When Haslanger talks about "our" concepts, I take it that she denotes ordinary language users in general and does not have any particular group of speakers in mind.

manifest *woman* concept encodes conditions having to do with femaleness, whereas our operative *woman* concept encodes a mixture of various conditions thus being applied on idiosyncratic grounds. And both the manifest and operative *woman* concepts have a claim to being our ordinary concept: we take ourselves to be applying 'woman' on the grounds of anatomical features, but in actual fact we apply it on various vague and idiosyncratic grounds. Because particular *woman* conceptions and our everyday linguistic usage diverge so widely, Haslanger takes ordinary speakers to be confused about the conditions that make someone a woman. And so ordinary speakers do not seem to have any introspective, privileged access to the content of gender concepts (Haslanger 2006, 106). It would, then, be politically unhelpful to analyze those ordinary concepts. The second reason that the conceptual and descriptive analyses are insufficient is that they are theoretically flawed. Ordinarily, to be a human female is thought to be sufficient to make one a woman. But Haslanger argues that (contra everyday beliefs) gender is socially constructed. Membership in women's type is ordinarily thought to depend on biological conditions when, in fact, it depends on social conditions. What makes the claim "I am a woman" apt are the social relations in which one stands, not one's biology. Haslanger's project is a debunking one and involves challenging the supposed truth conditions of gender ascriptions. She does not challenge the appropriateness of calling someone "a woman" or "a man"; rather, her project involves showing that gender terms ordinarily thought to track groups of individuals on the basis of some physical conditions are "better understood" as capturing groups that occupy some social positions (Haslanger 2003b, 318). Further, we are prone to make this naturalistic mistake (think that femaleness is the condition for womanhood) because oppressive ideologies interfere with our language use and mask what we really should be talking about (Haslanger 2006, 92).[6]

These factors motivate Haslanger to endorse an ameliorative analysis, which seeks to define *woman* for feminist theoretical and political purposes. Briefly put, feminists need *woman* in order to fight sexist injustices. In particular, they need gender terminology in order to (1) identify and explain persistent social inequalities between males and females; (2) identify how gender is implicated in apparently gender-neutral social phenomena (like the arts and philosophy); and (3) empower women as social agents (Haslanger 2000, 36). Haslanger's goals demonstrate that she too adheres to the prevalent normative outlook introduced in chapter 1 and that undergirds the gender

---

[6] Haslanger's debunking project is not to be confused with the gender skeptics' error theory about women (cf. Butler 1999). Haslanger is challenging *which* conditions make statements like "I am a woman" apt. But gender skeptics are challenging the view that there are *any* conditions that make such statements apt.

controversy: we need to articulate a thick enough conception of *woman* that can do the required feminist (descriptive and normative) work. Only an ameliorative analysis of *woman* ensures that the concept is suited for the task of fighting gendered oppression, and with this in mind Haslanger proposes the following:

> S *is a woman* iff [by definition] S is systematically subordinated along some dimension (economic, political, legal, social, etc.), and S is "marked" as a target for this treatment by observed or imagined bodily features presumed to be evidence of a female's biological role in reproduction.

> S *is a man* iff [by definition] S is systematically privileged along some dimension (economic, political, legal, social, etc.), and S is "marked" as a target for this treatment by observed or imagined bodily features presumed to be evidence of a male's biological role in reproduction. (2003a, 6–7)

Understanding gender concepts in this manner supposedly provides feminists with effective tools to fight sexism. They are therefore the ones that *should* be appropriated: our target concepts. These definitions require a radical rethinking of everyday gender terminology—something Haslanger acknowledges (2003b, 319). If some female (like, perhaps, the queen of England) escapes sex-marked subordination, she would not count as a woman on Haslanger's definition. Nor would she be part of the social kind that makes up feminism's subject matter. This is unproblematic, though: "It may be that non-oppressed females are marginalized within my account, but that is because for the broader purposes at hand—relative to the feminist ... values guiding our project—they are not the ones who matter" (Haslanger 2000, 46). If feminism aims to eradicate sexist oppression that women face, and (for argument's sake) the queen faces no such oppression, it seems reasonable that feminists should not concern themselves with the queen. In fact, from a feminist point of view it would be highly desirable to exclude as many females as possible from women's social kind: this would mean that there are plenty of nonoppressed females, and that feminists are achieving gender justice. For Haslanger, "It is part of the project of feminism to bring about a day when there are no more women (though, of course, we should not aim to do away with females!)" (2000, 46). Gender justice would eradicate gender since it would abolish sexist social structures responsible for sex-marked oppression and privilege.

Haslanger clearly defines *woman* in a way that enables feminists to pick out women's social kind: feminist politics will be organized around those who are sex-marked subordinates. Given the values guiding feminist politics, this theory of gender seems extremely helpful. Saying that, her proposal is strikingly counterintuitive. It seems that most people would be willing to call the queen a "woman," and their willingness to do so might suggest that

Haslanger is simply wrong about the content of gender concepts. This is not a reason to reject her analysis, though. Haslanger is not aiming to capture some commonsense understanding of *woman*; instead, (this part of) her proposal is revisionary. She articulates a theory of gender that *should* be appropriated on practical political grounds. The important point is that her target *woman* concept can be usefully employed to achieve certain political goals, not that it is intuitive. However, elsewhere Haslanger suggests (perhaps surprisingly) that her ameliorative analysis of *woman* may not be as revisionary as it first seems (2005, 2006). Although successful in their reference fixing, ordinary speakers do not always know precisely what they are talking about. Further, oppressive ideologies can "mislead us about the content of our own thoughts" (Haslanger 2005, 12). We might be utterly ignorant of the fact that the every-day *woman* concept we actually employ (our operative concept) is different from the one we think we are employing (our manifest *woman* concept). And although Haslanger's analysis of *woman* is different from the ordinary mani-fest concept, it could be the same as our ordinary operative *woman* concept— the concept we *in fact* employ. Perhaps Haslanger's analysis of the target con-cept has captured our operative *woman* concept and reveals to us the concept that we actually employ. Consequently, her proposal would be descriptive: we may be applying 'woman' in our everyday language on the basis of sex-marked subordination without realizing this.

In order to grasp this better, consider a different example. Manifest con-cepts are those that we take ourselves to be employing, whereas operative concepts are those that we in fact employ. Although our manifest and opera-tive concepts often coincide, at times they come apart. This seems to be so with *bachelor*. A conceptual analysis asks under which conditions x counts as a bachelor. The usual answer is x is a bachelor iff x is an unmarried male. This captures our manifest concept. But if we look at people's willingness to apply 'bachelor,' we arrive at a different concept. This descriptive analysis re-veals our operative concept: if many language users are unwilling to apply 'bachelor' to unmarried males in long-term partnerships or to the pope (and it seems plausible to suppose that many are), the term clearly does not apply to all unmarried males. The revealed operative concept is different from our manifest one. Different kinds of analyses may show that "our assumptions about what we mean are false, given our practice. This is not to propose a new meaning, but to reveal an existing one" (Haslanger 2006, 110). Now, the same could be true of gender: a conceptual analysis of our manifest *woman* concept conceivably concludes that all and only human females are women. But a de-scriptive analysis might reveal a different (operative) concept that our appli-cations of 'woman' in fact express. And given that we may simply be mistaken about and ignorant of what we mean, the target concept Haslanger proposes might be our operative *woman* concept. This would not make her proposal radically revisionist. By contrast, she would be pointing out something that we have been doing all along with our language use.

But showing that Haslanger's ameliorative analysis has captured our operative *woman* concept is tricky. Even if our applications of 'woman' were to track sexually marked subordinates (something that is contentious in itself), this would not show that being sex-marked for social subordination is *constitutive* of being a woman: 'woman' and 'sex-marked for social subordination' could simply be coextensive. Take the familiar case of being renate (having kidneys) and being cordate (having a heart). Although 'renate' tracks a type whose members are all renate and cordate, this does not show that the concept of *being cordate* is (even partly) constitutive of the concept that the term 'renate' expresses. The terms are simply coextensive, and the same could be true with 'woman' and 'sex-marked for social subordination'. I am not yet convinced that Haslanger's descriptive claim is true, and she needs to do more to show that her ameliorative analysis of *woman* has in fact captured our operative *woman* concept. Of course, what I have said does not show that Haslanger is wrong. This would require showing that our operative *woman* concept is different from Haslanger's target concept. But discovering *our* operative *woman* concept is extremely difficult (Saul 2006, 129). After all, if sexist ideology masks what language users ordinarily mean and thereby confuses them deeply about ordinary gender concepts, it is very hard to discern the grounds on which ordinary speakers in practice apply gender terms. Simply put: the prospects of showing that Haslanger's analysis of *woman* is not as revisionary as it first appears are not good. Subsequently, I will treat her analysis as revisionary.

4.2.2. BENEFITS OF THE REVISIONARY ANALYSIS

Accepting Haslanger's proposed revisionary theory of gender turns on evaluating its usefulness relative to feminist political goals. Haslanger herself holds that appropriating the proposed terminology is warranted if certain semantic and political conditions are satisfied. The semantic condition states:

> the proposed shift in meaning of the term ['woman'] would seem semantically warranted if central functions of the term remain the same, e.g., if it helps organize and explain a core set of phenomena that the ordinary terms are used to identify or describe. (2000, 35)

The political condition is satisfied provided that the appropriated terminology helps feminists fight gender injustice (2000). Haslanger's definition of *woman* should provide "a better explanation of how gender works" and be theoretically and politically useful (2003b, 319). But good questions can be raised about whether the political condition is satisfied.

My contention is that Haslanger's analysis of *woman* may not best serve the goal of fighting gender injustice. It seems fair to say that this goal encompasses certain (what I call) feminist normative demands: feminists should be able to elucidate how and why patriarchy damages women, to justify feminist critical claims about extant states of affairs, and to ground a vision of a feminist future. Our theory of gender should facilitate meeting these demands in order to foster social change. But I am unconvinced that appropriating Haslanger's terminology would yield such political benefits. Quite simply, if feminists appropriated her gender terms, this may create linguistic confusion between them and ordinary speakers that is unlikely to help in the task of challenging existing social conditions. Take Haslanger's own claim, "I believe it is part of the project of feminism to bring about a day when there are no more women" (2000, 46). Without previous knowledge about her definition of *woman* and taking this statement out of context, most ordinary speakers will probably think this is a call for femicide—something Haslanger clearly does not have in mind. If feminists appropriated Haslanger's gender terminology, a number of politically important claims would be in danger of being grossly misinterpreted by ordinary speakers. This would not be politically beneficial: if ordinary speakers fail to grasp feminist claims pertaining to women, getting the crucial "feminist message" across is compromised, and feminist politics is ineffective.

There are other ways too in which Haslanger's gender terminology may not help feminists. Ordinarily, people hold many questionable beliefs about women's capacities, psychologies, desires, and aspirations. One such extremely persistent belief pertains to supposed genetic differences in innate aptitudes for math and science, which has been used to explain why women do not excel in these fields. Beliefs about women's supposedly innate mathematical inferiority have played a significant role in excluding women from natural sciences, and such beliefs disadvantage women by suggesting that certain social arrangements are appropriate (like women being "unsuitable" for science jobs). The belief that women are innately inferior in math, however, is just a gender myth (Spelke 2005). Convincing people of this and of the fact that many stereotypical beliefs about women, men, trans*, and intersexes are false are important feminist tasks that foster gender justice. Now, imagine the following (somewhat odd) example. A group of feminist scientists aims to dispel the mathematical gender myth. In order to get their message across, they place info-advertisements in major newspapers. Imagine further that they are convinced of Haslanger's gender concepts, and the ad reads: "There are no differences in the innate aptitudes for math and science between women and men. (And by 'woman' and 'man' we mean occupying sex-marked subordinate or privileged positions). It is a gender myth because . . ." Juxtaposing 'woman'/'man' and social position occupancy in this manner may not be conducive to the scientists' aims to dispel the gender myth. First, ordinary gender concepts were deemed to be politically problematic because ordinary speakers are deeply confused about their contents. But ordinary speakers are likely to be confused by the juxtaposition of 'woman'/'man' and social position occupancy in the advertisement because doing is unintuitive. In this case, feminists would be replacing one kind of linguistic confusion with another. And so appropriating Haslanger's gender terminology might muddy the waters even more, which seems undesirable. Second, Haslanger took the ordinary manifest *woman* concept to be theoretically flawed in encoding conditions having to do with femaleness; but it may not be as flawed as she thinks. What underlies the above gender myth is the belief that women are somehow *innately* incapable of math. And pointing out that they are not so incapable qua social position occupants is entirely consistent with holding that women qua females nevertheless are incapable. Bluntly put: it is not social position occupancy that renders women incapable of calculating difficult sums; it is ovaries interfering with poor female brains! So those gender myths that trade on biologist conceptions of *woman* may not be countered by Haslanger's debunking project, unless we first convince ordinary speakers to debunk gender. Or to put the point differently: when aiming to counter biologically based stereotypical beliefs, it may be more appropriate and politically helpful to rely on the everyday manifest *gender* concepts rather than Haslanger's target concepts. This is because what we are trying to get across is precisely the view that female biology is not responsible for behavioral outputs and personality traits. In order to counter such gender myths, then, we must engage with ordinary speakers in their own terms and avoid talking past one another.

This raises two questions though: How high is the price of linguistic confusion? And might linguistic confusion be a precursor to political action in that it challenges existing meanings that are in some way insufficient or problematic? Consider the former question and the math myth-busting ad again. If the ad does not specify that the scientists have Haslanger's sense of gender in mind, ordinary speakers are likely to understand *woman* and *man* in their everyday manifest senses. Were there to be a subsequent conversation, feminists and ordinary speakers would probably talk past each other. Since (for Haslanger) the target concept should satisfy the semantic functions of our ordinary concept, both camps would broadly be talking about the same group of people—the extension of 'woman' would broadly be the same, although the intension would differ. It may even be that during the course of the conversation, no obvious confusion ensues because it remains undetected that the interlocutors are talking about different things. (Let's even imagine that both camps falsely believe that they are talking about the same thing, and have no reason to doubt this.) So communication is not prima facie compromised, despite interlocutors talking past one another. There are two ways in which the situation can go. If the difference in meaning were uncovered, this is likely to produce linguistic confusion and undermine communication. As long as feminists and ordinary speakers are talking about different things, there is always a potentially high price to pay for appropriating Haslanger's target concepts (it potentially compromises politically crucial exchanges that would prevent feminists' from getting their message across). Then again, if our everyday gender terminology does not pose any obvious semantic problems, and the differences in meaning remain undiscovered, the motivation for appropriating Haslanger's target concept is undermined. Haslanger's new conceptual tools should afford us some benefits, and they should be somehow better. Judging these benefits will trade on feminist political and pragmatic considerations, and (relative to these considerations) our everyday gender vocabulary is meant to be deficient. But if talking past one another poses no real communicative problems, and if relying on our manifest *woman* concept is at times even more appropriate, it is no longer so clear that our everyday gender vocabulary is deeply flawed and unsuited for feminist political endeavors.[7]

This pushes me to the second question posed: perhaps there will not be miscommunication and linguistic confusion; but there *should* be. So one political benefit of Haslanger's approach is that it alerts us to the need for such confusion. Haslanger's example of *parent* illustrates what I have in mind (2006, 99–101). Ordinary speakers intuitively seem to think that the (manifest) concept of *parent* encodes the condition of being someone's immediate biological progenitor. But, of course, many people are not brought up by their biological progenitors. This suggests a different—operative—*parent* concept: parents are primary caregivers, who undertake the social role of parenting. Adoptive parents, then, would satisfy the operative *parent* concept, though not the manifest one. Now, the distinction between manifest and operative *parent* concepts is politically important. For instance, if teachers were able to discuss the progress of their students only with the students' immediate progenitors, they would be barred from doing so with adoptive parents. Challenging the accepted manifest *parent*, then, would be warranted and extremely desirable: doing so is a necessary precursor to certain political action (like adoptive parents gaining rights and recognition qua parents) because the manifest *parent* concept is clearly insufficient for certain political and communicative tasks. In this case, political action requires that we complicate communication and create linguistic confusion.

Might the same be true of *woman*? I think not, and my contention is that with *woman* linguistic confusion would not be politically beneficial. This is because of the kind of confusion involved. With *parent*, the confusion boils down to our manifest and operative concepts coming apart, where both have

---

[7] One suggestion would be that Haslanger's target concept affords us some clear explanatory benefits. I will discuss this further in chapter 5. To anticipate: I do not think that it does. Still, I will postpone the point for now.

a claim to being our ordinary concepts. We take ourselves to be applying parent on (roughly) biological grounds, but our practice shows that we apply it on some other grounds too (referring to primary caretakers). Nevertheless, the confusion generated by feminists appropriating Haslanger's gender terminology is between our ordinary (manifest and/or operative) *woman* concept and her target concept: regardless of how we take ourselves to understand *woman* and how we actually do understand it, there is a different manner in which we should understand it. Here the confusion does not rest on how different ordinary speakers understand *woman*, but on how ordinary speakers in general and feminists in particular do. In the case of *parent*, both the manifest and the operative concepts are familiar to ordinary speakers—the dispute boils down to which of the two is more helpful given some political goals. But with *woman*, Haslanger's target concept would be utterly unfamiliar to ordinary speakers. And appropriating such an unfamiliar concept would have politically useful results only if feminists work extremely hard to avoid miscommunication between themselves and ordinary speakers by going to great lengths in order to ensure that ordinary speakers know what feminists are talking about when they use common, everyday terms like 'woman'. As I see it, this would be strategically undesirable: feminist resources would be better directed at tasks other than trying to explain in detail what feminists mean when they talk about women, thereby making sure that ordinary speakers have not misunderstood their claims.[8]

We might defend Haslanger further by going contextualist. Perhaps appropriating her gender notions is meant to be context sensitive, and so in certain contexts it would be entirely wrongheaded to do so. (In fact, she seems to suggest so [Haslanger 2000, 48].) My critique above would then be deflated because it would not be strategic to appropriate her gender terminology in all contexts, for example, when the scientists are aiming to bust gender myths. However, I am suspicious of this response. If Haslanger is arguing for contextualism, it becomes crucial to identify those contexts in which it is strategic to appropriate her terminology. For instance, perhaps feminist philosophers should do so. But this would make 'woman' a feminist technical term, which strikes me as a bad idea: if feminists use 'woman' as a technical term that differs from ordinary usage, communication between them and ordinary language users would again be

---

[8] Now, one might retort that perhaps appropriating *woman* in Haslanger's sense would be strategic after all. For instance, the notion of *queer* has been successfully reclaimed and with beneficial political consequences. Why not do the same with *woman*? However, the parallel does not hold, which undermines the objection. Bluntly put: reclaiming queer did not change the meaning or intension of *queer*, but its ethical assessment. Queerness was not debunked in Haslanger's sense (shown to be a social category, rather than a biological one). It was turned from a negative social identity into a positive one. Appropriating Haslanger's gender terminology would require something else, which is why the cases come apart.

compromised. I contend that feminists and ordinary speakers should be talking about the same thing. After all, the success of feminist goals depends on feminist concerns being taken up by ordinary social agents more widely. Consequently, feminist philosophers should stay methodologically grounded in everyday situations as much as possible and avoid positing technical terms unfamiliar to ordinary speakers. Let me clarify: it is not the positing of technical terms per se that I object to; rather, it is turning 'woman' into such a term. We may have good reasons to treat (say) "gender justice" as a feminist technical expression, but this is because (qua ordinary speakers) we have a rather bad grasp of it. However, ordinarily social agents tend to be secure in their grasp of gender terms (or at least they think that they are). Turning 'woman' into a technical term with an unfamiliar meaning would be like environmental activists turning 'nature' into a technical term that ordinary speakers would not recognize without large-scale educational efforts. My worry is that if *woman* as a feminist technical notion radically differs from the ordinary notion, there is always a potential for gross linguistic confusion. And this is not politically strategic. Or, to return to what I said earlier, if feminists and ordinary speakers can make use of the manifest *woman* concept in order to avoid talking past one another, I see little need to advance Haslanger's *woman* as a feminist technical notion.

That said, it is not entirely clear how contextualist Haslanger's proposal is meant to be, and she seems to think that her gender terminology should be appropriated more widely. One central function of her theory of gender is to empower women as social agents. She aims to provide a negative ideal of womanhood and asks us to "reject what seemed to be positive social identities": "we should refuse to be gendered man or woman ... [where this] involves an active political commitment to live one's life differently" (2000, 48). Haslanger seemingly hopes that ordinary speakers more generally will appropriate her gender terminology and that this will motivate a particular political response to undercut unjust social arrangements. However, in this case her proposal becomes rather demanding, and this again undermines the purported political benefits of revising *woman*: in addition to convincing ordinary social agents to alter structural arrangements that disadvantage women, feminists would have to convince them to use an ordinary term in quite an extraordinary way. Changing ordinary language use is not easy, and the difficult task of opposing gender injustice would become more demanding still. For strategic reasons, Saul too suggests that feminists should instead "try to use ordinary terms in as ordinary way as possible" (2006, 141).

To sum up: seeking to advance Haslanger's target gender concepts (I hold) would be more trouble than it is worth. This is partly because I think feminists should move beyond gender and embrace humanist feminism. But, I also contend, responding to the ontological and semantic puzzles along

Haslanger's lines would be politically quite demanding; and so a preferable strategy would simply be to give up the underlying focus on thick gender concepts. (I will return to this thought in chapter 5.)

4.3. Gendered Social Identity as Positionality

Linda Alcoff takes feminism to be facing an identity crisis: the concept *woman* is "the central concept of feminist theory" in being "the necessary point of departure for any feminist theory and feminist politics"; nevertheless, it is "a concept that is impossible to formulate precisely" (2006, 133). In response, she offers an account of gendered social identity to dispel the crisis. On Alcoff's general account, social identities (like gender and race) have three key features: (1) they are real; (2) they are visibly marked on the body; and (3) they provide us with interpretative horizons from which we act. First, Alcoff takes social identities to be real in being "relational, contextual, *and* fundamental to the self" (2006, 90). Social identities are extrinsic properties and exist relative to other human agents and institutions. Further, social identity attributions are contextually variable. For instance, our racial classification systems are notoriously context dependent: going from one country or region to the next can make one "from mulatto or Cuban to black, from Mexican to Latino, even from white to black" (Alcoff 2006, 91). Finally, although social identities are relational and context dependent, they are nevertheless fundamental: "they have causal determinacy over our epistemic and political orientations to the world—what we notice, what we care about—[and] they profoundly affect how we are seen and interacted with by others" (2006, 91). For Alcoff, something's being fundamental does not make it unanalyzable or reduced to some metaphysical primitives. The thought is rather that social identities are not additional and peripheral to the self, but rather central to our social agency.

Second, as social agents, we cannot escape social identity categories insofar as they are "essential to the way the self experiences the world." (2006, 92). The self cannot escape its gendered or racialized social identity because such social identities tend to be visibly marked on the body and determinant of various material realties (like economic or political status). The basic point is that bodily differences exist, and some of these differences are endowed with special social meanings. In order to adequately analyze social identity categories, we cannot ignore that they operate through bodily markers (2006, 102).

Third, *in* being so visibly marked, social identities constitute particular interpretative horizons. Such horizons denote

> the background, framing assumptions we bring with us to perception and understanding, the congealed experiences that become premises by which we strive to make sense of the world, the range of concepts and categories of description that we have at our disposal. (2006, 95)

Roughly: our social identities crucially shape our (epistemic, moral, intellectual) agency by situating and embedding us differently in the world. Our interpretative horizons situate us in ways that make a difference to how we interpret not only others but also ourselves.

Although Alcoff does not make use of this example, the idea of interpretative horizons is nicely elucidated by Miranda Fricker's (2007) work. Certain negative identity prejudices and stereotypical beliefs (about women, people of color) can result in two kinds of epistemic injustice: testimonial and hermeneutic. The former pertains to ways in which others judge us. Fricker discusses the example of Marge Sheerwood from the novel *The Talented Mr. Ripley*. In short: Marge's fiancée Dickie disappears under odd circumstances, and Marge (rightly) suspects that Dickie's newfound friend, Tom Ripley, has killed him. However, Marge's intended future father-in-law dismisses her accusations as "women's intuition" and brands her a hysterical woman who simply cannot face her fiancé's leaving her for another woman. The background assumptions framing the male characters' interpretative horizons (most prominently: 1950s gender relations) had the effect of diminishing Marge's status as a reliable witness and a knower—despite her fiancé's philandering past, she *knew* from the cues around her that Dickie had not left her, but was dead. In not being recognized as a knower, she was subject to testimonial injustice. Hermeneutic injustice, then again, affects the way that members of disadvantaged social groups comprehend their own experiences. Such injustices can arise when collectively shared interpretative systems prevent individuals from understanding (say) their own feelings. This was arguably the case prior to consciousness-raising about workplace sexual harassment: those subject to sexual advances could not articulate any specific harm done to them despite their discomfort because sexual advances were seen as part of normal workplace conduct. Only once the term 'sexual harassment' was coined did this become possible. The lack of shared conceptual resources diminished the subjects' ability to make sense of what was happening to them. Such agents were subject to hermeneutical injustice. Our particular interpretative horizons (our background beliefs, framing assumptions, and conceptual schemes) are the tools with which we aim to make sense of the world. Cases of epistemic injustice clearly demonstrate how our social identities shape our self- and other-directed interpretations, sometimes with detrimental results.

Being visibly marked on the body, real, and constitutive of our interpretative horizons are the general aspects of social identities. What then is it to have a specific gendered social identity, or "a sexed self" (Alcoff 2006, 128)? Alcoff elucidates this question with the notion of *positionality*. In short, gender is "a position one occupies and from which one can act politically" (2006, 148). This position is extrinsic to women, and its precise location in the matrix of social relations is fixed relative to a network of considerations, such as economic conditions, cultural and political institutions, and ideologies. At the same time, gender is not (strictly speaking) a relation, although it is relational: for Alcoff, women's social identity is constituted by their position. Further, this is politically important. Transcending women's gendered position should not be a political goal; instead, the position should be "actively utilized . . . as a location for the construction of meaning, a place from where meaning can be *discovered* (the meaning of being female)" (Alcoff 2006, 148). This position has a material basis, which comes down to the division of reproductive (biological) labor. That is, the material basis of gender comes down to distinguishing individuals on the grounds of their actual or expected reproductive roles: "*Women and men are differentiated by virtue of their different relationship of possibility to biological reproduction, with biological reproduction referring to conceiving, giving birth, and breast-feeding, involving one's body*" (2006, 172). The thought is that those standardly classified as biologically female, although they may not actually be able to reproduce, will encounter sets of practices, expectations, and feelings about reproduction that differ from those sets encountered by biological males. This differential relation to the *possibility* of reproduction is used as the basis for many cultural and social phenomena that position women: it can be the basis for various "social segregations, it can engender the development of differential forms of embodiment experienced throughout life, and it can generate a wide variety of affective responses, from pride, delight, shame, guilt, regret, or great relief from having successfully avoided reproduction" (2006, 172). Further, reproductive roles provide a way to conceive of females and males as genuine types. There is a nonrandom, principled, and nonarbitrary basis on which the types are unified: that of reproductive division of labor, which not only includes anatomical facts about reproduction, but also mutable social and cultural aspects (e.g., that we can alter the "natural" reproductive processes with technological interventions). The objective basis for distinguishing females and males takes on an even deeper cultural dimension when we bear in mind that our bodies are lived in a matrix of social relations. This being so, our lived experiences will differ greatly from one another.

Alcoff is not entirely clear on the precise connection between the reproductive division of labor and gender as positionality, but I expect the story to go something like this. The reproductive division of labor not only fixes one's membership in the type of females, but also positions one in a way that fosters the development of specifically gendered social identities. One's (lived) body socially and culturally situates one in certain ways: for one thing, acknowledging that one may become pregnant affects how one thinks about and views childbirth, sexual and familial relations, and career and caretaking possibilities (Alcoff 2006, 176). This then produces gendered social identities, which are real, embodied, and constitutive of those interpretative horizons from which we interact with the world and understand ourselves. In a sense, and Alcoff acknowledges this, her account is akin to the original sex/gender distinction: sex difference (the division of reproductive labor) provides the foundation for certain cultural arrangements (the development of a gendered social identity). But, with the benefit of hindsight, her view avoids the implausible claim that sex is exclusively to do with reified nature, and gender with culture. Rather, the distinction on the basis of reproductive possibilities shapes and is shaped by cultural and social phenomena that these possibilities gives rise to (2006, 175). Finally, since women are differentially positioned depending on the relation they have to actual or expected reproductive roles, Alcoff avoids reifying womanhood in the old-fashioned essentialist manner that took women to share some intrinsic, essential property qua women—there is no cross-cultural gender essence (2006, 147–148). Nonetheless, there is something women qua women share: positional, gendered social identity. Thus, Alcoff aims to avoid the gender skeptic view that gendered social identities are mere fictions and that women's social kind does not exist, while doing justice to women's diverse and particular experiences.

Alcoff's account is meant to provide the starting point for feminist politics. It aims to overcome feminism's identity crisis and to provide a helpful articulation of *woman*. Overcoming this crisis is pivotal. Otherwise feminism will be stuck in an impasse:

> What can we demand in the name of women if "women" do not exist and demands in their name simply reenforce the myth that they do? How can we speak out against sexism as detrimental to the interests of women if the category is a fiction? How can we demand legal abortions, adequate child care, or wages based on comparable worth without invoking the concept of "women"? (Alcoff 2006, 143)

If we keep overcoming this impasse in mind, gender on Alcoff's conceptualization will be a position from which one can act politically. Women's positionality should afford the location from where "meaning can be *discovered* (the meaning of being female)" (2006, 148). In my terminology, Alcoff is aiming to articulate the basis for feminist normative demands: she aims to articulate *woman* in a way that retains its centrality as "the necessary point of departure for any feminist theory and feminist politics" (Alcoff 2006, 133). The strategy is to provide a thick conception of *woman* in terms of social identities while avoiding gender skepticism, and by making good intersectionality. This should support feminist critical claims about the damage done by patriarchy and help form a future vision of gender-just social arrangements.

I find Alcoff's elucidation of women's social identities eloquent and phenomenologically deeply compelling. Nevertheless, I cannot see how her conception of gender satisfies feminist normative demands. That is, I cannot see how the conception of *woman* as positionality helps us in speaking against sexism and in devising policies that can help women—tasks for which Alcoff takes the elucidations of womanhood to be central. In a sense, her view alerts us to the fact that those positioned as women face sexism: we can tell this by looking at the specific ways in which sexed selves are positioned; and this helps us to discover what it is to be a woman. But I do not see how this formulation solves the feminist identity crisis. Bluntly put, how does gender as positionality enable feminists to make political demands in the name of women? Perhaps Alcoff intended her proposal all along to be more modest than this, and I am expecting too much from it. Maybe she merely intended her account to serve as a way to elucidate that—contra gender skepticism—women do exist, and that acknowledging this is a crucial first step of any adequate feminist project. The next step is to investigate empirically how patriarchy damages those sexed subjects positioned as women. In this sense, then, we should not "transcend" women's social positions but keep them in mind when explicating patriarchal injustices. But I am unconvinced that for the tasks of identifying women, elucidating that they exist, and empirically looking at women's lived experiences it makes much difference whether we endorse Alcoff's conception of gender or not. In pointing out that women exist, we can rely on some fairly thin conception of *woman*—even Haslanger's manifest gender concepts tell us that there are women. In order to merely identify women, there is no need for a thick account of gender like Alcoff's. For one thing, although (as Alcoff notes) the concept of *woman* has been a problem for many contemporary feminist theorists, this has not made feminist politics and activism impossible. Ending violence against women, guaranteeing women access to political decision-making, enhancing equal opportunities, and improving women's working conditions (to name but a few) have been included in the European Union's core policies under the Treaty of Amsterdam. (For a discussion of these measures, see Walby 2002.) Gender mainstreaming is a public policy notion employed by the EU (among other large international/corporate bodies) that aims to enable, facilitate, and foster gender justice by "looking at every step of policy—design, implementation, monitoring and evaluation—with the aim of promoting equality between women and men" (European Commission 2004). This exercise starts by looking at the everyday life situations of women and men in order to make visible how their needs and problems differ. As starting points for our public policies, even Haslanger's manifest concepts will suffice. So there must be some political benefits other than identifying women to be gained from advancing a thick *woman* notion. But what are they? I am genuinely unsure.

The upshot is this: feminist theorists have critiqued earlier essentialist theories of gender, and they have aimed to replace those with nonessentialist ones. Nevertheless, feminist philosophers (like Alcoff) aim to advance nonessentialist thick conceptions of *woman*, and supposedly in order to meet feminist political demands (e.g., to speak against sexism). I do not see as necessary, however, the move to elucidate such a nonessentialist *thick* conception, and it again illustrates the pull of those theoretical underpinnings that undergird the gender controversy. The crucial self-critical question is this: does feminist politics require a nonessentialist thick conception of *woman*, or might relying on some thin articulation suffice? My contention is that the thin articulation will do, and I cannot see what further benefits substantive conceptions like Alcoff's bring when we aim to speak out against sexism or demand legal abortions. Or we are owed a more fleshed-out story about the supposed political benefits of such thick conceptions—a story that Alcoff does not tell. This is not a problem that she alone faces; it is part and parcel of the gender controversy and of the assumption that articulating a thick *woman* conception is somehow theoretically required given feminist political concerns. However interesting Alcoff's proposal is, I hold that we should privilege a thin understanding of woman if it suffices relative to feminist normative work. In fact, the next chapter advances the view that, for the task of identifying and articulating women's social kind membership, feminists can rely on such a thin everyday conception. And this deflates the semantic worry.

4.4. Historical Essentialism

4.4.1. GENDER AS A NATURAL KIND

Contra the prevalent view that feminists must elucidate women's *social* kind, Theodore Bach's recent solution to the ontological puzzle holds that women make up a natural kind with a historical essence. In short:

> The essential property of women, in virtue of which an individual is a member of the kind "women," is participation in a lineage of women. In order to exemplify this relational property, an individual must be a reproduction of ancestral women, in which case she must have undergone the ontogenetic processes through which a historical gender system replicates women. (Bach 2012, 271)

This view supposedly resolves two common clusters of problems for feminists.

1. *Representation problem*: "if there is no real group of 'women,' then it is incoherent to make moral claims and advance political policies on behalf of women" (2012, 234).

2. *Commonality problems*:
    1. *Inseparability*: Gender does not exist and develop independently of other (social) features such as race, class, and religion.

2. *Universality*: There is no feature that all women cross-culturally and transhistorically share.
3. *Immutability*: "By defining women according to property *P* it follows that (i) the elimination of *P* entails the elimination of women, (ii) if an individual possesses *P* at time 1 and loses *P* at time 2, then that individual is no longer a woman."
4. *Normativity*: Delimiting women's social kind with the help of some essential property privileges those who possess it, and marginalizes those who do not (2012, 235).

One strategy to resolving these problems is (what Bach terms) "social objectivism," of which Haslanger's position is an example. It allegedly employs two dialectical moves. First, social objectivist accounts define women "according to a suitably abstract relational property" (2012, 236), which avoids the commonality problems. Second, they employ "an ontologically thin notion of 'objectivity'" (2012, 236), thus providing an answer to the representation problem. Haslanger's solution (Bach holds) is specifically to argue that women make up an objective type because women are objectively similar to one another. As he puts it, Haslanger's method of determining whether some collection of objects has unity is "to investigate if, and to what degree, they are in some sense similar. In order for a type to be objective, then, the axis of similarity must be objective as opposed to merely conceptual" (2012, 238). Social objectivism supposedly avoids the representation problem by arguing for a nonessentialist conception of gender that nevertheless tracks "a real structure of reality as opposed to a conventional aspect of our categorizing" (2012, 238). However, Bach claims, Haslanger's account is not objective enough. We can—in fact we *should* on political grounds—"provide a stronger ontological characterization of the genders *men* and *women* according to which they are natural kinds with explanatory essences" (Bach 2012, 238). A theory of gender in terms of historical essentialism is said to provide such an account.

Bach's model for understanding the natural kinds of women and men emphasizes historical properties' role in supporting inductive practices. On this view, "historical facts about genetic replication and past selective pressures explain why the members of a species share a phenotypic profile" (2012, 242)—that is, the "deep" historical properties are to do with genetic or cultural replication, and they explain surface manifest properties. Specifically, historical kinds have seven features:

1. Their essential property is *participation in a lineage*.
2. This property defines *kind*, not individual, essence.
3. In order to exemplify this essence, an individual must be a *replication* or *reproduction* of ancestors from a lineage.

4. Reproduction and replication are *ontogenetic processes* caused by mechanisms that produce historical kind members.
5. Historical kind members tend to be *similar* to one another in various ways because of their history; similarities that are due to something other than shared history are not necessary for kind membership.
6. Individuals reproduced from a selected-for historical lineage possess *teleological functions*.
7. This function is defined by "the contribution made by ancestral kind members to *the stability and effect of a more general historical system*" (Bach 2012, 245–246; italics mine).

With these features in mind, Bach argues that gendered kinds are historical kinds. Being a woman (or a man) is not a matter of having some biological or psychological properties, or of occupying certain social positions. These are mere indicators of a deeper shared history or origin. Instead, womanhood is about having "the right sort of origin and replicative history in relation to a more fundamental historical kind—a replicating gender system" (2012, 246).

To illustrate, Bach offers the following analogy. The historical kind "1990 Nissan Sentra" is a replicating system. All token Sentras have been reproduced from the same historical design, which is why the individual tokens have certain features (good gas mileage, front-wheel drive). The various subcomponents of Sentras were selected for and reproduced given the role that they played in the success of the replicating Sentra *system*, a system that met the demands and interests of consumers more than other competing car model systems did. Now, the subpart "Sentra transmission" is also a historical kind because individual Sentra transmission tokens are reproductions of a lineage of Sentra transmissions. Further, "On account of their history of reproduction under past selection pressures, Sentra transmissions also possess a teleological function" (Bach 2012, 246). This system-relative function is *shifting gears in Sentras*. So a piece of steel is a Sentra transmission provided it has been designed and produced to shift gears in Nissan Sentras. The case of gender is similar. Our gender system is a historical kind akin to the historical kind of "1990 Nissan Sentra," and the individual components of our gender system are like Sentra transmissions: they were selected for and reproduced given the role that they played in successfully replicating the overall gender system. Although there might not be anything ontologically necessary or ethically desirable about such a system, our gender system is homeostatic—"its various components have achieved a stability that is resistant, though not impervious, to change" (Bach 2012, 247). For Bach, such homeostatic gender system has seven components:

1. *Binary sex categories*: categories of male and female
2. *Conceptual gender dualism*: "the tendency for individuals to think and categorize in terms of the masculine and feminine binary"

3. *Gender identity*: identification with a particular gender, its roles, and taking certain gender norms to be applicable to oneself
4. *Binary gender socialization practices*: for example, sex segregation
5. *Social and legal institutions:* for example, gender differences in law
6. *Binary gendered artifacts:* for example, masculine and feminine toys and clothing
7. *Binary roles:* for example, gendered roles, sexual division of labor (2012, 247–248)

The idea is that these individual components have been selected for and reproduced because they play an important role in the successful replication of the gender system as a whole; they have made our gender system homeostatic.

On the picture put forward, these components possess certain teleological gender functions because of ancestral selection pressures and processes. It does not much matter whether these pressures were biological or social—both are consistent with the historical account. We can (for instance) tell a story about cultural processes doing the work. And cultural mechanisms that specifically favor the selection of gender include institutions like media, schools, and the medical profession that effectively transmit gendered norms, expectations, and other components of the gender system. Nevertheless, we cannot elucidate the teleological gender function via conceptual analysis—we must do some empirical investigation of our gender system and its history in order to do so.[9] In order to elucidate the teleological gender functions of the gender system's components, we must investigate "the contributions made by the historical lineages of men and women toward the stabilization of a gender system" (Bach 2012, 254). This requires social scientific research, and some such research already exists relative to the gender roles of men and women (component 7 above). Plausible candidate features for the teleological functions of gender roles then include (*a*) social hierarchy: women having less power and status than men; (*b*) division of labor: women performing more household chores, sex segregation of/in household and paid labor, gender differences in earning; (*c*) personality traits: men having more agentic traits, being aggressive; women having communal traits, being "tender-minded"; (*d*) body management: women wearing makeup, electing for cosmetic surgery, the increased frequency of women smiling, and so on (Bach 2012, 254–255). Those individuals in our ancestral past who acted in conformity with these features acted to stabilize the gender system. If the above characteristics

---

[9] For instance, a piece of clothing is gendered not by its "masculine" or "feminine" appearance; rather, "a type of clothing is women's clothing on the basis of the type's historical role in the gender system" (Bach 2012, 253). What makes a kilt a member of a historical, masculine artifact kind is that individual kilts are reproductions of earlier garments that had the role in our gender system of denoting masculinity. Further, we know that the kilt plays this role relative to the historical gender system via empirical investigation.

were culturally reproduced because of their stabilizing effects, we can conclude that they were culturally selected for. On the picture put forward, then, the above four binary sets of properties "constitute the teleological functions of men and women" (2012, 255).

So no one is born a man or a woman; instead, certain ontogenetic processes reproduce members of these historical kinds out of sexed individuals. The most important of such processes is differential socialization (component 4 of the gender system): parents attributing gender-stereotypic behaviors to their children and talking about them using gender-stereotypic language; sex segregation in schools and among tasks assigned to boys and girls. To sum up,

> both conscious and unconscious design mechanisms mold infants as reproductions of historical men and women from the moment they are born. Through these processes an individual comes to participate in a lineage of men or women and thereby becomes a member of the historical kind *men* or *women*. (Bach 2012, 260)

One's sex is not necessary for participation in a particular gender kind: sex merely marks individuals as targets for particular ontogenetic processes. Further, to be a woman does not require that one exemplify the properties outlined above that are constitutive of women's historical gender role ("to be subordinated, tender-minded, present her body according to the norms of the fashion-beauty complex, and perform more housework" [Bach 2012, 261]). For womanhood, it is necessary to have undergone an ontogenetic process through which one comes to take part in the lineage of women. In short: female gender socialization fixes gender, but one need not exemplify any typically female properties or enact stereotypical female roles. One is a woman because one has "the right history" (2012, 261). A robot woman that is relatively powerless, performs housework, is tender minded, and pays attention to feminine fashion norms would exemplify the properties that define women's historical gender role, but she would not therefore be a member of women's kind. This is because the robot woman has the wrong history and has not undergone the ontogenetic process of gender socialization.

We can capture Bach's picture in the following manner: at the most basic and overarching level, we find the replicating gender system. Next level up, we find seven components of this underlying system, which were biologically or culturally selected for given their success in making the gender system homeostatic. The components were replicated and reproduced precisely because of this success. Out of these components, gender socialization represents the most important ontogenetic process that produces and reproduces gender out of sex. So on the third level we find the historical kinds of women and men; they are created and recreated by the components of the gender system via the ontogenetic process of gender socialization. At the final, manifest level we find typical gender traits (like behavioral patterns or social position occupancy). These surface similarities are not definitive of gender. Instead, they are manifestations of the deeper, more fundamental similarity: having the right history, and shared ontogeny. What does the important ontological work and provides responses to the representation and commonality problems is the third level. This establishes the following: what makes *x* a woman is *x*'s participation in a lineage of women. In order to participate in this lineage, *x* must be a reproduction of ancestral women. In order to be such a reproduction, *x* must have undergone the right ontogenetic process. Undergoing this process (socialization) is the mechanism with which the base-level gender system replicates women.

4.4.2. FEMINIST POLITICS AND HISTORICAL ESSENTIALISM

Historical essentialism is meant to conceptualize women's kind in a *politically* helpful manner and thus overcome pressing feminist problems. I am unconvinced, however, that this has been achieved. In particular, Bach's model faces a serious concern relative to his solution to the normativity problem. Bach takes his response to the universality problem to respond to the normativity problem. A politically adequate theory of gender must be sufficiently inclusive and avoid positing some exclusionary universal feature. Haslanger posits such a feature, but takes this to be nonproblematic. Although nonsubordinated females won't count as women, this should not worry us since they are not the ones who matter for feminist politics (Haslanger 2000, 46). The historical essentialist view avoids this consequence and supposedly provides a better way to be inclusive. For Bach, the only individuals who will not be members of women's kind are those who have not undergone the right ontogenetic process (2012, 266). One need not possess any gendered features to be a woman; thus, nonsubordinated females will still count as women because they have the right origin and history. This does exclude (for instance) humanoid robot women from women's kind. Although such individuals still deserve moral consideration, Bach holds, they nevertheless should not gain feminist political representation. This hinges on a distinction between natural kind and ad hoc political representation. The former "advocates on behalf of categories for which members tend to share certain social and political properties (such as oppression and opportunities) for the same reason," whereas the latter "advocates for individuals who accidentally share similarities with natural political kinds" (Bach 2012, 267). The basic idea is this: although oppression is not definitive of womanhood, it is not a purely accidental feature of women that they tend to be oppressed. Rather, such a surface feature is a manifestation of a deeper shared essence: that women have undergone the right ontogenetic process of gender socialization. This makes the surface similarities nonaccidental and non-ad hoc, which supposedly provides a stronger basis for feminist political organizing. So, females-socialized-as-women will gain natural kind political representation. The robot woman's oppression, however, is not a manifestation of a deeper similarity with other women—it would be a feature that robot women accidentally share with females-social-ized-as-women. Thus, robot women only qualify for ad hoc political repre-sentation. Nevertheless, the historical account is allegedly more inclusive and will marginalize fewer individuals: only those who have not been socialized as women fail to count as women; but since the socializing ontogenetic pro-cesses are ubiquitous, Bach takes his account to be genuinely inclusive.

There are some individuals, though, who clearly fail to satisfy Bach's cri-teria for womanhood: trans* women. And this is deeply problematic. On Bach's account, they would not count as women, given that the right onto-genetic processes that fix one's gender status as a woman or a man take place "through events that occurred primarily before the age of ten" (Bach 2012, 268). In fact, this suggests that trans* women would be gendered men con-trary to self-identification, which raises serious questions about how genu-inely inclusive the historically essentialist account is—it looks instead highly marginalizing, and problematically so. Bach does very briefly consider tran-sitioning. He asks: when does an individual transition into a new gender? His reply, however, is less than satisfying. In Bach's view, this is a difficult question without a clear answer (2012, 269). All that we learn from the phe-nomenon of transitioning (in his view) is that historical gender kinds have vague boundaries. Admittedly, Bach is right to point out that gender kinds do not have rigid boundaries. But his treatment of trans* women is nonetheless deeply worrying, particularly given the history of trans* women's marginal-ization within feminist movements. Here is the rub: on his picture of histori-cal gender kinds, trans* women end up being either men or like robot women. If we conclude that trans* women having undergone male gender socializa-tion actually count as men, they won't be even prima facie candidates for feminist political representation. If we conclude that trans* women are like robot women, it follows that it is wholly accidental that they share features with females-socialized-as-women. Again, trans* women will be explicitly excluded from feminist political representation understood in Bach's natu-ral kind political representation sense—they merely deserve ad hoc political representation. Either way, the upshot of Bach's metaphysics is that trans* women will be excluded from women's kind and thereby marginalized within feminist politics, which is an unacceptable result.[10]

---

[10] Bach does claims that "as if" women like robot women may end up being systematically mis-taken for "real" women because of their surface properties and thus be treated as women. If such treatment is prolonged, the would-be women may convert over time into "real" women (2012, 266). This does not seem possible, though, since the ontogenetic process of childhood gender socialization is *constitutive* of one's gender kind membership. Further, many trans* women are likely to find this view deeply offensive.

Now, Bach can of course retort by claiming that this is politically less than ideal; but if the metaphysical facts pull us in one direction and ethical considerations in another, so much worse for the ethical considerations! Metaphysical facts trump political desiderata, and it is metaphysics that should fix the relevant political categories—our politics cannot fix metaphysics. Implicitly such a view seems to figure in Bach's metaphilosophical commitments: he is seeking to elucidate the metaphysical facts "out there," which may or may not be ethically desirable. But the metaphysical facts are distinct from our political and ethical values. The feminist philosophers I have discussed so far, however, have a different set of background metaphilosophical commitments. On more standard feminist views, the challenge is not merely to elucidate some ontological parts of reality. As Haslanger (and others) have helpfully put it, the challenge is to elucidate parts that *serve* feminist politics. Our assessment of (say) the appropriate ontological theory of gender must be made relative to feminist political and ethical considerations, just as much as feminist politics should make use of ontologically adequate conceptions of gender. This is because feminist philosophers usually reject the view that womanhood is carved in nature's joints. And they reject this view because social forces and structures causally and constitutively underpin the existence and nature of gendered social kinds. Bach, however, takes the need to elucidate a real (as opposed to a fictional) kind of women to express the need to elucidate gender as a natural kind. His metaontological commitments differ from standard feminist ones, and the responses to the normativity and universality problems demonstrate that Bach has a particular metaphysical background picture in mind. My contention is that this, however, skews his formulation of the politically pertinent issues.

In order to see this more clearly, consider some of Bach's background ontological presuppositions. He draws a sharp line between two ways in which we can conceive of kinds: some kind x is either part of reality's structure and therefore objective and nonconventional; or x is conventional and therefore nonreal and dependent on our conceptual schemes. Given this background ontological picture, the feminist quest for a *real* kind of women appears to be a quest for a kind that is objective (explanatory in the sense of supporting inductions), nonconventional (in the sense of not taking into account, say, political goals), and carved in nature's joints. Otherwise, feminists cannot make good the reality of women's kind: if the kind is merely conventional and conceptual, it won't be real. However, Bach's picture does not exhaust the available ontological options. Moreover, when feminists are after a real kind of women, they are after something other than Bach's real kinds. Feminists are more usually after a kind that is objective, conventional, *and* real. First, a kind can be objective *relative to* certain strongly normative practices; second, a kind may be conventional in the sense that its existence and persistence *depend* entirely on human agency, our practices, customs, norms, and institutions; third, a kind may be real insofar as it has causal and explanatory *powers*.

Consider traffic rules by way of example. UK traffic direction is left-handed, but the United States is right-handed. These driving conventions depend entirely on contingent human practices, and there is no mind-independent "fact of the matter" about which side is the *correct* one to drive on—in this sense, traffic rules are not to be found in nature's joints. Nevertheless, the rules are objective in another sense: relative to certain social frameworks, norms, and practices, the rules governing traffic are not "up to us" or up for grabs. I cannot simply decide to bunk the norms of driving—these norms are strongly binding on us, although they are conventional. Or, to put the point differently: I could drive however I wanted. But this would probably result in serious accidents, my own death or the death of others, fines, and even long prison sentences. So, in this sense, traffic rules are not up to me. They have (what Searle [1995] calls) deontic powers, although we confer on them the relevant authority. Finally, these objective and conventional traffic rules are real in the sense of having causal and explanatory powers. Were I to bunk the norms and drive on the right-hand side in the UK, I would very probably cause an accident. Were I to follow UK traffic rules while driving in the UK, the likelihood of my driving causing an accident would be diminished. If I have a serious accident, my bunking the objective and conventional traffic rules can be used to explain what caused the accident. So traffic rules support inductions and causal explanations.

The upshot is this: we have more than Bach's two ontological options available to us, and women's kind seems ontologically more akin to traffic rules. The response that trans* women are out of women's kind because our ontology tells us so is thus not only ethically problematic, but also metaphysically unwarranted. If women's kind is conventional, objective, and real in the manner outlined, we can spell it out in a way that includes trans* women. Since this is more congenial to feminist politics and does not problematically exclude trans* women, I see little reason to accept Bach's metaphysical picture of gender. He could, of course, reply that my "real" kinds are not really real, but supervene on properly real ones. So traffic rules supervene on psychological states of conscious agents, and these states *are* carved in nature's joints. This would undermine my alternative ontological position. But if it turned out that traffic rules are not real because they supervene on psychological states, then—I submit again—feminist philosophers simply are not after a *real* kind of women in Bach's sense. This (once more) would demonstrate that his way of framing the crucial political issue differs from more usual ways that feminists frame the problem.[11]

---

[11] Bach's presentation of the representation problem is also questionable. Gender skepticism generates this problem: as Bach puts it, the problem is whether there is a real group of women on behalf of which feminists can make moral claims and advance political policies (2012, 234). The

4.5. Upshot of the Discussion

In this chapter, I have discussed recent positions that aim to make good a politically useful genuine women's kind from a realist perspective. But, I argued, the theories discussed do not satisfy their own self-proclaimed political desiderata. This appears to leave us with an impasse: neither prominent gender nominalist theories nor gender realist ones have provided an articulation of womanhood that is thick enough to support feminist normative claims and political demands. The positions considered in this and the previous chapter take there to be a need to provide an inclusive and unified theory of gender that is substantive enough to do feminist political work. But they either fail to be inclusive (Bach), to be unified (Frye, Young, Stoljar), or to afford the needed political benefits (Zack, Haslanger, Alcoff). What is a feminist philosopher to do? I think that the game is far from over—we must simply change the terms of our engagement. In order to motivate this move, I will deflate next the semantic and ontological worries.

---

desideratum is to cash out a kind of women that is of Bach's real/nonconventional/objective sort. But, as I argued above, there is an alternative way to understand women's real kind that is more congenial to feminist politics, and more commonly appealed to by feminist philosophers. When feminist philosophers talk about the real or genuine kind of women, they have in mind something like my third option above: a kind that is not a mere fiction, one that is conventional, objective relative to certain strongly binding practices and norms, and has causal and explanatory efficacy. Thus, Bach's formulation of the representation problem already presupposes *his* background meta-metaphysical commitments, rather than those feminist philosophers more commonly hold. And this skews his manner of formulating the representation concern as well.

{5}

Deflating the Puzzles

The first part of this book argues that feminists should give up the gender controversy along with a certain theoretical outlook that keeps the controversy alive. This outlook is present in the feminist accounts examined earlier (among others), and it holds that feminist politics somehow hinges on a thick social conception of *woman*. First, it is presumed that feminists ought to elucidate womanhood in some sufficiently substantive sense: defining *woman* as *not-man* will not do because such an elucidation is empty, and it does not tell us what it is to be a woman under patriarchy. Second, an adequate theory of gender trades on how politically helpful the theory is; after all, since gender is not found in nature's joints, theoretical and ontological adequacy is to be measured against political usefulness. Third, the political benefits that articulations of gender ought to offer pertain to explicating the damage done to women by patriarchy, justifying feminist critical claims of the status quo, and providing a vision of gender-just social arrangements (i.e., feminism's normative demands). Overcoming the semantic and ontological puzzles supposedly affords feminism not only explanatory tools with which to analyze unjust social relations, but also normative tools with which to speak on behalf and in the name of women. This is not how gender talk in feminist circles began. Rather, the original sex/gender distinction aimed to explicate how biology is not destiny and show that commonly observed behavioral patterns and character traits are socially constructed, rather than biologically "given." But, as I have already noted, gender concepts have since taken on a life of their own, and feminist philosophical debates have moved on from providing merely explanatory accounts of gender.

Feminist challenges to the sex/gender distinction generated the semantic and ontological puzzles that seemingly threaten a basic tenet of feminism: that feminist politics should be organized around women, understood as a gendered social kind, since it is "a fundamental claim of feminism that women [as a group] are oppressed" (Frye 1983, 1). The previous two chapters demonstrate how feminist responses to these puzzles aim to salvage feminism's political viability. It is this move (I contend) that has unhelpfully turned the gender debate from an explanatory endeavor to an evaluative one. All of the positions looked at take the idea of social gender somehow to ground and support normative claims pertaining to feminist politics, which is why it is so important to provide an analysis of *woman*. My examination of feminist responses to the semantic and ontological puzzles offers a philosophical excavation to make this theoretical outlook explicit.

Now, I hold that the various positions discussed earlier are untenable, but they are not so merely because of their individual weaknesses. Rather, the positions are unsatisfying because of their theoretical underpinnings. That is, there is some common ground that undergirds these individual weaknesses. And the problem ultimately lies with those theoretical assumptions and normative commitments found at the center of philosophical elucidations of gender. Thus, my plea is that we surpass these assumptions and commitments and change the terms of our engagement. In this chapter, I will argue that the semantic and ontological issues are not as pressing as feminists make them out to be. We can talk about women without providing a thick articulation of *woman*, and we can understand the phenomena usually discussed under the rubric of the sex/gender distinction in a way that avoids certain unintuitive and undesirable ontological implications. My aim is to show that we can deflate the ontological and semantic worries, and so there is no need to seek solutions to them. This being the case, we can move beyond the gender controversy and embrace my proposed humanist feminism.

5.1. Deflating the Semantic Puzzle

Feminist theorizing about gender examined above buys into a particular line of thought: knowing "what it is to be a woman" and articulating a conception of *woman* in a thick and politically helpful manner enables feminists to do important emancipatory work. Doing so provides feminists an analytical tool with which to identify and explain gendered social inequalities (Haslanger 2000; Zack 2005), and it provides justification for political action in the name of women (Bach 2012; Stoljar 1995; Young 1997). Further, solving the puzzles retains the concept of *woman* as central to feminism and enables it to function as the necessary starting point for feminist politics (Alcoff 2006; Frye 1996). By contrast, I contend that we need not know "what it is to be a woman" or to define *woman* in order to identify and explain gendered social inequalities or in order to say why patriarchy damages women. Let me clarify: feminists must be able to refer to women, and our language use must pick out women's social kind. If we genuinely cannot distinguish women from other ordinary objects, feminism has lost its viability. But holding that unless we solve the semantic puzzle, we will be simply *unable* to talk about women does not follow. Feminism need not give up gender talk tout court in the absence of a thick conception of *woman*—a minimal conception will do. I will argue next for such a conception. Certain linguistic intuitions, which I call "extensional," are key to my proposal. With respect to 'woman', it seems intuitively easy to apply the term but hard to account for its application (or to state some conditions for being a woman). Reflecting on this common phenomenon in language use suggests that intuitions about gender terminology have two distinct, although not unrelated, functions: they guide gender terms' *deployment* and provide insight into gender concepts' *content*. I will call these "extensional" and "semantic" functions, respectively. Very roughly: although I agree with other feminist philosophers that ordinary language users' semantic intuitions about *woman* are unhelpful, I hold that their extensional intuitions are not so unhelpful. And this enables feminists to pick out women's type and to refer to women. Now, this is a separate issue from whether feminism ought normatively to be grounded in the gender concept *woman*. My view is that it should not be, despite holding that feminists must have some way to talk about women as a group in order to theorize systematic injustices that women face. But (my argument goes) being able to talk about women is much less problematic than current feminist debates take it to be, and the semantic puzzle is far less pressing than assumed.

The above-mentioned extensional and semantic functions are akin to applicability and reference-fixing conditions. The former specify "*what it takes* for a concept to apply to an object—that is, they specify the concept's intension by means of certain semantically basic features" (Schroeter 2004, 429). However, semantic externalism has demonstrated that we need not grasp precisely what it takes for something to count as an elm tree, water, or arthritis in order to get our reference-fixing right—we can correctly refer to *that* colorless, odorless, clear liquid in my glass with 'water' even when we do not exactly grasp what it takes for something to count as water (i.e., its chemical composition). So there are ways to satisfy the reference-fixing conditions in the absence of satisfying the applicability conditions. Satisfying either condition is sufficient for reference; but while the applicability conditions single out the reference by citing some essential features of the object, the reference-fixing conditions typically achieve this "by citing some inessential but epistemically accessible features of the reference, such as the subject's own causal interaction with it" (Schroeter 2004, 430). The moral of the story is this: we need not precisely specify what it takes for someone to count as a woman (or satisfy the intension of *woman*) in order to make good our reference fixing. Thus, my proposal is that in order to retain gender talk for politically relevant social explanations, we can merely rely on the reference-fixing extensional intuitions.

Before I go on to specify what I mean by such intuitions, a note about intuitions themselves is in order. Relying on intuitions in our philosophical theorizing is not uncontentious (for a detailed recent survey of their role, see Cappelen 2012). Relying on intuitions when accounting for our gender talk is even more questionable; some, including Haslanger, maintain that common intuitions about gender terminology are utterly unhelpful. Ordinary language users' intuitions about what *woman* means or amounts to vary, being unclear and inconsistent. In fact, Haslanger's ameliorative analysis of *woman* is motivated by the desire to avoid an appeal to ordinary speakers' idiosyncratic everyday intuitions about gender. Saul also holds that ordinary speakers' uses of gender terminology are muddled, and so their intuitions are a poor source of information about the content of gender concepts. Thus, "When people are deeply confused about a subject matter, it is not a good idea to look to them as sources of information" (Saul 2006, 132). I agree that ordinary language users are poor and unhelpful sources of information about the *content* of the concept *woman* (or, about its intension). Nevertheless, they find it easy to apply gender terms, and there is a high degree of uniformity in everyday gender ascriptions. Ordinary speakers' intuitions about the deployment of 'woman', I propose next, can be more useful than Saul and Haslanger allow. Actually, it seems to me that what underlies our disagreement is that we implicitly understand the nature of intuitions differently. Two accounts of intuitions, the doxastic and the perceptualist, help us to diagnose how my account differs from Haslanger's and Saul's. If we understand intuitions in Saul's and Haslanger's sense, I agree that we should not find them particularly helpful. My claim is not that my implicit understanding of intuitions is the correct one, and for my purposes not much hangs on settling what intuitions "really" are like. Rather, my thought is the following: the account of intuitions that I favor—the perceptualist one—allows us to explain and make sense of the common phenomenon, where ordinary speakers find it easy to apply the term 'woman' but struggle to account for its applicability conditions (for instance, to state some essential conditions for being a woman).

The doxastic view of intuitions states that intuitions are (or are acquisitions of) doxastic attitudes and dispositions: most simply put, intuitions are judgments or inclinations to form judgments. By contrast, the perceptualist view holds that intuitions are predoxastic experiences that "represent abstract matters as being a certain way" (Chudnoff 2011, 626). Roughly, intuitions are more like immediate "gut feelings." More specifically, on the perceptualist view

> in having an intuition, it seems to you that abstract matters are a certain way. But it is only if you take your intuition at face value that you judge or even form an inclination to judge that abstract matters are the way they seem to you to be. (2011, 626)

A key to this proposal is that there is a predoxastic intuition experience, which plays "the role of presumptive justification for our beliefs about abstract matters" (2011, 626). Given this presumptive justification, we then go on to make judgments about some abstract matters, or form an inclination to make such judgments. On Chudnoff's view, this intuition experience may be either sui generis ("not identical to and not analyzable in terms of thoughts, imaginings, etc."), or it can be colocated with thoughts, imaginings, and the like in our streams of consciousness (2011, 645). In the latter case, our intuition experience may be constituted by our thoughts, imaginings, and such like. In this case, intuitions are not some free-floating, mysterious experiences alongside our thoughts, imaginings, and so on—intuitions are rather colocated with other mental entities (2011, 650).

This distinction diagnoses the dispute between myself, on the one hand, and Haslanger and Saul, on the other. They seem implicitly to have a doxastic view of intuitions, while my proposal that appeals to extensional intuitions is more akin to a perceptualist view. So, roughly on the former: when I have an intuition that Jill is a woman, I judge or have the inclination to judge *that* Jill is a woman. One suggested way to make sense of such judgments is in terms of conceptual competence (Ludwig 2010). So on this formulation my judgment that Jill is a woman would be an expression of my competence to employ the concept *woman*. Such competence is likely to be further based on some supposed extralinguistic beliefs and attitudes about what it takes for someone to be a woman. On Haslanger's formulation, our judgment that Jill is a woman can be made on the basis of femaleness (our manifest *woman* concept) or based on some mixture of anatomical and social features (our operative *woman* concept). Since our everyday intuitions appear to direct us in two ways and prompt us to make two distinct judgments, this suggests that our intuitions about gender may not express conceptual competence. This fits with Haslanger's claim that our ordinary intuitions about womanhood are vague and idiosyncratic: were we conceptually competent, our intuitions would direct us to make only one kind of judgment (the one that expresses our competence). If we further interrogate ordinary speakers' doxastic intuitions (their judgments), we may find as Saul suggests that ordinary speakers are rather confused about what grounds their judgments. Both Haslanger's and Saul's remarks about everyday gender intuitions fit the view that our intuitions understood as judgments are confused, where conceptual *incompetence* underpins this confusion. This doxastic conception of intuitions elucidates why we should not look to ordinary speakers' linguistic intuitions when analyzing gender concepts.

Now, consider the perceptualist view. On this understanding, when I have an intuition that Jill is a woman, I have a predoxastic representation, which functions as a presumptive justification for my (possible) subsequent judgment about Jill's womanhood. Further, this intuition experience (the predoxastic representation) is constituted by other components in my stream of consciousness: by my thoughts, imaginings, and the like. My suggestion is that extensional intuitions tap into such predoxastic experiences. And so extensional intuitions guide our deployment of gender terms even in the absence of semantic intuitions about gender concepts' precise applicability conditions. Or, to put the point differently: the perceptualist view of intuitions helps to explain the nature and structure of extensional intuitions, which enables us to make sense of the common phenomenon that ordinary language users find it easy to apply gender terms, but they struggle to elucidate the grounds for their applications.

To explicate this further, it is worth clarifying what extensional intuitions are *not*. Again, recall Haslanger's distinction between manifest and operative concepts (cf. section 4.2). Manifest concepts are those that we take ourselves to be applying and that are arrived at by appealing to native speakers' intuitions about particular cases. Operative concepts are those arrived at by examining our terms' extensions. So a conceptual analysis of *bachelor* relies on common intuitions, which usually suggest that all and only unmarried males satisfy the concept (the manifest concept). People's unwillingness to apply the term 'bachelor' to unmarried males in long-term partnerships provides a different analysis and reveals our operative *bachelor* concept (the one we in fact employ). Both analyses appeal to some (for now unspecified kinds of) linguistic intuitions. One might be tempted to suppose that semantic intuitions inform us about the content of our manifest concepts, whereas extensional intuitions inform us about the content of our operative concepts. But this is not what I have in mind. For me, ordinary language users' intuitions about the contents of our manifest and operative concepts are *both* semantic intuitions. By contrast, our (perceptualist) extensional intuitions about 'woman' are simply about which individuals we think the term applies to. They do not, then, inform us about the content of *any* concept, manifest or operative. Extensional intuitions may, of course, be taken to provide the starting point for inquiring into the content of our operative *woman* concept. Again, this fits my characterization of extensional intuitions as perceptualist: our predoxastic intuitions may lead to doxastic attitudes like judgments, and we could go on to analyze those doxastic attitudes in detail. But, I submit, we *need not* take this further step. Extensional intuitions understood as predoxastic perceptualist intuitions give feminists what they need: a way to retain gender talk in a deflated manner.

I noted earlier that intuition experiences are constituted by components in our streams of consciousness. How does this fit gender talk? Ron Mallon has distinguished properties that are *indicative* of category membership from those that are *central*. A property is of the former kind if "having the property increases the likelihood that one is a member of a category" (Mallon 2004, 652–653). For instance, Mallon claims, wearing a dress is indicative of being a woman in the United States, but this property is neither necessary nor sufficient for womanhood. As I see it, common everyday experience suggests that language users deploy the term 'woman' on the basis of the kinds of traits deemed indicative of womanhood (cf. Stoljar 1995; Hale 1996). These include features feminists commonly link with gender: dress codes, roles, social position, hairstyles, makeup, particular behavioral patterns, and self-ascription. Ordinary speakers also seem to deploy 'woman' on the basis of anatomical sex features such as body type; 'woman' is not a purely gender term for them, but a mixture of both sex and gender. My view is that these features are conceivably part and parcel of the components in our streams of consciousness out of which the gendered intuition experiences are constituted. That is, these sorts of indicative features of womanhood undergird our extensional intuitions and are the grounds on which we ascribe gender (and I am sure there are others, too, that I have not mentioned).

The indicative features outlined constitute the very common grounds on which we deploy gender terms—namely, they are the building blocks of our extensional intuitions. Nevertheless, these intuitions should not be taken to inform us about some underlying *concept* that our language use supposedly expresses. My contention is that trying to figure out which concepts underlie our gender talk is more trouble than it is worth. The prospects of explicating gender concepts via traditional conceptual analysis are unpromising because language users take them to be about a variety of things (sex, femininity/masculinity, associated traits, self-ascription, a mixture of these). Social and cultural diversity, historical change, and vagueness seem to make it impossible to analyze *woman* so that some precise social conditions for satisfying it are uncovered. The prospects of an adequate revisionary analysis of *woman* also look unpromising since this tends to make gender terminology unfamiliar to ordinary speakers. Common gender terms become feminists' theoretical terms, which, I argued in the previous chapter, is politically unhelpful. Given the insurmountable difficulties that feminists have faced when aiming to define *woman*, we should simply not aim to do so. Hanging onto the view that, in order to pick out women's social kind, the applicability conditions for the concept *woman* must be elucidated generates more debate about the content of gender concepts and unnecessarily perpetuates worries about the social kind many take feminism to be organized around. Quite simply: focusing on ordinary language users' willingness to apply 'woman' is enough to pick out women's type, and this is sufficient to answer the representation problem (how to fix feminism's subject matter). In order to avoid getting bogged down by conceptual problems, this is what feminist philosophers should settle for.[1]

---

[1] It might appear that I am endorsing predicate nominalism about women, where the tokens of women's type have in common that they are all picked out by the term 'woman'. However, I wish to resist this view and (at least for now) keep the metaphysical and linguistic issues separate. This is because endorsing predicate nominalism would suggest that what makes individual women members of the same type is that they are all called "women." And this would commit me to the metaphysically weighty view that individuals are women *by virtue of* being picked out by 'woman'. But I do not

I am clearly focusing on the *use* of gender terms. With this in mind, it is worth stressing two ways in which my proposal differs from more usual descriptive projects that also focus on language use. For Haslanger, descriptive projects pick out a social kind into which our paradigm *x*'s fall, thereby disclosing some operative concept of *x* that our language use expresses (2005, 19). But, as already noted, I am not aiming to elucidate any concept supposedly undergirding our language use. Whether or not gender terms express any single concept and what that concept might be are questions I simply won't take up because I see no political gain in doing so. My project differs in its goal from the kind of descriptive analysis Haslanger discusses. Roughly, both projects start by looking at our everyday uses of gender terms (or, what I have termed "extensional intuitions"). But, unlike other descriptive analyses, my project goes no further: it does not take the step to examining what our extensional intuitions disclose about the content of the concept *woman*. Rather than trying to get at conceptual content via use, my proposal simply attends to the use of 'woman' without drawing (or aiming to draw) any conclusions about conceptual content. My view is that this suffices for fixing women's social kind.

Moreover, although some descriptive analyses start by identifying paradigms or exemplars of a kind and then examine whether our vocabulary tracks those kinds (cf. Haslanger 2005, 19), my analysis does not. I am not advocating that some exemplar or paradigm women should be singled out in order to see whether our uses of 'woman' track a kind into which these paradigms fall. My contention is, quite simply, that feminists need not rely on woman paradigms to mark off women's type: such an appeal is unnecessary because there is *not* much extensional confusion over 'woman'. If language users were often confused about the term's extension, perhaps a good case could be made for appealing to paradigms. For instance, students taking introductory logic courses are often confused about the applications of 'validity'. In order to dispel the confusion, it is customary to point out some paradigm valid arguments and show how they work. In this context a good case can be made for introducing paradigm valid arguments, as this helps students to pick out the right cases. But this is so only because students qua ordinary speakers are confused about proper ascriptions of validity. Ordinary language users, nevertheless, apply 'woman' with a high degree of uniformity. They are seldom confused about its extension, and subsequently an appeal to paradigm women is unnecessary.

This also responds to a closely related worry. One might challenge my proposal claiming that our extensional intuitions differ. Take 'marriage'. Ordinary language users' willingness to apply the term to same sex-unions differs: some people are willing to do so, whereas others are not. One might,

---

wish to commit myself for now to any such metaphysical view, and so my position should not be understood to support predicate nominalism.

then, claim that concentrating on intuitive uses of terms simply encounters the same problems that intuitions about the content of concepts did since deployment of terms is also often idiosyncratic. So, just as language users' semantic intuitions about the content of *woman* differ, so do our extensional intuitions about our willingness to apply 'woman'. And this (the objection goes) undermines my suggestion. Now, I agree that our semantic intuitions differ and that ordinary speakers have different views about what *woman* means (they employ various different conceptions of the concept, or their intuitions express a variety of doxastic attitudes). But again, I submit, extensional intuitions about 'woman' are not that idiosyncratic: to a high degree of uniformity, different speakers pick out the same group of individuals with 'woman', and they are usually *not* confused about the term's extension. Actually, even some feminist philosophers considered earlier acknowledge this: they hold that ordinary speakers are deeply confused about their grounds for calling someone 'woman', even though different speakers pick out basically the same group of individuals with the term (Haslanger 2003b, 318; Zack 2005, 27). As Zack put it, feminists do not worry about the denotation of *woman*; they worry about its connotation (2005, 27). Marilyn Frye's remarks about oppression are also illustrative (I will discuss her view in more detail in chapter 7). She holds that a system of gender oppression works to "reduce, immobilize and mold people who belong to a certain group, and effect their subordination to another group" (1983, 33). However, Frye continues:

> Such a system could not exist were not the groups, categories of persons, well defined. Logically, it presupposes that there are two distinct categories. Practically, they must be not only distinct but relatively easily identifiable; the barriers and forces [of oppression] could not . . . be applied if there were often much doubt as to which individuals were to be contained and reduced, which were to be dominate. (1983, 33)

So the very existence of gendered injustices suggests that ordinary speakers are usually not that confused about the denotation of *woman*. Thus, extensional intuitions do not seem to be that idiosyncratic after all.[2]

Now, it may be that extensional intuitions are far less idiosyncratic than Haslanger holds. But are they at all helpful? My proposal is that they are:

---

[2] One might further argue in response that it would be more beneficial to try to curb ordinary language users' willingness to use gender terms because they are loaded with undesirable connotations. For instance, if a frustrated football coach tells their male team that the team members are a bunch of women, this is meant as an insult and reflects people's attitudes about women's supposed inferior physical abilities. I agree that part of feminism is to try to change language use of this kind. However, when I claim that feminists should concentrate on language users' willingness to apply the term 'woman', I do not have this kind of use in mind. I have in mind everyday willingness to ascribe genders: willingness to say whether someone is a woman. The football coach, however, is not applying 'woman' in this way.

such intuitions deliver a very thin conception of womanhood, but one that can fix women's social kind. This raises an issue about those instances where language users are genuinely confused about applying gender terms. That is, how does my proposal deal with trans* people, who do not conform to prevalent gender expectations "by presenting and living genders that were not assigned to them at birth or by presenting and living genders in ways that may not be readily intelligible in terms of more traditional conceptions of gender" (Bettcher 2009)? Ordinary extensional intuitions may guide language use in a way that either 'woman' or 'man', or both, or neither applies to (say) trans* women. In fact, some confusion in language use may be generated by our extensional intuitions: we may (for instance) have conflicting predoxastic intuitions, so that we have different sets of presumptive justifications for our beliefs. This being the case, one might argue that women's social kind remains undetermined because there are unclear cases. And it might seem that I have not offered a way the settle the issue that I am aiming to settle: my appeal to extensional intuitions (the argument goes) is insufficient. More worryingly, it might be that extensional intuitions guide language use in harmful ways: they may guide language use in a way that speakers denote trans* women with the term 'man'. Focusing on extensional intuitions might then give us highly problematic results in excluding some trans* women from women's social kind. The exclusion of trans* women is a serious issue and merited the rejection of Bach's position discussed earlier. Might my proposal then have similar results? I think not. Let me elaborate on this.

Trans* people and intersexes helpfully demonstrate that the precise boundaries of gendered social kinds are not fixed and rigid. So in appealing to extension intuitions, which I do take to be highly uniform, I am not proposing to cement the kinds' boundaries. Furthermore, disagreements generated by extensional intuitions that involve trans* people and intersexes are not primarily to be settled by semantics—they are a political issue. So, in some contexts, our gender ascriptions and the materials out of which intuition experiences are constituted in our streams of consciousness will be indecisive. But where to subsequently draw the lines cannot be answered with philosophy of language. This is a political, not a semantic, question. As I see it, there is no right answer to the question of whether trans* women are "in" or "out" of women's social kind that we can discover via *conceptual analysis* and philosophy-of-language tools. This does not mean that there are no right answers: theory of gender that point-blank excludes trans* women from women's social kind is simply unacceptable. But just as I find it politically problematic to propose such an exclusionary theory, I find it problematic to propose a view that unquestionably includes trans* women. After all, not all trans* women want to be part of women's social kind because this implicitly denotes cis women's kind. Some want to be identified specifically as trans* women rather than women. Arguing for a position that uses philosophy-of-language tools that prescribe how to deal with trans* persons in every single situation, and contrary to some trans* people's explicit wishes, would be equally problematic and seriously misguided. Political concerns are critical when deciding how to proceed.[3]

Thinking about feminist political practice further elucidates what I mean. Feminist politics and practice incorporate different feminisms that have specific goals and aims. Different campaigns focus on different aspects of women's lives and on particular groups of women. In every feminist context, the broad general aim is the same: to undercut sex- and/or gender-based injustices. In some contexts, cis women are subject to such injustices; in others, the subjects are trans* women and intersexes (and sometimes they are even cis men). But *which* people are at issue, and *how* to proceed in order to achieve feminist aims, diverge. Those working to improve women's visibility in certain academic professions will focus on the women academics in their field; those feminists working to improve postnatal care for new mothers will focus on that particular group of women, explicitly excluding childless women. Feminists who fight against sexist-cum-homophobic violence that queer women face focus on queer women that face such violence. Focusing on particular groups of women is not problematic per se. But focusing on particular issues, and excluding those whom others judge not to be affected by them, becomes problematic when this exclusion is discriminatory and when individuals who are affected by some issues are ignored or even silenced by more dominant others. Unfortunately, in the history of feminist movements cis feminists have far too often and far too quickly judged trans* women's concerns to be outside of feminism's purview on the basis that they are not "really" women. For instance, if trans* women are excluded from the scope of campaigns aiming to improve women's visibility in some professions contrary to the concerns and wishes of trans* women in those professions, this would be discriminatory. But our effective response to such discrimination does not lie with improved semantics, it lies with improved politics. And this demonstrates that fixing women's social kind membership is not a purely semantic issue—it is also about politics, power, and ideology, which is why there is only so much that philosophy of language can do for us.

The upshot is this: cis feminists must be extremely careful about their judgments. They must engage in a dialogue with trans* people in order to

---

[3] This claim draws on cultural differences between Anglo-American and German contexts. In Germany, the expression "Frau" is not taken to be inclusive because it is taken to connote just cis women. Instead, the expression "Frau*" is used to denote a class inclusive of cis and trans* women. Furthermore, many trans* people find it oppressive and insulting to be designated by others as simply women or men because this buys into a heteronormative and heterosexist gender binary. So there are many pertinent questions about inclusion and exclusion; and different trans* communities have different views on this. Context-specific trans* activism shows that such questions are not to be settled by doing more philosophy of language.

negotiate together where the boundaries of women's social kinds in particular circumstances fall. This is an issue that requires something other than philosophical reflection; it cannot be settled without consulting those whose daily lives will be (perhaps significantly) affected. For instance, when feminist campaigns are about (say) improved treatments for ovarian cancer, it may be entirely appropriate to exclude those who have no ovaries. Nevertheless, such campaigns must include not only cis women, but also some trans* men and some intersexes. The same goes for campaigns to improve breast cancer screening: cis men are, statistically speaking, highly unlikely to develop breast cancer, cis women more so. But it would be inappropriate to focus just on cis women—after all, some trans* men are also in higher-risk categories and so should be included. Then again, childless cis women do not directly benefit from good postnatal care, and their exclusion from the group of women who matter for this issue does not strike me as problematic. So in appealing to extensional intuitions I am not proposing to settle the boundaries of women's social kind once and for all. But this does not render my proposal unhelpful. Rather, my view helps further to illustrate that in fixing social kind boundaries it is also politics, and not just semantics, that matters. (For a similar view, and how this tells us important methodological lessons when doing philosophy of language, see Saul 2012a.)

With the above in mind, my proposal might nonetheless be further challenged: one might claim that it is incomplete precisely *because* I do not consider what our language use tells us about what it is to be a woman. Presumably discerning the applicability conditions of *woman* (articulating womanhood in some thick-ish sense) affords important political benefits. It perhaps elucidates the oppressive social conditions constitutive of womanhood and thereby enables us to meet some important feminist political demands. Or the applicability conditions tell us something that will be crucial for our social explanations of gender oppression, which in turn helps us fight gender injustice. We could name this the "gender controversy strikes back" response. After all, debates over gender concepts and kinds are perpetuated precisely from such an outlook. I contend, by contrast, that nothing hangs politically on providing a substantive account of gender that elucidates the applicability conditions of *woman*. The thin conceptualization advanced here can do the required feminist work: for instance, it delivers terminology that can be used in feminist social theory to identify and explain persistent social inequalities. To illustrate, compare my proposal with Haslanger's. One might claim that Haslanger's gender terminology is better suited for the task of explaining and identifying inequalities: just by calling someone a woman we have identified the person as occupying a socially subordinate position and noted that her subordination is tied to (actual or imagined) bodily features, which position her as someone societies in general tend not to privilege. Unlike Haslanger's proposal, my focus on extensional intuitions and the uses of 'woman' tells us nothing about the social situations and circumstances of those designated as women. Still, my proposal can equally well be used to single out and to explain persistent social inequalities. For Haslanger,

> The explanation of persistent inequalities between females and males would begin from the fact that females tend overwhelmingly to be women, and that women are systematically subordinated to men. The next step would be to analyse this systematic subordination and how it is perpetuated. (Saul 2006, 136)

If we rewrite this strategy with my proposal, no crucial explanatory force is lost:

> The explanation of persistent inequalities between females and males would begin from the fact that females tend overwhelmingly to be designated as women, and that those individuals designated as women are systematically subordinated to those designated as men. The next step would be to analyze this systematic subordination and how it is perpetuated.

Nothing in my proposal prevents feminists from identifying and explaining persistent inequalities, since this is a separate task. In the second part of this book, I will provide feminist social theoretical tools with which we can advance such an examination. So Alcoff is right to point out that we cannot undertake practical and explanatory tasks without using certain terms: she rightly points out that we need the term 'woman' to demand legal abortions and to close the gender pay gap (cf. section 4.3). But for these tasks (and for explanations of persistent social inequalities) we need not rely on a thick conception or on any semantic intuitions about the content of the concept *woman*. Feminists can rely on our uses of 'woman' that trade on thin extensional intuitions combined with a feminist social theory (to be articulated in Part II). Extensional intuitions can mark off women's social kind, and we need not consult our semantic intuitions to do so. Despite a high degree of uniformity, extensional intuitions do not deliver rigid kind boundaries since there are times when "our" intuitions come apart. But, as noted, in these cases the debate is not to be had on the level of semantics, but on the level of politics. Subsequently, if one takes feminism to be organized around women, and if extensional intuitions provide a way to pick out this kind, not being able to articulate a solution to the semantic puzzle by explicating the applicability conditions for *woman* does not present a serious political concern. Feminist work can advance with a thin conception of *woman*, although (as I will spell out in the chapters to come) this is not all that feminist philosophical work requires. Relying on extensional intuitions is merely part of the story; in the following section, I will explicate another part that pertains to ontological issues.

Now, I should note that for me feminism is not just about women, and I reject the view that feminism should be exclusively organized around women's social kind. Feminism should have a broader scope, and this is something that my humanist feminism aims to supply. My argument in this section has been theory internal: even if we think that feminism orients itself around women's social kind, the semantic puzzle is not that pressing. We can pick the kind out and talk about women in my deflated sense, which is needed to advance feminist social theories. But we need not respond to the semantic puzzle by explicating *woman*'s applicability conditions. And there is no need for a thick conception of *woman* to support feminist normative demands (such as elucidating how and why patriarchy damages women—more on this in subsequent chapters). This should aid in forging alliances with those who are engaged in more empirical projects. After all, given that effective feminism requires practical responses and cannot be done simply via conceptual analysis of any kind, answering the question of *how* to achieve gender justice must be an interdisciplinary and cooperative endeavor. Understanding the term 'woman' in my proposed manner facilitates this by removing conceptual barriers to progress and by putting forward a semantically nonweighty account that (I expect) should have broader appeal.

5.2. Deflating the Ontological Puzzle

As I see it, the sex/gender distinction is part of the unhelpful theoretical outlook undergirding feminist theorizing about gender, which takes a thick social conception of *woman* normatively to support emancipatory feminist claims. This is because the distinction posits womanhood as a substantive social position crucially connected to gendered oppression. Since I reject the need for a thick conception of *woman*, I will argue next that we should give up the underlying sex/gender distinction too. I go on to propose a way to rethink the phenomena usually discussed under the rubric of the sex/gender distinction by developing an alternative: the trait/norm covariance model. My model redraws the boundaries of the sets of gender and sex traits and divides these traits into new sets: *descriptive traits* (traits of which there are "facts of the matter") and *evaluative norms* (normative reactions to descriptive traits). For instance, the paradigm gender trait of wearing makeup and the paradigm sex trait of having ovaries will *both* count as descriptive traits for me (one either has ovaries/regularly wears makeup or does not). But my proposal also acknowledges the influence of social normativity: certain evaluations and reactions (being perceived to act, be, or appear "feminine") covary with particular descriptive traits, which accounts for why some traits are supposedly appropriate for women and others not. This proposal (I submit) has three distinct benefits: it provides a better way to conceptualize the phenomena usually discussed under the auspices of the sex/gender distinction; it deflates the on-tological puzzle by thinking anew the underlying ontology; and it provides a model that (along with the deflated semantics argued for above) will be an aid to feminist social theory building. A quick clarification is in order: I am not intending to spell out yet another *theory of gender*. Rather, I am offering some-thing that is more radically an alternative to the distinction: a framework that goes beyond sex and gender. In short, my view is that although the sex/gender distinction did some helpful work to begin with, it has outlived its helpful-ness. This is because it founds and perpetuates the gender controversy that has generated a theoretical impasse (in the form of the semantic and ontological puzzles), which hinders progress in feminist political and social philosophy. So when thinking about contemporary social injustices that those designated as women face, I submit, more theorizing about the content of gender concepts and about women's social kind membership along existing lines will not do. My alternative aims to move feminist thinking forward by providing a radi-cally different framework. Admittedly, this task is somewhat hindered by the lack of available linguistic resources, and it is at times difficult to articulate my proposal without using the more usual language of gender and sex. Still, I wish to stress that my goal is not to engage in more theorizing about gender (as standardly conceived) but to offer a framework with which we can discuss the relevant social and cultural phenomena anew. After all, I am ultimately aiming to advance a new paradigm of humanist feminism that requires us to go beyond current understandings of gender.

The ontological puzzle consists in certain problems that arise out of preva-lent presuppositions about the nature of gender. Specifically, I have in mind problematic ontological commitments arising from *conventionalist* and *ab-olitionist* implications that are underpinned by the sex/gender distinction.[4] First, the conventionalist implication holds that women and men exist mind *dependently*, or because of productive human activities. Paradigmatically, some social conditions must be met in order for one to count as a woman or a man because (as the slogan goes) gender is socially constructed. This implies that the existence of gendered individuals ontologically depends on some social institutions, practices, conventions, social agents, and their acceptance of such institutions, practices, and conventions. Women and men could not

---

    [4] In chapter 2, I considered influential problems with the sex/gender distinction. These prob-lems generated the semantic and ontological puzzles that a number of contemporary feminist phi-losophers have responded to. However, since these responses did not radically rethink the nature of gender, they still explicitly or implicitly rely on a problematic ontological picture not unlike that of the original sex/gender distinction. Thus, the worries discussed next are present both in the older feminist positions (cf. chapter 2) as well as in the newer ones (cf. chapters 3 and 4). I take these wor-ries to show that the distinction does no helpful theoretical or political work. Further, we can see that the sex/gender distinction is problematic in ways that the earlier critiques did not bring up (cf. chapter 2). Therefore, we need to rethink the distinction in more radical, rather than reformist, ways.

exist unless the relevant institutions, practices, conventions, and conscious agents upholding them existed. Gendered individuals are ontologically akin to wives, landlords, and prime ministers. Thus, it should be possible to eradicate the gender part of social agents while leaving them otherwise intact: we simply alter those social conditions on which gender depends so that individuals no longer *count as* women and men. The same is true of US senators: they depend for their existence on certain institutionalized political conventions, so that were a bloodless revolution to alter those conventions by abolishing the US Senate, US senators would literally vanish overnight. Just as one need not execute US senators in order to eradicate them, eradicating women and men does not putatively require physically altering those individuals we think of as women and men—we simply alter the salient social conditions, so that no one counts as gendered anymore.[5] Second, the abolitionist implication holds that gender depends ontologically on *oppressive* social conditions. As a result, changing our social environments would not only unwittingly eradicate women and men; doing away with gender should be feminism's political goal. The different theories of gender previously considered are all in some way (explicitly or implicitly) committed to these implications. For instance, Haslanger (chapter 4), Rubin, and MacKinnon (chapter 2) are committed to both. Then again, Stoljar, Young, Frye (chapter 3), Zack, and Alcoff (chapter 4) are (at least) conventionalists about gender.[6] Since both of these implications are explicitly present in Haslanger's position, I will focus on it to illustrate why they are problematic.

For Haslanger, gender is constitutively constructed: in defining it we must make reference to social factors (1995, 98), and specifically we must make reference to hierarchical social positions (2000, 37–43). The existence of women and men is mind dependent in the sense of depending on oppressive human social practices and conventions. What it is to be a woman or a man (for Haslanger) is to occupy a sex-marked subordinate or privileged position

---

[5] A quick clarification is in order. We can think of ontological dependence as a kind of ontological "non-self-sufficiency" (Correia 2008, 1013). In a trivial sense, many aspects of reality are ontologically non-self-sufficient. For instance, if all human organisms suddenly zapped out of existence, that would obviously abolish wives and US senators *because* only human organisms can occupy these social roles. It would also abolish all social institutions, since human social agents are needed to uphold those institutions. Further, had there never been any human agents, artifacts would not have existed because all manufactured goods depend in this causal sense on the existence of their (human) makers. But I am not interested in trivial or causal non-self-sufficiency here. The existence of paper causally depends on human agency. Still, that some pieces of paper count as money depends on us in a different non-self-sufficient sense. If social agents suddenly zapped out of existence, money would cease to exist, although those pieces of paper that counted as money would survive. This social fact is anything but a trivial form of non-self-sufficiency, and it is the kind of dependence that I am interested in here.

[6] Although all abolitionist views are conventional, not all conventional ones are abolitionist. That is, although one may hold that the existence of women and men ontologically depends on some social conventions, one need not hold that these conventions are oppressive. Further, although all

(2003a, 6–7). This being the case, Haslanger takes gender justice to eradicate gender by abolishing those social structures that produce and maintain sex-marked subordination and privilege. Women and men could not exist if sexist oppression did not exist. Feminism's goal, then, should be to dismantle those social structures underlying oppression. The implications of Haslanger's position are not unproblematic, though. Ordinarily, women are thought to be human females, men human males. As a result, their *existence* is not thought to depend on productive human social conventions, practices, and institutions in such a way that we could abolish women and men simply by altering our social landscapes. Conventionalism, then, has highly *unintuitive* ontological commitments. Further, many ordinary social agents find the abolitionist implication that "after the revolution" women and men will no longer exist objectionable. Anecdotally, students often tell me that they do not see being a woman or a man as problematic per se; rather, the problem is how we are viewed and treated as representatives of currently prevalent gender kinds. The idea that feminists should aim to do away with women and men, then, harbors *undesirable* ontological commitments.

These unintuitive and undesirable commitments seem to result from a clash between the paradigmatic feminist and everyday conceptions of womanhood. Ordinarily, 'woman' is not purely a gender term, but rather a mixture of sex and gender. For feminists, it is standardly a gender term to be distinguished from sex. Now, we can avoid this clash by modifying the everyday conception so that it is in line with the conventionalist and abolitionist views. Or feminists can endeavor to employ 'woman' as ordinarily as possible, thereby preventing it from turning into a feminist technical term. In my earlier discussion of Haslanger (cf. chapter 4), I already provided some reasons against the former option. Seeking to radically modify everyday usage of 'woman' would be hugely demanding, and at times prima facie unwarranted; therefore, the latter option seems more attractive to me. Two important points are worth flagging, though. First, the significant point for my purposes is that 'woman' is a mixed term for ordinary speakers. Taking this insight seriously (I submit) is beneficial in that we can do away with the unhelpful division

---

conventional accounts of gender are (in some sense) constructivist, not all social constructivist accounts have the conventional implications mentioned. This is because there are different ways to understand social construction and the distinction between mind-dependent and mind-independent features of reality (for more on different conceptions of social construction, see Haslanger 1995). Note, however, that the expression "mind dependent" should not be understood to commit one to any kind of idealism about women or to the claim that our immaterial thoughts literally create material entities. It is simply meant as shorthand for dependence relations that involve human agents and broader social conditions, where human agency and requisite social relations are crucial for the dependent entities' existence. This does not yet tell us anything about the nature of those dependencies, and there are different ways for things to be mind dependent. Gender being constitutively constructed is one way to be so. I will say more about the notion of *mind dependence* shortly.

between sex and gender.[7] It is not so much the particular ways in which ordinary speakers think about women and men that matters, but rather the underlying structure. The division into social gender and biological sex is unfamiliar to ordinary social agents, and trying to convince them to appropriate this distinction is not worth the effort. Second, we should not, of course, simply take ordinary language usage at face value. For instance, some ordinary speakers endorse gender myths (like ovaries interfering with women's brains), and taking our cue from ordinary language considerations does not mean we *endorse* all such considerations. Bear in mind further that feminists and trans* and intersexed people are also ordinary speakers. So although I think that ordinary language use matters, this does not mean that only the language use of some "average individual" (who is probably a white, middle-class, heterosexual, cis man) matters. There are many different groups of ordinary speakers, and sometimes we have good political and practical reasons to privilege the language use of some groups over others. Take just a banal case: if we wish to know about the ordinary usage of snow-related terminology, we should not look at ordinary language use of speakers who have no conception of snow. Rather, it would seem more appropriate to consult Finns, Greenlanders, Alaskans, and other northern peoples. This echoes Talia Mae Bettcher's (2013) view that in order to analyze gender concepts, we should not take the dominant cis conceptions as our starting point, but rather privilege resistant trans* conceptions. Subsequently, taking ordinary language use seriously does not entail that all ordinary use should be taken *equally* seriously. At times, there are good pragmatic grounds to privilege some use over others.

The next two sections will outline in more detail why the conventionalist and abolitionist implications harbor problematic ontological commitments. I will then spell out my alternative ontological model and show how it avoids the problems outlined.

5.2.1. CONVENTIONALISM IS UNINTUITIVE

Start by considering in more detail what is problematic about the conventionalist implication. That gender depends on something social and extrinsic means that being a woman or a man is prima facie ontologically on a par with being a wife, a landlord, or a scapegoat (cf. Haslanger 2002; Mikkola 2006). This implies that just as one can cease to be a wife or a landlord by changing one's extrinsic social environment (by getting a divorce, selling off

---

[7] I am not alone in rethinking the sex/gender distinction: for example, Stoljar and Alcoff also offer alternatives to it. Nonetheless, they still retain a commitment to the distinction in some form. My view is that we should give such commitments entirely up, and this makes my proposal more radical than reformist.

one's property), one should be able to cease to be a woman by changing those extrinsic social relations constitutive of gender. On closer scrutiny, though, drawing the above comparisons is misleading: being a woman turns out *not* to be ontologically on a par with social positions like being a landlord. To tease this out, I will advance linguistic and metaphysical arguments. Take the linguistic one first and consider the following claims:

(1) For a week last summer, James was a woman.
(2) For a week last summer, James was a landlord.
(3) After seeing John's body, I realized that John is a woman.
(4) After seeing John's body, I realized that John is a landlord.

Statements (1) and (2) take 'woman' and 'landlord' to express social notions (e.g., the first takes womanhood to be about easily perceptible gender markers, like clothing and appearance). By contrast, (3) and (4) are not making claims about social factors. Nevertheless, claims (1) and (3) make sense to us, although in (1) 'woman' is used as a social gender term, and in (3) it is used as a biological sex term. But when we substitute 'woman' for 'landlord' in (4) the statement no longer makes sense to us. 'Woman' is not on a par with 'landlord': it is not a purely social term since it can quite sensibly be used to denote both sex and gender.[8] We can advance a metaphysical argument to demonstrate the above further. Think about ontological dependence relations in terms of explanations (cf. Correia 2008). The conceptual explanations regarding these examples go as follows:

(5) *S* is a landlord in virtue of owning a property leased.
(6) *S* is a woman in virtue of occupying a sex-marked subordinate
     social position.

Now, given that womanhood and landlordyness are meant to be socially constructed, these conceptual explanations prima facie should entail particular metaphysical explanations.

(7) Landlords exist in virtue of there being social agents who lease
     their properties owned, which is made possible by the institution of
     private property.
(8) Women exist in virtue of patriarchy positioning some individuals
     as socially subordinate on sex-marked grounds.

I take it that we would not have trouble accepting that (5) entails (7). But we are less willing to accept that (6) entails (8). Again, the sticking point seems to be that the conceptual and ontological commitments of ordinary speakers

---

[8] I am not alone in thinking so. For instance, Stoljar (1995) and Hale (1996) also hold that 'woman' picks out individuals by virtue of a mixture of sex and gender traits. For Saul (2012a) this suggests that 'woman' may be a contextually shifty term.

differ from standard feminist ones, where the former contain a mixture of (traditionally speaking) sex and gender traits. The property of *being a woman* seems to be disanalogous to that of *being a landlord*. And this renders the conventionalist implication unintuitive: it is not obviously true that women's and men's existence is mind dependent in the sense that the existence of landlords is. It seems that one cannot cease to be a woman (or a man) just by altering one's social relations because womanhood involves not just social relations.

The above arguments appear to deduce ontological states of affairs from linguistic and conceptual considerations. And (one might claim) this is unwarranted: just because we can employ 'unicorns' in a sensible manner does not ontologically commit us to their existence. So the worry is that although we can sensibly employ 'woman' as both a sex and a gender term, this does not yet tell us anything about the underlying ontology. In many ways I agree that our language use does not fix what exists. But here the *kind* of ontology we take ourselves to be elucidating makes a difference. Think back to Bach's discussion of gender in the previous chapter (cf. section 4.4.). He aimed to show that women's kind is real in the sense of being found in nature's joints. This kind, for Bach, was nonconventional in the sense of being nonconceptual. It is not entirely clear what this means, but I take it to mean the following: women's kind is not a strong pragmatic construction, where social factors entirely determine the use of our conceptual and classificatory schemes, and these schemes fail to represent accurately any "facts of the matter." Such pragmatic construction would make women's kind nonreal and wholly conventional. If we presuppose Bach's realist ontology, appealing to language use would be inappropriate, and we should not take it as evidence of the underlying ontology of women. After all, one of the main features of realist views like Bach's is that some kinds exist and have their natures independently of human conceptual schemes and representations. And genders are (perhaps surprisingly) such kinds. However, as I argued earlier, Bach's ontology does not exhaust the available options. That is, the only options available to us are not gendered kinds being either fictitious, pragmatic constructions or carved in nature's joints. Rather, I suggested that we can understand women's kind (as many contemporary feminist philosophers do) as being conventional *and* real. This renders women's kind less objective than on Bach's ontology, but it does not make it nonobjective and fictional. Being conventional, women's kind does (at least partly) ontologically depend on our conceptual schemes and classificatory practices. When thinking about conventional kinds like women or landlords, we should not subsequently expect a sharp and thoroughgoing distinction between conceptual representations and the elucidated ontology. Rather, given that our language use is part of what constructs the ontology, I submit, it can helpfully tell us something about that ontology. And one informative insight that our language use tells us (I suggested above) is that being a woman is not conventional in *the same way* as being a landlord is.

A defender of conventionalism might hold that claim (3) does not really make sense either, but we are fooled into believing that it does precisely because sex and gender are falsely tied together. If we thought about womanhood in the right way, we would see that (3) is also senseless. And this would debunk *woman*: it would show that it is a social notion, dispel my worries about unintuitive ontological commitments, and enable us to eradicate women just by altering some social relations. I have no knockdown argument against this response: after all, if we can be deeply confused about the contents of our thoughts (as Haslanger claims), it becomes impossible to prove that *woman* really is a social notion or that it really is a mixed one. But I think that a defender of conventionalism hence has to do more: since we can be deeply confused about the contents of our own thoughts, why should we accept the conventionalist position? In order to justify conventionalism, one might wish to know: precisely what kind of social change would abolish women and men? Which beliefs, social conventions, institutions, linguistic practices, and relations would have to be altered and dismantled in order to achieve this? In order to stop conventionalism from descending into dogmatism, these questions must be systematically addressed. In fact, doing so has largely been the stuff of feminist philosophy on gender over the past couple of decades. But as the previous chapters testify a variety of answers have been proposed, and the nature of gender is a point of contention.

Admittedly, the inability to provide satisfying answers may simply be down to gender being such an incredibly complex phenomenon that discerning the kind of social change that would eradicate it is extremely difficult. We may simply be ignorant of the kind of change needed. But it may also be that feminists cannot agree on what social changes would do away with women and men because doing so just by altering one's social environment is not possible. Bluntly put: perhaps it is just plain wrong to think that women and men's *existence* ontologically depends on social factors. I am not concluding that it is, although I feel the pull of this view. My point is strategic: the issue of which social conditions ground the existence of women and men is so intractable as to be unhelpful. If gender really is so complex that feminists cannot agree on the social conditions that underpin it, the most useful move is to give up the quest. Pragmatically, I think, feminists should not try to uncover which social factors are responsible for the existence of women and men. Instead, we should settle for the much less contentious view that human action and social normativity significantly *shape* the way we are—they shape our social identities. No feminist (to the best of my knowledge) denies this claim. My concerns are not decisive and do not rule out conventionalism about gender. But, as I see it, the less contentious view I have floated here is the one that feminists ought to endorse precisely because of its less weighty ontological commitments.

I am not calling for a lighter ontology on the more usual grounds of explanatory simplicity and parsimony. I do not much care about parsimony or simplicity. Reality is complex and messy; and for our philosophical theories to say something plausible (even true) about that reality, we should at times favor complexity of explanations and the proliferation of ontological categories. But relative to the above conventionalist implication, I am urging feminist philosophers to accept "ontology light" on practical, political grounds. This further demonstrates an important aspect of my metaphilosophical commitments, which I already introduced in chapter 1: sometimes the contextual (political, practical) values of a theoretical practice should trump constitutive values (cf. Longino 1990). Sometimes political and ethical considerations provide good reasons for accepting or rejecting certain ontological positions with respect to gender. Thus, I am urging the acceptance of a lighter ontology that is committed to the view that *how* women and men exist crucially depends on social factors. And we should reject the more demanding view *that* their existence depends on social factors alone.

5.2.2. THE ABOLITIONIST IMPLICATION IS UNDESIRABLE

On views like Haslanger's, gender is a product of oppressive social circumstances and thus something feminists should seek to abolish. But this may not be conducive to feminist interests since it appears to harbor undesirable ontological commitments. To tease this out, compare the abolitionist strategy to a re-evaluative one. They both have the same starting point: feminism is about ending sex- and/or gender-based injustices. But feminist ways of achieving this goal differ. Abolitionist accounts take womanhood to be *by definition* tied to oppression so that it is not possible to be a woman and not be (in some sense) oppressed. Re-evaluative accounts do not take being a woman per se to be oppressive. Instead, they recognize that our social circumstances create environments where women are viewed and treated in ways that disadvantage them—perhaps by associating with women some traits and using this association to ground unjust social arrangements. It is possible to be a woman and yet not be oppressed, provided that we have successfully altered how women are viewed and treated. So, on the former view, gender justice would dismantle unjust social hierarchies, thus doing away with women and men; on the latter, gender justice would dismantle such hierarchies while retaining women and men without (say) the earlier oppressive association in place. Now, our choice of strategy comes down to a pragmatic political choice, and there is no a priori criterion to favor one over the other. But if ordinary social agents think that eradicating gender is undesirable, it may be strategically wrongheaded to endorse an abolitionist view. Some anecdotal evidence supports this: students tell me time and again that the abolitionist strategy aims to eradicate something that seemingly need not be eradicated. As they see it, "the feminist revolution" need not do away with gender, and *being* a woman or a man is not primarily the problem—the real problem is how people are viewed and treated.

One might immediately question whether the distinction between being *F* and how one is treated qua *F* is as clear-cut as this. After all, being viewed and treated in some way can *make* one that way. Consider MacKinnon's view of the construction of reality. For her, reality is always constructed from the dominant perspective, and since males are the dominant social group, it is constructed from *their* perspective. The mechanism of construction is sexual objectification: male power has the ability to create "the world in its own image, the image of its desires" through women's objectification (MacKinnon 1989, 118). The idea is something like the following. Pornography falsely portrays women as being sexually submissive, and this conditions male desire to find dominance and submission "sexy." As a result, men desire women to be submissive, and since this is the perspective of the dominant group, they have the power to project and enforce their desires (make their desires "real"). The male perspective then takes women *in fact* to be submissive: sexual submissiveness is thought to be an independently existing fact about women's "nature." And treating women accordingly makes it the case that women become submissive in patriarchal societies.[9] Against this backdrop, one might claim, it is not enough merely to focus on how people are viewed and treated; we must also focus on the projected consequences of such treatment. If "what it is to be a woman" turns out to be deeply problematic because of projected sexual objectification, it might be appropriate to aim to abolish not just the insidious ways of treating people, but the results of such treatments too. In this case, we should prefer the abolitionist strategy.

However, my contention is that MacKinnon's underlying metaphysics is suspect, and this undermines the response that we should aim to abolish gendered individuals (qua products of oppressive projection). Against her antifeminist opponent, MacKinnon's political position aims to show that being sexually submissive is just a contingent fact about women. But since she rejects the existence of a perspective independent reality that fixes what *really* is the case, MacKinnon cannot show that women are not in fact submissive by appealing to some supposedly hidden true reality covered up by the male reality. Rather, a new feminist reality must be constructed to replace the male one. It is possible to construct any reality provided that one has enough social power to do so. Haslanger helpfully describes MacKinnon's view as follows:

> [For her] different points of view generate competing realities, and to decide between them is to take a moral stand. MacKinnon's own moral stand is unequivocal; she proposes that we stop acting on the basis of what

---

[9] I won't consider whether MacKinnon can plausibly maintain the link between objectivity and objectification; I recommend Haslanger's (2002) illuminating discussion on the issue.

is real *to men* and instead begin to take seriously what is real *to women*. (1995, 123–124)

A feminist reality is better than the male reality because the latter oppresses women. Women's oppression is not just "in the head"; in fact, male reality literally hits women in the face (MacKinnon 1987, 57). So, even though our choice of realities is an evaluative decision, MacKinnon still thinks that our evaluative judgments rest on some facts about reality: because the male reality *in fact* oppresses women, we ought to choose a feminist reality and start taking seriously what is "real" to women. As a result, feminists (and women generally) must gain enough social power to project and make real their conception of reality to replace the male one.

Unfortunately, MacKinnon's metaphysics undercuts her powerful political message. MacKinnon claims that by treating women in submissive ways, women become submissive—they become "walking embodiments of men's projected needs" (1989, 119). But then the feminist claim that women are not in fact submissive comes out *false*. If the male perspective constructs reality, feminist critiques do not describe or capture reality as it is, thus undercutting critical claims about oppression (feminists are crying abuse when there is none). The upshot is that if our metaphysics is too radically constructivist in the service of those with social power, feminist politics will be undermined. We cannot tell truths about women's oppression from a feminist perspective, if that perspective is one of relative powerlessness (our claims come out as false). In this sense, there might be good political grounds to favor a re-evaluative strategy that does not reify or congeal projection and social construction in the manner that MacKinnon does.

One might further favor a re-evaluative strategy on the grounds that gender identity is a source of positive value for many ordinary social agents. Anecdotal evidence suggests that many doubt the viability of eradicating gender because it is seen at least partly as a positive social identity, rather than a wholly negative one. Trying to do away with gender, then, would result in something good being unnecessarily lost. It is certainly true that, although one may be discriminated against because of one's gender, one can still positively value it; in a similar sense, one can take pride in one's racialized group membership despite being socially disadvantaged by it. The abolitionist strategy, then, runs into difficulties if many social agents are unwilling to follow it through. Haslanger, for instance, is asking for a significant shift in people's self-conceptions, and she acknowledges asking social agents to understand themselves in ways that are not ordinarily part of their gendered self-understandings (2000, 48). In so doing, she is asking us to reject putatively positive social identities and to refuse to be gendered women and men.

I agree with Haslanger that a change in our self-understandings is called for. But I am less convinced that she is calling for is the right kind of change, given that ordinary social agents do not always see the viability of eradicating gender. Again, my point is strategic: abolitionist accounts are likely to be extremely demanding. It will take a lot of convincing to make social agents refuse to be gendered women and men, if they do not believe gender to be a wholly negative social identity. Such demandingness makes it much harder to achieve positive social change. And, as I have already noted, scarce feminist resources may be better spent on something other than trying to convince social agents to give up prima facie positive self-understandings. Clearly Haslanger wants to see an end to gendered oppression, just like those who would endorse a re-evaluative strategy. This may suggest that we are merely talking past each other, since everyone wants gender justice. Haslanger's rhetoric just differs from how we ordinarily talk about women and men, and it has a specific purpose: to motivate particular social and political responses to undermine sexist oppression. I admire Haslanger's strategy; but I worry about it being the most effective one. Instead, I hold that a more effective response can be motivated by reconceiving sex and gender in a way that no longer implies the revolution will abolish women and men. Again, my concerns are not decisive. But I think that they motivate an alternative way of thinking.

5.2.3. THE TRAIT/NORM COVARIANCE MODEL

In order to deflate ontological worries about the nature of gender (and womanhood), I will argue next for an alternative framework to replace the sex/gender distinction. My alternative deals roughly with the same phenomena as the distinction; but it apprehends the relevant phenomena anew in a way that helps feminist social theory and provides a pretheoretically more congenial understanding of the matter at hand. The first step is *not* to understand the term 'woman' as a purely social gender term. This fits ordinary language use, where speakers seem to have (the already mentioned) indicative features in mind when they use the term 'woman' (cf. Mallon 2004). These indicative features include one's appearance (clothing, hairstyles, makeup); behavioral patterns; social roles; self-ascription; anatomical and bodily features (body type, shape, size, amount of body hair, how one "carries" one's body). These are not necessary and sufficient for membership in gendered social kinds, but conceivably involved in everyday gender ascriptions and constitutive of our extensional intuitions (as I argued in section 5.1.). Standardly, feminists hold that the indicative features mentioned are not exclusively gender traits; they also include features that are taken to be paradigm sex traits. But ordinary speakers seem to treat 'woman' as a mixed term. Relative to this insight, my contention is that feminists should use the term 'woman' as ordinarily as possible. And my trait/norm covariance model will be sensitive to these reflections about ordinary language use.

The second step in developing my alternative model is to redraw the boundaries of the sets of gender and sex traits and give up the labels "sex" and "gender" to denote those traits. Subsequently, we divide the old sex/gender traits anew into sets of descriptive traits and evaluative norms. The former, in a sense, describe "the way the world is" and include (among others):

- Physical/anatomical traits (e.g., chromosomes, ovaries, testes, genitalia, body shape and size)
- One's appearance (e.g., clothing, makeup, haircut, amount of body hair)
- Roles (e.g., whether one undertakes caretaking roles, engages in childrearing tasks)
- Self-conceptions (calling oneself, say, a woman) (cf. Stoljar 1995)

Having these features is not mysterious or down to value judgments—in this sense, there are "facts of the matter" pertaining to descriptive traits. This does not mean that values and norms were not involved in singling out descriptive features like anatomical traits, or that descriptive features are not socially malleable (more on this shortly). The simple point is that there is a fact of the matter as to whether (for example) I call myself a woman or not—either I do, or I do not. Evaluative norms, by contrast, are to do with stereotypical reactions and judgments: whether one is viewed or judged to be, to appear, and/or to act in feminine, masculine, or neutral ways. The attributed evaluations include explicit judgments, but they also capture implicit social values and cultural norms that form the basis of further explicit cognitive attitudes (like judgments or beliefs). Although not developed with anything like the trait/norm covariance relation in mind, Tamar Szabo Gendler's notion of *alief* nicely illustrates this latter idea. For Gendler, aliefs are mental states distinct from beliefs and desires. They are associative, automatic, arational, antecedent to other cognitive attitudes we may develop, affect laden, and action generating (2008, 641). Social distancing provides a conceivable example of an alief in action; for instance, someone automatically holding on to their purse more tightly when entering an elevator with a black male. This seemingly demonstrates an associative, automatic, and arational affect-laden state ("black male, thief, danger!") that is action guiding (one holds onto the purse more tightly). Something similar is conceivably at play when (say) the trait of wearing makeup is automatically associated in an action-generating manner with femininity, and this association is due to prevalent cultural and social norms. Of course, one may also have the explicit belief that wearing makeup is feminine. Our evaluative reactions about traits like wearing makeup then plausibly contain both belief- and alief-like states.

The basic difference between my account and the paradigm feminist schemas is captured in table 5.1.

In short, my model aims to provide a systematic account of some very ordinary social and cultural behavior—one that we might characterize as "gender-stereotype ascription" in the more traditional feminist language.

TABLE 5.1 Paradigm Feminist and the Trait/Norm Covariance Models

Paradigm feminist model		Trait/norm covariance model	
Sex	Gender	Descriptive traits	Evaluative norms
Having ovaries	Wearing makeup Being "feminine"	Having ovaries Wearing makeup	Being "feminine"

What I aim to elucidate is why we so easily accept claims like "wearing makeup is feminine" and think that something has gone wrong when one claims that wearing makeup is masculine. My alternative aims to account for this kind of apparent obviousness (for lack of a better word), with which our social reality is saturated.

Let's spell out the model in detail. First, what does it mean for descriptive traits to *covary* with evaluative norms? Simply put: we take certain traits to be of a certain kind. The trait/norm covariance relation is constituted by particular descriptive traits being viewed in a particular evaluative manner *by us*— they *count as* feminine, masculine, or neutral to us. So, depending on how we view particular descriptive traits or what we take them to count as, they covary with either femininity, masculinity, or neutrality. I take *femininity* to mean associated with women, *masculinity* to mean associated with men, and *neutrality* to mean associated with neither or both. The classification scheme of feminine, masculine, and neutral evaluative norms is a strong pragmatic construction: social factors wholly determine our use of the scheme, and the scheme fails to represent accurately any agent-independent "facts of the matter" (Haslanger 1995, 100). The feminine/masculine/neutral scheme is a *mere* social construction and exists because of human-made fashions, styles, cultural beliefs, and social conventions (among other social forces).

Of course, these reactions or evaluations are not the only ones we have. The scheme does not exhaust social normativity, and there is usually considerable conceptual spillage between different norms. For instance, certain norms govern domesticity: the "good mother" norm expects mothers to have all the time and love in the world to devote to their children, and outsourcing child care allegedly makes one a "bad" mother (Williams 2000). This norm is clearly not unrelated to the feminine/masculine/neutral classification scheme. But it is, if you like, one normative step further. The evaluative norms that I am focusing on are to do with basic stereotypical reactions and judgments. These reactions provide the basis for a wider normative framework that deals with further stereotypical ascriptions. My description of the evaluative reactions as norms is perhaps misleading, and such reactions are not fully-fledged norms, like the "good mother" one. But my thought is this: without some initial evaluative reaction that (say) binds the descriptive trait of child caring with femininity, richer norms like the "good mother" norm would not have gotten off the ground. It is this base level that I am aiming to elucidate here, a level that makes ascriptions of femininity and masculine seem so natural to many social agents.

What *kind* of a relation is the trait/norm covariance relation? Or, to put the point differently: what kind of a relation is the *counts-as* relation mentioned above? I will suggest next that the relation is one I term "quasi-essentialist." To understand what I have in mind, let's start by considering the "counts as" expression and John Searle's account of constitutive rules. In his elucidation of social and institutional reality and of institutional facts like "Herkel married Merkel," Searle draws a distinction between constitutive and regulative rules. The basic idea is that while the latter regulate antecedently existing forms of behavior, the former create and define new forms of behavior (Searle 1969; 1995).[10] Further, constitutive rules are of the form "x counts as y in context C." Now, Searle provides two ways to understand what x and y in such rules refer to: either one (x) is a brute fact and the other (y) an institutional fact; or neither can be said to be brute. An example of the former would be "certain physical movements on Jones's part constitute Jones's scoring a touchdown," whereas an example of the latter would be "Jones's possessing the ball in the opponents' end zone while a play is in progress constitutes Jones's scoring a touchdown" (Cherry 1973, 305). In the latter example, it is clear that we cannot treat the state of affairs in the x position as brute in any sense—rather, it only makes sense to us relative to an already existing rich institutional framework. Now, think back to the trait/norm covariance relation. In saying that this relation involves a *counts-as* relation, which of these two ways of understanding "counts as" do I have in mind? I noted earlier that although some facts of the matter pertain to descriptive traits, this does not mean that values were not involved in singling out descriptive features, or that such features are not socially malleable. This makes the trait of wearing makeup akin to Jones's possessing the ball in the opponents' end zone while a play is in progress: both are descriptive in the sense that there is some fact of the matter (either I wear makeup or not, either Jones possesses the ball in the opponents' end zone or not), but neither makes sense to us without being embedded in some broader social-institutional framework. Neither is brute in the sense that Jones's physical movements are. So, in order to even begin to comprehend the "counts as" expression relative to my proposal, we should understand the "counts as" expression to relate two pieces of institutional reality.

So far the idea is the following: the proposed trait/norm covariance relation involves a *counts-as* relation that binds together two pieces of institutional reality (namely, a trait and a normative evaluation). I noted earlier that

---

[10] This way of characterizing the difference is rudimentary, and it has been critiqued as being unsustainable: for instance, Cherry (1973) has argued that ultimately the distinction so understood collapses because some regulative rules also constitute new forms of behavior. I am inclined to agree, but for my purposes here nothing hangs on this.

this *counts-as* relation is quasi-essentialist. What do I mean by this? In order to clarify this, it helps to consider first what an essentialist *counts-as* relation would look like. I should stress that I am not endorsing this sort of essentialist relation or arguing for its plausibility. I am merely formulating a possible way to conceive of an essentialist *counts-as* relation in order to use it as a heuristic device that helps to elucidate the quasi-essentialist relation. My formulation of an essentialist *counts-as* relation draws on the aforementioned work by Searle, along with Kit Fine's work. Searle's formulation of "*x* counts as *y* in C" that connects two pieces of institutional reality is in a sense definitional: one institutional fact seems to provide (at least partly) the definition of another institutional fact. Moreover, on a prominent account of essence advanced by Fine (1994), we should understand essences too as definitional. That is, just as we can define a word, we can define an object—this tells us *what* the object is, what is its *nature*. Putting together the essence-as-definitional and counts-as-as-definitional views yields the following: if one institutional piece of reality provides (partly) the definition of another, then the one tells us something about the other's *nature*—what the other essentially is. On the Searlean account of counts-as-as-definitional, an entailment relation between *x* and *y* exists; a relation that taken together with Fine's essence-as-definitional turns out to be of a complex conceptual-metaphysical kind.

To illustrate, take the case of scoring a touchdown. Possessing the ball in the opponents' end zone (*x*) counts as scoring a touchdown (*y*). It then follows that the former entails the latter: I have scored a touchdown, only if I possess the ball in the opponents' end zone while play is in progress. It looks further that possessing the ball makes up part of the definition of scoring a touchdown: it tells us (at least partly) what it is to score a touchdown. This appears to tell us something about the nature of scoring a touchdown—what kind of a phenomenon it essentially is. And this quickly lends itself to the following: if we wish to explain to someone what it is to score a touchdown, we quite probably will say that this amounts to possessing the ball in the opponents' end zone while play is in progress.

I take this to be the structure of possible essentialist *counts-as* relations. Again, I am not arguing that this is a plausible structure—I am merely using the above as a device to introduce and elucidate the structure of quasi-essentialist *counts-as* relations. So what are these relations like? Simply put, they are like the essentialist relations, except that they merely *purport* to capture some facts about the world. It is *as if* they pertain to some essential/definitional facts of the matter, when they do not. Consider the following: wearing makeup counts as acting in a feminine way—this is a typical evaluative reaction to the trait. I wish to suggest that we can elucidate this *counts-as* relation in a manner parallel to the above example, *except* that in the case of makeup and femininity the *counts-as* relation does not capture any genuinely essential or definitional relation; it merely appears to do so. Here's how the story goes.

The statement "wearing makeup counts as acting in a feminine way" suggests that wearing makeup entails acting in a feminine manner: in wearing makeup, I appear to be doing something feminine—something associated with women. Wearing makeup then (partly) defines or elucidates what it is to be, act, or appear feminine. And, conceivably again, this tells us something about the nature of femininity: what femininity essentially is about. As above, doing so quickly lends itself to the following: if we wish to explain to someone what it is to be "feminine," we quite conceivably might say by way of elucidation that wearing makeup is a way to be so. The difference to the essentialist *count-as* formulation is simply that in the latter case of makeup and femininity we have not captured any genuinely essential definitional relation. The relation between the descriptive trait and the evaluative norm is merely conceived *as if* it were essential. What then explains this apparent essentialism? The trait/norm pairings ontologically depend on us; and hence relative to our current social, cultural, and normative frameworks, we have *congealed* particular pairings so that there appears to express an essentialist relationship. But this merely appears to be so—thus, I have termed the elucidation of this fairly common everyday phenomenon of certain descriptive traits being normatively evaluated in particular ways "*quasi*-essentialism." We (social agents, our attitudes, and actions) have congealed particular accidental relations between traits and norms to make them appear essentialist.

The general picture is thus: certain traits are paired with particular norms, and these pairings are bound together via a covariance relation, which I take to be quasi-essentialist. Specific pairings are currently linked to women, others to men, and still others to neither or both. And there are different modes by which the pairings are linked to us—or better, different modes of congealment that explain the pairings' apparent essentialism. Further remarks on congealment are in order. It can be global. Being shortsighted globally covaries with neutrality: as far as I know, the trait is nowhere associated exclusively with either women or men. Then again, the possession of testes appears to be globally masculine, possession of ovaries globally feminine. More often, though, the trait/norm pairings are local. They differ from one context to the next, and depend on particular social and cultural arrangements. So, although all cultures have traits that covary with femininity and others that covary with masculinity, the configurations of these pairings are contextually variable. To illustrate, take the descriptive trait of having long hair. At the time of writing this, in many UK communities it is not strongly associated with women and often covaries with neutrality. However, in UK Asian-Indian communities, where it is not considered appropriate for those picked out by 'woman' to have short hair, having long hair covaries more strongly with femininity. But, of course, other social and cultural axes affect this covariance relation even within a culture: in UK Indian Sikh contexts, both men and women are expected to have long hair, which suggests that in these social contexts having long hair covaries with neutrality. Other social and cultural practices having to do with hair additionally covary with femininity and masculinity, like the practice of Sikh men wearing turbans. The trait/norm pairings are intertwined: for those picked out by 'man', the pairing "having long hair/neutrality" is intertwined with "wearing a turban/masculinity." But for those picked out by 'woman', the former pairing is not intertwined with the latter pairing. The covariance pairs also change over time. Wearing trousers is a good example: until quite recently in many Western Anglo-European contexts, masculinity covaried with it. But, relatively quickly, it has become largely neutral. The social value attached to this trait has changed.

The above demonstrates that the ways in which the covariance relations pan out are not always straightforward, clear-cut, and simple since the particular relations depend on aliefs, beliefs, and conventions that change over time and place. Mapping out extant trait/norm covariances will be a slow and arduous task—and one for which social scientists, sociologists, and cultural anthropologists are better suited than philosophers. However, sometimes seeing how the relations pan out is uncomplicated, and usually social agents (relative to a context) do not significantly differ in their ascriptions of some evaluative norm. This is unsurprising because normative evaluations are in a sense public and always ascribed from within a social framework and setting. This public nature conceivably explains why those from similar social settings display a high degree of uniformity in their evaluative reactions.

This relates back to congealment: although the particular (congealed) trait/norm pairings may be highly contextually variable, they can also be extremely resilient. Just think how difficult it is to dissociate caretaking traits from evaluations of femininity. What explains the durability of such quasi-essentialist congealment? I suspect that something akin to Frank Hindriks's acceptance dependence is going on. (He focuses on the example of money, but the position has wider applicability.) On this account, the concept of *money* is acceptance dependent: x is money in some context C, if and only if some group G in that context has the attitude of accepting something as money (or believing it to be money) toward x (Hindriks 2006, 491). With this in mind, we can prima facie explain why congealment is so resilient: social agents in a particular context have specific attitudes toward some descriptive trait, in that they accept the trait as evaluatively being of a certain kind. On Hindriks's account, the relevant attitudes that figure in acceptance dependence are belief-like states (2006, 491). Although the sort of congealment I discuss here at times depends on acceptance dependence in Hindriks's sense, I suspect that much of what sustains congealment boils down to *implicit* non-belief-like attitudes. Earlier I suggested that the trait/norm pairings conceivably involve alieving and that the mechanism by which we pair some descriptive traits with evaluative reactions involves implicit non-belief-like automatic states. Here my speculative point goes further: the mechanism by which such pairings are sustained and congealed also involves implicit non-belief-like attitudes. The existence of such implicit attitudes has been amply documented by social psychologists (for a great overview, I recommend Jost et al. 2009). Social psychological research on implicit attitudes relies on and is an extension of an established cognitive science principle that "knowledge is organized in memory in the form of semantic associations that are derived from personal experiences as well as normative procedures and roles" (Jost et al. 2009, 43). Implicit attitudes work via automatic associative links in memory that are (somehow) meaningful—like the associations between child care and femininity. These links are rendered meaningful partly, but in an influential manner, by shared cultural stereotypes (2009, 60). So the mechanism of implicit attitudes comes down to automatic associations that fit common stereotypical views, and these associations tend to take place even when subjects explicitly reject the stereotypes. The relevant point here is this: even though acceptance dependence is conceivably going on *sometimes* when quasi-essentialism is at play, I suspect that our implicit attitudes are responsible for much of the resiliency of quasi-essentialist covariance relations outlined above. This fits the view that implicit attitudes are not immediately under the agent's rational control and easily amenable to belief revision. For instance, according to a recently pregnant acquaintance of mine, no matter how often she mentioned to her father that her obstetrician was female, her father still kept referring to the obstetrician as a "he."

To recap: trait/norm pairings involve covariance relations that are quasi-essentialist. Specific pairings are linked to women, others to men, and still others to neither or both. Different modes of congealment explain the pairings' apparent essentialism: some pairings are global, most are local, and despite contextual variability many are highly resilient to change. To explain the resiliency of quasi-essentialist covariance relations, I invoked acceptance-dependence and implicit attitudes. Now, I already noted that I take the existence of particular covariance relations to be a thoroughly agent-*dependent* matter. If you like, wearing makeup and engaging in childrearing are not inherently or mind-independently feminine—they are merely quasi-essentially so. With this in mind, let me briefly clarify the notions of *mind independence* and *mind dependence* to finish elucidating my alternative model. For me, the claim "Jane is feminine because Jane wears makeup" does not capture an agent-independent fact about the world. But my model also takes wearing makeup to be a descriptive trait of which there is "a fact of the matter." This generates two worries. First, it appears that I am saying something inconsistent here. Second, how sustainable is the distinction between descriptive traits and evaluative reactions really? Let me say something to this latter worry first. One might worry that finding "facts of the matter" descriptive traits is not as easy as I have made it out to be. For instance, is someone who is wearing red face paint wearing makeup? Are those wearing kilts wearing skirts? How do we fix the relevant facts of the matter here—isn't this going to depend on a huge amount of evaluative and normative considerations? Well, the short answer is yes. But the normative factors at play when fixing facts of the matter relative to descriptive traits are different in *kind* from those reactions I have here termed "evaluative norms." I noted earlier that descriptive traits are not socially immutable, and that they do not come to be factual sui generis. The distinction between kilts and skirts (for instance) is fixed relative to certain social norms, historical properties, and aesthetic features. In short: there are background frameworks and public meanings at work that fix descriptive traits' factuality. These frameworks do not have cemented borders, and the background social norms and functions are certainly open to revision. But they regulate social interactions. Were Jack to show up at a ceilidh (a Scottish dance event) wearing a black, tight, stretchy, down to his ankles, tube-formed garment and claim that he is wearing a kilt, others would take him to be mistaken. And this seems warranted given what currently fixes the artifact class of kilts. That is, there are public frameworks that are involved in fixing meanings; those who are unfamiliar with the frameworks may get things wrong (for instance, those unfamiliar with Scottish culture and the existence of kilts might falsely think that Jack is wearing a skirt to a ceilidh when he is wearing a kilt). All of this shows that there are framework-relative facts pertaining to descriptive traits, although these facts are (of course) in no sense carved in nature's joints. And spelling those frameworks out requires empirical investigation, not a priori armchair reflection.

To elucidate this further, consider the former worry. To dispel the air of inconsistency, consider again driving. Which driving convention is the correct or "true" one: left- or right-side driving? This question strikes me as unanswerable. We cannot answer it because the context-specific conventions governing driving are agent dependent; they depend for their existence on productive human social practices and require that certain human-made background conditions be in place. There is no convention independent way to answer the question, which is why it is unanswerable. The relevant driving conventions are clearly socially mutable; nonetheless, there is no agent-independent "fact" about which side is the correct one for driving. Still, that UK motorists drive on the left is agent independent in another sense. When I state, "UK motorists drive on the left," I am stating something agent-independently true, and the truth of the statement is not up for grabs. I cannot just decide that this statement is false for me. Or, I could, but probably with quite tragic results. So, *given* certain background conditions, it is an agent-independent fact that UK motorists drive on the left, and this is irrespective of driving conventions being agent dependent. Descriptive traits are akin to this: they are agent dependent in that their existence depends on factors that require particular human-made background conditions to be in place. Still, there is another sense in which descriptive traits like Jane wearing makeup and Jack wearing a kilt are agent independent. The truth or falsity of the statement "Jane wears makeup" is not up for grabs, *given* our current conventions: either she does or she does not. The same goes for "Jack wears a kilt." And although wearing makeup and wearing a kilt are agent independent in this sense, that Jane acts in a feminine and Jack in a masculine way *because* of their respective actions is thoroughly agent dependent. These latter evaluative judgments do not capture any genuinely agent-independent facts, but merely quasi-essentialist ones that obtain because of productive human activities—because of us. Fortunately, this means that we can alter the existing states of affairs, thereby undercutting quasi-essentialist trait/norm covariance relations.[11]

5.2.4. ONTOLOGICAL COMMITMENTS AND THE TRAIT/NORM COVARIANCE MODEL

I argued above that the sex/gender distinction harbors some unintuitive and undesirable ontological commitments, and that a feminist ontology should aim to avoid these commitments. How then does my trait/norm covariance model fare? Consider first the conventionalist implication. That there are certain conventional trait/norm pairings linked to women and men does not commit one to the view that their existence nontrivially depends on some social forces. So feminists need not take the *existence* of women and men to be conventional, although the ways in which the covariance relations pan out are. This is theoretically more beneficial in being ontologically less weighty than conventionalism considered earlier. To clarify: I am not claiming that being linked to particular trait/norm pairings somehow settles what it is to be a woman or a man. I am simply providing a way (*a*) to account for the ubiquitous fact that such pairings are linked to women and men; (*b*) to conceptualize this in a way that takes into account the vital role of productive human social activities. As a result, my model holds that social change can significantly affect those individuals we call "women" and "men" without implying that this does away with them: it will alter what is associated with us and how we are subsequently viewed by others. The locus of social change is the descriptive trait/evaluative norm covariance relation, which leaves the

---

[11] One might wonder whether all descriptive traits are agent dependent, or whether only socially constructed ones are. There is a way to see all descriptive traits as being agent dependent (being products of human social practices). However, this requires understanding social construction quite broadly, and it requires that we acknowledge the existence of not only *object* construction, but also *idea* construction (cf. discussion of sex in chapter 2). Social forces and human practices bring certain objects into existence, like one-dollar bills; but they also bring certain ideas into existence, like the idea of money. So even though we either have ovaries or don't, the idea or concept of *ovaries* is a product of human social practices, broadly speaking. After all, the history of scientific research on human anatomy is deeply intertwined with many ideology-laden practices and cultural beliefs that have guided (and still guide) such research. This further demonstrates that the factuality of descriptive traits is not somehow metaphysically preposterous.

existence of women and men ontologically intact. So we start by looking at those individuals designated women and men (cf. section 5.1.) and by examining which trait/norm pairings are linked to them. For such tasks, discourse-analytic tools might be particularly useful (cf. Herbelot, von Redecker, and Müller 2012). We should then examine whether there is anything morally or politically problematic about the pairings—after all, not all pairings are problematic (e.g., neutral ones). Finally, we would work to undermine those that are insidious. The aim is for our reactions and judgments to change radically over time, so that future individuals picked out with 'woman', 'man', and other identity designators will be associated with different and more just pairings than those associated with extant women and men. The aim is to undermine problematic quasi-essentialism and those forces that are responsible for resiliency. As a result, a change in the trait/norm covariances does not do away with women and men because (for me) no particular features must be had for one to *be* a woman or a man. We thus avoid the unintuitive conventionalist implications.

One might object that my classification scheme of evaluative norms (femininity/masculinity/neutrality) ignores trans*, intersex, and queer identities and lives. There is some truth to this insofar as I have so far focused on the traditional woman-men binary. The reason for doing so is twofold: first, elucidating my model is easier with a more restricted focus; second, I am aiming to show that the standard ontological conceptualization of cis women's and cis men's gender fails in important ways. That is, there are many ways to complicate ontological theories of gender, and critiques from trans* and queer perspectives have done a good job at that. However, I wanted to show that even putatively *uncomplicated* cases are not so uncomplicated—and that this warrants a rethinking of the sex/gender distinction. Still, my model is not limited to the standard binary. In order to expand our classificatory scheme of evaluative norms, we would start by looking at everyday usage of terms like 'trans*' and 'intersex'. Here Bettcher's (2013) view, noted earlier, becomes particularly pertinent: for this move, we have excellent reasons *not* to take the dominant cis usage as our starting point, but rather privilege resistant (trans* and inter) usage. On this expanded model, our classificatory scheme would be (at least) feminine/masculine/queer/trans*/intersex/neutral. The new evaluative reactions and norms would be defined in a manner parallel to "feminine" and "masculine": they would be associated with queer/trans*/intersex individuals, respectively. Neutrality would also have to be redefined to reflect the plurality. Particular descriptive traits would then covary with the expanded list of evaluative norms, and some pairings would be linked to those individuals picked out with 'queer', 'trans*', and 'intersex'. The subsequent critical point would be to see whether these pairings are problematic or not. For instance, a trait like wearing makeup may generate in some context a feminine evaluation, but in another a queer one. And the moral assessment of the pairing may vary depending on who is associated with the trait: when associated with cis women, it may well be deeply insidious (as when employers impose appearance codes and demand that their female employees wear makeup). Then again, when the pairing is associated with queer individuals, it may well have emancipatory effects. Nevertheless, when the pairings are morally or politically worrisome, the emancipatory strategy will be the same as with all pairings: to drive a wedge between the descriptive trait and the evaluative norm (more on this shortly). In short: even though my focus so far has been on women and men, my proposed model can deal with a broader range of evaluative norms and judgments.

My alternative conceptualization also bears on the issue of what happens "after the revolution" and avoids undesirable abolitionist commitments. For me, gender justice eradicates problematic trait/norm pairings (along with material and structural forces sustaining them). This enables feminists to conceptualize positive social change that dismantles unjust social hierarchies and normative expectations while retaining women and men reconceived. Here is an example of what I have in mind. Many traits and activities associated with women are devalued in comparison to traits and activities associated with men. And many difficulties women face appear to be due to such trait/norm pairings being associated with them—just think of so-called women's work being badly paid and of low status. Now, childcaring tasks conceivably covary with femininity, which seems to devalue them. This situation disadvantages women: it makes it hard for them to combine work and family life commitments and fuels the expectation that women undertake the bulk of child care. But it also disadvantages men. For instance, in the UK men have found it hard to take up parental leave partly because of employers' unwillingness to grant them leave—after all, what kind of a man would want to stay at home with a child! The UK Department for Trade and Industry revealed that, in 2007, "a quarter of men working in the private sector who asked to work flexibly had their requests refused, compared with only one in 10 women. Almost a fifth of men in public sector jobs have had requests turned down" (Ward 2007).[12] Even with the best will in the world, parents find it hard to combine equally work and family lives. If child care were not so closely paired with femininity but, rather, associated with all parents (thus becoming neutral), those with children might conceivably find it easier to combine work and family lives, and employers would hopefully be more willing to grant everyone flexible working conditions. As long as child care solely covaries with femininity, the covariance relation is likely to be insidious. So driving a wedge between this

---

[12] It is worth noting that the rules have since changed with a view to offering parents better leave possibilities. This has not, however, hugely improved the situation for fathers. According to the Trade Union Congress (a federation of UK trade unions), two in five fathers do not qualify for the new rules (BBC News, April 5, 2015; http://www.bbc.com/news/business-32130481).

and other problematic pairings will be a mechanism for change: doing so should make it easier (for instance) for men to obtain parental leave, and for women not to be disadvantaged relative to their career prospects simply by becoming a parent. On my model, the revolution would render childcaring tasks neutral human activities.[13]

For me, as for Haslanger and other feminist philosophers, fighting gender injustice requires active normative commitments in our daily lives. Among other things, it will involve acting in ways that undermine extant trait/norm pairings: by men taking on caring roles and refusing to act in stereotypical ways; by challenging stereotypes in one's own behavior and when interacting with others; and by trying to bring up one's children in ways that undermine the current pairings and so educate them about the diversity of bodies, desires, and possibilities. But meaningful social change also requires revisions in our public policies and institutions. One relatively easy way this could be done is by making sure that public baby-changing facilities are not always located *in* women's toilets, although much more radical structural changes are also needed. For instance, in Sweden, the government has attempted (in my terms) to drive a wedge between child care and femininity via parental leave legislation. Each couple has the right to take a total of 480 days leave, of which each parent is allocated 60 nontransferable days (the rest are transferable). The thinking is that by encouraging fathers to take parental leave, gender equality in the family is fostered (Sundelin 2008). A more recent newspaper article highlights that through such public policies, personal lives can change in ways that alter problematic trait/norm pairings. Richard Orange, a Brit living and raising his child in Sweden, writes that during his share of the parental leave, he has come to realize that "when I thought I was being understanding [to my wife during her parental leave], I didn't understand a thing." He continues that the main qualities required to look after babies "don't now seem to me intrinsically feminine" (Orange 2012). Further, in the free-of-charge playgroup that Orange attends, fathers on parental leave sometimes outnumber mothers. Another (female) British expat in the playgroup comments:

> My whole parenting experience had been played out in England, and you just don't see that many dads at playgroup or in the playground with small

---

[13] Another possible way to sever the links would be to try to undermine the associations between particular trait/norm pairings and women and men. So it would leave the child care/femininity pairing intact but would aim to dissociate this pairing from women. But insofar as *femininity* on my account means "associated with women," I cannot see how this strategy would work. It would still leave in place an implicit normative suggestion that child care really should fall within women's purview. As a result, leaving the pairings intact would be the wrong strategy. The insidious pairings themselves must go.

kids, and then I came here, and sometimes the majority are dads. . . . It just shows how skewed my perspective had become that when I see so many dads involved in their children's lives, I am shocked. (Orange 2012)

Of course, this is merely anecdotal and a single example. But in many ways it demonstrates how incredibly *easy* it might be to alter even the most resilient pairings with different public policies.

One might worry, however, that my account of quasi-essentialism undercuts this sort of change. After all, I hold that implicit attitudes are probably responsible for much of the durability of worrisome quasi-essentialist pairings. Such implicit attitudes are typically automatic, beyond agents' rational or introspective control, often nontransparent to the agents themselves, and notoriously difficult to eradicate. In fact, many (myself included) hold that we cannot eradicate all implicit attitudes. This seems to undermine the suggestion above: how is it actually possible to undermine the resiliency of quasi-essentialism, if such resiliency in part trades on impossible-to-eradicate implicit attitudes? I do not think that the situation is as bleak as this, though. It may be impossible to do away with all implicit associations, but we can certainly diminish their hold and influence on us. For instance, Saul has outlined interventions that can reduce the hold of implicit attitudes. One effective strategy is exposure to counterstereotypical exemplars: members of a stigmatized social group who do not fit group stereotypes (Saul 2012b, 259). My speculative point is that the case of Swedish fathers on parental leave while Swedish mothers are at work plausibly contributes to minimizing implicit associations between child care and femininity in providing precisely such counterstereotypical exemplars. Another way in which we can mitigate the effects of our implicit biases is via implementation intentions. Again, Saul writes:

> there is recent work on the potential for implementation intentions to reduce implicit bias. Implementation intentions are very specific intentions of the form "if I'm in situation S, I will do F" (as opposed to "I'll try to do F as much as I can"). Forming an intention like "if I see a black person, I will think safe" or "if I see Ina, I will ignore her gender" has been shown to reduce implicit bias. (2012b, 259)

Much more work is still needed to determine the most effective ways to reduce the influence of implicit attitudes. Nevertheless, my contention is that the situation is not that bleak, and even though implicit attitudes are conceivably responsible for much of quasi-essentialism, my proposal does not make meaningful social change unachievable. Change is possible.

5.3. The Gender Controversy Deflated

This chapter aimed to deflate the semantic and ontological puzzles: in short, to show that they are not so pressing once we reconceive the central phenomena under discussion. With respect to the former, I argued that an elucidation of a thick *woman* concept is not needed for political purposes. Rather, thin and superficial extensional intuitions enable us to pick out women's social kind. Feminist social theory requires certain terminological and theoretical tools, and feminist theorists must be able to talk about women. This is what the thin understanding of the term 'woman' that I articulate above offers (cf. section 5.1.). The terminological tools that I have proposed here enable feminists to identify and explain persistent social inequalities in order to justify their critiques of the status quo. (Though of course the thin understanding of 'woman' alone does not accomplish all of the required feminist work, and is only part of the whole story—more on this shortly.) The dilemma of either providing a substantive definition of *woman* or being unable to pick out women's social kind is a false one. The urgency of the semantic puzzle is thus deflated.

Relative to the ontological puzzle, I argued that the phenomena usually discussed under the rubric of the sex/gender distinction can be reconceived in a way that avoids problematic ontological commitments—commitments that arise from taking gender to be socially constructed through oppressive social relations. As an alternative, I proposed a model that avoids these commitments and thus bypasses the second puzzle. First, it avoids the view that we can eradicate "gendered" individuals just the way we can eradicate political posts. Second, it avoids the political commitment to eradicating women and men. On my model, the task is to eradicate problematic trait/ norm pairings associated with those our extensional intuitions pick out as women and men. In plain terms, it amounts to altering our social reactions and normative judgments about descriptive traits. This deflates the puzzle by reconceiving the underlying ontology. It also stays close to our social realities and (I submit) can be more helpful in feminist social theory building than the contested notions of *gender* and *woman*. My arguments in this chapter then should diminish the pull of the gender controversy. As I see it, feminists should move on from analyzing gender concepts, and the remainder of this book argues that the concept of *dehumanization* should be the focal point of emancipatory feminism. In short, the damage done by patriarchy is that women (understood as a social kind picked out by extensional intuitions) are treated in dehumanizing ways. *This* is what justifies feminist action on behalf of women, not some thick articulation of the gender concept *woman*.

PART II

Normativity Anew

{ 6 }

Dehumanization

6.1. Introduction

The previous chapters advanced this book's first substantive claim: to leave behind the gender controversy and embrace a paradigm shift toward feminist philosophy that is humanist. My subsequent discussion continues on from this and offers a vision of such humanist feminism that is to be grounded in a particular notion of *dehumanization.* This notion (I argue) serves not only to undergird feminist philosophical investigations of injustice, but also to elucidate the wrong of social injustice per se. This twofold role that dehumanization plays enables us (1) to avoid the pitfalls of current gender debates in feminist philosophy; (2) to provide a more nuanced account of gender injustice by giving up those theoretical presumptions that the gender controversy harbors and that steer feminist philosophical debates in unhelpful ways; and (3) to facilitate social theory building (both in feminism and more generally) by better understanding the wrongness-making feature of social injustice. With my understanding of dehumanization, I go on to explicate this feature of social injustice, and in the chapters still to come I provide a regimentation of social injustice from a feminist perspective. This also spells out the specifics of the proposed humanist feminism. My discussion in Part I should already engender support for point (1) above; the forthcoming chapters will address the second and the third benefits.

What, then, is dehumanization? In short: an act or a treatment is dehumanizing if and only if it is an indefensible setback to some of our legitimate human interests, where this setback constitutes a moral injury. Or so I will propose in this chapter. My position draws on some existing humanist ideas in feminism. Louise Antony holds that

> feminist theory needs an appeal to a universal human nature in order to articulate and defend its critical claims about the damage done to women

under patriarchy, and also to ground its positive vision of equitable and sustaining human relationships. (1998, 67)

In order to say what is wrongful about patriarchy, feminists must affirm women's humanity by asserting that they are "essentially beings of a certain kind" (namely, humans), and that "there are modes of treatment that are appropriate, and others that are inappropriate, for beings of this kind" (Antony 2000, 11). For Antony, Martha Nussbaum's capabilities approach exhibits this sort of humanist thinking. Nussbaum proposes a list of "the most important functions and capabilities of the human being, in terms of which human life is defined" (1995b, 72). This list should be used to frame our public policies and social arrangements: making sure that citizens possess the *capability* to function in particular areas of life constitutes for Nussbaum the acceptable social minimum that every government should guarantee. These areas include life, health, bodily integrity, emotions (capacity for pleasure, pain), certain cognitive abilities and practical reasoning, the need for affiliation with others, play (recreation, humor), the recognition that we are not the only living creatures, and control over one's environment (Nussbaum 2000, 78–80). Furthermore, out of these Nussbaum singles out practical reason and affiliation as especially important: they suffuse and organize all other capabilities, so that the pursuit of the above capabilities will be distinctly human (2000, 82).

In arguing for her version of humanist feminism, Nussbaum distinguishes externalist and internalist essentialism. The former takes facts about what is essentially human to be "matters of natural scientific fact, not of ethical value" (Nussbaum 1995a, 88). Internalism, however,

> constructs its account of what is essential to a human being by drawing explicitly on the norms and values embodied in human practices, using human beings' own judgments about what makes their lives "human" to sort human characteristics into the essential and the accidental. (Antony 2000, 14–15)

Nussbaum favors this latter approach and explicitly seeks to define *human being* as a normative ethical concept, rather than in some value-neutral manner. Antony, however, takes issue with Nussbaum's position; she argues that there is no notion of *human being* that can be employed to single out how women are damaged under patriarchy and that can justify positive feminist ethical and political claims (cf. Antony 2000)—contra her earlier appeals to humanism in feminism (cf. Antony 1998). First, in order to define *human being* in a genuinely inclusive manner, it must be defined in terms of certain human universals. Prima facie the externalist strategy is fitting for this task. But it fails: the only traits that have a claim to being genuine human universals are biological or genetic traits that have no ethical or normative importance in themselves. Externalism, then, does not "generate reasons for accepting ethical propositions about what human beings should and should not do" (Antony 2000, 15). Second, Nussbaum's internalism makes values and norms part of the definition of *humanity*. This provides the required normative element and generates ethical conclusions. However, Antony holds, "the crucial premise about human nature will only be acceptable to someone who antecedently endorses the value judgments embodied therein" (2000, 16). An internalist definition will not persuade those who disagree about which values and norms should define a human life. So the prospects of cashing out *humanity* in a way that can ground feminist ethical and political claims, Antony holds, seem unpromising. Bluntly put, the definition will either be too normative or not normative enough. And this undercuts the prospect of developing humanist feminism: we cannot make sense of dehumanization if we are unable to cash out a genuinely inclusive concept of *human being* that can support normative claims about how women should and should not be treated qua human beings.

I think that Antony is right to claim that the prospects of cashing out a genuinely inclusive, ethically thick concept of *human being* are not good. Furthermore, I hold that our theorizing should not rely on such a notion. This is methodologically demanded by my rejection of ideal theory: as I see it, idealizations like Nussbaum's cannot serve as acceptable foundations for a feminist theory of injustice. Nevertheless, we can develop a humanist—or, rather, neohumanist—feminism that makes sense of how patriarchy damages women *without* relying on an idealized, internalist conception of *human being*.

My strategy has two basic steps. First, we must understand *human being* in broadly externalist terms as picking out the biological kind of human beings, as we commonly understand this kind in everyday speech. Members of such a kind are of the *homo sapiens sapiens* species (anatomically modern humans); they are typically "featherless bipeds" with certain dispositional cognitive capacities (like language and reasoning skills), which develop given the appropriate environmental conditions. Contra Nussbaum's internalist sense of *humanity*, my externalist conception is not equivalent to personhood, and it does not designate those who are members of "our" moral community. Further, the kind of human beings that my notion picks out will not have clear and rigid boundaries, and there are many difficult questions about when biological humanity begins and ends. I will not say more about these concerns, though, since they do not bear on my argument here. My aim is merely to capture an everyday conception of humanity as a biological kind, where this conception trades on typical paradigm features of human beings. Second, I take it as an incontrovertible fact that members of this kind can be and often are treated in deeply damaging and dehumanizing ways. Specifically, I take rape

as a paradigm case of such treatment.[1] Taking these two claims as my starting point, I develop a notion of *dehumanization* in the aforementioned sense
that can be employed to ground feminist ethical and political claims. That
is, having accepted that rape is a paradigm damaging kind of treatment, let's
examine what are the key features that make it damaging, and then use the
insights gained to develop a general account of dehumanization as a property
or feature of acts and ways of treating people. My proposal does not require
cashing out *human being* as an evaluative ethical concept, and yet it can do
the required normative work: the definition of *dehumanization* proposed can
be used to single out treatments that are damaging to women (as well as to
men and trans* people), and to frame positive responses to such treatments.[2]

A word of warning regarding the subsequent discussion is in order. Given
my commitment to nonideal theorizing, I will base my discussion on actual
examples of rape. Some forthcoming descriptions are rather vivid and graphic;
thus, I am issuing a trigger warning. The examples are not gratuitous descriptions of violence, though, but serve important argumentative purposes: they
enable our theory of injustice to stay grounded in actual (albeit disturbing)
instances of injustices. Moreover, they demonstrate something important
about philosophical methodology. In short, extant armchair philosophical
discussions of rape are insufficient and fail to pass muster once we take actual
instances of sexualized violence seriously.

6.2. Why Humanism

The earlier chapters argued for giving up the gender controversy. Clearly
this does not yet fully motivate humanist feminism. Why then endorse my

---

[1] A brief clarification is in order: for me, rape is about nonconsensual sex. This does not mean
that we can determine for every alleged case whether rape has definitively taken place. After all,
there are many difficult questions about how to define *nonconsensual* and *sex*. These difficulties will
be put to one side for now since nothing hangs on them for my purposes. My point is that every case
of nonconsensual sex is rape, although there may be disagreements about whether some cases are
nonconsensual or sex. Further, the cases that I will be looking at shortly are clear cases of nonconsensual sex (for views that take 'rape' to be a vague term or an essentially contested notion, see Burgess-
Jackson 1995 and Reitan 2001). I should also note that although the cases I will be shortly examining
are attacks perpetrated by men against women, I take *rape* to be an essentially gender-neutral notion.

[2] Recall that dehumanization for me is not about an assault to "our" human dignity or value as
Kantian ends in ourselves (cf. section 1.3). And so since on my account dehumanization is a characteristic of *acts* and ways of *treating* others, it is not about forces that render individuals *dehumanized*.
Dehumanization is not about objectification or treating someone as a mere means in a Kantian
sense that reduces the individual to some subhuman state. This is because instances of contemporary social injustices work via setbacks to interest of *human* agents. Hence, in order for human
interests to be violable, it is a necessary precondition to acknowledge these interests as being those
of *someone* (not of something). Thus, I hold that we should not understand dehumanization as being
about reducing someone to something.

proposed paradigm shift toward such a conception? That women should not be treated in dehumanizing ways hopefully strikes most of us as obvious. Nevertheless, arguing for humanism in feminist philosophy is contentious. Appeals to humanity have tended to exclude members of marginalized groups as well as to mask their particular needs and interests in an assimilationist fashion. Consider the exclusion claim first. As Antony puts it, feminist philosophers have often viewed appeals to humanity or "human nature" when framing ethical and political visions as "conceptually bankrupt" and "inevitably pernicious" (1998, 67). This is because eminent philosophers like Aristotle, Rousseau, and Kant seemed either to exclude women or to take them to be deficient exemplars of humanity, while advocating equality among all members of humanity. Moreover, social roles and gendered behaviors have all too often been explained and justified by appeal to our supposed "human natures." In order to avoid such dubious aspects of humanism, feminist political and ethical claims are more commonly founded on the social concepts of *gender* and *woman*. However, as I argued in Part I, this gender paradigm is far from theoretically costless in having generated apparently intractable semantic and ontological puzzles. Providing definitions of *gender* and *woman* that everyone can agree on, that are in some sense social, and that can be employed to justify positive feminist visions is not possible, in my view. The problems encountered and discussed in chapters 2–4 are parallel to the problems Antony takes Nussbaum's internalist definition of *human being* to face. Certain social norms and values are built into the definitions of *gender* and *woman*; but feminists disagree among themselves about which values and norms should do the work. The various definitions, then, will persuade only those who antecedently agree on what the relevant and important values and norms are and should be; there are no independently obtaining states of affairs to settle the matter. Given that the gender controversy is so intractable, I submit, feminists would do well to change the terms of the debate. Thus, my plea for the proposed shift from the gender paradigm in feminism to a humanist paradigm: this will avoid current theoretical pitfalls and prevent feminist discussions from getting bogged down by unnecessary conceptual problems about the proper understanding of *woman*.

Avoiding conceptual problems is not the only consideration that motivates my humanism, though. As briefly introduced in section 1.3, it is familiar feminist terrain to claim that patriarchy damages women, and it is not unusual to find this damage described as disadvantaging women *as women*. In very general terms, feminism is committed to "bringing about social change to end injustice against women, in particular, injustice against women as women" (Haslanger, Tuana, and O'Connor 2015). More specifically, Rubin held that women are oppressed *as* women and by having *to be* women (1975, 204). And Haslanger claims that women are oppressed as women (for instance) by cultural representations of women as sex objects in context C at time t iff being a woman in *C* at *t* "nonaccidentally correlates with being subjected to systematic violence, and cultural representations of women as sex objects creates, perpetuates, or reinforces the systematic violence" (2004, 112). Moreover, Frye holds that gender oppression is about being a member of women's social kind: "Women are oppressed, *as women*" (1983, 16). For her, "The forces which make us mark and announce sex are among the forces which constitute the oppression of women, and they are central and essential to the maintenance of that system" (Frye 1983, 33). Sexism and patriarchy do not merely accidentally and contingently make women unhappy; they systematically target women and prevent them from being able to lead certain kinds of lives.

This usual view that patriarchy damages women as women is ambiguous and affords two readings. One is about social explanations: my being a woman is part of the explanation for why I suffer (say) systematic violence due to cultural representations of women as sex objects. The other is more constitutive and justificatory: patriarchy targets women because they are women, and this crucially *renders* some instances of oppression sexist instances. I suffer because of patriarchy since instances of sexist oppression track something about me (my gender), and so they damage me accordingly qua woman. Qua man, one is not damaged by patriarchy (though, of course, some other form of oppressive damage might—say—in virtue of one's race). So the first is more about what causes patriarchal damage; the second is about what (at least partly) constitutes such damage. These two readings are often not carefully distinguished. And my contention is that this lends itself to potentially misleading descriptions about the damage done by patriarchy. If by the locution "women are oppressed as women" we have the first explanatory sense in mind, I have no objection to it. But the second reading is trickier. Since patriarchy tracks something about me (my being a woman), its damage seems also to be to me qua woman. After all, patriarchy does not damage men qua men. So the constitutive reading of the locution "damage to women qua women" suggests that patriarchy's damage turns on damaging women as particular kinds of *gendered* beings. For instance, the idea that patriarchy damages women first and foremost as gendered beings appears (at least implicitly) to underlie feminist separatism. Radical feminism does not contend that being a woman is merely something that explains oppression; rather, it is committed to something stronger than this—that it is *as women* that we are damaged by sexism. Or to put the point differently: it may be that patriarchal damage is enacted via withholding from me certain rights and privileged that I am qua human entitled to. But in so doing, the treatment is an affront to a crucial aspect of my social identity: namely, to me qua a certain kind of gendered being.

Taking gendered social injustices to damage women qua gendered beings, in my view, gets the normative underpinnings of sexism and patriarchy wrong. It bypasses what I take to be the main issue: that when women are treated in disadvantaging and damaging ways, they are (as Antony puts it) "treated in ways that prevent or impede the full development of their *human* capacities" (1998, 85). The damage done by patriarchy is not to women qua gendered beings, but to women qua human beings. Clearly feminist philosophers do not typically reject the view that women qua human beings are damaged by patriarchy. But they often too quickly note that patriarchy damages "women as women" without sufficiently elucidating the thought.

There is a further sense in which the talk of "damage to women as women" lends itself to unhelpful interpretations. As I see it, there is a crucial distinction between damage as *harm* and as *wrong*. But the haphazard talk of patriarchy damaging women unhelpfully runs harm and wrong together by running together the explanatory and constitutive readings of "qua woman" claims. It is not unusual to find in the literature indiscriminate talk about patriarchy harming and wronging women. However, this is insufficiently precise. There are specific harms that women suffer because of patriarchy, such as certain patterns of sexualized violence. Being a woman is clearly a relevant aspect in our explanatory accounts of these patterns (what motivates the violence, which forces perpetuate it, what strategies of resistance could end it). The talk of patriarchy's harms then fits the explanatory "qua women" talk.

But wronging is a *different* phenomenon. Not all harms that we suffer are wrongs; for instance, if my computer breaks down without me having properly backed up my academic work, my carelessness is clearly harmful to me (I have lost some work)—but this does not wrong me. So I have not been wronged, although I have been harmed. And even though being harmed may be an indicator (even a good one) that I have been wronged, it does not yet elucidate how and on what grounds I have been wronged. Hence, patterns of sexualized violence harm differently "gendered" individuals differently. It harms those designated as women by levying on them extra burdens and costs generated by efforts to avoid such violence (among other things). These harms are not ones that those designated as men face. Oppressive social patterns then harm women, men, trans*, and intersexed individuals differently (for example) by imposing differential burdens and costs that depend on our "gendered" identities. But, I submit, oppression wrongs everyone qua human alike. For example, sexualized violence like rape (of which I will have more to say shortly) wrongs everyone qua human beings, although individuals are differently harmed by such violence qua women, men, trans*, and intersex. Hence, I hold the following: "damage to women as women" in the explanatory sense pertains to patriarchal harms that women face; in the constitutive sense this expression is about what the wrong of patriarchy consists in.

Appreciating this point is helpful in feminist analyses of social injustice because it enables us to articulate not only the harm, but also the wrong, of injustice. After all, these are not equivalent, but analyzing both is crucial for emancipatory feminist efforts: they both play a central role in hampering women's lives, but in different ways. Even though feminist philosophical work on gender-based oppression, domination, and discrimination is laudable in many ways, the distinction I am highlighting here is not always appreciated or spelled out as carefully as it should be. What precisely is wrongful about gender injustice is often left implicit or articulated in unclear ways, and harms are sometimes conflated with wrongs in an unhelpful manner. Now, in order to elucidate the wrong of patriarchy, we need a normative theory. The position developed in subsequent chapters—my theory of injustice—offers precisely that: it elucidates the nature of sexist/patriarchal social injustices by focusing on dehumanization as that which undergirds the wrong of these social injustices. In so doing, my humanist feminism, I believe, better captures the damage done by patriarchy, where damage is understood as both harm and wrong. This (I submit) further motivates the view that our normative focus ought not to be on gender concepts. A thin understanding of the term 'woman' is needed as an analytical tool in feminist social explanations of injustice's harms. But dehumanization, not gender, supports core feminist normative claims and demands.

The above may suggest that my proposal falls prey to assimilationist problems forcefully argued against by Young. It is important to clarify how my view differs from assimilationist positions that also appeal to humanism. Young describes humanist feminism of the past as being analogous to an ideal of assimilation "in identifying sexual equality with gender blindness, with measuring women and men according to the same standards and treating them in the same way" (1990, 161). This sort of view supposedly posits an ideal of shared humanity that does not acknowledge group differences and thus ends up perpetuating "cultural imperialism by allowing norms expressing the point of view and experience of privileged groups to appear neutral and universal" (Young 1990, 165). Such a move problematically creates a picture of supposedly neutral and universal humanity that is nonsituated and insensitive to difference. My proposal certainly does not intend to reproduce an assimilationist ideal, and I think that it does not. First, the kind of humanity Young has in mind is understood in an internalist manner. But with my externalist conception I avoid thick ethical judgments that would threaten difference and situatedness. Second, my humanism is not "gender/race blind" in the manner Young outlines. This point is somewhat tricky: in a sense, I am advocating a single standard to measure the treatments of women, men, trans*, and intersexes from all racialized groups alike—that of dehumanization. But, as will become clear shortly, this standard can accommodate difference because it is realizable in multiple ways. So I am not advocating a single and strictly speaking identical standard. Further, as I will clarify in chapters 7–9, my proposal does not have the upshot that men and women ought to be treated in an identical manner. This is because my understanding of dehumanization aims to identify and elucidate illegitimate ways of treating others, where such judgments can only be made context sensitively. So, since dehumanizing treatments will differ from one case to the next, the requisite responses will differ too. My humanist feminism might best be characterized as neohumanist insofar as it aims to avoid the pitfalls of earlier humanist projects in feminism that did succumb to the assimilationist ideal. Nonetheless, as I see it, the humanist view argued for here is perfectly compatible with (what Young [1990, chap. 6] calls) the politics of difference.

6.3. Rape as Dehumanizing

My argumentative strategy involves starting with two claims, which I take to have prima facie plausibility. First, I understand *human being* in broadly externalist terms as a concept that picks out the biological kind of human beings, as we ordinarily think of this kind. Second, I take rape to be a paradigm case of treatment that damages those who fall under this everyday concept. Not everyone agrees with this latter point: for instance, Baber (2002) argues that certain jobs are more harmful than rape. Rape is just an episodic harming of the victim, whereas especially bad and low-paid work that women are forced to undertake poses long-term harm. It is certainly true that sexualized violence is not experienced in the same way by all survivors and that attacks differ in the harms they cause, given their brutality, for instance. But I take it that rape per se is dehumanizing because of its underlying damage qua wrong, even though the individual harms suffered and the survivors' experiences vary. Interestingly, what grounds my claim is precisely what grounds Baber's claim too (namely, an appeal to certain welfare interests articulated by Joel Feinberg). Later on, I will argue that Baber is wrong about rape being merely an episodic harming. Prior to that, however, I will cash out what makes rape dehumanizing by focusing on two arguments that provide the most worked-out accounts of its wrongfulness: the "objectification argument" of John Gardner and Stephen Shute (2000), and the "soul murder argument" of David Archard (2007). I think that Archard's argument captures more accurately and plausibly what makes rape morally wrongful and dehumanizing; ultimately I will develop my general account of dehumanization by drawing on Archard. But, first, what is lacking in Gardner and Shute's account?

6.3.1. THE OBJECTIFICATION ARGUMENT

Gardner and Shute argue that what is wrongful about rape is that the perpetrator *objectifies* the victim by treating the latter as a mere thing or instrument to be used. Qua persons we have a certain worth due to which "to use people without at the same time respecting this [worth] involves treating them as something other than people. It means treating them as things" (Gardner and Shute 2000, 203–204). This is the familiar Kantian picture: one should treat others, not as mere means to one's ends, but as ends in themselves. And rape violates this by objectifying the victim. Drawing on Nussbaum's (1995c) discussion of objectification, the authors hold that the rapist is objectifying the victim by instrumentalizing them: they are treating a person as a *mere* tool or instrument for the rapist's own end. In being the "sheer use" of a subject, rape denies someone personhood, and this makes it "literally dehumanizing" (Gardner and Shute 2000, 205). However, I submit, this view leaves something to be desired: first, many instances fail to fit this model of dehumanization, and yet we think of them as dehumanizing; second, I am unconvinced that rape necessarily involves instrumentalization as understood by Gardner and Shute.

Let's start with my former point. Gardner and Shute take rape to be dehumanizing because it is the sheer instrumental use of a person. They do not clearly say that it involves the sheer instrumental use of a person for some *sexual* ends. But they must hold this view—otherwise they cannot distinguish the wrongfulness of rape from the wrongfulness of other merely instrumental uses of persons, which is something Gardner and Shute clearly aim to do. They hold that although rape usually involves some physical, psychological, and/or emotional harm, it need not—these are merely epiphenomenal to rape. So Gardner and Shute present the following example:

> It is possible, although unusual, for a rapist to do no harm. A victim may be forever oblivious to the fact that she was raped, if, say, she was drugged or drunk to the point of unconsciousness when the rape was committed, and the rapist wore a condom . . . [W]e have a victim of rape whose life is not changed for the worse, or at all, by the rape. She does not . . . "feel violated." She has no feelings about the incident, since she knows nothing of it [and] . . . the incident never comes to light at all. (2000, 196)

This example supposedly homes in on the core wrong of rape: objectification understood as instrumentalization. Following Gardner and Shute, rape's wrongfulness consists in the perpetrator treating another as a mere instrument for their end.

Now, compare the above example to the following case.[3] Imagine an identical situation where the perpetrator makes sheer use of another for some other end; for instance, one is drugged and mouth swabbed so that one's DNA can be extracted for scientific research, when (for some reason) the person would not have consented to its extraction. This is done in a way that leaves no physical markers, and the person is forever oblivious to what has happened. They have been used as a sheer instrument. So in this respect the mouth swab

---

[3] The example is my variant of Archard's (2008) nonconsensual mouth swab example.

case is on a par with the above example of rape, and the two are morally indistinguishable. But Gardner and Shute should not want this result: they are explicitly aiming to cash out what is *specifically* wrongful about rape that sets it morally apart from other heinous crimes. The way to distinguish the two cases is in terms of their ends: in the mouth swab, the end is to extract DNA; in the rape case, it is "sexual pleasure" (Gardner and Shute 2000, 204). So Gardner and Shute must say that the wrongfulness of rape consists in it being a sheer use of a person for some *sexual* ends. Any old sheer use will not do.

With this qualification, their picture of the rapist becomes that of Rae Langton's sexual solipsist. The sheer sexual use of a person dehumanizes them; it turns human beings into things. For Langton, this kind of sexual solipsist fails to see that in sexual contexts women are not things: they treat women as "mere bodies, as merely sensory appearances, as not free, as items that can be possessed, as items whose value is merely instrumental" (1995, 153). And what instrumentalizes the victim in this way is the solipsist's sexual desire toward the object of their desire due to which they display some objectifying attitudes—namely, they view a person as thing-like (Langton 1995, 165). The rapist on this picture treats another person as a sex *object* to be used merely as a tool for their sexual ends and gratification.

However, the objectification argument subsequently fails to capture the wrong of rape: the criterion of wrongfulness will leave out some important cases, which we pretheoretically think of as dehumanizing and morally wrongful. In order to see this, consider the practice of rape used as a weapon of war, or martial rape. At the time of writing this book, aid agencies and human rights organizations consider the Democratic Republic of Congo (DRC) to be the epicenter of wartime sexual violence against women. In the DRC, the rape of civilians by combatants is a systematic practice and used as part of fighting a war "for a variety of purposes, including intimidation, humiliation, political terror, extracting information, rewarding soldiers, and 'ethnic cleansing'" (Amnesty International 2005, 1). Rapes are part and parcel of general attacks on communities where soldiers and other combatants also kill or injure civilians and destroy their property.[4] Rape is used "to terrorize communities into accepting [the combatants'/soldiers'] control or to punish them for real or supposed aid to opposing forces" (Human Rights Watch 2002). As a practice, it aims to "win and maintain control over civilians and [their] territory," particularly by terrorizing and humiliating women, who in this cultural context are seen as the representatives of their communities (2002). For instance, women and children are often attacked in public in front of their husbands and parents.

---

[4] I will talk of "combatants" and "soldiers" without distinguishing which soldiers or combatants I have in mind. This is because the political situation in the DRC is hugely complex, with many different factions fighting one another. Actually, this makes no difference since all sides have been reported to practice martial rape.

Relative to the DRC context, perpetrators do not appear primarily to use their victims for sexual ends but for fighting a war. The independent web initiative *Women Under Siege Blog* (http://www.womenundersiegeproject.org/) documents the use of rape and sexualized violence as weapons of war. It provides a detailed and comprehensive account of the recent situation in the DRC as well as of the apparent ends for which women and children are subject to sexualized violence. These include the already mentioned ends: humiliation, control of people and natural resources, retaliation (women whose husbands are community leaders or supporters of rival militia are often raped in retaliation). The *Women Under Siege Blog* lists other ends too:

- Soldiers' protection: some combatants believe that raping a woman fortifies them for battle, and so they must rape in order to "beat the enemy."
- Termination of pregnancies: some evidence suggests that pregnant women are targeted for rape in order to induce miscarriages.
- Avoidance of violence from superiors: combatants are reported to suffer severe beatings from their superiors if they refuse to attack women. Some combatants admit perpetrating sexualized violence in order to avoid violence themselves.

The point I wish to make is this. The perpetrators of martial rape use other persons as means to their ends for sure; but given the purposes for which the practice is used, their ends do not appear to be primarily sexual. So the martial rapist simply does not fit Langton's picture of the sexual solipsist, to which Gardner and Shute's account is wedded. The objectification argument holds that rape dehumanizes because the perpetrator uses another for sheer sexual ends. But this does not capture what is dehumanizing about martial rape: the martial rapist instrumentalizes another, *not* for sexual ends, but for ends that have to do with warfare. The distinction between sexual and sexualized ends clarifies this point. The former include ends that are directly to do with sex, like sexual gratification. However, the latter involves instrumentalization for some (nonsexual) ends by sexual *means*. To a large extent, this seems to be the case in the DRC: violent sexual means are used to achieve ends that are to do with warfare. However, in relying on the view that rape is about instrumentalization for sexual ends, the objectification argument fails to account for the wrong of martial rape. So even if the sheer use of persons for sexual ends is dehumanizing, *this* is not what makes martial rape dehumanizing.[5]

Moreover, rape does not necessarily involve instrumentalization as understood by Gardner and Shute: the *kind* of instrumentalization involved

---

[5] The so-called corrective rapes also ill fit the objectification argument. In such cases, nonheterosexual females are raped in order to "cure" them of homosexuality. Again, the end is not sexual gratification but to induce heterosexuality by using sexual means.

does not obviously involve treating persons *literally* as things. Again, looking at the harrowing situation in the DRC is instructive. Women in the conflict areas are sexually violated (among other reasons) because they are seen as the representatives of their communities and the facilitators of the communities' continuation. Given this, and the broader goals of the practice, martial rapists do not appear to view the affected women as thing-like. They are viewed as persons with goals, life plans, and a desire for well-being; martial rape as a practice is aimed at precisely thwarting these aspects of women's lives, thereby destroying whole communities and making it extremely hard for people to rebuild them. The victims of the practice are not treated as inert things simply to be destroyed, like dwellings. Actually, martial rapists are more akin to sadistic rapists, who want their victims to fight back and thereby affirm that they are subjects rather than inert things. A kind of autonomy affirmation is a necessary feature of sadistic rape (cf. Langton 2009). In the above examples, women's personhood is affirmed insofar as their social roles as community representatives are recognized; and this is a necessary prerequisite for violating their personhood. Otherwise the practice of wartime rape would not be such an effective weapon. The situation is akin to David Sussman's discussion of Abu Ghraib–like torture. A person becomes an accomplice in their own violation in that the torture "involves not just the insults and injuries to be found in other kinds of violence, but a wrong that, by exploiting the victim's own participation, might best be called humiliation" (Sussman 2005, 30). Inert objects cannot partake in their own violation; only persons or subjects with agency can. So the kind of mere use in martial rape that violates others presupposes that the affected subjects are persons with life plans and particular social roles. And the wrong committed by the rapist is precisely aimed at exploiting *that* in order to violate the affected persons.

Considerations like these, then, suggest to me that the sort of dehumanization relevant for understanding social injustice is not one where someone is literally treated as something. So, in this sense, injustice does not trade on literally dehumanizing those individuals subject to it. Rather, since the affirmation of autonomy or humanity is a necessary prerequisite for the kind of violation at issue, understanding dehumanization in a more traditionally Kantian sense is misguided. I may be treated in dehumanizing ways, which underpins the violation that I face; but this does not turn on others taking me as some*thing* as opposed to some*one* in the manner that Gardner and Shute hold.

6.3.2. THE "SOUL MURDER" ARGUMENT

A more plausible account of what makes rape dehumanizing is put forward by David Archard, who takes rape to be wrongful in being "an indefensible harming of a legitimate interest in safeguarding what is central to our personhood" (2007, 390). Let's unpack this claim. Archard distinguishes an act's hurtfulness, harmfulness, and wrongfulness: "hurt" denotes the pain, discomfort, and displeasure of the act; "harm" the setback to one's interests; and "wrong" the indefensible (inexcusable and unjustifiable) setback to one's interests (Archard 2007, 378). Archard further maintains that hurtfulness and harmfulness may be evidence of rape's wrongfulness, but not constitutive of it. In order to see this, we must distinguish core and aggravating harms. The former are those done by *any* act of rape; the latter are harms additional to the particular instances (like violence, brutality, the circumstances of the attack, or features of the survivor's society). Rape's aggravating harms compound the core harm. Still, for Archard, "the essential wrong of any instance of rape is the set of indefensible core direct harms it causes" (2007, 382).

Since wrongfulness is defined as a setback to one's interests, we must identify which interests rape indefensibly sets back. Archard outlines two models for understanding interests: network and spatial models. Joel Feinberg (1984) discusses the former: all persons have some ultimate goals and aspirations, and certain welfare interests are general (often indispensable) means to advance such ulterior goals and aspirations. These are the basic requisites for well-being, and minimally include

> continuance for a foreseeable interval of one's life, and the interests in one's own physical health and vigor, the integrity and normal functioning of one's body, the absence of absorbing pain and suffering or grotesque disfigurement, minimal intellectual acuity, emotional stability, the absence of groundless anxieties and resentments, the capacity to engage normally in social intercourse and to enjoy and maintain friendships, at least minimal income and financial security, a tolerable social and physical environment, a certain amount of freedom from interference and coercion. (Feinberg 1984, 37)

The above make up a whole network of interests, which are components of personal well-being. By contrast, Archard endorses the spatial model that takes interests "to occupy a space which helps to define the self or personhood, and the most important interests are those that are closest to, are at the core of, a person or the self" (2007, 387)—the most important interests are those that define *who we are*. Archard takes rape to violate these latter interests, a view that he claims fits some survivors' descriptions of their attacks as "soul murder" and the ultimate violation of the self. The interests that are at the core of the self have to do with sexuality. For Archard, then, if sexuality is one interest that defines who and what we are, it is at the very core of our selfhood. Thus, rape is dehumanizing in that it violates the self because "rape attacks and damages something crucial to our being and personhood" (Archard 2007, 388).[6]

Archard's view draws on Shafer and Frye, who take there to be a person-defining domain that is "the physical, emotional, psychological and intellectual space [the person] lives in" (1981, 338). For them, in failing to respect the victim's autonomous power to consent, rape intrudes on and attacks this person-defining domain, thus coming very close to "treading upon the person itself" (Shafer and Frye 1981, 338). Archard takes rape to disrespect something at the very center of this domain: the sexually embodied self. This, in Jean Hampton's terms, amounts to a moral injury. The setback to one's interest in sexual integrity is a moral injury in that it damages "the realization and acknowledgement of the victim's value," where "value" is understood as the worth we have as Kantian ends in ourselves (Hampton 1999, 123). Although neither Archard nor Hampton employs this terminology, I find it useful to denote this damage as lack of recognition respect: such respect involves weighing appropriately "in one's deliberations some feature of the thing in question and [acting] accordingly" (Darwall 1977, 38). Recognition respect tracks some fact that "one ought to take into account in deliberation" (1977, 40). So a failure of recognition respect involves a failure to give appropriate consideration to some salient fact about a thing in one's deliberation and conduct; and this underpins rape's moral injury for me. The motivation for understanding the moral injury claim in this manner is to avoid relying on Hampton's Kantian conception of humanity (on which Archard also relies). After all, and this will become clearer later on, what is doing the work for me is that certain *facts* about people are not taken into account, where these facts can be accounted for using the thin externalist conception of humanity.

I find much in Archard's position deeply appealing. However, my contention is that violations of Feinberg's network interests may also violate the self in the manner Archard holds. And so, relegating network interest violations to mere aggravating harms of rape may lose sight of something deeply important. Archard can, of course, accept that network interest violations worsen some individual instances of rape. Nonetheless, the wrong of rape is constituted by the indefensible core harm (the violation of one's interest in sexual integrity), and this makes rape a violation of the self for Archard. Still, as I see it, rape can violate the self in other ways too. Again, consider the situation

---

[6] Archard's key claim is conditional: if sexual integrity is a core interest defining who we are, rape indefensibly violates it. But why should we think that the antecedent is true? Archard holds (and I agree) that nothing particularly contentious is being claimed here. It seems uncontroversial that humans are sexed beings. But this does not mean that we are beings who value having sex or even exercise our sexuality. It just means that we are beings who value sexual *integrity*. Even those who choose not to have sex, value the fact that they are able to so decide—sexual autonomy is an important human good, which nonconsensual sex clearly hampers.

in the DRC. The practice of martial rape undoubtedly sets back the affected women's interest in sexual integrity. But given the ways in which attacks in the DRC are conducted, along with the social beliefs and cultural taboos surrounding it, victims come to suffer indefensible setbacks to crucial welfare interests in ways that can also amount to violations of the self. That is, martial rape can violate certain welfare interests in ways that result in a damage to something "crucial to our being and personhood" (Archard 2007, 388) because these violations are so severe as to prevent the affected women and children from achieving future personal well-being in a meaningful sense. And, as Feinberg puts it, "Without [such] fulfilment, the person is lost" (1984, 37). So martial rape violates our legitimate interest in sexual integrity; but it *also* indefensibly sets back other interests in ways that constitute violations of the self.

How can setbacks to one's welfare interests constitute such a violation? Martial rape in the DRC sets back nearly every interest in Feinberg's list of network interests. (The reader should be warned that the following contains some distressing descriptions of the situation in the DRC.) For a start, rape carries a huge social stigma, and female victims are often ostracized from their communities as well as rejected by their families and husbands. This is particularly problematic since many women become pregnant following their attacks and come subsequently to suffer severe economic hardship. A Congolese woman recounts how, after her attack, "[my husband] left me alone with my eight children and two of them have died since because of starvation. I have lost a lot of weight. I am suffering from insomnia and I don't have any strength to look after my children" (Médecins Sans Frontières 2004, 28). According to another Congolese woman, "When I ask my husband to give me some food he replies to me, why don't you go and ask for food to your husband in the forest," referring to the man who raped her (2004, 31). Further, many women are attacked while working on the fields, where such work is for them "the only way of ensuring that they can feed their children" (2004, 31). Knowing the risks of getting attacked deters women from undertaking such work, and this compounds their dreadful economic situation. Those trying to avoid these economic consequences are forced to work under constant fear, which hampers psychological well-being.

The affected women in the DRC also tend to suffer profound health problems. Sixty percent of the soldiers and combatants are estimated to carry HIV. Given the prevalence of rape in the region and the fact that perpetrators are reported not to use condoms, the long-term effects are feared to be extremely bad.[7] Attacks are also reported to be particularly brutal, leaving their victims

---

[7] According to the UN, forty-five hundred rapes were reported in *one* eastern province of the DRC during the first six months of 2007. This figure, however, is believed to represent only a fraction of the actual number of rapes taking place: because of cultural stigmas and the impunity with

with long-term, even permanent physical problems. For instance, many survivors suffer from horrific cases of genital mutilation: women have been shot in the vagina after being attacked; their clitoris and breasts have been cut off; and "many have been so sadistically attacked from the inside out, butchered by bayonets and assaulted with chunks of wood, that their reproductive and digestive systems are beyond repair" (Gettleman 2007). As a Congolese gynecologist and human rights activist, Denis Mukwege, put it: "[The combatants] rape a woman, five or six of them at a time—but that is not enough. Then they shoot a gun into her vagina. . . . In all my years here, I never saw anything like it.. . . [T]o see so many raped, that shocks me, but what shocks me more is the way they are raped" (Nolen 2005). All of this profoundly and completely alters the "future lives, livelihoods and prospects" of the women affected by martial rape in the region (Human Rights Watch 2002).

On Archard's account, one's personhood is violated if one's person-defining domain is attacked in a way that counts as morally injurious. And, I submit, the setbacks to one's welfare interests by martial rape can be so severe as to constitute such violations. That is, for Archard rape violates the person-defining space that (following Shafer and Frye) includes physical, psychological, and emotional dimensions. The DRC cases show that these dimensions are clearly attacked and invaded; this being so, violating the welfare interests of those who are attacked ends up invading the domain definitive of who they are. Martial rapes disrespect something that *is* at the center of our person-defining domain, but that is *other than* our interest in sexual integrity. They disrespect those basic welfare interests, without the fulfillment of which there is no person. Further, martial rape clearly counts as morally injurious in that it involves a failure to grant recognition respect: the martial rapist fails to respect the fact that others' welfare interests will be severely set back, and that they ought not to be violated in a way that prevents the achievement of basic welfare. This being so, I disagree with Archard when he claims that on the network model rape is wrong because "it stops a person from doing what she chooses," but on the spatial model because it "denies that she is, in regard to what is central to her personhood, worthy of respect" (2007, 393). Violations of welfare interests in the cases looked at deny that the attacked women and children are worthy of respect precisely by preventing them from being able to pursue a way of life that facilitates well-being, or to live a life characterized by minimal welfare. Focusing just on how rape sets back one's interest to sexual integrity is too narrow. It is clearly one interest that defines who we are, but not the only one.

---

which rapes take place, many women in the region simply do not report being attacked (BBC News 2007). A more recent 2011 report showed that 12 percent of Congolese women have been raped at least once. The report also estimated that 1,152 women are raped every day, which is about one per minute (Peterman et al. 2011).

We are now in a position to see why Baber's view mentioned earlier (that rape is not as bad as having to endure long-term drudgery at work) is mistaken. Baber also appeals to Feinberg's welfare interests to make her case. For her, the seriousness of harm—either of rape or of work—should be determined relative to the importance of the violated interest within the affected person's network of interests (2002, 252). So the greatest harms are those that affect the individual's most vital interests. With this in mind, Baber claims that although rape is seriously harmful, it is not the greatest harm one can suffer:

> Rape interferes with a person's freedom to pursue his [sic] own projects and is, to that extent, a harm. It does not, however, render a person altogether incapable of pursuing his ulterior interests. Having a certain minimally tolerable amount of liberty is a welfare interest without which a person cannot pursue any further projects. While rape diminishes one's liberty, it does not diminish it to such an extent that the victim is precluded from pursuing other projects which are in his interest. (2002, 254)

Having to endure some chronic (rather than episodic) harmed condition supposedly interferes with one's freedom in a more serious manner. And one such condition is being forced to undertake badly paid, low-status, unsatisfying, unpleasant, dull, routine, tedious, mind-killing, and regimented work that women typically are forced to undertake. The time that women must devote to work like this "prevents them from pursuing any other projects that might be conducive to their well-being" (Baber 2002, 257). And anyone (male or female) who does a good deal of this kind of work is "in a more seriously harmed state than one who is raped" (2002, 257). Although rape deprives its survivors of some degree of freedom, bad jobs chronically deprive a person the minimal amount of freedom required to pursue those interests that are conducive to personal well-being.

I find Baber's case unpersuasive and take the example of martial rape to demonstrate where her account goes wrong. First, it is unclear to me why freedom is the most important interest Baber focuses on. Recall Feinberg's basic requisites for well-being.[8] These interests make up a whole network of interests, which are the components of personal well-being. Now, if the seriousness of harm is determined by "the importance of the interest which is violated within the network of the victim's interests" (Baber 2002, 252), and

---

[8] The continuance of one's life; physical health and vigor; the integrity and normal functioning of one's body; the absence of absorbing pain, suffering, grotesque disfigurement; minimal intellectual acuity, emotional stability and the absence of groundless anxieties; the capacity for normal social intercourse; maintenance of friendships; minimal means of subsistence; a tolerable social and physical environment; a certain amount of freedom from interference and coercion. (Feinberg 1984, 37).

bad work crucially violates one's freedom to pursue one's ultimate aims, then freedom would be one of the most important interests in our network. But it is not obvious to me why this should be the case, and Baber assumes the importance of freedom from the outset. Now, one might account for freedom's importance by appealing to negative and positive liberty. For Feinberg, freedom *from* coercion is one key welfare interest. And so negative freedom in some form is part of our network of interests that facilitates personal well-being. Baber nevertheless talks about the freedom *to* pursue one's own ends, which is positive freedom. This suggests that the important kind of freedom, which marks the ethical distinction between rape and chronic bad work, is precisely the violation of one's positive liberty to pursue one's goals. But, again, more needs to be said to motivate the importance of positive freedom.

In order to provide this motivation, Baber could claim that Feinberg's welfare interests have an implicit positive liberty built into them. And having to undertake time-consuming and unsatisfying jobs violates such positive liberty in a way that rape does not; therefore, the former is a greater harm. However, the examples I have offered do precisely what Baber assumes rape does not do because she takes it to be episodic. The situation in the DRC chronically violates the affected women's and children's liberty to pursue their own aims. So the instances of rape violate not only the subjects' negative, but also their positive, freedom by undermining the victim's opportunities to achieve even the most basic minimal requisites for personal well-being. Further, given what we know about post-traumatic stress syndrome, the psychological harms of such widespread sexualized violence are unlikely to be episodic in the sense that Baber assumes. Just as certain bad work can deprive one of important positive freedoms, so can rape, as illustrated by my examples. Of course, I cannot claim that all instances of rape do so and that all instances diminish one's freedom "to such an extent that the victim is precluded from pursuing other projects which are in his interest" (Baber 2002, 254). But then again, I am not convinced that all terrible jobs have this feature either, or that it is prima facie impossible to attain personal well-being in Feinberg's sense while having a tedious job. The upshot is this: both Baber and I take Feinberg's welfare interests to be key to elucidating rape's wrongfulness. However, I take my example case of DRC martial rape to demonstrate that Baber's episodic understanding of rape's harmfulness is in need of revision.

6.4. Dehumanization in General

Rape on Archard's account is wrong in that it is (a) an indefensible setback to certain interests (b) where these interests are spatial (not network) ones and (c) the setback constitutes a moral injury. Above I argued against (b): my contention is that rape can set back both spatial and network interests in a way that threatens the self. However, there is something valuable about (a) and (c) that I wish to retain. Drawing on this, I propose a general definition of *dehumanization* that can be used as a humanist feminist tool when discerning which modes of treating women (qua human beings) are inappropriate and why.

> An act or a treatment is dehumanizing if and only if it is an indefensible setback to some of our legitimate human interests, where this setback constitutes a moral injury.

Let's unpack this claim.

6.4.1. OUR LEGITIMATE INTERESTS

Dehumanizing acts indefensibly set back some of *our* interests. But who are we? I have in mind here the everyday kind of anatomically modern humans outlined at the beginning of this chapter. For me, the relevant kind falls under the externalist conception of *human being*, and its members are *homo sapiens sapiens*, "featherless bipeds" who typically develop certain cognitive capacities given the appropriate background environmental conditions. Relying on this sort of thin externalist account has theoretical benefits that are acknowledged even by Antony, who rejects the view that *human being* can be defined in a manner that grounds humanist feminism. She writes that although externalism is not able to undergird a sufficiently thick normative account of humanity needed for feminism, it can nonetheless

> tell us two kinds of things that will be relevant to ethical thinking: the first is that we can indeed expect lots and lots of similarity among human beings [picked out on purely biological criteria]. . . . Second . . . given the way our embodiment works, we are extremely apt to have a variety of fundamental wants and needs in common. (2000, 35)

Antony's claims strike me as uncontroversially true. Thus, by and large those picked out by the term 'human being' understood in an externalist sense— one that takes into account general human embodiment—share Feinberg's network interests. Externalism provides the foundation for thinking about the legitimate human interests set back by dehumanizing acts: it tells us something about their content and shared nature.[9]

---

[9] Jean Hampton claims that a successful feminist contractarianism includes two crucial normative aspects central for emancipation: a conception of human worth and an account of legitimate human interests. Hampton frames our legitimate interests relative to an Aristotelian idea of flourishing: "Human beings' unique and considerable value requires that they be properly cared for" (2002, 355). This involves detailing "who we are and what interests of ours are urgent given our nature. These interests would include not only having enough to eat but also having the psychological conditions that allow us to function well and the liberty that, as autonomous beings, we need"

With the above in mind, my proposal will focus on interests central to our basic well-being. However, these can be network or spatial interests, and violations of both can violate the self (as I argued above). In fact, I will simply talk of "welfare interests" henceforth, as I take the distinction between network and spatial interests not to be that helpful. Being able to set one's own life plan (following Archard) appears to be a spatial interest: being able to do so plausibly helps define who we are. But being able to devise one's own life plan is also a network interest: many other interests and goals are hampered if this interest is curtailed. So if women are treated in ways that prevent them from being able to set their own life plans, perhaps by denying them access to education, this would damage a whole network of interests that are necessary means for achieving other goals. Furthermore, it would also conceivably have profound effects on people's self-conceptions. Being "the author of one's own destiny," then, can function as both a spatial and a network interest, and this renders the division unhelpful. Subsequently, the legitimate interests that dehumanizing acts violate are (in my view) better captured as welfare interests that help define who we are and that foster the achievement of other interests.

Some important interjections should be made. First, I do not take *well-being* to be equivalent to *human flourishing*, but rather something prior to it. Well-being figures in the building blocks of a tolerable human life and is a factor that enables subsequent human flourishing. Whether individual lives are characterized by flourishing depends on a different set of considerations, though. I will have more to say about this later. For now, it is important to bear in mind that flourishing is not well-being in my sense. Second, it is vital to stress that interest violations on my account must be *indefensible*: they must be inexcusable or unjustifiable. The setback may (for instance) be unjustifiable on epistemic grounds: it may be founded on some false or unjustified beliefs, as when particular courses of action are justified by false beliefs about women's "nature." Or the setback may be inexcusable in causing or foreseeably causing certain harms: for instance, systematic and arbitrary police brutality against members of certain racialized groups sets back their interests in indefensible ways by conceivably causing physical and psychological harms. The point to note is that not all setbacks to our welfare interests are indefensible. In an unprejudiced employment competition, my interest in financial

---

(Hampton 2002, 355). On the face of it, Hampton's proposal is akin to mine. We both start with the idea of shared humanity, which provides the foundation for discerning our legitimate human interests that ought to be protected. However, Hampton elucidates both our shared humanity and the relevant interests in much more normatively loaded spirit than I do. For her, we would start from an internalist conception of humanity. Subsequently, our legitimate interests would figure in an Aristotelian project that involves explicating what is good for us as humans. So both our shared humanity and the relevant interests are elucidated in deeply normative terms, which makes Hampton's proposal more akin to Nussbaum's. Mine differs precisely in its appeal to an externalist conception of humanity as the foundation of our legitimate interests.

security may be set back if I fail to get the job. If this is because the chosen candidate is genuinely better qualified, my legitimate interests have not been *unjustifiably* set back. And so this treatment would not count as dehumanizing on my definition.

Third, given the theoretical goals driving my work and my focus on the normative grounds of social injustice, the unjustifiability of setbacks will in the end partly be a function of structural conditions. I will have more to say about this in the chapters to come. But to anticipate: if my interest in living in a tolerable social environment is hampered by systematic police brutality toward my racialized social kind, this interest violation is indefensible (in being inexcusable) not only because of the physical and psychological harms caused, but also because the brutality is an expression of institutionalized racial prejudice. This captures a crucial structural and systemic aspect of the proposed notion of *dehumanization*: setbacks to individuals' interests are indefensible not merely because of unjustified beliefs others may hold and harms that individuals subsequently suffer, but also because of wider and more diffuse social prejudices and structural arrangements sustaining those beliefs and harms. Bearing this in mind also helps to highlight that there is a difference between morally wrongful conduct per se and dehumanization: my suggestion is not meant to account for moral wrongfulness as such, and there are many ways in which actions may be morally wrong. I am aiming to elucidate one particular kind of wrongfulness, namely that found at the core of social injustice.[10]

For me, our shared human embodiment has the consequence that those who fall under the externalist conception of *human being* by and large share Feinberg's list of interests. That said, these interests include (for example) "the integrity and normal functioning of one's body" and the absence of "grotesque disfigurement" (Feinberg 1984, 37). Such supposedly shared welfare interests may, and have, come under attack from disability activists and philosophers working on disability issues. Feinberg's list is implicitly (if not, explicitly)

---

[10] One might, nevertheless, worry that in fixing indefensible interest violations, we need to appeal to some prior normative notion: in order to say why the violation is indefensible, we need to know what makes it so—namely, what makes it unjust. And so my argument would be circular: I am trying to elucidate injustice in terms of indefensible interest violations; but in order to fix those violations, I must already presuppose some *thick* moral standards that render them wrongful. My contention is that I do not appeal to such standards. Rather, I make use of the practical and descriptive standards noted above (like the epistemic ones). These elucidate the indefensibility of interest violations without bringing in some thick moral criteria. This, of course, does not make the standards utterly nonevaluative. For instance, false beliefs about women's "nature" tend to draw on social normativity (e.g., what is expected of women, what is taken to be their "proper" social role, etc.). Harms stemming from structural prejudices also trade on social normativity: for instance, arbitrary police brutality against one's racialized group resulting in physical harms is an expression of institutionalized prejudice. And it is the harms coupled with institutionalized prejudice that renders brutality inexcusable. Escaping all evaluative and normative judgments would be simply impossible; but relying on some prior normative (social or theoretical) commitments is not equivalent to relying on some hidden thick moral premise. I will say more about this in chapter 8.

committed to an ableist view that having a nonnormal or "abnormal" bodily functioning impedes well-being. This buys into the idea that nonnormal, abnormal, or "disabled" bodily functionings are defective, imperfect, nonideal, and insufficient in some sense.[11] Appealing to "normal" bodily functioning (whatever that means) as providing one basic requisite for minimal well-being can be reproached on the following grounds: it grossly misunderstands the experiences of people with atypical bodily functioning and helps to maintain the normative connection between ability and normalcy. This further buys into the patronizing idea that atypical, "abnormal" embodiment cannot be combined with personal well-being. Those who endorse social models of disability understand disability in a relational fashion, rather than as a physical or mental impairment of an individual. What renders certain atypical bodily functionings disabling is

> the exclusion of people with certain physical and mental characteristics from major domains of social life. Their exclusion is manifested not only in deliberate segregation, but in a built environment and organized social activity that preclude or restrict the participation of people seen or labelled as having disabilities. (Wasserman et al. 2013)

On this view, well-being is not hampered by one's physical or mental impairments, but by the stigma and discrimination that result from perceived and labeled impairments. A more nuanced account of basic well-being, then, should not appeal to "normal" bodily functioning or the lack of disfigurement, in that (properly understood) something other than physical impairment reduces well-being.

I am sympathetic to the above critiques and take there to be a need to modify some of Feinberg's interests. However, there are at least two difficulties when trying to do so. First, there are no agreed-upon definitions of *disability*, *ability*, or *impairment*. Philosophical disputes about how we do or should understand these notions are alive and well. Second, there are some clear cases of atypical bodily functioning that plainly do hamper personal well-being and even render it unachievable. We can see one such case again in the example of rape in the DRC. Many victims suffer from traumatic fistulas: as a result of violent rape, the vaginal wall between the bladder or rectum is torn, resulting in urine or feces leaking into the vagina. This condition is painful and makes the person easily susceptible to infections. Now, there is an obvious sense in which such a condition impairs the "normal" functioning of the body and hampers well-being. The same is true of violent attacks that render one's reproductive and digestive organs irreparable. So we must be

---

[11] For a good introduction to philosophical engagements with disability, see Wasserman et al. 2013; for feminist philosophical engagements, see Silvers 2012.

able to frame the basic requisites of well-being in a way that is sensitive to the critiques from disability theorists and activists, *but* in a way that enables us to acknowledge some degree of typicality and normalcy, where these notions are not just understood statistically, but also normatively pertaining to how our bodies ought to be. After all, no bodies *should* suffer from debilitating and painful conditions like traumatic fistulas. With this in mind, I suggest replacing Feinberg's "normal functioning of one's body" with two more nuanced welfare interests: first, the interest in being nonstigmatized and excluded because of one's atypical body or bodily functioning; second, the interest in being free from debilitating and painful bodily conditions. This second interest covers the interest to be free from (descriptively and normatively) disabling conditions, like traumatic fistulas. But it can also deal with critiques from a disability perspective insofar as I take common "disabilities" (like impaired vision, hearing, or mobility) not to be necessarily debilitating. Silvers (2012) describes how people can learn to cope with such conditions: for instance, some visually impaired individuals identify "objects in their physical environment by echolocation, having cultivated the skill of making clicking noises with their tongues and identifying the different qualities of sounds bounced back toward them" (Silvers 2012). If one can find new, and actually rather impressive, ways to negotiate and cope with one's environment, atypical bodily functioning does not ipso facto debilitate.

The account of dehumanization I am proposing begins with our shared humanity, understood in an externalist sense. This tells us that we can expect there to be many similarities among human beings and that, given human embodiment, we are likely to have some basic welfare interests in common. For me, these include (at least) the modified list of interests in

- The continuance of one's life, and in one's own physical health and vigor
- The absence of absorbing pain and suffering, being nonstigmatized and excluded because of one's atypical body or bodily functioning, being free from debilitating and painful bodily conditions
- Minimal intellectual acuity, emotional stability, the absence of groundless anxieties and resentments
- The capacity to engage in meaningful social intercourses, to enjoy and maintain friendships
- At least minimal income, financial security, or means of subsistence
- A tolerable social and physical environment, a certain amount of freedom from interference and coercion.[12]

---

[12] Let me briefly pause on a possible objection. Human beings are not the only living creatures to have these sorts of interests. This might suggest that my definition of *humanity* is too broad: it will encompass many living creatures insofar as they also share some of the stated welfare interests. And so our moral community will include many nonhuman animals too. However, this objection rests

Now, one might ask: from which perspective do we judge whether these basic welfare requisites are satisfied? Given the history of disregard for the first-personal stories of poor women and women of color within feminist theorizing, it may seem that we ought to privilege precisely such a first-personal perspective. After all, any adequate account of what normatively grounds emancipatory feminism ought to avoid chauvinism and patronizing attitudes and not treat poor women and women of color as helpless, ignorant, and to be educated by white, cis, middle-class Western women. However, determining well-being from a first-personal perspective encounters notorious worries with adaptive preferences (Khader 2011; Nussbaum 2001). This is the phenomenon of individuals adjusting their preferences and desires relative to the options available to them and relative to what sorts of lives they live. One way in which we could understand personal well-being is in terms of preference satisfaction that is conducive to (something like) flourishing. Well-being in this sense would be measured with first-person experiential reports: whether one takes their preferences to be satisfied or not, whether this amounts to flourishing or not, and so on. However, this strategy demonstrates an obvious problem with adaptive preferences. For instance, one coping mechanism women in sexual slavery make use of is to convince themselves that their lot is just part of the natural order of things, or that they are somehow responsible for their situation (cf. Bales 2012). Another is to be thankful for not suffering (more) severe abuse from their "owners" or pimps. The women themselves might not describe their lives as lacking in well-being when this is measured against the satisfaction of their preferences and expectations. But because these preferences and expectations have been insidiously shaped by the deeply problematic situations they are in, the experiential measure of well-being leaves something to be desired.

I will subsequently take a third-personal perspective that enables us to hold that the lives of women in sexual slavery fall short of well-being, even if they have adapted their preferences, and report (relative to these preferences) not to be suffering from attacks on personal well-being. I also aim to do so in a way that avoids charges of chauvinism. The crux of my case is the (already noted) distinction between well-being as flourishing and well-being

---

on a mistake. First, there may be many living creatures that have the same interests, but this does not make them human. Humanity is about satisfying the thin externalist conception of *human being*, from which certain interests follow. It is entirely acceptable that other living creatures may have a kind of biological makeup that generates similar interests. But this does not collapse the distinction between human and nonhuman animals. Second, satisfying these interests is not what delimits our moral communities. So even though some nonhuman animals also have the above interests, this does not mean that they are part of our moral community and that violating those interests would counterintuitively dehumanize some animals. I do not wish to take a stance here on the vexed issue of animal rights—I merely wish to point out that even if nonhuman animals share some legitimate human interests with human animals, this alone makes them neither human nor part of our moral communities.

as satisfaction of basic welfare interests. For me, well-being as flourishing is a function of preference satisfaction and to be determined relative to experiential considerations. It may well be that I enjoy a high degree of flourishing because my preferences are satisfied, even if my preferences have been abominably formed. By contrast, whether some treatment is dehumanizing is a function of nonexperiential and structural concerns. Delimiting dehumanization trades on whether some welfare interests have been indefensibly set back, and part of what makes such setbacks indefensible is a function of structural arrangements. Thus, responding to such treatment does not aim to change the affected individuals' mindset, but some institutional conditions. And this importantly avoids being patronizing. My approach does not involve claiming that those subject to some dehumanizing treatment have deformed or defective desires and preferences, which would open up the charge that the account is patronizing. My proposal requires additional social theory to elucidate the background conditions leading to some interest violations and to explicate the social structures enabling them. This is needed not only for social explanations of current practices, but also for future-oriented theories of resistance. Still, regardless of how one's legitimate welfare interests came to be indefensibly set back, and regardless of how one has come to view such interest violations, my approach can avoid charges of being patronizing and chauvinist because it aims to elucidate the wrongness-constituting feature of social injustice. And so delimiting dehumanization does not involve a conception of how we ought to live in order to have a flourishing life; rather, it involves flagging up structural nodes and arrangements in need of fixing.

6.4.2. MORAL INJURY

In order for a treatment to count as dehumanizing in my terms, it must set back a legitimate human interest in a morally injurious way: it must damage the realization and acknowledgment of the person's value. I framed this above as a failure of recognition respect, which is a failure to give appropriate consideration to some salient *fact(s)* about an x both in one's deliberation and in one's conduct. For me, the saliency of a fact is tied to our legitimate human interests. For instance, consider the practice of denying females access to education. This denial has repercussions for a wide range of basic welfare interests and constitutes an indefensible setback to such interests where the indefensibility is partly explicated in terms of underlying patriarchal social arrangements. Of course, in this case such social arrangements also *cause* women's welfare interests to be hampered. Now, such denials are usually based on certain supposed facts about women and their "nature." In so doing, the treatment clearly fails to recognize that there is nothing intrinsic about women that makes them incapable of being educated or choosing their own life plans—it simply gets the relevant facts about women qua human wrong. Furthermore, the denial is indefensible in being unjustifiable and inexcusable. It is unjustifiable on epistemic grounds: namely, it is simply empirically mistaken to think that there is something about women's "nature" and natural abilities that justifies the denial of education. Thus, the belief grounding the interest violation is unwarranted, which makes the interest violation indefensible. Moreover, denying education would also be inexcusable in causing certain harms: lack of education tends to render women economically dependent on others, which makes them vulnerable to domination and exploitation. Thus, the anticipated results of the interest violations would have harms that make the interest violation indefensible. Denying women education, then, involves an indefensible hampering of welfare interests and a moral injury (failure of recognition respect). It is, therefore, a dehumanizing mode of treatment. In fact, it makes no difference whether the denial is aimed at women, men, or trans* people; *anyone* who is treated in this manner on prejudicial grounds is treated in a dehumanizing way.

That said, what if one holds that there is no (real or purported) fact about women that makes them incapable of choosing their own life plans, but one nevertheless thinks that women ought not to be allowed to do so? Prima facie there would be no failure of recognition respect and, so, no morally injurious setback of interests (i.e., no dehumanization). I am unconvinced that such a situation is psychologically plausible or that the normative claim could be justified without relying on some putatively factual claims about women's "natural" abilities. That one's evaluative judgment ultimately relies on such putative facts may not be initially obvious. But a closer scrutiny of one's reasons, I would suspect, reveals some putative facts about women that one is basing the evaluative claim on. The trait/norm covariance model I outlined earlier provides a further elucidation of how exactly the lack of recognition respect trades on a failure to appreciate some salient facts about individuals. On the model I outlined, certain traits are paired with particular norms, and these pairings are bound together via quasi-essentialist covariance relations. Specific pairings are linked to women, others to men, and still others to neither or both. Different modes of congealment explain the pairings' apparent essentialism: congealment can be global or local (and contextually variable) but it is often highly resistant to change. To explain the resiliency, I invoked acceptance dependence, and implicit attitudes. Against this backdrop, consider the following way to think about the failure of recognition respect: person A fails to appreciate a salient fact about a person B because of a problematic association of a norm with a trait that B possesses. We have an insidious quasi-essentialist trait/norm pairing at work, which is standing (so to speak) in the way of recognition respect.

Again, consider the DRC by way of example. (As before, a trigger warning is in order.) I claimed earlier that the martial rapist fails to respect the fact that the victim's welfare interests will be severely set back, and that they ought not to be violated in a way that prevents the achievement of basic personal well-being—thus, there is lack of recognition respect, where the salient facts ignored trade on our humanity in the externalist sense. We can further explicate this with my model of congealed trait/norm pairings: physical traits having to do with femaleness are evaluatively viewed in a "feminine" way that makes those possessing such traits sexually violable. And this pairing is quasi-essentialist: given wider cultural beliefs and customs, the physical traits are viewed *as if* their femininity licenses such violations. These and other widespread beliefs are responsible for the continuation and resilience of the pairing, which hampers the attainment of recognition respect. The congealed trait/norm pairing is standing in the way of respect because the martial rapist fails to appreciate that there is nothing agent-*independently* factual about the pairing. Rather, the congealed pairing licensing sexual violence is a result of widely held sexist beliefs about those with female bodies. Now, the prevalence of sexualized violence in the DRC goes together with cultural attitudes that justify such violence. This is not somehow inherent to the Congolese culture; rather, the prevalence and impunity of rape have had the effect of shaping general attitudes about sexualized violence in problematic ways. In a recent study of such attitudes, a male shopkeeper (aged forty-eight) recounts his attack of a young girl (under eighteen), who came into his shop asking for water: "When a girl is asking for water in such a way, she wants sex. So I took her in the middle of my shop, I think she liked it, because her body accepted me to enter" (Slegh et al. 2012, 10). Here the girl's request for water was viewed as if her femininity (her supposed "way of asking for sex") licensed and justified the attack. In my terms, there is a disquieting trait/norm pairing at work, which stands in the way and hampers the achievement of recognition respect.[13]

One might further worry that the above relies too heavy on individual intentions and deliberation. In so doing, my view of recognition respect fails to capture structural aspects of wrongdoing. On the one hand, it seems mistaken to say that what undergirds the wrongfulness of patriarchal treatment of women is that individuals deliberate badly about women and miss some empirical facts. After all, it is plausible to hold that unwarranted structural relations have a huge role to play in explicating the damage of patriarchy. On the other hand, it also seems that many people simply do not deliberate about social identity categories: the background ideologies among which we live are so strongly and deeply ingrained that some way for women "to be" just seems natural—it is never called into question. In such cases, the objection

---

[13] Unfortunately, there are plenty of similar examples from around the world: a recent US case in Steubenville involving two male high school students sexually assaulting an unconscious female (and documenting the abuse) also demonstrates the lack of recognition respect, the achievement of which (I contend) is hampered in a parallel fashion.

goes, the failure of recognition respect cannot explain what goes wrong.[14] Let me start with the latter worry. As I see it, a failure to deliberate *is* a deliberative failure. So my view is that when one simply fails to consider some facts pertaining to women in one's conduct, one is making precisely the kind of mistake that hinders recognition respect. That is, there are many ways in which deliberation can fail—and one way is simply to fail to deliberate at all. This hinges on epistemically responsible agency. Given the kind of world we live in, it seems extremely difficult to avoid encountering counterexamples to one's beliefs about the way things are (at least in Western Anglo contexts). Imagine that I believe women to be "by their nature" mere baby incubators. This would be getting the facts about women's "nature" wrong, and there is plenty of evidence to the contrary. Now, the failure to even question one's belief in one's conduct despite available counterevidence suggests to me that the subject must engage in active ignorance. And this is a failure that signals epistemic irresponsibility precisely of the kind that hampers recognition respect. So a failure to deliberate because one actively ignores evidence to the contrary does not present a counterexample to my view, but is another way in which recognition respect can be blocked.

However, what about the structural aspect—is my view too individualistic? I hold that social structures make a huge difference to the story, and they play an integral role in the damage patriarchy does to women. I will have much more to say about this in chapter 7. But let me briefly say something to anticipate: the explication of different forms of injustice (oppression, discrimination, domination) and their various contours (sexism, racism, ableism, trans*phobia) cannot but refer to social structures. After all, I am aiming to elucidate systematic, structural, social injustices. So there are harms that are directly due to social structures and institutional arrangements (of which I will say more in the next chapter). For now, however, I have been aiming to elucidate the underlying wrong of such structural arrangements and what explicates the unjustness. So, understanding the damage of patriarchy as *harm* must make reference to structural factors. Still, for me, understanding the damage as *wrong* has a more individualistic component, and this involves deliberative failures (among other things). In this way, the explication on offer does not ignore social structures and their influence. But structures come into play more when we are elucidating a slightly different part of the whole story.

Finally, it is worth clarifying that although all dehumanizing modes of treatment are morally injurious, not all morally injurious acts are dehumanizing. Take the case of lying to your friend, which also seems to involve a failure of recognition respect: the liar fails to appreciate some facts about the friend in their conduct, which is that the friend qua friend ought not to be

---

[14] Thanks to an anonymous referee for this objection.

deceived.[15] But it seems odd and wrongheaded to say that each act of lying to one's friend is dehumanizing just because it is morally injurious (for instance, consider something like telling a "white lie" to one's friend in order not to hurt their feelings). If all instances of lying were dehumanizing, this would make the conditions for dehumanization intuitively too loose. My contention is that although a lie may be morally injurious, it need not be dehumanizing: it may not clearly set back some legitimate human interest, or the setback may be defensible (there might be mitigating circumstances that make lying justifiable and excusable). The lie might also be morally wrongful on some *other* grounds. After all, I am not aiming to elucidate moral wrongness per se, but the wrong of social injustice in particular. On the face of it, lying to one's friend may not fall within the scope of systematic social injustices despite being wrongful, though there may well be cases of lying that do. Since structural considerations (at least partly) determine whether some action is indefensible, some systematic ways of misleading social agents may well count as dehumanizing on my definition. But discerning the cases that do from those that do not crucially depends on the details of the particular cases.

Now, an act can be morally injurious without being dehumanizing, but an act cannot be dehumanizing without being morally injurious. This is because indefensible setbacks to legitimate interests involve a moral injury understood as a failure of recognition respect—part of what *makes* the interest violation indefensible is the moral injury that it involves. Consider again the example of employment competition. My interest in financial security may be set back if I fail to get the job. If this is because the selection process involved sexist, racist, or homophobic discrimination, my legitimate interests have been indefensibly set back: the interest violation involves false or unjustified beliefs pertaining to some social identity marker. In this example, the moral injury is already present. The hiring committee members have committed a failure of recognition respect in failing to appreciate in their deliberation and conduct some facts about me as a candidate—namely, that (contra the committee members' beliefs) my social identity and background do not as a matter of fact make me unsuited for the job, provided that these are irrelevant for the post. The treatment indefensibly sets back my legitimate interests (because the interest violation is unjustified) in a way that amounts to a moral injury (because it involves a failure of recognition respect). And so the treatment is dehumanizing. There is no *further* moral injury, which is committed in addition to my interests being set back. The setback is morally injurious in involving a prejudicial failure of recognition respect.[16]

---

[15] Thanks to Jules Holroyd for raising this issue.

[16] One might be tempted to say that if one brings the interest-violating action upon oneself, this would be an instance of self-dehumanization. Doing so would yield an odd account of dehumanization: one indefensibly sets back one's own legitimate interests in a morally injurious way. For instance, imagine one deliberately (and without prima facie good reason) sets out to live in a country

6.5. Dehumanization and Feminism

This chapter has developed a notion of *dehumanization* that is meant to ground emancipatory feminism. As I see it, it is dehumanization that normatively underpins feminist claims and enables feminists to speak on behalf of women: simply put, when those picked out by 'woman' (cf. section 5.1) are subject to dehumanizing treatments, feminists can (1) articulate and identify instances of patriarchal harm, (2) justify critical claims about that treatment's wrongfulness (3), and call for changing the treatment. Feminists have normative resources at their disposal to show that their critical claims do not rest on fabrications of injustice and that they are not crying abuse when there is none. I contend that my notion of *dehumanization* further elucidates the wrong of social injustice per se, of which I will say more in subsequent chapters. But prior to that, let me say more about how my conception connects with some extant feminist concerns.

A number of phenomena like humiliation, degradation, and objectification seem pretheoretically dehumanizing too. For instance, Ann Cudd (2006) thinks that humiliation and degradation are direct forces of oppression. And Nussbaum (1995c, 257) has proposed that objectification, or the idea of treating a person as a thing, involves seven features:

- *Instrumentality*: treating a person as a tool for the objectifier's purposes
- *Denial of autonomy*: treating a person as lacking in autonomy and self-determination
- *Inertness*: treating a person as lacking in agency
- *Fungibility*: treating a person as interchangeable with other objects
- *Violability*: treating a person as lacking in boundary integrity
- *Ownership*: treating a person as something that can be traded
- *Denial of subjectivity*: treating a person as something whose experiences and feelings need not be taken into account[17]

---

where one's interest in a tolerable living environment is hampered because the country's police force perpetrates systematic violence against members of one's racialized group. Would this be a case of self-dehumanization? I think not, and I do not think that one can self-dehumanize in my sense. I noted earlier that my approach requires additional social theory that elucidates the background conditions leading to the interest violation and that explicates enabling social structures. For my elucidation of the wrongness-constituting feature of social injustice, it is not crucial to spell out *how* one's legitimate welfare interests came to be indefensibly set back. Such an elucidation is needed for social explanations of current practices and for future-oriented theories of resistance. Still, for the task at hand (for the elucidation of dehumanization as the wrong of injustice) the causal issue of how the dehumanization came about is not crucial. So even if I bring racist police brutality "upon myself" in the manner described, the crucial point is that the actions of the police officers set back my legitimate welfare interests in an indefensible way that is morally injurious. This is what renders the treatment wrongful, and it is this *constitutive* point that matters for my purposes here.

[17] Langton has added three more features to Nussbaum's list: reduction to body (identifying people with their body parts); reduction to appearance (treating people in terms of how they look); and silencing (treating people as lacking the capacity to speak) (2009, 228–229).

These features strike many as prima facie dehumanizing. How does my proposal then deal with humiliation, degradation, and objectification? Although these phenomena may resonate with pretheoretical conceptions of dehumanization, I submit, we should resist intuitively coupling dehumanization with humiliation, degradation, and objectification. First, whether objectification can be morally benign is a feminist philosophical point of contention, and some hold that objectification is not per se morally problematic. (For a helpful introduction to feminist views on objectification, see Papadaki 2012.) By contrast, dehumanization cannot but be wrongful. Thinking about moral wrongfulness, then, gives us prima facie grounds to hold that the two come apart. Second, as I see it objectification is a way of bringing about dehumanization. For instance, take ownership: in treating someone as something that can be bought or sold, I contend, one's legitimate human interests are indefensibly set back in a way that constitutes a moral injury. But the normative work is not being done with the claim that one can be bought or sold (i.e., with objectification in this sense); rather, what does the work is the claim that this treatment amounts to an indefensible interest-setback (i.e., dehumanization). Once more, the distinction between harms and wrong elucidates this: objectification in the ownership sense is the harmful means with which dehumanization (as the underlying wrong) is instantiated. Third, I contend that humiliation and degradation are consequences and resultant harms of dehumanizing treatments, but they are not constitutive of injustice's wrongfulness. Again, consider DRC cases of martial rape. It is very common for victims to report a deep subsequent sense of shame and humiliation. But if my argument above is right, their attacks are dehumanizing on other grounds. Humiliation and degradation are harms that result from being subjected to dehumanizing treatments, but they are not equivalent to such treatments and so are not part of injustice's normative core.

Finally, dehumanization is commonly taken to involve treating persons as things, and (I suspect) many would intuitively hold that an assault on "our" human dignity or worth as Kantian ends in ourselves underlies the wrong of objectification, humiliation, and degradation. But, as already noted, I take this view to be misguided. On my view, I may be treated in dehumanizing ways, which underpins the oppression that I face; but this does not turn on others taking me as something as opposed to someone. This is because instances of contemporary social injustice work via setbacks to *human* agency. Hence, in order for human interests to be violable, it is a necessary precondition that these interests are of *someone* (not of something). This point was also made apparent in my earlier discussion of the damage done by rape: contra Gardner and Shute, I argued, instrumentalization in their sense does not capture what is wrongful about at least some instances of sexualized violence. If the wrongfulness of injustice turns on something like the affirmation of humanity or agency, the idea that objectification makes social injustice wrongful is untenable. Moreover, if different forms of injustice work via instrumental-ization that renders human subject literally dehumaniz*ed*, it is hard to make sense of resistance. On the face of it, things cannot resist what is done to them or fight back. But this would make social change, emancipation, and empowerment simply impossible—something that I take to be, as a matter of fact, false. Those facing contemporary social injustices do resist, and there are many extremely subtle ways to do so. Acknowledging the existence of resis-tance is in tension with the idea that social injustice turns on objectification qua instrumentalization. My sense of dehumanization as a characteristic of *acts* and ways of *treating* others, which does not dehumanize human subjects, does justice to these insights: it can better capture the idea that paradigm instances of injustice seem to involve some affirmation of humanity, and it leaves room for resistance in denying that injustice literally renders individu-als *dehumanized*.

Nonetheless, one might wonder how my gender-neutral definition of *de-humanization* helps feminist philosophy. One might immediately worry about my argumentative strategy: dehumanization relies on a gender-neu-tral understanding of rape, and this may strike one as inadequate insofar as rape is predominantly a crime against women. A number of feminist phi-losophers take it to be a wrong done to women as a *social kind* (cf. Brison 2002; Card 1991). Keith Burgess-Jackson takes rape as an act and practice to "subjugate an entire class of individuals (women) to another (men) . . . every woman, qua woman, is wronged by it" (2000, 289). These views take rape to damage women and men differently—it damages women qua women, and men qua men because rape is an apparatus of patriarchal oppression that is used against women as a group. If the damage done by rape is to women qua women and to men qua men, my gender-neutral conception is inadequate, and it insufficiently supports the developed gender-neutral idea of dehuman-ization. Consequently, one might find my account deeply dubious.

This objection is helpful in elucidating a number of things. For a start, it elucidates the already-mentioned ambiguity with making "qua woman" claims. Whether we are talking about "damage to women as women" in the explanatory or constitutive senses outlined earlier is not entirely clear, which is illustrated by Burgess-Jackson's claim. Whether he intended to or not, the quote reads in the constitutive rather than in the explanatory sense. The claim is not about whether being a woman figures in the explanation of sexualized violence. Instead, the claim is that women as gendered beings are wronged by rape. And this is precisely exemplary of the view that misplaces the locus of patriarchy's damage: rape does not wrong women's "gender part," and the damage in this sense is not to women as gendered beings—it is a wrong to women as human beings. Appreciating this point demonstrates that the moral wrongness-making features should not be thought of as gender specific. So even though we may accept that rape as a practice is a tool of patriarchal oppression, we must understand the locution "damage to women as women" in a manner that does not smuggle in the implausible reading that patriarchy wrongs women's "gender part."

My suggestion is (again) that we can do so by keeping in mind the different senses of *damage*. Rape undoubtedly *in one sense* damages women as a group differently than men as a group. But in this case we are talking about the harm of rape. Sexual violence harms women and men differently: for instance, most men do not live with a fear of being attacked, they need not take extra precautions to avoid sexualized violence, and they relatively seldom come to experience trauma resulting from such violence. I won't say much more about the harms of sexualized violence here; other feminist philosophers provide helpful and comprehensive outlines that I can only recommend (cf. Cudd 2006; Whisnant 2013). Rather, my point is that even though the harms differ, the idea that patriarchy damages women as human beings supports the view that the underlying wrong of rape is the same for everyone. After all, if rape wrongs women qua human beings, it would be strange to maintain that it wrongs men and trans* people qua human beings too, but that this wrong is nevertheless different in *kind*. And so I take it that every instance is wrongful on the same underlying grounds. In a similar vein, dehumanizing acts do not differ in kind for me—qua dehumanizing acts, they have the same constitutive and wrongness-making conditions. However, these conditions are clearly realizable in multiple ways and depend on the situations, circumstances, background conditions, contexts, and the subjects' embodiment and self-identification. Still, these differences alter the harm, not the underlying wrong. This being the case, I do not see my reliance on a gender-neutral conception of rape to be problematic.

One might wonder further what my definition of *dehumanization* contributes to feminism in particular and what it has to do with feminist ethical and political claims. Bluntly put: the definition per se is independent of such claims. But this is benign. Every first-order moral theory should be feminist in facilitating the quest for gendered social justice. If one's theory fails to do so, it is time to revise the theory. My aim here is to provide an elucidation of a concept that can do the required feminist normative work; but (as I will discuss in subsequent chapters) it can do more. Relative to feminist concerns, the notion developed here ought to explicate how and why patriarchy damages women and help to articulate and defend feminism's critical claims with the view to attaining gender justice. And these are tasks that we can accomplish with my notion of dehumanization. Let me spell out how. First, it can be used to delimit the damage as harm that is done to women by patriarchy in that my definition picks out harmful ways of treating women. This tells us which acts or ways of treating women are impermissible—namely, those that count as dehumanizing. Doing so will require further social theoretical tools that I will outline in the next two chapters. But the basic idea stands:

combining the descriptive social theoretical tools (e.g., a notion of *discrimination*) with my normative tools (i.e., dehumanization) enables us to pick out those treatments that are harmful to individuals designated as women. Second, my approach elucidates the role that patriarchy plays in such harm: if the indefensible setbacks to women's welfare interest (qua human) trade on sexist beliefs or patriarchal social structures, we can clearly see that the setbacks have their roots in forces oppressive to women. Third, since sexist beliefs and patriarchal social structures make the setbacks indefensible in morally injurious ways, feminists are afforded strong justificatory tools in their subsequent critiques of the status quo. These critiques in turn offer resources to articulate and justify a positive vision of human relationships that strives for justice. Finally, the definition of *dehumanization* tells us how patriarchal damage as harm is also wrongful: it captures the wrongness-making feature of patriarchal treatment of women, in addition to its harm. In short: even though my notion of *dehumanization* can be employed independently of feminist concerns, it is also a tool with which we can advance humanist feminism.

With this in mind, it is helpful to highlight how my proposal avoids earlier difficulties that were discussed with respect to the gender controversy and internalist conceptions of humanity. The above elucidation of how we can advance humanist feminism in no way relies on substantive or thick notions of *woman, gender,* or *human being*. It avoids the pitfalls of both the internalist and the externalist conceptions of *humanity*, on the one hand, and of the gender controversy, on the other. First, *dehumanization* for me does not rely on cashing out *human being* in an ethically thick way. I started with some fairly common externalist claims about us qua human beings. I then claimed that members of humanity (so understood) can be and are treated in damaging ways, where rape is a paradigm case of such treatment. These two claims were used to develop my notion of *dehumanization*. Hence, the account that I have proposed starts with quite easily acceptable assumptions and does not rely on any controversial evaluative understanding of humanity. Second, although I rely on an externalist conception, I avoid the charge that this generates no ethical conclusions that are relevant for emancipatory feminism (or for other emancipatory social movements). This is Antony's objection to externalism outlined at the beginning of this chapter, with which I agree. However, I avoid this charge because I am not trying to ground normative feminist claims on the externalist conception of *human being*. On my account, this thin externalist conception is first used to develop a notion of *dehumanization* that has a normative ethical component; *dehumanization* is then used to ground ethical claims about how women should and should not be treated. So it is this notion that provides the required bridge between nonnormative and normative considerations. Third, my proposal avoids debilitating conceptual worries over *woman* because in elucidating and making good feminist normative claims, we need not rely on any such thick conception. The thin understanding of the term 'woman' argued for in chapter 5 suffices and can be used in feminist explanations of gendered social injustices. We avoid the worry that unless feminist philosophers can provide a satisfactory elucidation of *woman* that is in some substantive sense social and inclusive, we cannot justify feminist critical claims on behalf of women. After all, this justificatory work will be done with my notion of *dehumanization*, whereas the thin understanding of womanhood will figure in our social explanations and theory. This further demonstrates that emancipatory feminism can move beyond the gender controversy.

Although humanist feminism has not been widely defended in recent years, there are two notable such positions put forward by Martha Nussbaum (2000) and Susan Moller Okin (1989). I will conclude this chapter by considering how my position differs from theirs. First, for Nussbaum gender injustice amounts to women not being treated as "ends in their own right, persons with dignity that deserves respect from laws and institutions" (2000, 2). Rather, they are treated as mere means to others' ends. Women (qua women) lack the essential support to lead "fully human" lives (2000, 4). Nussbaum's capabilities approach elucidates how and why this is the case: women lack certain capabilities to function in truly human ways. Her aim is to provide a philosophical foundation for basic constitutional principles that governments of all nations should respect and implement. Doing so guarantees "a bare minimum of what respect for human dignity requires" (2000, 5). Nussbaum aims to articulate a threshold level of capability beneath which truly human functioning is not possible. Her strategy is the following: we measure quality of life in terms of certain capabilities to function in core areas of life. We then argue that in these areas of human functioning

> a necessary condition of justice for public political arrangements is that it deliver to citizens a certain basic level of capability. If people are systematically falling below the threshold in any of these core areas, this should be seen as a situation both unjust and tragic. (2000, 71)

So certain functionings are central to human life, and there is way to "do" them that is truly human, rather than merely animal. For instance, someone who is starving does not use food in a truly human manner. This connects to the ideas of dignity and dignified life: these are about being able to shape one's life in certain ways and in cooperation with others. Thus, a truly human life is "one that is shaped throughout by . . . human powers of practical reason and sociability" (2000, 72).

Nussbaum's list of capabilities provides the moral basis for basic constitutional guarantees of "what a complete good life for a human being would be" (2000, 74). Certain capabilities (in her view) are central to any human life, irrespective of whatever else an individual may choose to pursue. The list goes thus:

- Life (e.g. ability to live a life of normal length)
- Bodily health (e.g., being able to have adequate shelter, and nourishment)
- Bodily integrity (e.g., being able to be secure from assaults)
- Sense, imagination, and thought (e.g., being able to do things in "truly human" ways informed and cultivated by adequate education; being "able to search for the ultimate meaning of life in one's own way")
- Emotions (e.g., being able to form attachments)
- Practical reason (e.g., being able to form a conception of the good)
- Affiliation (e.g., being able to live with others, having the "social bases of self-respect and non-humiliation")
- Other species (e.g., being able to live with animals and "the world of nature")
- Play (e.g., being able to laugh and to play)
- Control over one's political and material environments (e.g., having the ability to participate in political decision-making and hold property) (Nussbaum 2000, 78–90)

These capabilities can be realized on different levels. Humans have, first, basic capabilities: "the innate equipment of individuals that is the necessary basis for developing the more advanced capabilities, and a ground of moral concern" (2000, 84). Second, they have internal capabilities: "developed states of the person herself that are . . . sufficient conditions for the exercise of the requisite functions" (2000, 84). Third, combined capabilities are "internal capabilities *combined with* suitable external conditions for the exercise of the function" (2000, 84–85). For instance, citizens of repressive nations have the internal capability to exercise free speech and thought, but not the combined one because they are externally restricted in their exercise of the capability. Nussbaum's list above is one of combined capabilities. However, it is the capability to function that matters for justice, not actual functioning.

One might wonder how different my human interests are from Nussbaum's capabilities. After all, they do share many aspects (like the focus on bodily functioning). Now, I admit that there are many particular capabilities and human interests that we share. Nevertheless, this is not the issue. My qualms with Nussbaum's approach pertain to her justification of the list: Nussbaum starts by articulating an evaluative notion of *human being* and then uses this to fix social and institutional arrangements. On her approach, women (and all people) are ends in themselves and bearers of value (Nussbaum 2000, 73). And protecting our capabilities to function should be geared toward protecting and realizing such value. Her view of humanity, then, is internalist. My list is drawn from an externalist conception of humanity that hinges on our shared biology and embodiment. For me, Nussbaum's justificatory strategy is a nonstarter on methodological grounds. It buys into an idealized internalist conception of humanity, and ultimately *that* does the justificatory work. But, as Antony argues, the internalist conception will be acceptable only to those who already endorse Nussbaum's list of the central human capabilities, perhaps doing so implicitly. Such prior acceptance thus explains why the list resonates with some philosophers but not others. My alternative, externalist conception of humanity, however, should resonate more widely.

This difference helps further to clarify a point already recurrently made. Dehumanization is often taken to be the tendency to render groups less than human (cf. Smith 2013). For instance, treating persons as mere means to others' ends underlies Nussbaum's view of what violates humanity. Humanity (for her) is conferred in terms of uniquely human capacities (like practical rationality), and dehumanization is about moral exclusion and social devaluation of *persons*. So from the outset Nussbaum takes there to be a much more intimate conceptual connection between humanity and personhood than I do. Clearly I do not deny that by and large the types of human and person are coextensive. But for me, the two come conceptually apart insofar as I rely on an externalist conception of humanity. Because of this, dehumanization for me is not about conceiving some individuals as "lesser" persons, or about reducing human subjectivity to some subhuman state. On my view, being treated in dehumanizing ways tells us something important about that treatment: namely, that it is wrongful, impermissible, and in need of societal responses. But it does not literally turn a someone into a something.

So much for how my position differs from Nussbaum's; what about Okin's humanist feminism? Okin aims to elucidate a theory that "treats women, as well as men, as full human beings to whom a theory of social justice must apply" (1989, 23). What stands in the way of justice is gender, which means "*the deeply entrenched institutionalization of sexual difference*" (Okin 1989, 6). Gender is the linchpin of unjust family arrangements. And such arrangements along with unequal distribution of unpaid work underlie structural inequalities, like the gender wage gap, the dearth of women in powerful positions, and women's poverty (1989, 4). Social justice thus demands that our family structures be revised. To motivate this, Okin makes use of Rawls's thought experiment of the original position. Behind the veil of ignorance, it would be rational for us to choose not only principles of justice that guarantee basic rights and liberties, but also those that ensure, were one to end up as a single mother, one would not be rendered vulnerable to poverty. That is, justice requires that we have access to affordable child care facilities and a basic income provision in order to alleviate women's oppression that is due to social and institutional structures. Encouraging and facilitating the sharing of paid productive and unpaid reproductive work (among other things) would counter women's economic and social vulnerability that is due to gender-structured families. This will allow us to move beyond gender and toward a just future "without gender" (Okin 1989, 171). In particular, this would mean that

> in its social structures and practices, one's sex would have no more relevance than one's eye color or the length of one's toes. No assumptions would be made about "male" and "female" roles; childbearing would be so conceptually separated from child rearing and other family responsibilities that it would be a case of surprise ... if men and women were not equally responsible for domestic life or if children were to spend much more time with one parent than the other. It would be a future in which men and women participated in more or less equal numbers in every sphere of life, from infant care to different kinds of paid work to high-level politics. (1989, 171)

As impressive and admirable as Okin's humanist feminism is, her strategy and methodology have problematic aspects that my approach hopes to avoid. Okin advocates surpassing gender, which seems close to my view. But we are farther away from each other than might at first seem. First, Okin's position is abolitionist in the manner that I discussed in chapter 5. For her, gender is a product of oppressive social conditions. Thus, the appropriate feminist response is to do away with gender (i.e., with oppressive gender roles) while retaining females and males. However, as I argued in section 5.2.2, this ontological picture is not without its problems. Second, I take us to mean different things with the idea of surpassing gender. For Okin, this means doing away with those social forces that socially construct gender. This includes public policies and family arrangements that assume and institutionalize a social differentiation between the sexes and socialize us accordingly. For me, the idea of surpassing gender is put forward in subtly different spirit: it is about the paradigm shift in focus when thinking about the justification and grounding of normative feminist claims. The move that I am calling for is more radical than Okin's in that mine goes to the heart of emancipatory feminism. That said, in many ways her description of what eradicating gender involves resonates with mine. For instance, her proposal that childbearing should be conceptually separated from gendered expectations is not that far from my idea (cf. section 5.2.4) that public policies should aim to drive a wedge between caretaking (the descriptive trait) and femininity (the normative evaluation). In this sense, although we mean different things with "moving away from gender," there are still many points on which we agree.

Nevertheless, a greater sticking point for me pertains to Okin's theory justification. Okin is offering a critical feminist appropriation of Rawls's original position. Bluntly put, if we take the reality of gender injustice seriously and posit that the agents behind the veil of ignorance know that they may end up being deeply disadvantaged as women by current family arrangements, it would be rational to choose principles of justice that ensure our social arrangements and family structures are characterized by justice too. This strategy is less grounded in a thick conception of *woman* than those I discussed earlier (cf. chapters 2–4). Still, I wish to resist Okin-inspired humanist feminism also on methodological grounds: feminists have reasons to be wary of idealized theories like Rawls's theory of justice, and I take my nonideal approach to provide a preferable methodology. Let me clarify: Okin's work contains an impressive discussion of practical strategies for bringing about gender justice, and her theorizing retains an acute sensitivity to actual injustices women suffer. Nonetheless, the justification for her theory is not nonideal. *This* is the part of Okin's methodology that I take issue with. As noted earlier, I contend that an explication of injustice should not trade on a prior theory of justice. Elucidating justice and injustice come apart; and thus, we should not aim to understand injustice by theorizing it via the lens of justice. Instead, we need different theoretical tools, or (as I put it) an interim theory of injustice that can subsequently be employed to develop a fully-fledged theory of social justice. Okin's method, however, is precisely of the sort I object: we explicate injustice through the lens of a prior idealized theory of justice in order to measure which actual social relations fall short of that idealization. In this sense, her theory is not nonideal, although Okin applies it to actual nonideal social relations.

Finally, much of Okin's humanist feminism is developed relative to considerations of justice in the family and the private realm. Although this has been immensely influential and important in the history of feminist philosophy, I consider my approach to provide a more contemporary picture of humanist feminism—one that moves on from Okin's second-wave feminist considerations. With its focus on gender-binary family arrangements, Okin's work is susceptible to queer feminist critiques. Okin's picture of the family, for instance, is heteronormative. Further, in taking the family to be the linchpin of gender, Okin fails to theorize other sites of injustices, like those hinging on racialization, atypical bodily functioning, and trans* and homophobic violence. In focusing on the heterosexual family, feminism for Okin is squarely about cis women; it thus seemingly fails to take into account injustices that are due to other social identifications as well as ways in which these injustices are intertwined. My humanist feminism on offer can better deal with concerns of queer and trans* people. I reject the view that feminism is just about women's concerns; feminism is about fighting particular injustices, which are not just faced by those designated as women. Instead, some cis men, trans* people, and intersexed individuals also face injustices due to sexist beliefs and patriarchal social arrangements, and this also falls under the purview of feminism. The relevant injustices will be delimited with my proposed definition of *dehumanization*, not with the notions of *gender* and *woman*. (In fact, the injustices will be fixed by *dehumanization* and a particular emancipatory social theory that I develop in due course. But more on this shortly.) As I see it, the paradigm shift toward humanist feminism enables us to understand the political project of feminism anew and so garners it a broader base. For me, feminism is politically committed to ending sexist and patriarchal injustices. And achieving this end will require *more* than ending just women's oppression.

Feminism, then, is not antithetical to political projects aiming to advance the rights of trans* people and intersexes, and these political projects are different aspects of the same struggle against patriarchy. In understanding feminism this way, the hope is to build bridges between feminist and trans* movements—something that has been fraught with difficulties given the acrimonious historical exclusion of trans* persons from feminism's purview. My position also avoids problematic and false background presumptions about cis men, such as that cis men cannot identify as feminists or that a male feminist is an oxymoron. Injustices that men encounter on prejudicial grounds due to (roughly put) gendered expectations will also be feminist issues: an example would be men being denied the possibility to work part-time in order to look after their children. Thus, I am proposing a reformist conception of feminism that is broader in scope. Anecdotally, such a conception is welcomed by some cis men and trans* people. In particular, I have in mind cis men who wish to avoid any association with politically problematic and regressive men's rights movements, but identify as feminists and would wish to be acknowledged as such. The basic take-home message is this: patriarchy is not a problem just for women; it is a problem for everyone. Overcoming it will involve changes that affect us all. And if feminism plays a pivotal role in this, then feminism is for everyone—not just for women.

Forms of Injustice and Emancipatory Social Theory

7.1. Introduction

Iris Marion Young writes that without a social theory "normative reflection is abstract, empty, and unable to guide criticism with a practical interest in emancipation" (1990, 5). Any attempt to formulate a good normative theory (say, of how women ought and ought not to be treated) "cannot avoid social and political description and explanation" (1990, 5). I agree with Young; but I hold that the relation goes both ways. Any attempt to formulate an adequate social theory requires and cannot avoid a normative theory in order to articulate and undergird *why* some ways of treating others are wrongful and thus illegitimate. A theory of injustice then requires both descriptive and normative components: a normative theory devoid of social and empirical content is empty, while a social theory divorced from a normative one lacks guidance. In chapter 6, I developed the normative part. There I proposed a definition of *dehumanization* that does not rely on cashing out *human being* in an ethically thick way and that can be employed to make good a version of humanist feminism. In this chapter, I will develop the descriptive social theoretical aspects of injustice from a feminist perspective. The overall goal is to offer a feminist regimentation of social injustice. This will impact feminist philosophy by further spelling out the specifics of my proposed humanist feminism; the regimentation also offers us a better grasp of what social injustice involves and improves some extant ways of understanding injustice that do not originate from a distinctly feminist viewpoint.

In regimenting social injustice, we must first identify the core forms of injustice (discrimination, domination, oppression), their central defining features along with various contours that social injustice takes (e.g., sexist, racist, homophobic, ableist, classist injustice). These contours are the basis on which one suffers injustices, although we know from intersectional critiques that sharply dividing them is always slightly unhappy. In reality, the shapes that injustices take are enmeshed and messy. My intention here is to provide analytical tools, albeit in reality the bases of injustices turn out to be less clearly discernible. Second, our regimentation must elucidate the normative basis of the above kinds of injustice. I take my earlier developed conception of *dehumanization* to do this. Finally, the regimentation involves outlining some resultant states of affairs. These include (among other things): inequality, lack of freedom, exploitation, subordination, and marginalization. That is, the core forms of injustice generate certain individual and structural harms. The former include (for instance) physical and psychological hurt via violence and trauma; the latter include inequalities in material resources, marginalization of certain groups as well as exploitation of vulnerable individuals (to name but a few). In this sense, my typology comes apart from other ways to theorize injustice. Sometimes unfairness, inequality, and exploitation are included as forms of injustice. I disagree with this picture: for me, they are not forms of injustice, but states of affairs that result from prior instances of injustice. So I will next provide a typology of different forms (oppression, domination, discrimination) that all share the descriptive features of being social, structural, and systematic. Moreover, I hold, dehumanization constitutes their wrongness-making feature. Finally, these forms have certain effects like dividing individuals into "haves" and "have-nots." The insights gained here, in the previous chapter, and in the coming one provide the constituents of a unified account of injustice. The account is unified in the sense that the individual instances have a core set of defining features in common, though these conditions are multiply realizable. Thus, the resulting states of affairs and individual experiences of those subject to social injustices are hugely divergent.

I have already set out what I take dehumanization to consist in. But what do I mean by social, structural, and systematic? First, I am concerned with injustices that are grounded in socially salient self- and other-directed identifications—or, as I put it, injustices that have the various aforementioned contours (to be discussed in chapter 8). There are many different ways to understand subsequent social groupings, and philosophers have written extensively on what social groups amount to (if anything at all). A rather simple and rudimentary conception suffices for my purposes here. I take my cue from Ann Cudd, for whom social groups are voluntary or nonvoluntary "collections of persons who share something that is socially significant" (2006, 41). The former sorts of groups share perhaps joint commitments or projects (Gilbert 1989); the latter sorts may be subject to shared social constraints that are externally imposed on group members, regardless of whether individuals see themselves collectively so constrained or not (Cudd 2006, chap. 2). This fits the position that I argued for in chapter 5 with respect to women: certain extensional intuitions guiding our deployment of 'woman' help pick out women's social kind. These extensional intuitions are grounded in both voluntary and nonvoluntary public indicative features that are taken as socially significant (e.g., physical traits, behavior, social roles, self-ascription). Those so picked out are then subject to various trait/norm pairings that may be problematic and thus warranting intervention. Being designated as a woman may also be a source of individual, subjective identity or sense of self. For me, then, the social kind of women is situated somewhere in between fully voluntary and fully nonvoluntary social groups, where both self-ascription and being ascribed certain normative expectations by others figure in the requisite social identifications. The second feature of social injustices is their structural nature. This means that such injustices have their causes in norms, habits, symbolic meanings, and assumptions unquestionably embedded in and underlying our institutional and social arrangements (cf. Young 1990). Third, in being systematic social injustices exist "throughout a society, usually over a substantial period of time," where "the institutions of society interlock and reinforce each other in ways that create and maintain" the injustices (Clatterbaugh 1996, 290).

By way of example, consider the following case. Imagine that my employer has idiosyncratic beliefs about employees with tall foreheads (e.g., that they perform worse than those with "shorter" foreheads). If only my employer holds such beliefs, my failure to get promoted due to the size of my forehead would not count as an instance of social injustice: although I would have been discriminated against as an individual exemplar of an idiosyncratic kind (tall-foreheaded people), my discrimination would not be social, systematic, and structural—it would be incidental, idiosyncratic, and nonsocial. Socially relevant kinds are not individuated by a single individual's idiosyncratic beliefs. The kinds relevant for social injustice must be somehow socially salient and public: they are groups "important to the structures of social interactions across a wide range of social contexts" (Lippert-Rasmussen 2006, 169). Further, this instance of discrimination is neither systematic nor structural: having a tall forehead is not coupled with public symbolic meanings, and there is no system of interlocking barriers and institutions that constrain tall-foreheaded people. With these three conditions in mind, then, the barriers and obstacles experienced by women, people of color, atypically bodied, poor, queer, and trans* individuals make up paradigm cases of contemporary systematic social injustices.[1]

---

[1] Two immediate clarifications are in order. First, the idiosyncratic case should fall, of course, under legislation that outlaws workplace discrimination based on traits irrelevant for performance. However, relative to social injustice, discrimination is to be understood in somewhat different and broader terms. And the example of being denied promotion because of my forehead size does not fit this broader social conception of discrimination. Second, it is true that the employer's idiosyncratic beliefs about foreheads and job performance indefensibly set back my legitimate human interests in a morally injurious way. But this does not render the treatment dehumanizing in my sense, despite being impermissible on other grounds. That is, there is a difference between individual wrongdoing and systematic social injustice. The point relevant to social injustice is this: the indefensibility of the setback in this example does not trade on systematic public beliefs or institutional arrangements. It is indefensible and clearly wrongful, but not because the behavior displays the hallmarks of *social* injustice.

This chapter provides a typology of different social injustices and demonstrates how dehumanization provides their wrongness-making feature. This will help us meet two of the three motivating factors introduced at the start of the previous chapter: that my proposal provides a more nuanced account of gender injustice, and that it facilitates social theory building (both in feminism and more generally) by better understanding the wrongness-making feature of social injustice. In order to see how, let's start with the desiderata and adequacy conditions of emancipatory social theories.

7.2. Emancipatory Social Theory: Desiderata

The gender controversy discussed in Part I connects straightforwardly to feminist social theory. For instance, Zack (cf. section 4.1) holds that such a theory is needed for feminist political purposes. It should be "unapologetically normative" (that is, grounded in "facts about the existence of real women"), it should explain women's oppression in a comprehensive manner, and it should acknowledge that women's oppression is not "in the head" (2005, 63). These desiderata make use of the term 'woman', which (to recap) for Zack is about being designated female at birth, a mother, or a primary sexual choice for men. Zack's conception of *woman* is meant to be thick enough to guide us in satisfying the aforementioned desiderata and inclusive enough to avoid gender-skeptical critiques. Haslanger (cf. section 4.2) also aims to cash out womanhood in a way that satisfies the desiderata of a feminist social theory: her gender concepts should provide us with conceptual tools with which we can explain and identify persistent gendered social inequalities and empower critical social agents. And Bach's account of gender as a historical, natural kind is supposedly better than existing alternatives at undertaking certain explanatory tasks that serve feminist political goals (cf. section 4.4).

Compare this case to the same employer not promoting me but their nephew instead. In this case, my interests have been set back too, but (given our current social arrangements) not in a manner that is idiosyncratic. This is because those who enjoy certain social privileges due to possessing social power are systematically treated in beneficial ways. Were nepotism and "old boy networks" not forms of systematic privileging of certain socioeconomic groups, promoting one's nephew over me would be akin to the case of having a tall forehead. It would be morally wrong, but not an instance of systematic social injustice. However, so long as the indefensibility of setbacks trades on certain patterns of systematic privileging, these setbacks fall under my investigation too. To offer yet another example to elucidate: if my legitimate interest in living in a tolerable social environment is hampered by systematic police brutality toward my racialized social kind, this interest violation is indefensible not only because of the physical and psychological harms caused, but also because the brutality is an expression of institutionalized racial prejudice. Further, the individual harms are grounded in systematic and institutional prejudices, which make the latter ontologically prior to the individual harms. The brutality is social and systematic in a manner that the idiosyncratic employer's actions are not. In the subsequent chapters, I will focus on such social and systematic cases.

In responding to the semantic and ontological puzzles, these philosophers (among others) aimed to provide analytical tools that can be used in a feminist social theory in order to ground feminism's "positive vision of equitable and sustaining human relationships" (Antony 1998, 67) and to make good feminist critical claims about the damage done by patriarchy. They aim to elucidate something *normatively* important about gender, which would justify feminist claims on behalf of women, and explicate what it is that underpins women's oppression as a social kind. Doing so can presumably help feminists advance good theories of resistance.

Given my earlier argument (cf. Part I), feminist social theory should not rely on the conceptions of *gender* and *woman*. Rather, we should proceed with my deflated terminology and ontology (cf. chapter 5) along with dehumanization (cf. chapter 6). The "gender" terminology and ontology that I offered earlier will help with the descriptive social theoretical parts of humanist feminism, while dehumanization provides the required normativity.[2] To spell this out in detail, consider the desiderata and adequacy conditions of feminist social theory. Ann Cudd (2006) has provided one of the most comprehensive theories of oppression inspired by feminist concerns. She aims to elucidate an ameliorative sense of *oppression*, which we ought to appropriate in order to meet certain explanatory and emancipatory needs. Cudd outlines three adequacy conditions that should be met in order to satisfy these needs. First, our analysis of oppression ought to provide "a clear and coherent definition of oppression and conditions to pick out the right cases of oppression" (Cudd 2006, 20). Second, a comprehensive theory of oppression must answer and give guidance to the following more specific questions:

- Who are oppressed, and who benefits from oppression?
- How does oppression originate?
- How does oppression endure over time?
- How do institutional structures of oppression form?

Out of these, the third endurance question is central, and (for Cudd) answering this question will inform our answers to the rest. The final adequacy condition is that our theory of oppression should provide some way to conceptualize overcoming and reducing oppression (2006, 21). With these conditions in mind, Cudd develops her theory (to be discussed shortly).

---

[2] I say "gender" terminology and ontology for a reason. The trait/norm covariance relation and the positions put forward in chapter 5 that elucidate a thin 'woman' conception are not strictly speaking elucidations of *gender* terms and ontology. After all, the take-home message of Part I is that feminists should move on from the gender controversy and embrace my proposed paradigm shift in focus. However, as already noted, articulating this postshift state of affairs is not easy because of the lack of alternative linguistic resources.

Cudd's desiderata for a feminist social theory are on a par with those views examined in Part I: such a theory should be able to provide a good and systematic articulation of why women as a group are and continue to be oppressed, so that we can conceptualize overcoming such oppression. Feminist social theory is made good by empirical accuracy, correctly describing the existing states of affairs (descriptive components), and by plausibly accounting for some conditions that help us overcome oppression (evaluative component). However, this strategy fails to articulate *why* some ways of treating others are wrongful and illegitimate—an articulation that extant feminist social theories lack. Let me clarify: prior theories do not lack normative components altogether. Cudd, for instance, provides a detailed theory of resistance to complement her theory of oppression (2006, chap. 7). And Young holds that "no empirical investigation of social structures and relations can avoid normative judgments" (1990, 29). Nevertheless, the normative commitments of extant positions *differ* from the normative commitments that I take to be central to a feminist social theory. Other positions focus on the question, What should we do about oppression in order to advance social justice? But my contention is that an adequate feminist social theory requires a satisfying account of a different normative component too: why oppression is wrongful. That is, we need a further underlying normative theory, but one that does not elucidate a theory of justice. Rather, we need a theory of *injustice*, which extant positions have not sufficiently put forward.

So, although Cudd is right to include the three aforementioned conditions as adequacy conditions of a feminist social theory, I contend that the set of conditions is incomplete—we require a further normative criterion to make good an account of social injustice. For me, then, a feminist social theory must (1) provide clear and coherent definitions of different forms of patriarchal injustice; (2) explain injustices women face under patriarchy; (3) provide some way to account for the conditions of justice for women; *and* (4) say why patriarchy wrongs women. This final requirement is needed in order to meet the first three adequacy conditions and to make good the descriptive aspects of our explication of injustice. After all, feminist philosophers usually understand 'injustice' and its cognates in moralized senses (cf. Cudd 2006; Haslanger 2004; Young 1990). 'Injustice' is not a nonevaluative term; still, extant positions do not sufficiently elucidate the term's evaluative component and often leave this implicit. By contrast, I submit, if we aim to delimit different forms of injustice that are understood in moralized senses, we need an account that explicates those moralized senses. My earlier articulation of dehumanization aims, then, precisely to do that.

I take the above desiderata to generalize. So any emancipatory social theory, or henceforth EST, should satisfy the above four conditions. Our theory of social injustice should (1) provide clear and coherent definitions of different forms of injustice; (2) explain injustices on various different grounds; (3) provide some way to account for the conditions of social justice; and (4) say why these forms of injustice are wrongful, where this component is sensitive to actual nonideal states of affairs. With these adequacy conditions in mind, I will propose next a typology of different forms of injustice (oppression, domination, discrimination). I go on to argue that my proposed normativity (i.e., dehumanization) helps to elucidate and refine these forms of injustice. I will say more about the different contours of injustice, or the basis on which one suffers injustices, in the following chapter.

7.3. Forms of Injustice

7.3.1. DISCRIMINATION

At its most basic, discrimination amounts to group-based differential treatment. It can be understood in a moralized or neutral sense. For instance, adults and children are treated differentially along many social axes (e.g., one group is allowed to drive, the other is not). We do not usually find such differential treatment problematic, though. In its moralized sense, discrimination consists in differential treatment of one group relative to another insofar as some acts, practices, or policies impose a *wrongful* disadvantage on that group. Young takes intent to be a defining feature of discrimination, though not of oppression: for her, the concept of *discrimination* should be restricted to "intentional and explicitly formulated policies of exclusion or preference" in the distribution of benefits and social positions (1990, 196). Although one can be oppressed without someone explicitly doing the oppressing (more on this shortly), one cannot be discriminated against without someone doing the discriminating.

However, this rudimentary understanding neglects some important distinctions (cf. Altman 2011; Moreau 2010). First, there are different types of discrimination, most basically (1) *direct discrimination*: some people are explicitly and intentionally singled out for disadvantaging treatment because of socially salient features; (2) *indirect discrimination*: some rule disproportionately affects a group of people because of a socially salient feature they possess, although the rule is at face value neutral. Second, in picking out discriminatory acts we can rely on *intentions* or *outcomes*. The former considers whether the discriminator explicitly intended to discriminate (e.g., hanging a "Whites Only" sign in a cafe); the latter looks at whether some rule or conduct disproportionally affects and excludes some social group(s), regardless of the underlying (perhaps even good) intentions of the actors. Third, how we understand the claim that some course of action disadvantages a group "because of" or "on the basis of" a socially salient identification makes a difference. We can understand this as a claim about *internal reasons* for action: the discriminator's motivation hinges on the social background of the discriminated. Or we can understand "because of" as picking out *explanatory factors*: socially salient group membership provides a part of the explanation for social disadvantages. These three distinctions map onto one another. Direct discrimination is about intentional exclusion because of one's social kind membership, which trades on discriminators' internal reasons for action (namely, they intend to discriminate against some individuals because of those individuals' social identity). Indirect discrimination is about outcomes that disproportionately disadvantage and exclude people, where social identity markers (at least partly) explain the disadvantages and exclusions suffered.

Discrimination obviously results in various harms, like inequalities in the distribution of social goods. But since I distinguish harm and wrong, the important question for me is, Why and when is discrimination wrongful? Some differential treatments are not wrongful either intuitively or following my definition of dehumanization. Take a case of a women's shelter hiring only female care workers. Male and female applicants are differentially treated, but this does not strike me as a case of wrongful discrimination: the male applicants' legitimate interests may be set back, but not indefensibly so. This is because we have good grounds to hire female care workers in order to prevent further harm and trauma to the shelter's inhabitants, which makes the differential treatment excusable. So not all discrimination is wrongful for me—only that which is dehumanizing will count as wrongful and be of the sort that social justice should counter. In this sense, my normative component enables us to home in on the right cases of discrimination; the fourth adequacy condition of EST helps us to meet the first three. However, others have suggested different grounds for wrongfulness. How does my proposal, then, fare against competing conceptions of discrimination's moral wrong? Consider two recent proposals.

Deborah Hellman (2011) suggests that wrongful discrimination consists in drawing distinctions among people based on some trait they possess that results in harmful consequences *and* that counts as demeaning. That is, so long as some social classification does not demean, it is not wrongful—even if it has some harmful consequences. "Demeaning" for Hellman means the following: "to treat someone in a way that denies her equal moral worth. . . . To demean is not merely to insult but also to put down, to diminish or denigrate" (2011, 29). It is to treat another as "not fully human or not of equal moral worth" (2011, 35). What makes discrimination wrongful is that it violates (what Hellman takes to be) a bedrock moral principle: the equal moral worth of all persons. Two further principles comprise this "bedrock" principle: first, "there is a worth or inherent dignity of persons that requires that we treat each other with respect"; second, this worth is not gradual, and we are all equally worthy (Hellman 2011, 6). So, a "Whites Only" sign in a cafe is not discriminatory because it divides people along racialized lines. Rather, the sign is discriminatory because by dividing people the cafe owner demeans nonwhites in failing to treat them with respect—the owner does not accord everyone equal moral worth.

Pretheoretically, many would probably take the notion of *demeaning* to be equivalent to *dehumanizing*. I disagree, however, and take my notion to capture something else. For Hellman, demeaning ranks people as inferior. But this is not necessary for dehumanization. Being treated in dehumanizing ways has a consequence of differentially distributing social agents in social milieus, where doing so is unjust. Differential distribution of social agents is nonetheless not equivalent to ranking them hierarchically or to this ranking literally diminishing one's intrinsic worth. Some indefensible interest-violations might prevent a person from pursuing a career in x and pushing her to a career in y instead. If this constitutes a moral injury in my sense, we have dehumanization. (For instance, think of social mechanisms like women being left out of professional networks or being ignored in meetings and thus stymied in careers in certain male-dominated fields.) There may nevertheless be no obvious inferiority ranking between the two careers, provided that we are not committed to some contentious ranking of professions. Still, something impermissible from the point of view of social justice has taken place—some structural exclusion mechanisms are at play—even without an obvious inferiority ranking.

Another important difference pertains to our methodologies. Hellman relies on the "bedrock" moral principle of equal worth of all persons without arguing for this principle. I have no pretheoretical qualms with the principle, but I find it methodologically problematic. The principle's acceptance is part of the background presumptions guiding Hellman's analysis of discrimination's wrong. And she seems to assent to the principle because it is inscribed in the US Constitution: Hellman's desideratum is to elucidate why some discriminatory behavior is wrongful in a way that fits the US system of laws; thus, her reliance on the principle of equal worth. My goals are different, and I am not bound to follow this principle simply because some legal jurisdictions rely on it. I see no reason therefore to build a general theory of discrimination on it. Moreover, I wish to actively resist relying on Hellman's bedrock moral principle because it buys into an internalist conception of humanity. On methodological grounds, then, Hellman's proposal is a nonstarter for me. I start my investigation from an externalist conception, which avoids Antony's critique of internalism and Young's attack on assimilationism (cf. sections 6.1. and 6.2). Precisely because my proposal avoids having to assent to an ethically thick conception of *humanity*, I take it to afford methodological benefits. For me, dehumanization underpins the wrong of discrimination. But my normative work is done by morally injurious and indefensible interest setbacks, where none of these component parts rely on some traditionally Kantian and typically primitive conception about "our" inherent worth.

Sophia Moreau has also recently explicated why discrimination is unjust in that (for her) discrimination injures our crucial interest in *deliberative freedoms*: "freedoms to deliberate about and decide how to live in a way that is insulated from pressures stemming from [normatively] extraneous traits of ours," such as skin color or reproductive organs (2010, 147). Being about interest violations, Moreau's position is prima facie not far from mine. However, I contend, her account is in need of some revisions, and dehumanization can helpfully deliver what is missing. For Moreau, discrimination is wrongful in that the discriminator has interfered with another's right to certain freedoms (to undertake and engage in deliberative activities and to make decisions about some aspect of one's life). In this sense, discrimination is a personal wrong, which fits existing legislation. The key ingredients of this account are *deliberative freedoms* and *normatively extraneous traits*. Let's briefly clarify these. First, deliberative freedoms are those that we appear to think members of liberal societies have a right to, namely freedom of thought and action (Moreau 2010, 148). Decision-making and deliberation are about making commitments and taking steps to bring about what we are committed to. A necessary condition for me having a particular deliberative freedom is that "I really have the opportunity to do the thing I may decide to do" (2010, 170). Second, normatively extraneous traits are those that

> people should not have to factor into their deliberations . . . *as costs*, even if they are deeply important to the person and relevant to her decisions . . . [T]o say that a person's race is normatively extraneous . . . is to say that people should not be constrained by the social costs of being of one race rather than another when they deliberate about such questions as what job to take or where to live. (2010, 149)

So discrimination (both direct and indirect) is wrongful in that our right to deliberative freedoms is not insulated from pressures based on extraneous traits. In direct discrimination, some people are explicitly singled out for disadvantaging treatment because of a trait they possess; with indirect discrimination, some rule disproportionately affects a group of people because of a trait they possess, although the rule is at face value trait neutral. And the mark of discrimination in these cases turns on whether the trait in question is normatively extraneous: whether the trait burdens its possessor's deliberative opportunities when the trait ought not to be a factor in deliberation. When extraneous traits interfere with our right to deliberative freedoms, we can descriptively fix the relevant class of discriminatory acts and articulate the wrongness-making feature of discrimination.

That discrimination is about differential treatment that disadvantages certain groups has pretheoretical appeal, and I am happy to endorse this as a core component of discrimination. However, Moreau's method for fixing those traits that should be taken as *prohibited* grounds for differential treatment leaves something to be desired. She takes this to be a normative question, and our answer will depend on "whether people have a right to make decisions in a manner that is free from the sorts of institutional and attitudinal

pressures that are encountered by those with the trait" (Moreau 2010, 156).
Now, Moreau admits that this leaves her account open to the complaint that
she fails to provide a unified account of discrimination's grounds. The normatively extraneous traits seem to be too disparate and gerrymandered to
account for how discrimination wrongs its recipients, and the account seemingly fails to provide a "principled explanation of that wrong" (2010, 157).
Although Moreau admits that her account does not offer an explanation that
elucidates the wrong of discrimination in terms of some single normative fact
operative in each case, nevertheless, it can still provide a principled explanation of discrimination. This is because

> On the account of discrimination that I am proposing, victims of discrimi-
> nation have been denied an equal set of deliberative freedoms. Which de-
> liberative freedoms we are entitled to depends on which traits should be
> recognized as normatively extraneous. And the fact that we cannot answer
> this question by appealing to some single further kind of normative fact in
> all cases is not a problem. Rather, it reflects the complex nature of the type
> of injustice that we are trying to explain. (2010, 157)

Moreau is surely right that discrimination is a complex kind of injustice (as
are all social injustices). But I fail to see why it is *therefore* unproblematic not
to elucidate the further unifying normative fact. First, such a fact is apparently not needed since we can determine the relevant normatively extraneous trait(s) in legal contexts and on a case-by-case basis (2010, 159). However,
in relying on legal cases we lose sight of the moral issue: why discrimination
is wrongful. If we are after a purely legal conception of *discrimination*, I am
happy to fix the relevant traits in courts of law and on a case-by-case basis. But
if we are interested in understanding discrimination in a way that has import
in moral and social theory more widely, this does not seem satisfying. And
given that Moreau is after an account of discrimination that not only fits US
and UK antidiscrimination laws, but *also* elucidates "what discrimination involves and why it is unjust" (2010, 145), more needs to be said on the moral side.

Second, once we keep in mind the goal of explicating discrimination
more broadly as a form of social injustice, it seems that we must account
for which traits are normatively extraneous. I take it that a principled explanation of discrimination must contain descriptive and normative elements: at the very least, which instances are correctly or plausibly identified
as discrimination, and what renders those instances wrongful (the first and
the fourth adequacy conditions of EST, respectively). But unless we have
an account of the traits that are normatively extraneous, the prospects of
providing such an explanation will be poor. Or rather: it will be difficult
to distinguish systematic from incidental/idiosyncratic discrimination. In
order to fix the former systematic cases, we must appeal to denials of deliberative freedoms that hinge on some normatively extraneous and socially

salient traits. Otherwise it is hard to see how Moreau's account satisfies the adequacy conditions of EST.

My suggestion is that dehumanization can provide the "further normative fact" that fixes the extraneous traits on the basis of which deliberative freedoms are denied. In short: if some trait undergirds dehumanizing ways of treating others, it is the sort of trait that counts as normatively extraneous and that discrimination tracks. Recall that for me, an act or a treatment is dehumanizing iff it is an indefensible setback to some of our legitimate human interests, where this setback constitutes a moral injury. Given our shared embodiment, we have basic welfare interests in common.[3] If some trait (like my ethnic background) is indefensibly used to justify setbacks to such interests (where the setback involves unjustified beliefs about the "nature" of my ethnicity, for example), the trait would count as normatively extraneous in Moreau's sense: it ought not to be a factor in one's deliberation, and so one is constrained by social costs in deliberating (e.g., about what job to take or where to live) on the basis of the trait. Or take the example of my interest in living in a tolerable environment being setback by arbitrary police brutality against members of my racialized group. If such setbacks take away some deliberative freedoms and force me to take my group membership into account when I ought not to, then those traits indicative of my group membership would be normatively extraneous. We can fix such traits to pick out cases of discrimination. In this way, my account of *dehumanization* enables us to satisfy the first desideratum of EST by satisfying the fourth.

7.3.2. DOMINATION

In her deeply inspiring book *Justice and the Politics of Difference*, Young outlines two phenomena that she takes to define injustice: oppression and domination. These are distinguished by their correspondence to two constituents of a good life. First, a good life requires that we develop and exercise certain capacities; second, that we have the opportunity to participate in determining our actions and their conditions (1990, 37). With these two constituents of flourishing in mind, Young defines *oppression* and *domination*. The former consists in "systematic institutional processes which prevent some people from learning and using satisfying and expansive skills in socially recognized settings" (Young 1990, 38). Domination describes the condition where others

---

[3] To recap: the continuance of one's life and in one's own physical health and vigor; the absence of absorbing pain and suffering; being nonstigmatized and not excluded due to one's atypical bodily functioning; being free from debilitating and painful bodily conditions; minimal intellectual acuity, emotional stability, the absence of groundless anxieties and resentments; the capacity to engage in meaningful social intercourses and to enjoy and maintain friendships; minimal means of subsistence; a tolerable social and physical environment.

can without reciprocation prevent or inhibit socially and morally relevant participation in determining one's course of action (1990, 38).[4] In short: oppression prevents people from *acquiring* certain skills needed for a good life, whereas domination inhibits people's *participation* in choosing (the conditions of) their actions that enable them to realize a good life. The dominated are forced to follow rules set by others and to do so "under institutional conditions they have not had a part in deciding" (Young 1990, 218). These forms of injustice usually overlap, albeit being asymmetrically related. Although oppression usually includes some domination (oppressed people are typically constrained to follow rules set by others), oppressive situations are not all generated by dominance relations. Further, domination does not entail oppression. Common societal decision-making practices are usually dominating in being constituted by constraining rules set by others. Nevertheless, many still enjoy "significant institutionalized support for the development and exercise" of capacities needed for flourishing (1990, 38). Just think of those who are privileged in virtue of their assigned racial category and have subsequently access to good educational opportunities. Although they may be dominated by some societal practices, those who are privileged in educational opportunities on racialized grounds are not oppressed in the sense of being denied the opportunity to acquire important skills needed to live a good life.

I will say more about Young's sense of *oppression* in the following section. But first consider her conception of domination. Rationalized bureaucratization both in the workplace and in everyday life is a major dominating force for Young:

> Both government and private agencies subject clients and consumers to meshes of microauthority. Clients and consumers submit to the authority of hospitals, schools, universities, social service agencies, government offices, banks, fast-food restaurants, and countless other institutions. Officials in these institutions not only prescribe much of the behavior of clients or consumers within the institutions, but perhaps more importantly, through social scientific, managerial, or marketing disciplines, they define for the client or consumer the very form and meaning of the needs the institutions aim to meet. (1990, 79)

Intuitively I agree with Young that domination is about someone else determining my actions and their conditions. But defining domination in so diffuse a manner is not unproblematic. On Young's picture, we are conceivably *all* dominated in one way or another. And although this may be true loosely speaking, assenting to such a diffuse picture of domination would mean that we all

---

[4] Feminists and social philosophers also often speak of subjugation being a form of injustice. I take it that this is just another ways of speaking about domination and that there to be no substantive difference between the two.

suffer from injustice, regardless of the ways in which we may be privileged by our institutional settings and social structures. That is, Young's view makes social, systematic, and structural domination too widespread, which fails to satisfy the first adequacy condition of EST: to capture the right set of cases. To illustrate, consider the following examples. The rich can (and do) complain that government-imposed taxes force them to submit to rules set by others. The US gun lobby complains that gun ownership restrictions would prevent them from determining the conditions of their actions in ways that would hamper individual safety and flourishing. On the face of it, both cases involve Young's sense of domination. But to think that the people in question *therefore* face social injustice gets the conditions of injustice wrong. That is, domination is a core form of social injustice; but if on Young's criteria we are all dominated in having to follow rules set by others, everyone will therefore face social injustice—a result that hampers meaningful social analysis and critique.

How should we understand domination then? Young's understanding of domination has prima facie plausibility; but (I contend) not every instance of following rules set by others is unjust. I will propose next that we can distinguish unjust and permissible domination with my notion of *dehumanization*, which improves Young's account. Roughly put: if the domination one is subject to fulfills the conditions of dehumanization in my sense, it counts as unjust and falls under the purview of liberatory political movements. If the domination is not dehumanizing, it is not unjust and need not concern us from a social justice point of view. This enables us to say that even though prevalent bureaucratic institutional processes and structures dominate everyone, not everyone *therefore* suffers from social injustice.

To test this criterion, consider the case of US gun controls. Do gun controls indefensibly setback some legitimate human interests? It seems to me that they do not. First, the right to bear arms in the sense advanced by the US National Rifle Association is hardly a basic human welfare interest in my sense. For me, satisfying the basic requisites of well-being subsequently makes (something like) flourishing possible—but welfare interests are not constitutive of flourishing. So even though one's personal flourishing may be hampered by gun controls, such controls do not undermine the basic human welfare interests. Moreover, such welfare interests may legitimately be hampered *if* we have defensible reasons to do so—after all, dehumanization is about unjustified and inexcusable setbacks to these interests. And arguably, there are good reasons to restrict access to guns in the United States on rather obvious consequentialist grounds: just think of the harms generated by firearm-related incidents.

Defenders of gun ownership can of course retort: we should not think about the justifiability of the setback in consequentialist terms, but in terms of *rights*. Because US citizens have a constitutional right to bear arms, any restrictions on gun ownership are unjustified and thus indefensible. This response is unlikely to persuade many outside the United States insofar as the US Constitution is an amendable legal document made by people, and there is nothing necessary about its particular contours. In fact, debates that boil down to the proper understanding, significance, and import of the US Constitution are rather frustrating from a moral point of view. Still, we can again appeal to the basic welfare interests that derive from our shared embodiment: nothing about *those interests* would make gun restrictions indefensible or justify the right to gun possession. The right that defenders of gun ownership appeal to is a legal-political notion; dehumanization is a moral one. So on the more basic moral level, the story goes thus: restricting gun ownership would be domination in Young's sense, but since it does not count as dehumanizing, such restrictions would be morally permissible. Thus, though they are instances of domination, they would not *therefore* count as socially unjust. On the next legal-political level, we can debate the merits and consequences of restricting gun ownership further: namely, whether this instance of morally justified domination is also legally justified given the Second Amendment right to bear arms. If *on this level* the restrictions were upheld, the relevant instance of domination would be both morally and legally permissible. On my amended version, restricting gun ownership would be a case of justified domination, albeit of domination in Young's sense nonetheless.

Contra Young, Frank Lovett suggests an arbitrary power conception of domination: domination is "a condition experienced by persons or groups to the extent that they are dependent on a social relationship in which some other person or group wields arbitrary power over them" (2010, 2). Lovett further argues for a conception of social justice with his idea of *justice as minimizing domination* (JMD): since avoidable domination is a grave wrong, social and political institutions should be organized in a way that minimizes domination. I will have more to say in chapter 9 about Lovett's conception of social justice, which (to anticipate) I find implausible. But let's briefly consider his view of domination, which encompasses three individually necessary and jointly sufficient conditions: the dependency, imbalance of power, and arbitrariness conditions. First, what matters for domination is not the outcome of any particular relation between persons or groups; rather, when persons or groups are structurally related to one another in ways that constitute dependency relations, they are likely to be dominated. Examples of such relations are slaves' dependency on their masters and nineteenth-century marriage relations that make women dependent on their husbands. Second, in order for these dependency relations to constitute domination, they must involve social power imbalances. To have social power is to have power over someone; and to have power over someone is (among other things) "to have the ability to change what they otherwise prefer to do, whether one happens to make use of this ability or not" (Lovett 2010, 82). Third, for some treatment to be an instance of domination, the dependency relation involving the exercise of power over someone must be arbitrary—at the discretion of the powerful. This means that the exercise of social power is "not externally constrained by effective rules, procedures, or goals that are common knowledge to all persons or groups concerned" (2010, 96). This conception supposedly captures the "core cases" of domination: feudalism, slavery, domination in the family, autocratic governments, and the domination of workers (2010, 93).

Some differences in Lovett's and Young's conceptions are immediately obvious. Young's view of domination turns on established, public, and externally constraining rules and procedures, rationalized bureaucratization being one major dominating force. For Lovett, the situation is quite different. Whenever the exercise of power is externally constrained by effective rules or procedures, its exercise is not arbitrary and there is no domination. Legally regulated gender discrimination, for example, would not count as domination for Lovett. So Young takes domination to be precisely about externally imposed effective rules that enable some individuals or groups to have power over other individuals or groups. For Lovett, domination is the lack of such rules, though externally constraining rules and procedures can open up the space for arbitrary exercises of power. For instance, traditional family law that prevented any external interference with husbands' power over their wives and children created a space within which husbands could wield such power arbitrarily and unchecked (Lovett 2010, 111). Nevertheless, the law simply created the conditions for domination, and the law itself would not count as dominating. This does not render the law fair. But (Lovett maintains) not everything that is unfair or bad is equivalent to domination:

> It is bad to starve, for example, but it does not follow that to be starving is to be subject to domination. It is also bad to treat others unfairly in the distribution of goods and opportunities, but it does not follow that this is, as such, to subject them to domination. Domination is one thing, and unfairness is another. (2010, 119)

Lovett accepts that many will find this intuitively unsatisfying. But, he holds, we should give up the intuition that the above are instances of domination and that instances of discrimination, coercion, exploitation, and oppression are prima facie instances of domination. On Lovett's view, discrimination and exploitation are likely outcomes of domination—but since his account of domination is not outcome based, discrimination and exploitation are not equivalent to domination. Then again, coercion is a likely enabling factor of domination, but again not constitutive of it. Finally, oppression (in Lovett's view) is too broad to be helpful: it covers too many problems that have too divergent origins. Therefore, his account of domination is to be preferred as being more useful (Lovett 2010, 123).

For Lovett, undermining domination is "the exclusive concern of a conception of social justice" (2010, 170), and domination is exemplified by "the

core cases" of feudalism, slavery, domination in the family, autocratic governments, and domination of workers (2010, 93). What is striking about this
position is its restricted scope, which generates two problems. First, Lovett's
conception of domination ill fits contemporary paradigm cases of social,
structural, and systematic injustices. Second, his privileging of domination over other forms of injustice is unpersuasive. I will address the second
point in chapter 9. But why do I hold the former view? My contention is that
Lovett's historical focus does not address contemporary social injustices, and
domination in his sense is less widespread than he seems to hold. Or, to put
the point differently: domination in Lovett's sense is not so widespread in
many supposedly democratic, Western societies (like the United States and
UK), but this counterintuitively renders such societies relatively just. Key to
my concern is Lovett's notion of arbitrariness. For him, the exercise of social
power is arbitrary insofar as its exercise is "not externally constrained by effective rules, procedures, or goals that are common knowledge to all persons
or groups concerned" (2010, 96). This fits his conception of social justice as
being about curbing the exercise of arbitrary power over others. Social justice
is about instituting effective rules and procedures that externally constrain
exercising power "at will." But where in the contemporary Western world is
domination of this kind to be found?

Lovett's only nonhistorical example of "clear sites of domination" is the
contemporary US prison system (2010, 179–180). However, it is far from obvious
to me (and Lovett does not elaborate) why this involves arbitrary use of power
over the prisoners. Prison guards' use of power is externally constrained by
rules and procedures—these rules and procedures perhaps just give the guards
relatively wide scope to exercise power. But there is no arbitrary wielding of
power akin to cases of slavery and political tyranny. Furthermore, take the example of people of color being disproportionately affected by stop-and-search
policies, where police officers have no other grounds for suspicion but the individuals' racialized group membership. That is, the police officers are acting
on a perception of danger, which does not reliably track empirical facts about
how "dangerous" members of this racialized group are. Many of those affected
would say that this is a case of domination in the sense of involving unjust
wielding of power over them. But, again, what makes this exercise of power
problematic from a social justice perspective is not that it is arbitrary—that
there are *no* externally constraining effective rules and procedures to govern
police behavior. The problem is that the rules and procedures for stop-and-
search policies are badly formulated and justified, and they result in particular
groups being disproportionately affected on prejudicial grounds.

Here Lovett might appeal to the notion of *effective* rules. He might retort
that the rules involved in stop-and-search policies are not effective, which
enables arbitrary wielding of power. Rules and laws are effective when they
have the actual capacity to constrain the exercise of social power (Lovett 2010,

96–97). It is not enough that there should be some normative standards of "fairness" or "with moderation" that constrain social power; rather, effectiveness requires that there be some formal mechanisms to enforce the rules, like formal laws. So, one might say, stop-and-search policies do not contain effective rules and merely contain some normative standards. Therefore, the example is one of wielding arbitrary power. But this is unconvincing since Lovett's notion of *effectiveness* leaves something to be desired. There are many ways for laws and rules to be effective: for instance, there are formally codified rules that enable citizens to seek legal recourse. Those who are unjustly affected by stop-and-search policies can and do complain to the Independent Police Complaints Commission in the UK. Of course, such complaints do not always yield the right results. But that should not matter: what matters for Lovett's conception is that there be no effective rules that have the capacity externally to constrain the exercise of social power—not how successfully we in fact can enforce those rules. Given that there are ways for rules and laws to be effective that Lovett fails to consider, I am genuinely unsure how widespread contemporary domination in his sense is.

The upshot is this: cases of indirect discrimination and diffuse oppression due to abject structural conditions ill fit Lovett's core case of social injustice. If we are interested in contemporary social injustices, his core examples of domination are woefully out of date. The sort of outright slavery and feudalism Lovett notes no longer exist in contemporary Western societies; but I hardly think that these societies are therefore characterized by social justice. I say "outright slavery" for a reason: implicit, often covert, and hidden slavery still takes place. This is particularly so because of the trafficking of women and children into sexual slavery. So there are some clear and serious contemporary cases that fit the conception of domination as the arbitrary wielding of power. Nevertheless, there are many other cases that Lovett's account fails to capture that should concern us deeply from a social justice perspective. To put the point somewhat differently: as I see it, *social injustice* is not a transhistorical notion; rather, it is a historically and locally specific one. This does not imply some sort of relativism, whereby we can judge history and say that (e.g.) slavery is not an instance of unjust domination given what we now take social injustice to amount to. Instead, my point is that the nature of social injustice is not static in the sense that we can unproblematically use examples of past injustices to explicate contemporary ones. I agree with Lovett that relative to the past, his examples do capture paradigms of social injustice. But since human societies and social interactions evolve and transform, I am not convinced that these past paradigms help capture contemporary ones. The pool of paradigm social injustices changes, which does not render older paradigms innocuous. But it does mean that if we wish to understand social relations characterized by injustice in the contemporary world, historical examples may be deeply unhelpful (as I have suggested here). A feminist social

theory, and emancipatory social theories in general, should thus not endorse
Lovett's conception of domination. Its relevance to the contemporary world
is rather questionable, due to which it fails to satisfy the first and second adequacy conditions of EST: to pick out the right cases and to provide satisfying
explanations of injustices suffered by groups of individuals based on their
socially salient identities.

7.3.3. OPPRESSION: A FIRST STAB

Oppression as a phenomenon appears to be more diffuse and less clear-cut
than discrimination and domination; thus, it is harder to define precisely. At
its most basic, oppression has to do with unjust *constraints*. As Alison Jaggar
puts it, oppression is "the imposition of unjust constraints on the freedom
of individuals or groups" (1983a, 6). We can understand the imposition of
constraints in many different ways, though. Kenneth Clatterbaugh (1996)
provides a helpful preliminary understanding. First, psychological theories
hold that oppression is some constraining internal state or feeling. Second,
on inequality theories, oppression amounts to one group being denied some
scarce and valuable resources. Third, limitation theories take oppression to
name a condition that denies options available to individuals on the basis
of their social kind membership. All three are implausible on Clatterbaugh's
view: people are not oppressed just because they feel oppressed; and resource
denials and opportunity constraints are not per se oppressively constraining (just think of cases that are due to bad luck or weather). By contrast,
Clatterbaugh advances a dehumanization theory of oppression, which allegedly well befits our pretheoretical intuitions: oppression is the systematic
dehumanization of some identifiable human group, and to dehumanize is to
deny that the members of the group "possess the complete range of human
abilities, needs, and wants that are valued at that time as important for being
a human being" (Clatterbaugh 1996, 295). (Or they are treated as if they lack
the aforementioned human qualities and thus are treated as defectively
human.) When social structures (like social institutions, practices, policies,
laws, humor, ideology, and work relations) assume, promote, or treat a target
group as if it were defective relative to any of the relevant human-defining
abilities and needs, the structure is oppressively constraining.

   Clatterbaugh's theory of oppression may appear to be similar to mine in
that we both take dehumanization to play a pivotal role in social injustice.
However, there are significant differences worth flagging. First, Clatterbaugh's
notion of humanity is internalist, whereas mine is externalist. As noted already, I consider this starting point to be unacceptable on methodological
grounds. Second, his conception of dehumanization is committed to the view
that individuals are treated as lacking some qualities and that this makes oppression wrongful. For me, dehumanization is a feature of acts, and it is not

wrongful in denying some supposedly human qualities; instead, dehumanizing acts hamper the fulfillment of certain human interests. Now, what matters for Clatterbaugh is that some abilities, needs, and wants that "the broader society [at some time] *values* as human-making" be denied (1996, 295). This runs into problems, though, unless we fix the human-making features as those that the broader society *ought* to value. Imagine that some society takes having blue eyes as the important and valued human-making feature. Those without blue eyes would appear to be denied humanity and thus be oppressed; something that fits Clatterbaugh's own example of US slavery, where black slaves were denied the then-valued human-making traits and thus treated as chattel and as non-persons. But apparently the blue-eyed case would not be oppressive because "a group is not oppressed if there are qualities included in being a human being that are denied them and that they in fact lack" (Clatterbaugh 1996, 295). So if having blue eyes is a valued human-making quality, then those who lack the quality are not oppressed because *in not possessing* the quality, they cannot be denied it. And only when groups are denied valued qualities that they prima facie possess do we have oppression in the dehumanization sense.

My contention is that this fixes the conditions of oppression wrong. Imagine a society (and I doubt that this requires much) that values consistent and lifelong opposite-sex-directed sexual desire as an important human-making quality. Since this is something that queer people do not possess, it is a human-making quality that cannot be denied. So queer people are not oppressed as a group in Clatterbaugh's sense. They may be denied housing, equal access to social benefits, and be disadvantaged on the job market because they lack the relevant human-defining quality. But this sort of treatment will not count as group oppression because the salient group simply does not possess the quality of opposite-sex-directed desire to be denied. I suspect that many will find this pretheoretically unpersuasive. Further, the problem is not the denial of some human-making qualities, but the fact that the broader society has homed in on the *wrong qualities*. This elucidation of oppression fails to meet the first adequacy condition of EST: that our account of oppression should pick out the right cases. Clatterbaugh must fix some particular right values that societies ought to focus on, which will be a much more difficult undertaking.[5]

As already mentioned, domination for Young consists in preventing individuals from participating in processes that foster a good life and from

---

[5] Clatterbaugh might claim that, in fact, homophobic denial of housing is not oppressive since he differentiates oppression from other forms of injustice. In his words, social philosophers "often treat oppression as a more serious injustice than being discriminated against, treated unfairly, or unequally" (1996, 290). The severity of oppression is further meant to show that overcoming oppression requires "often a revolution or some great social upheaval, while [overcoming] inequality and discrimination typically seem to require only reform" (Clatterbaugh 1996, 290). Whether social philosophers treat oppression as a more severe wrong than discrimination or unfair treatment is

determining their own actions, whereas oppression consists in systematic processes that prevent people from developing or acquiring certain capacities needed for flourishing. In fact, the term 'oppression' names a family of constraining conditions: exploitation, marginalization, powerlessness, cultural imperialism, and violence (Young 1990, chap. 2). These are the *wrongs* that oppression names (1990, 40), and 'oppression' refers to

> the vast and deep injustices some groups suffer as a consequence of often unconscious assumptions and reactions of well-meaning people in ordinary interactions, media and cultural stereotypes, and structural features of bureaucratic hierarchies and market mechanisms—in short, the normal processes of everyday life. (1990, 41)

Causes of oppression can be found in accepted norms, habits, symbols, institutional rules, and their consequences. This makes oppression systemic and structural. Young's forms or "faces" of oppression are meant to capture a plurality of different conditions that members of various social kinds encounter. Exploitation, marginalization, and powerlessness refer to "relations of power and oppression that occur by virtue of the social division of labor—who works for whom, who does not work, and how the content of work defines one institutional position relative to others" (Young 1990, 58). These forms of oppression express structural and institutional relations that affect people's material existence, such as which opportunities are open to them. The other two forms of oppression are somewhat different. Violence is not directly tied to the division of labor but rather aims to humiliate, damage, and destroy the oppressed persons or to engender the threat of violence. Cultural imperialism, then again, has a symbolic dimension and denotes the experience of "how the dominant meanings of a society render the particular perspective of one's own group invisible at the same time as they stereotype one's group and mark it out as the Other" (1990, 59).

For Young, the five faces of oppression capture not only the constraining harms of oppression, but also oppression's *wrongs*.[6] However, I find this

---

contentious. In any case, thinking about how (on his view) we can overcome oppression ill fits actual queer rights struggles. If the sorts of homophobic treatments I have noted were not instances of systematic oppression, but "just" inequalities, the required social change would be one of reform rather than revolution. Now, much will depend on how one understands *revolution*, which is something Clatterbaugh does not elucidate. But, I contend, gay rights movements across the world have achieved and are achieving something revolutionary, not just something reformative. So thinking about how oppression can be overcome further suggests that Clatterbaugh's proposal does not meet the first adequacy condition of EST or pick out the right cases. If my example were not a case of oppression, mere reform would suffice to remedy the situation. But I am unconvinced that deeply homophobic societies (like at the time of writing, Russia) can be fixed just by correcting some of the society's unfortunate hitches.

⁶ Actually, Young's position a somewhat ambiguous. Since she takes oppression to hamper self-development, and domination to hamper self-determination (1990, 37), this might suggest

unsatisfying on two grounds. First, Young's five faces do not capture what the wrong of oppression consists in. Instead, they capture states of affairs that more properly elucidate the means to enact oppression (e.g., violence and cultural imperialism) along with oppression's harms (e.g., exploitation, marginalization, and powerlessness). Second, Young's normativity does not go far enough: it does not tell us what makes the five putative forms of oppression wrongful.[7] To elucidate these claims, consider exploitation, or "who works for whom" (Young 1990, 58).

Young describes such oppression in largely Marxist terms, where one group's labor benefits another group. Still, she seems to want to extend the notion to nonlabor relations too. Hallmarks of such broader exploitative relations are asymmetry and dependence. For instance, under patriarchy women's and men's familial relations tend to be asymmetric (e.g., women's double shift versus men's single shift) and characterized by dependence (e.g., the gendered wage gap tends to make women financially dependent on their male partners). However, as I see it, the sheer possibility of exploitative relations depends on some prior enabling conditions. That is, exploitation may be a materially harmful relationship but only because there is something that enables the formation of such relationships. Young's initial definition of oppression seems to be the underlying factor that captures the enabling conditions: that certain constraining conditions prevent individuals from developing or acquiring capacities needed for flourishing. In this sense, then, running oppression together with the five faces gets the story slightly wrong. Oppression understood in terms of constraints on our actions

---

that Young takes the wrong of social injustice to amount to something like autonomy violation. However, Young does not explicitly frame her view in such terms. In fact, she discusses autonomy in the context of oppression relative to feminist critiques of the liberal tradition, which assumes that moral agency requires persons to be autonomous and independent, where this leads liberalism to ignore ways in which women's lives have been characterized by dependence relations (1990, 55–54). Since Young does not explicitly frame the wrong of injustice in terms of autonomy violations, but she does explicitly state that the five faces name oppression's wrongs, I will focus on these five faces.

[7] Haslanger's (2004) position is akin to and draws on Young's, but she too fails to articulate the wrongfulness of oppression. Haslanger offers an account of structural oppression, where *F*s are oppressed as *F*s (as a social kind) by an institution *I* in a context C iff (by definition) there exists some relation *R* where being an *F* nonaccidentally correlates with being disadvantaged by standing in an unjust relation *R* to others, and *I* creates, perpetuates, or reinforces that relation. Even though Haslanger provides helpful and detailed elucidations of what it is for one's social kind membership to nonaccidentally correlate with a disadvantage and of what it is for an institution to create and perpetuate a harmful relation, she does not spell out in detail what makes the relation *R* unjust. Haslanger notes that the harm is about constraint (2004, 106) and that oppression involves Young's five faces. But she also refuses to spell out the normative underpinnings of these harms or what makes them unjust. This is because (Haslanger holds) doing so would require a theory of justice, and one cannot articulate such a theory in just one article. This is fair enough; but elucidating the unjustness of the harms does not require a theory of justice. It requires a theory of *injustice*, which is something that I develop here. Furthermore, I think that Haslanger must account for the normative underpinnings of her theory of oppression because she understands *oppression* in a moralized sense. Appealing just to the harms suffered will not do the job.

produces certain human relationships that end up being exploitative in Young's sense (and I would think that domination relations further impact and undergird the formation of exploitative human relationships). But exploitation is not equivalent to oppression—it is the result of oppression. Therefore, contra Young, I do not take exploitation to be a core form of injustice, though this does not, of course, render exploitation any less morally significant.[8]

Moreover, I disagree with Young that the relations indicative of exploitation are per se morally problematic; an obvious example of a morally innocuous asymmetric dependence relation is that between children and parents. We need something further to render these relations morally problematic, which will render the relationship one of (unjust) exploitation. Feminists often argue that under patriarchy such relations are problematic because of the relative powerlessness of women (cf. Okin 1989). Intuitively I agree; but again, power differentials alone do not render asymmetry and dependence oppressive. Parents undoubtedly have more power than their children, regardless of whether we mean *power over* or power in some more diffuse sense. Nonetheless, this does not suffice to render the parent-child relationship oppressive. So the relations that mark exploitation do not in and of themselves explicate what makes exploitation wrongful.

To illustrate the above further, consider marginalization: "Marginals are people the system of labor cannot or will not use" (Young 1990, 53). Young notes that this is conceivably the most dangerous form of oppression because it potentially subjects a whole group of people to severe material deprivation, which is clearly unjust "in a society where others have plenty" (1990, 53). But again, this difference in material goods cannot underpin the wrongfulness of marginalization. It is entirely conceivable that some social groups choose positions that render them marginal in Young's sense: Cudd's (2006) example of such a group is the Amish. Of course, more often than not marginals do not choose their positions. Still, my point is a conceptual one: Young is right that exploitation and marginalization are gravely unjust; but focusing on material differences seemingly does not capture the wrongness-making feature of marginalization. This is where my notion of *dehumanization* comes in: even though I hold that Young's five faces go a long way to satisfying the first adequacy condition of EST, employing my normative criterion provides an improved overall account because it also satisfies the fourth adequacy condition.

How does my proposal go? I will not rehearse all the ways in which dehumanization provides oppression's normative grounding. Consider,

---

[8] For parallel reasons I do not think that subordination is a form of injustice: it also describes a resultant state of affairs that is enabled by prior oppressive conditions and relationships. That is, subordination implies a hierarchical ranking of some kind (e.g., when some group is ranked as inferior relative to another), which conceivably turns on oppressive constraints experienced by subjects with respect to some material conditions.

nevertheless, the most important case for Young: marginalization. For her, single mothers make up one marginal group. In order to see whether (say) not hiring a single mother constitutes dehumanizing oppression that results in marginalization, we must consider whether doing so constitutes an indefensible setback to some legitimate human interests in a morally injurious manner. If it does, the hiring decision is dehumanizing and unjust. Now, clearly a single mother's interest in financial security is set back if she fails to get some job. If this is because there are no prejudicial considerations underlying the decision, her legitimate interests have not been unjustifiably set back. In the case of marginals, though, the setbacks to interests are more likely to be indefensible insofar as they tend to involve morally injurious structural considerations as well as false or unjustified beliefs and implicit attitudes about people deemed marginals. I have in mind here prevalent social institutions, practices, policies, and work relations that tend to be insensitive to the needs of single parents along with attitudes about single parents' poor job performance and inflexibility. As I put it earlier, if the prevalent social arrangements involve explicit or implicit trait/norm pairings that stand in the way of recognition respect, the setback to legitimate human interests will be morally injurious in my sense. We have an indefensible setback to a legitimate human interest that is morally injurious; thus, the requisite act will count as dehumanizing. This delivers us an account that satisfies both the first and fourth adequacy conditions of EST. And so Young's five faces of oppression tell us something about oppression's harms and ways in which oppression is enacted. This provides helpful social theoretical tools, but it does not elucidate what is wrongful about oppression: the social relations she cites as grounding the wrong must be grounded by some further normative criterion. I take dehumanization to provide this criterion, which delimits instances of oppression by elucidating their wrongfulness.

At this point, I wish to return to Part I. There I argued that feminist philosophers should move on from the gender controversy since we need not articulate a thick conception of *woman* for feminist political endeavors. The outlook that underlies the gender controversy was as follows. A conception of *woman* should be thick enough to support feminist normative claims (e.g., to help elucidate how and why patriarchy damages women, to justify feminist critical claims, and to ground a vision of a feminist future). This conception should enable feminist theorists to articulate the social kind of women, so that feminism can make claims in the name and on behalf of women—something that gender-skeptical critiques apparently jeopardized. Subsequently, responding to the semantic and ontological puzzles that resulted from such skeptical critiques should prevent the rug from being pulled out from under emancipatory feminism. Above I considered Young's theories of oppression and domination, which are clearly motivated by feminist concerns. But these theories seem prima facie divorced from Young's theory of gender outlined in section 3.2. So her theory of injustice seems to be freestanding from her theory of gender—does this not, however, undermine the motivation for my entire project? If feminists have offered freestanding theories of injustice and these (as opposed to their theories of gender) are really doing the work, the first part of this book is simply redundant and the motivation for the second part is missing.

Let me briefly discuss this objection. On closer examination, it becomes clear that Young's putatively freestanding theory of oppression is not as freestanding as it first appears. The same is true of Frye's (1983) birdcage notion of oppression, which prima facie also seems independent of her theory of gender (cf. section 3.1). Consider Frye first. For her, oppression names a "system of interrelated barriers and forces which reduce, immobilize and mold people who belong to a certain group, and effect their subordination to another group" (1983, 33). It involves a network of systematically related barriers, none of which alone are sufficient to encage members of certain social groups, but that in relation to one another are deeply confining. Frye subsequently holds that forces and barriers that systemically reduce and immobilize women constitute gendered oppression (1983, 7). She writes:

> The image of the cage helps convey one aspect of the systematic nature of oppression. Another is the selection of occupants of the cages, and analysis of this aspect also helps account for the invisibility of the oppression of women. It is as a woman . . . that one is entrapped. . . . When you question why you are being blocked, [the answer] has to do with your membership in some category understood as "natural" or "physical" category. The "inhabitant" of the "cage" is not an individual but a group, all those of a certain category. (1983, 7–8)

One is marked as a target for certain oppressive pressures by one's category membership; in the case of gendered oppression, this hinges on the membership in the category of women (Frye 1983, 15–16). Therefore, identifying and naming oppression requires that we be able to pick out those who are confined. And in order to "recognize a person as oppressed, one has to see that individual *as* belonging to a group of a certain kind" (1983, 8). This means (following Frye) that women are subject to certain oppressive pressures as women—as members of a particular gendered social kind. In order to pick out and name these pressures (i.e., to recognize women as an oppressed group) and to articulate the damage done by patriarchy, we must be able to identify women's social kind. If we cannot do so, feminism lacks resources to respond to oppression skeptics: those people who fail to see women as a category of oppressed people (1983, 9).

Now, an objection to my view would go as follows: Frye's theory of oppression does not hinge on solving the semantic and ontological puzzles, and this undermines the argument made in Part I. This is because (contra my

diagnosis of the problem) feminist philosophers do not presuppose that feminism requires an elucidation of a thick *woman* conception for political purposes. Given Frye's comments about oppression, though, this objection does
not succeed. Making good her birdcage theory of oppression for feminist purposes hinges on first being able to elucidate women's social kind. Otherwise
we cannot recognize and identify specifically *gendered* oppression. Her elucidation of oppression in terms of interrelated barriers and forces that reduce,
immobilize, and mold individuals can only proceed for feminist purposes if
we first explicate what it is to be a woman and thus a target for certain oppressive group pressures. Frye's account of gendered oppression is not freestanding of gender because identifying and articulating the former presupposes a
conception of the latter; and so questions about how to understand gender are
simply one step removed and lurking in the background.

The same (I submit) is true of Young. She starts her analysis of injustice
from New Leftist social movements (feminism, black liberation, gay and les-
bian liberation) that typically make group-based claims: that there is gendered, racist, and homophobic oppression and domination. In taking such
claims seriously, Young's analysis of oppression explicitly starts by attending
to the conditions of putatively oppressed social groups (1990, 40). Her argument in *Justice and the Politics of Difference* is that "where social group differences exist and some groups are privileged while others are oppressed, social
justice requires explicitly acknowledging and attending to those group differences in order to undermine oppression" (1990, 3). This is because oppression
happens to social groups, where social groups "reflect ways that people identify themselves and others, which lead them to associate with some people
more than others, and to treat others as different" (1990, 9). Structural oppression does not turn on the tyrannical power of the few. Rather, as noted above,
it designates the vast and deep injustices that some groups suffer through
well-meaning actions of others (among other things). Having reflected on
the conditions of the groups that the New Left claims are oppressed enables
Young to articulate her five faces of oppression. This strategy requires that we
explicate what social groups are. And for Young, they are "collections of persons differentiated from at least one other group by cultural forms, practices,
or ways of life. Members of a group have a specific affinity with one another
because of their similar experiences or way of life, which prompts them to associate with one another" (1990, 43). Groups are not first and foremost defined
by share attributes, but "by a sense of identity" (1990, 44). In short, the dia-
lectic of Young's theory of gender injustice goes thus: feminism takes women
to be oppressed; women are a social group; hence, part of the elucidation of
oppression comes from looking at the specific situation of women as a group,
where group membership hinges on a shared sense of identity.

Again, good questions can be raised about whether this theory of injustice escapes worries about gender. In my view, it does not. Young's strategy

is also only one step removed from taking up the question, What is it to be a woman? Feminism requires a way to fix the social group relevant for its political concerns (i.e., women) in order to investigate gender oppression and make good the claim that women as a group are oppressed. After all, Young holds, "Whether a group is oppressed depends on whether it is subject to one or more of the five conditions" or faces of oppression (1990, 47). This requires that we can identify the relevant groups, a task that consists in explicating the special affinity that grounds a shared identity and (relative to sexist injustices) defines women's social kind membership. In fact, if there is no shared gender identity (as Young [1997] actually argues), there is no way of analyzing gendered oppression because we cannot identify the relevant group subject to this oppression. Once more, the theory of oppression on offer is far less freestanding from an analysis of gender than might at first seem, and employing it for feminist efforts does ultimately require that one take up an analysis of women's social kind membership. Analyzing *woman* lurks in the background and threatens attempts to provide freestanding accounts of injustice for as long as we accept that it is "a fundamental claim of feminism that women [as a group] are oppressed" (Frye 1983, 1). Let me be clear: articulating feminist theories of injustice that are freestanding from a substantive theory of gender is exactly the direction that I think we should be heading. Despite having done valuable work in elucidating patriarchal injustices, Frye and Young nevertheless stop halfway. My proposal on offer here aims to take those final steps and to motivate feminist philosophers to pursue genuinely freestanding accounts of injustice.

7.3.4. OPPRESSION: A SECOND STAB

Contra Frye and Young, perhaps a more properly freestanding theory of oppression is on offer after all. Ann Cudd (2006) has provided the most worked-out recent theory of oppression from a feminist perspective. The key idea for Cudd is that various social institutions like "government, legal systems, schools, banks, gender rules and norms, rules of etiquette, media outlets, stereotypical beliefs, class, caste systems, racial, or ethnic classification systems" (2006, 50) constrain our actions; and oppression takes place when we are unjustly constrained by these institutions. It is crucially a *social* phenomenon: perpetrated through the said social institutions, along with practices and norms connected with them, on social groups by other social groups. In particular, oppression is created and maintained via certain material and psychological forces. First, the material forces encompass oppressive mechanisms that work through violence and economic deprivation (having one's material resources like wealth, income, access to healthcare reduced). Second, the psychological forces capture cognitive and affective mechanisms that create and sustain oppression. Psychological oppression takes place "when one is oppressed through one's mental states, emotionally or by manipulation of one's belief states, so that one is psychologically stressed, reduced in one's own self-image, or otherwise psychically harmed" (Cudd 2006, 24). Finally, these forces can be direct or indirect: in the former case, the said forces externally affect individuals' choices; in the latter, the forces affect "background social beliefs and desires with which we perceive and behave toward others" (2006, 52). For instance, direct economic forces may require me to take up a second job in order to earn a living wage; indirect psychological forces may result in me rationalizing economic hardships in ways that pervert my sense of self-worth. For Cudd, these forces are crucial in explaining the endurance of oppression: they are the motivational factors due to which the oppressed submit or acquiesce to their circumstances (2006, 22).

In short, oppression "names a harm through which groups of persons are systematically and unfairly or unjustly constrained, burdened, or reduced" by the above material and psychological forces (Cudd 2006, 23). Morally benign oppression cannot exist. Rather, Cudd's understanding of oppression supposedly captures both normative and explanatory conceptions of damage: oppression is about harms (damage-explanatory) that are unjustly inflicted (damage-normative) (2006, 25). It is about coming to suffer "inequality, limitation, and dehumanization, among many other harms" in ways that are unjust (2006, 25). Further, since oppression is social and structural, social *groups* are the subjects of unequal or unjust institutional constraints. Cudd conceives such groups along the lines I outlined at the beginning of this chapter: they are collections of persons who share something socially significant. This significant feature is elucidated in terms of social constraints and includes "legal rights, obligations and burdens, stereotypical expectations, wealth, income, social status, conventions, norms, and practices" (2006, 41). Constraints are both action enabling and hindering depending on whether they are just or unjust. 'Constraint' as such, though, is a neutral term. So oppression takes place when direct or indirect material or psychological forces with the help of social institutional arrangements unjustly constrain a social group due to which the group comes to suffer unjust harms.[9]

This account of oppression is developed with the three aforementioned adequacy conditions of a feminist social theory in mind. A feminist theory

---

[9] In other words, oppression takes place when the following individually necessary and jointly sufficient conditions are satisfied (Cudd 2006, 25):
  (1). *Harm condition*: There is a harm that comes out of an institutional practice.
  (2). *Social group condition*: The harm is perpetrated through a social institution or practice on a social group whose identity exists apart from the oppressive harm in (1).
  (3). *Privilege condition*: There is another group that benefits from the institutional practice in (1).
  (4). *Coercion condition*: There is unjustified coercion or force that brings about the harm.

of oppression must clearly define *oppression* to pick out the right cases, explain women's oppression, and point to some conditions of justice for women. There is much that I find compelling in Cudd's theory, and her focus on action constraints seems to capture the right core feature of oppression, which can be highly diffuse and covert. Nonetheless, there are two issues that demand closer scrutiny: first, does Cudd provide a theory of oppression that is freestanding of gender which would undermine the first part of this book? Second, does Cudd's theory satisfy the fourth adequacy condition of a feminist EST? After all, my contention is that the descriptive adequacy conditions must be supplemented with a fourth normative condition that elucidates the wrongness-making feature of oppression. Otherwise we cannot explicate why oppression is an *unjust* harm, as Cudd claims.

Let me discuss the second concern first. Cudd explicitly, albeit quite briefly, elucidates the normative issue. For her, social constraints are "unequal when they differentially affect the life outcomes of the individuals subjected to the constraints"; further, the constraints are unjust when they unequally fall on different groups *and* are "unjustifiedly unequal" (2006, 51). Cudd's own example is the social constraint of segregated public restrooms. This constraint is unequal if it is on average worse for one group: if segregation leads (say) to longer waiting times for one group than the other, or if one group has to endure worse conditions due to the lack of cleanliness and maintenance. Such unequal social constraints may be justified if there are other good reasons for the constraint (for example, if sex-segregated restrooms reduce sexual harassment). In addition to being unequal, the constraint must be unjustified in order to count as unjust: for instance, if the justification for unequal social constraints is "manipulated to rationalize injustice" (Cudd 2006, 51).

However, this explication of what makes unjust harm or oppression *unjust* is not entirely helpful. A social constraint is unjust in being (1) unequal *and* (2) unjustifiably so (perhaps by rationalizing injustice). Nevertheless, in order to determine whether the constraint or harm incurred satisfies the second conjunct, we must have a prior normative theory at our disposal. Otherwise we cannot say whether the inequality is unjustifiable or not. Demonstrating that the inequality is harmful or worse for one group does not suffice. We must show that the harm incurred is *unjustly* worse and harmful for one group (Cudd 2006, 25)—namely, that the harm is unjustifiedly unequal. In this sense, Cudd too separates harm and wrong. But in order to make good her account of oppression, we must say something more about the latter and account for what makes harm wrongful. I will examine Cudd's forces of oppression more closely next in order to see how oppression harms and what founds the wrong of harmful oppression. In fact, Cudd's theory implicitly relies on three further sources of wrongfulness. However, I submit, they are all inadequate. Ultimately, I contend that dehumanization can supply the missing normative feature.[10]

The three implicit sources of wrongfulness come from reduction of choices, human nature, and intuitions. In order to elucidate these, consider Cudd's material and psychological forces of oppression. The former include violence, economic deprivation, and the credible threat of either. They are crucial to answering the endurance question: what are the forces that maintain oppressive social structures? First, violence is defined as the "*intentional, forceful infliction of physical harm or abuse*" (Cudd 2006, 87). Its immediate harms are easy to spot. Violence causes physical injuries, psychological effects like PTSD, and the loss of self-esteem. In particular, systematic violence is oppressive "because it alters the sense of the possible for its victims. . . . Systematic violence circumscribes their choices to their own detriment and for the benefit of others" (Cudd 2006, 116).

Second, economic oppression takes both direct and indirect forms. Note that economic oppression is not equivalent to economic inequality (2006, 120). The latter is necessary but not sufficient for the former because *oppression* is defined in terms of inequalities that are unjustifiably imposed on social groups. So economic oppression presupposes economic inequality, but it requires more: the inequality must be unjustified in order to count as oppressive. For instance, inequalities that come about fairly (as for example with the Amish, in Cudd's view) are not oppressive. Economic deprivation becomes unfair when a group encounters reduced economic opportunities relative to another group whose members have more opportunities (Cudd 2006, 121). This sort of oppression involves institutional coercion: "An institution (economic system, legal system, norm) is coercive if the institution unfairly limits the choices of some group of persons relative to other groups in society" (2006, 131). "Fairness" denotes the equal distribution of burdens, benefits, and choices. So, for Cudd, the decision about whether capitalism or socialism is a fairer or less oppressive economic system boils down to comparing "the choice situation of workers under capitalism with the choice situation of persons under socialism. If the benefits to capitalists are not at the expense of workers but rather also increase the workers' choices, then there is no coercion" and no economic oppression (Cudd 2006, 131).

Now, indirect forces of economic oppression are particularly insidious and cover (what Cudd calls) "oppression by choice." This involves subtle and often

---

[10] In order to elucidate *unfair* coercion, Cudd admits that we need a background moral theory that accounts for the unfairness. She writes: "That background moral theory has not been elucidated in this book, and I will not set out to do that now in the final pages of the work" (2006, 231). Nonetheless, we gain some insights: Cudd briefly notes that has in mind Rawls's (1971) liberal contractarianism or David Gauthier's (1986) libertarianism.

covert ways in which inequalities are generated through oppressed persons' individually rational choices that end up having harmful and suboptimal long-term outcomes. An example is the decision to become a stay-at-home mother in a heterosexual relationship in order to maximize the family's disposable income: under conditions of wage disparity and lack of affordable child care, it is rational for the mother (instead of the father) to stop working and take care of the children. This decision, however, makes the mother—along with women as a group—more vulnerable to economic oppression by hampering individual career prospects and portraying women as a group as carers rather than workers (cf. Okin 1989; Saul 2003, chap. 1; Williams 2000).

Psychological harms as forces of oppression also take direct and indirect forms. As with the material economic forces, direct psychological forces cause inequalities through intentional actions of the dominant group on the oppressed, and they result in the harms of terror, trauma, humiliation, and degradation. Indirect psychological forces cause inequalities through subsequent choices and decisions of the oppressed group and harm the oppressed by causing them to assimilate the oppressors' beliefs and values in their self-conceptions and value schemes (Cudd 2006, 176). Shame, low self-esteem, false consciousness, and deformed desires mold the psychology of the oppressed and make them co-opt harmful choices and decisions.

What does the above tell us about the unjustness of oppressive harm? To begin with, Cudd repeatedly notes that the forces of oppression reduce *options* and *choices* available to the oppressed. For instance, sexual slavery "harms the slaves by robbing them of choice," among other things (Cudd 2006, 97). Direct economic oppression causes inequalities through intentional actions of the dominant group in limiting the choices available to the oppressed; and indirect oppression causes inequalities through the choices and decisions that the oppressed make (2006, 135). Even more strongly, indirect economic forces are crucial to oppression's endurance (2006, 154): that is, "oppression by choice" is a key factor that creates and maintains oppression. So choice reduction plays a pivotal role in Cudd's theory of oppression and is used to elucidate why certain conditions are oppressive. This fits Cudd's theoretical building blocks: her analysis of oppression advances from a liberal perspective that embraces rational-choice theory. Such analyses commonly assume that "for the rational individual more choices are always preferable to fewer" (G. Dworkin 1988, 63). But what is the supposed value of choices, and what is the supposed value of *more* choices? Although Cudd does not provide clear answers to these questions, we can glean some hints from her discussion. Direct psychological harms harm the oppressed by "robbing them of the material and psychological wherewithal to successfully compete in the marketplace and keep themselves safe from further harm" (Cudd 2006, 175). So the value of choice derives (at least partly) from being able to successfully compete in the marketplace—increased choices enable us to better navigate the contours of our capitalist economic structures.[11]

I am unconvinced, however, that having fewer choices grounds the un-justness of injustice. For Cudd, the term 'fairness' denotes the equal distri-bution of burdens, benefits, and choices. In usual rational-choice theories, one justification for why more choice is better than less comes from desire or preference satisfaction. The presumption is that individuals want to satisfy their desires (they want various goods and services). Having more choices allegedly facilitates our desire satisfaction: being able to choose from a wider range of options will increase the probability of us finding and getting what we want, which presumably contributes to human flourishing. But I am unconvinced that having desires and preferences satisfied will make for a just society. Imagine one with perfectly functioning Jim Crow laws. There would be thoroughgoing de jure segregation of two racialized groups that is based on the "separate but equal" dictum. The choices available to and the burdens imposed on the segregated groups are equally distributed. Both groups have their own social institutions like schooling and courts of law, which give the youth of both sides the opportunity to become competitive members in the (segregated and group-specific) marketplaces. Both mar-ketplaces offer individuals choices, and members of these groups are able to satisfy a high proportion of their desires. Further, both social groups have the same opportunities relative to the other: for instance, members of both groups will face job discrimination if they attempt to cross racialized lines, and mixed relationships are not socially or legally sanctioned on either side. Bluntly put, the range of available choices and the opportunities for desire satisfaction are equally distributed.

But let's imagine that these conditions were unilaterally created. One group (namely, the one with more social power to begin with) is responsible for cre-ating the segregation. Now, from the perspective of social justice, it seems to be neither here nor there whether we can increase the choices available to the groups' members equally. What matters is that one group did not take part in creating the *structural conditions* that underlie the available choices. One group can create segregation laws because it is more powerful. And as long as this is the case, the situation does not strike me as fair or nonoppres-sive even though the choices, benefits, and burdens are equally distributed.

---

[11] Admittedly I have a visceral reaction against the idea that we should strive toward successful competition in the economic marketplace. Such extensive focus on choices and the elucidation of their supposed value have a rather unpleasant neoliberal flavor. Since I am skeptical of the value capitalist economic arrangements afford, I do not see the value of having more choices simpliciter. Nevertheless, this trades on our preexisting commitments to particular socioeconomic models, rather than engaging in systematic argumentation about the benefits and harms of the neoliberal economic model. Unfortunately, settling the issue is beyond the scope of my discussion here (see Cudd and Holstrom 2011 for a further discussion).

Decreased choices may be symptomatic of unfairness, but they elucidate neither unfairness nor injustice.

Of course, Cudd is right to claim that women living in sexual slavery have diminished choices and cannot do what they want. But it is not the lack of choice that renders this situation unjust. It is that the women whose families sold them to sexual slavery in societies like Thailand (which Cudd discusses) cannot influence the underlying structural conditions that render this possible. The problem is not that the women cannot do what they want; the problem is that they cannot prevent that which is done to them. The women lack the requisite social power in part because the social institutions framing their situations enable social injustices to continue. Giving these women more choices is not what ultimately changes the situation; rather, enabling them to gain more social power would, so that they can alter the structural and institutional arrangements underlying harmful choices made on their behalf.

Cudd's discussion of objectification (which is a further direct psychological force of oppression) brings up a new source of wrongfulness. Objectification is about treating "persons as mere objects, ignoring their full and equal status as persons" (2006, 165). Given this definition, objectification is "necessarily an unjust harm" because it involves "disregarding the deep moral equality of human persons" (2006, 166). This disregard boils down to the following: humans have some qualities and abilities that make us special, and "humans ought to be preserved and protected *for these qualities*" (2006, 166). Humans are special because of our sense of the good and the right, as well as our capacity to desire, to value, and to plan for future lives that express our desires and values. "Dehumanizing objectification," however, robs someone of their "right to express these unique qualities, and that is what makes it deeply morally wrong" (2006, 166).

This appeal to our valuable human natures is not something Cudd argues for, and it emerges rather unexpectedly in her discussion. Since I reject internalist accounts of humanity along with idealization as a helpful method, it should come as no surprise that I find Cudd's appeal deeply unconvincing. She offers us no justification to accept the unique human qualities as valuable; I see no reason, then, to take this as something normatively binding. Let me clarify: I agree that humans by and large have the capacities Cudd outlines. But I see no reason to think that *therefore* our theory of oppression should be grounded in an internalist conception of humanity that trades on these qualities. My point is methodological: Cudd's appeal to humanity will convince only those who antecedently accept her internalist conception. And, as I have stressed repeatedly, we ought not to base EST on intuitive appeals to deeply evaluative understandings of humanity. Doing so renders our justifications too precarious because accepting or rejecting a theory turns on something more akin to faith: whether we antecedently feel the pull of the evaluative understanding or not. My thin externalist notion of humanity stands on sturdier grounds, which is why I take it to be methodologically preferable.

Finally, at times Cudd bases her judgment of unfairness on pretheoretical intuitions in a manner that I find questionable. For instance, employment discrimination is said to be harmful in that (1) wage discrimination reduces the income of some groups (typically, women and people of color) and (2) occupational discrimination harms by enforcing job segregation. And since in these cases "discrimination is based on nonvoluntary social group status, it is unfair" (Cudd 2006, 140). Pretheoretically I agree, which appears to be what Cudd relies on. But more needs to be said on the normative side. For one thing, Cudd herself repeatedly stresses that economic inequality is not sufficient for economic oppression. So even though wage discrimination reduces the income of some, this does not yet render the reduction unfair. And if we accept (as was discussed above) that discrimination can be either wrongful or not, demonstrating income differences does not yet show that the discrimination is wrongful. We must show that reducing the income of some groups relative to others constitutes *wrongful* wage discrimination.

So what would make the discrimination wrongful? As Cudd notes, being discriminated against on the basis of nonvoluntary group membership undergirds the wrongfulness. But (I contend) this gives us the wrong results. Imagine that men across the board (who, following Cudd, make up a nonvoluntary social group) had their incomes cut in order to achieve gendered income parity. Prima facie, in being based on nonvoluntary social group membership, the cut should constitute an instance of wrongful discrimination. And perhaps it does—but much will depend on further details (like how much income men will be left with, which surely will differ for different men). In fact, if the wage cut merely on the basis of social group membership matters, we would have oppressive discrimination against some men that strikes me as neither oppressive nor wrongful.

To illustrate, compare the following two situations: (1) a CEO earning a seven-figure salary has his income cut down to a six-figure salary; (2) a bus driver has his wages cut below the living-wage threshold. If discrimination based on nonvoluntary social group membership were unfair simpliciter, both cases would count as oppressive discrimination against the individuals qua men. But holding that the CEO is subject to oppressive discrimination due to the wage cut is unpersuasive given that he will still have plenty left. Now, consider the wage cut with my notion of dehumanization in mind. The action will be dehumanizing (and thus impermissible) only if it unjustifiably hampers some legitimate human interests and in so doing constitutes a moral injury. On my model, cutting the CEO's wages would not count as dehumanizing because no legitimate human welfare interests would have been hampered (receiving a six-figure salary in dollars suffices, I take it, for basic material welfare). However, the bus driver's case would be different: if the cut in wages forces the bus driver into relative poverty, it would seem to set back basic welfare interests in an indefensible manner (it would be inexcusable precisely because of the conceivable material harms caused). And so it would count as dehumanizing assuming, for argument's sake, that the other conditions are satisfied too. The same surface action (a wage cut) might or might not count as dehumanizing and thus either would or would not ground an instance of injustice. With my normative component, we can achieve the desiderata of EST better: we can home in on the right cases of injustice by elucidating whether they count as wrongful or not.[12]

Now, what about the challenge that Cudd provides a feminist theory of oppression that is freestanding from a theory of gender, which undermines the motivation for my humanist feminism? I argued earlier that this line of argument fails with respect to the positions put forward by Frye and by Young. And I admit that out of these three notable feminist positions, Cudd's is the most freestanding. In fact, I think that Cudd and I are pursuing something very similar, and I think that she too is on the right track. Nevertheless, Cudd's theory also smuggles in the gender controversy through the back door (so to speak). This hinges on her account of social groups. Cudd clearly holds that oppression is a group-based social injustice: it is by definition "perpetuated through social institutions, practices, and norms on social groups by social groups" (2006, 23). What then are social groups? Generally speaking, they are "non-accidental groups that are formed by or maintained by some social fact, or action, either intentionally or as an unintended consequence of some social fact or action" (2006, 35). Or, to put the point differently: they are collections of individuals who share some set of social constraints on their action (or would share these constrains when similarly positioned) (2006, 44). Through such constraints voluntary and nonvoluntary social groups are formed. What unifies the latter are constraints shared because of decisions made by others. For all such social groups, then,

> membership is assigned by others through default assumptions that go into effect when they recognize or think they recognize some typical trait or behavior that is very salient in the culture for grouping. So, for instance, skin color, hair length, dress, voice pitch, word choice, size, walking or sitting

---

[12] Of course, there may be other grounds on which the CEO suffers injustices that the bus driver escapes: for instance, the former may be discriminated against, but the latter privileged, on the basis of their racialized group memberships. But the point of this example, and my entire position, is that dehumanization is a feature of acts and ways of treating others. This enables us to examine different situations with more fine-grained tools. And precisely because of intersectionality individuals may be subject to some dehumanizing treatments, but not to others. So my point is not to elucidate when individuals are on the whole dehumanized. This would miss the gist of my position, and I have noted throughout the book that my proposal aims to avoid the view that dehumanization reduces individuals *wholesale* to some subhuman state. It attaches to actions and ways of treating others. And ultimately, the details of each situation will make a crucial difference to whether some particular treatment is unjust, as this example of cutting men's wages because they are men demonstrates.

style are all well known signals of race, gender, class, and sexual orientation. (2006, 45)

In other words, social groups are collections of individuals whose common
constraints are structured by social institutions, like gender norms and rules
(2006, 50–51).

How freestanding is Cudd's theory of oppression from a theory of gender?
It is true that Cudd does not explicitly offer an account of gender. But in order
to elucidate group-based social injustices, we must identify the relevant social
groups experiencing such injustices. And in order to individuate those social
groups, we need to rely on identifying certain shared unjust constraints that
unify social groups. This strategy runs into trouble, though, when we think
about Cudd's own adequacy conditions of a feminist social theory. Such a
theory must make sense of oppression from a feminist perspective: it must be
able to identify gendered oppression, explain the roots of such oppression, and
provide some way to account for the conditions of gender justice. All of this
hinges on there being a particular social group that suffers gendered oppression, and Cudd accepts (as Frye puts it) the "fundamental claim of feminism
that women [as a group] are oppressed" (1983, 1). So meeting Cudd's own adequacy conditions requires that we have a conception of women as a group at
our disposal, since women make up the group relevant for feminist political
endeavors. After all, in order to explain the specifics of gendered oppression,
we must be able to identify and pick out the relevant social group that is nonaccidentally constrained by gender norms and rules in facing such oppression.

Prima facie this task requires taking a stance on what unifies women's
social kind; it therefore seems that Cudd cannot escape worries about gender
after all. In taking oppression to be essentially a group-based phenomenon,
her conception of *social group* smuggles in the gender controversy. Cudd
notes repeatedly that gender stereotypes, norms, and expectations play a
crucial role in the social group-defining constraints experienced by women.
But what exactly are these stereotypes, norms, and expectations, and what
grounds them? How can we fix the group defining constraint(s) in order
to fix women's social kind? To answer this, Cudd is faced with two options. On the one hand, she can refuse to elucidate them further and insist
that feminists rely on some unspecified understanding of those gendered
constraints that define women's social group membership. But this would
be in tension with Cudd's own normative feminist assumptions. Different
women are likely to face different clusters of constraints. In fact, when individuating social groups by focusing on certain harmful constraints on
our actions, we probably end up with social groupings very different from
those that emancipatory social theories typically have in mind. Perhaps
we cannot single out women's kind, but (say) a group of persons who face
action-constraining street harassment. Nonetheless, this group is likely to

include trans* people, queer individuals, and some gender norm-bunking cis men in addition to individuals typically designated as women. If we go with more fine-grained social groups like these and cannot single out some women's social group-determining constraints, Cudd will have to give up her claim that women as women face *systematic group-based* oppression.

On the other hand, if she wishes to retain the idea that women make up a social group or kind, which specific systematic injustices nonaccidentally target, Cudd must take a stance on what the relevant gender kind constituting social constraints and institutions are. Hence, in order to make sense of the constraints that women in particular face, one needs to articulate gender to distinguish (e.g.) those stereotypical expectations and norms that women face from those that men and trans* individuals do. One must partake in the gender controversy: what constraints are women *as women* subject to that individuate their social group? So in order to satisfy Cudd's own adequacy conditions of a feminist social theory, we seemingly need to know who the women are and what is it to be a woman. And this (I hold) demonstrates that the gender controversy lurks in the background of Cudd's view too, despite its being in other ways deeply valuable for feminist social theory.

Contours of Injustice and Feminist Social Theory

8.1. Introduction

The previous chapter explicated three different forms of injustice and their key features. In short:

- Discrimination is about unjust differential treatment that results in indefensible inequalities in the distribution of socially relevant goods (where the traits on the basis of which disadvantage is conferred count as normatively extraneous).
- Domination is about unjust wielding of power over others that forces the dominated to follow rules set by others and prevents them from determining the conditions for their own actions.
- Oppression is about systematically imposing unjust constraints on social agents and their actions through various material and psychological forces.

This satisfies the first adequacy condition of EST: we have coherent and clear definitions of different forms of injustice at our disposal. Further, my notion of *dehumanization* (I argued earlier) not only elucidates the wrongness-making feature of these injustices, but also helps to fix the correct definitions. This satisfies the fourth adequacy condition: it tells us why these forms of injustice are unjust. My typology of social injustices also advances our explanatory accounts, which enables us to satisfy the second adequacy condition of EST: the different forms can be employed to elucidate how injustices are damaging and harmful. The final third condition is to provide some way to account for the conditions of social justice. Although I will not put forward a fully-fledged theory of social justice here, I will consider what overcoming dehumanization requires in chapter 9 in order to pave the way for a theory of justice.

Now, it seems that my theory of *injustice* is nevertheless still incomplete: it does not yet fully satisfy the second adequacy condition because I have said nothing about the different contours of injustice. Moreover, how we understand them is highly significant since different prejudices (sexist, racist, homophobic, trans*phobic, classist, ableist attitudes) are part of what makes interest violations indefensible and thus dehumanizing. I need to flesh out these contours in more detail so that my proposal can provide the required explanatory tools. I will undertake this task in the present chapter. However, my argument in Part I puts certain constraints on this endeavor. After all, since I have argued against the gender controversy, I cannot simply appeal to interest violations being indefensible because they unduly burden women as women. Such a strategy to explicate sexist and patriarchal injustices would fall prey to the same problems that Young, Frye, and Cudd's strategies did: it would smuggle in the gender controversy through the back door. Different theoretical tools are needed; in this chapter, I take up the challenge to develop such tools. Doing so not only completes my regimentation of injustice, but also elucidates further theoretical tools that we can employ in the service of humanist feminism.

8.2. Contours of Injustice

Delimiting indefensible interest violations is not just a matter of focusing on harms experienced. Whether some interest violation is indefensible or not trades also on whether the violation involves some delineation or "flavor" of injustice that is associated with social identity groupings (like racism). Although such delineations take different shapes, they often trade on epistemic grounds (e.g., false beliefs about our "natures" and abilities) in addition to causing or foreseeably causing certain harms (e.g., psychological harms caused by systematic police brutality against members of certain racialized groups). These roughly correspond to what makes interest violations on my view unjustifiable and inexcusable—something that is vital when determining whether some treatment is dehumanizing or not. Insofar as I take injustice's contours to trade on, for example, false beliefs and various harms, my general picture is twofold: injustice works on both *individual* and *institutional* levels, working on the level of subjects' attitudes and beliefs and on the level of social structures, respectively.

This picture is meant to be flat rather than hierarchical. Institutionally prejudiced arrangement resulting in harms can exist without the individuals comprising the institution having similarly prejudiced beliefs; and individual prejudices may not cause prejudicial institutional arrangements (although, of course, institutional prejudices can sustain individual prejudices and vice versa). Moreover, it is helpful to adopt particular terminology to denote these levels. For me, the individual level is exemplified in sexist, racist, homophobic, trans*phobic, classist, and ableist beliefs and attitudes. In short, they name some conative or cognitive states and are thus fundamentally about individual psychologies. Let me offer two clarifications: first, although the attitudes are individually held, the ones that hamper social justice cannot be individually determined. Rather, the relevant prejudices are publicly available, and they crucially pertain to some socially salient groupings. So my prejudicial attitudes about tall-foreheaded people would not constitute an individual contour of injustice: they are simply idiosyncratic and nonpublic beliefs or sentiments that I hold. Second, the individual level comes in degrees: at one end of the spectrum are straightforwardly hateful attitudes (like misogyny, neo-Nazism, or "white power"); at the other end are less hateful attitudes against out-groups and more preferential attitudes toward one's own group or way of life. Examples of the latter would be sentiments like "I'm not a racist (but there are too many ethnic food shops in my neighborhood)." So (for me) sexist, racist, homophobic, trans*phobic, classist, and ableist beliefs and sentiments are expressions of some psychological and often affective states (fear, reservation, disrespect, contempt, outright hatred). And since they involve beliefs (among other attitudes), we can see how this level fits the epistemic story noted above. There is a rather clear and obvious way in which some interest violations can be (say) homophobic in this sense. If one is denied housing and social security, one's basic welfare interests are hampered. If the person making housing decisions harbors outright hatred toward the subject's socially salient identification as a queer person or holds false beliefs about them "spreading diseases" *and* because of this the person's interests are hampered, the interest violation is indefensible (the violation hinges on unjustifiable false beliefs and is thus justified in a way that is morally injurious). In this case, we have a form of injustice (discrimination) that has a particular attitudinal shape (homophobia). Of course, since our social identities are intersectional, the contours that injustice takes are usually less clear-cut and more intermingled. Still, this is the basic idea.[1]

Consider the institutional level next. This level has less to do with individual psychologies than with diffuse and covert social-structural arrangements. To denote these and to differentiate them from the more individualized phenomena, I reserve the following terminology to capture institutional contours of injustice: patriarchy, race- or ethnicity-laden dominance, heteronormativity, class elitism, and able-bodiedness. They denote the idea that some group has social power over other socially salient groupings and that our prevalent social arrangements tend to be organized in ways that benefit

---

[1] One might wonder where implicit biases and attitudes fall: are they part of the conative or cognitive states, or something utterly separate? I will have more to say about implicit biases shortly. However, for now, I wish to avoid saying much about them. This is because philosophical research on the nature of implicit bias is still very much ongoing. Some take implicit attitudes to be mental states unlike desires, beliefs, or intentions (Gendler 2008), whereas others dispute this (Mandelbaum 2013). Since this research is moving forward fast, I will for now refrain from saying anything too committal about where these influences fall on my picture.

those who hold social power. Patriarchy means that our social arrangements are structured in ways that take being a cis man as the norm and standard. Heteronormativity is about social arrangements and structures that take heterosexuality as the norm and standard. Class elitism structures our social institutions in ways that privilege those from already privileged socioeconomic backgrounds. And able-bodiedness frames our structures, practices, and intuitions in ways that render those with atypical bodily presentations "defective" in both descriptive and normative senses.

The case of race- or ethnicity-laden dominance is somewhat trickier to describe.[2] The term 'dominance' is not to be equated with that of 'domination.' I spelled out in the previous chapter what domination amounts to: unjust wielding of social power over others. By contrast, dominance is akin to predominance and primacy (e.g., cycling is the dominant/primary form of transport in Amsterdam). So the idea is this: insofar as the societal arrangements are organized, maintained, and perpetuated to the privilege and benefit of some racial or ethnic group, this renders that racial or ethnic group the dominant one—its members come to possess more social power. Further, such socially powerful groupings differ depending on the context. For instance, there is no question that German societal arrangements are characterized by race- and ethnic-laden dominance of white Germans born German.[3] So white Germans have much more social power than (say) black Rwandan Tutsis living in Germany. But in Rwanda, ethnic Tutsis have social power over ethnic Hutus. And so in this context societal arrangements are characterized by ethnicity-laden dominance of Tutsis. Since such societal arrangements conceivably do or may be foreseen to result in harms to individual social agents, this institutional-level story fits the idea that some interest violations are indefensible in being inexcusable: insofar as patriarchy, race- or ethnicity-laden dominance, heteronormativity, class elitism, or able-bodiedness tend materially or socially to disadvantage those lacking social power, and the possession of social power does not trade on anything like "natural" rights or entitlements, the resultant disadvantages and harms hinge on inexcusable institutional contours of injustice.

To illustrate these levels further, consider Mary Anne Warren's (1977) discussion of sexism. My two-tier picture roughly corresponds to what Warren has called "primary" and "secondary" sexism. For her, sexism means "*unfair discrimination on the basis of sex*" (1977, 241). On my typology, sexism itself is

---

[2] I borrow the idea of race ladenness and ethnicity ladenness from Haslanger: institutions are race laden when they "perpetuate racial injustice without doing so explicitly" (2004, 111). I should add that although Haslanger too distinguishes between more overt individual and more covert institutional levels of racial discrimination, she takes the term 'racism' to cover both (2004, 122).

[3] I say "Germans born German" for a reason: as a general rule, one can gain German citizenship only if one has at least one parent who is a German citizen. Being born in Germany does not give one an automatic right to citizenship.

not a kind of discrimination (and thus it is not a form of injustice). Rather, there would be primary sexist or secondary sexist discrimination. The former denotes dislike, distrust, or contempt (in this case) of women or "sincerely held but objectively unjustified beliefs" about them (Warren 1977, 241). Secondary sexism is indirect and covert, being about apparently sex- or gender-neutral but de facto discriminatory criteria used (e.g.) in employment selection. For example, job requirements that prevent flexible working hours are on the surface nondiscriminatory and gender neutral; in fact, they end up disadvantaging those with caretaking responsibilities, who are typically female. So, the prima facie neutral criterion is de facto discriminatory. Relative to my two-tier picture, only primary sexism would be sexism. By contrast, secondary sexism falls under (what I call) "patriarchy": social structures and institutional arrangements take cis men's experiences as the norm and work to benefit them in particular. This also fits with what Jean Harvey calls "civilized oppression" as opposed to violent oppression: apparently small actions that can generate "long-term patterns of exclusion, subordination, and denigration that can have a devastating cumulative impact, not only on the psychological well-being of the victims, but also their opportunities, life-path, and chances of fulfillment" (2010, 15; see also Harvey 1999). As I see it, this form of oppression is precisely exemplary of many contemporary systemic, hard-to-detect social injustices. The sort of oppression Harvey has in mind involves covert patriarchy, which can be difficult to detect, as opposed to outright sexism. In order to analyze such supposedly "civilized" oppression, the second institutional level is pivotal.

This differentiation in the terminology we use (or ought to use) to denote the individual and institutional levels affords certain benefits. It enables us to clarify what we are taking about. For instance, "racism" has been used to cover a whole range of phenomena: "racial hatred and racial contempt (whether overt or covert), explicit discrimination, subtle exclusion, unintentional evasion, cultural bias in favor of Eurocentric norms of behavior and beauty, negative racial stereotypes portrayed in the media, arts, and public discourse" (Haslanger 2004, 97).[4] "Racism" is often used as a morally contemptuous epithet when talking about particular people, some beliefs, attitudes, social and legal institutions, or behavior. In everyday discourse, racism is still often taken to express a commitment to some form of racial superiority, where the term 'race' is falsely taken to track biological kinds. Separating out the individual and institutional levels helps to dispel the "mystery" around (rather

---

4 In an equally broad manner, Frye writes that sexist "characterizes cultural and economic structures which create and enforce the elaborate and rigid patterns of sex-marking and sex-announcing which divide the species, along lines of sex, into dominators and subordinates. Individual acts and practices are sexist which reinforce and support those structures, either as culture or as shapes taken on by the enculturated animals" (1983, 38).

frustrating) debates about whether some action, person, or social arrangement is sexist or racist. It undermines a certain mistrustful complaint that feminists and antiracist campaigners are crying out sexism and racism too easily, and when there is no belief in race- or sex-based superiority. After all, on my view the lack of such beliefs does not morally absolve or vindicate some action, person, or social arrangement—the individual and institutional levels are both worrisome because they both crucially feature in dehumanizing ways of treating others, albeit being variously realizable. Still, I hope that the division of individual and institutional levels helps to dispel unhelpful moral panic on the part of some interlocutors in social debates: some social arrangements may not be sexist or racist; but if they are patriarchal or characterized by race-laden dominance, this renders them no less morally problematic.

Finally, my division can help resolve some philosophical disputes about whether (say) racism is "in the heart" of social agents or not (cf. Garcia 2001; Shelby 2002). Bluntly put, my distinction can make sense of how racism both is and is not so. Let me briefly say something more detailed about this. Jorge Garcia has put forward an influential volitional account of racism as "fundamentally a vicious kind of racially based disregard for the welfare of certain people" (2001, 259). Such disregard is most clearly and problematically manifested in hatred or ill will toward some persons due to their racialized group membership; less viciously, it is manifested in undue regard for their welfare. Racism, for Garcia, is "in the heart" of the racist: it is about conative rather than cognitive states and demonstrates the morally corrupt and evil nature of the racist. In this sense, Garcia's position is close to mine: he also takes racism to be (roughly put) an individual contour of injustice. Now, Garcia claims that racism does not involve beliefs, but rather affective states like contempt, disrespect, and hatred. In this way, our positions come apart: I take racism along with all individual contours of injustice to be about both cognitive and conative states. (See also Shelby [2002], who argues contra Garcia that racism involves beliefs.) However, I will put this concern to one side. A more noticeable difference between Garcia and me is his infection thesis: not only individuals but also institutions can be racist for Garcia, in that the former infect the latter with vicious racist attitudes. That is,

> institutional racism occurs and matters because racist attitudes (desires, aims, hopes, fears, plans) infect the reasoning, decision-making, and action of individuals not only in their private behavior, but also when they make and execute the policies of those institutions in which they operate.... Institutional racism begins when [individual] racism extends from the hearts of individual people to become institutionalized. (Garcia 2001, 266)[5]

---

[5] In fact, this quote undermines Garcia's own claim that individual racism is about conative attitudes: such attitudes are said to include racist *plans*. But it is very difficult to imagine how one could device racist plans of action without any cognitive attitudes.

For me, the institutional counterpart would not be racist; rather, some institutions or institutional arrangements would manifest configurations of race-laden dominance. First, institutional racism strictly speaking does not make sense on my account because institutions cannot have the requisite mental states—only social agents (so to speak) behind the institutional wheels can. Second, those individuals making up a social institution may genuinely fail to be racist in Garcia's sense, but the institutional arrangements may not therefore be characterized by social justice. The road to injustice tends to be paved with many good intentions, and some institutional arrangements end up discriminating against members of particular racialized groups even with the best individual intentions in the world. This is important to acknowledge and bear in mind on explanatory grounds (cf. Haslanger 2004).

Garcia would have to claim in response that, despite the explicit individual antiracist sentiments, some further implicit racist resentment is really doing the work. This is the basic point of (say) antiblack implicit bias. Such attitudes can be measured in various ways (for an outline, see Jost et al. 2009). One of the most widely used methods for testing implicit biases is the Implicit Association Test (IAT). Roughly: an IAT measures how quickly we associate individuals as representative exemplars of a social category with evaluative adjectives. So the racial IAT measures how fast we associate and pair positive words (like "good," "pleasant," "safe") with white and black faces, and how fast we associate and pair negative words (like "bad," "unpleasant," "dangerous") with those same faces. Those who take longer to associate black faces with positive words than negative ones and are quicker to pair white faces with positive words than negative ones are "theorized to have internalized a stronger preference for whites relative to blacks, compared to people who respond more equivalently across different category-valence pairings (or in the opposite direction)" (Jost et al. 2009, 45)—they have an implicit antiblack racial bias. Importantly, such bias does not correlate with explicit bias measures: many individuals who are explicitly and genuinely committed to antiracist or feminist goals have antiblack and antiwomen implicit biases. Garcia, then, could say that it is these implicit attitudes that are infecting our social institutions in the absence of more explicit affective sentiments.

I have no doubt that implicit biases do in some way insidiously infect our institutional arrangements. But I am less convinced that we should therefore call the requisite phenomenon "racism." This is in part because doing so opens up conceptual disputes and again muddies the waters about what racism is or amounts to. Further, although it is clear that outright racial hatred is deeply condemnable from a moral point of view, it is far from clear that implicit biases are equally or at all morally condemnable (for a discussion, see Holroyd 2012; Kelly and Roedder 2008). For one thing, many African Americans are implicitly biased against other African Americans (and many women are implicitly biased against other women). It strikes me as an unhelpful strategy in fighting racist injustices to be calling those subject to such injustices themselves *also* racist on the basis of their harboring some ubiquitous implicit biases that form relative to public stereotypes—especially when we have little or no control over their formation. Pragmatically, I submit, it would be more helpful to call those institutional arrangements that result from implicit racial bias as being characterized by racial or race-laden dominance, rather than racism. After all, implicit biases against one's own stigmatized group do help perpetuate precisely such race-laden dominance relations, and this makes a difference to our moral evaluation of implicit bias. Thus, I wish to reserve the term 'racism' for the individual level and 'race-laden dominance' for the institutional one. In this way, my typology captures the spirit of the claim that (loosely speaking) racism both is and is not in the heart.

Two immediate objections may be leveled at my proposed nomenclature: first, that I equate racism, sexism, homophobia, and other contours of injustice in an essentializing way; second, that the manner in which I define the second-level institutional phenomena makes it impossible to uncover ways in which our interest violations involve the more diffuse and covert shapes of injustice. Let me address these worries in turn. Although I take sexist, racist, homophobic, trans*phobic, classist, and ableist beliefs and attitudes to ground injustices, I do not thereby equate (say) sexist and racist oppression. Oppression is about being systematically and unjustly constrained by various material and psychological forces. How oppression in particular instances plays out will depend on which contour(s) it takes. So sexist oppression is not identical to racist oppression, although both involve the same *form* of injustice. This is because oppression (along with other forms of injustice) is realizable in multiple ways. That said, sexist oppression and racist oppression are both wrongful on the same ground: they are both made wrong by dehumanization. But since *harm* is not equated with *wrong*, nothing problematic is implied. The specific harms of different oppressions will clearly differ depending on the circumstances. And the severity of different oppressive harms will depend on the effects of the requisite interest violations. For instance, consider job-market marginalization that takes sexist or racist shape. (Of course, intersectionality in actual fact makes examples like this one much less clear-cut. But here I am assuming clarity for argument's sake.) Imagine a white, middle-class, married woman who is made "marginal" (or nonemployable) on sexist grounds, and a black, working-class, single mother, who is marginalized on racist grounds. Undoubtedly, both have their interests indefensibly setback in morally injurious ways. Nevertheless, this may and probably does harm the women differently: the interest violation may subsequently push the latter woman into relative poverty but not the former woman, because she will have her partner to rely on financially. So the material harms suffered may be more severe for the black woman—that is, the interest violation may be more harmful for her. Of course, all things considered, this is difficult to judge: the white woman may be further harmed by having to rely financially on her partner, which may render her vulnerable within the family in some other ways. In any case, the take-home message is this: the harms suffered (e.g., humiliation, economic deprivation, dependence on others) differ from one case to the next and depend on the particular details; this nevertheless does not alter the underlying *wrong*. That stays the same, albeit it can be realized or exemplified in different ways. And so my regimentation of injustice does not collapse different oppressions into one; the forms of injustice can be realized in multiple ways, as can be the harms involved.

Second, uncovering covert shapes of injustice can indeed be quite tricky. For one thing, this may be because some injustices are intertwined with patterns of social privilege in ways that make those injustices invisible (just think of white, economically privileged, cis women, who nevertheless do not escape patriarchal social arrangements). Furthermore, that some social relations are problematic may be hidden by ideological hegemony. I appealed earlier to Haslanger's definition of *ideology*: ideologies are "representations of social life that serve in some way to undergird social practices" (Haslanger 2011, 180). They provide the "background cognitive and affective frame that gives actions and reactions meaning within a social system and contributes to its survival" (2011, 181). An ideology has become hegemonic when it is no longer seen for what it is: it is not seen as a piece of ideology, but (perhaps) part of the "natural order" of things. In terms of my earlier terminology (cf. chapter 5), hegemony takes hold when ideological arrangements and attitudes become congealed and subsequently involve quasi-essentialist "counts as" relations. How can we then explain injustices and fight against them? How can we in fact demonstrate that some interest violation is indefensible in morally injurious ways due to, say, patriarchy? This is the stuff of critical social theory. My response will be limited in scope, but (I contend) still instructive.

To begin with, even though I distinguish harm and wrong, I take harms to be *indicative* of wrong. Were one constantly to find oneself materially or psychologically harmed in the ways that (for example) Cudd outlines, this should give us pause about the treatments that one is subject to—it should motivate us to consider whether some covert contours of injustice are at play. Further, it is well known that those in positions of power not subject to certain interest setbacks are often not in the best position to judge whether some policy or arrangement will hamper or advance basic welfare interests. But luckily, hegemony is like a frictionless plane: it is never fully realizable, and there are always some societal groups whose experiences constitute eye-opening rifts in the social fabric. We can uncover these rifts and make them explicit by listening, communicating, and documenting others' and our own experiences—in short, by acting in epistemically responsible manner (among other things). Moreover, even though my account distinguishes well-being in the senses of basic welfare and flourishing, when human flourishing is hindered this should raise alarm bells about our basic welfare provisions. This would be another indicator that some more basic social injustices are taking place, injustices that are characterized by dehumanization in my sense. These three putative ways of uncovering covert institutional interest violations point out that we do have some critical resources available to us.

That said, one might wonder, relative to my second comment above, how effective listening and communicating are given how deeply our interactions with others are affected by unconscious influences and attitudes. For example, Rudman and Ashmore (2007) measured white US college students' willingness to impose budget cuts on racial/ethnic groups that IAT scores showed their implicit biases to target. The participants in the study were asked to recommend ways to spread the university budget across different student organizations when faced with cuts. These included the marching band, drama club, political action groups, and Jewish, Asian, and black student organizations. The researchers found that the IAT scores were highly predictive of which student organizations' budgets the participants disproportionately slashed: namely, those of the Jewish, Asian, and black student organizations. The IAT scores were highly predictive of discriminatory behavior even after being adjusted for explicit discriminatory attitudes. How can we uncover these sorts of attitudes and change them?

I think that the situation is far from hopeless, and certain educational projects and safeguards can mitigate the insidious influences of implicitly held ideological attitudes. First, it helps to engage in (what social psychologists call) "unconsciousness raising": to device educational programs that make explicit how our communication and decision-making practices hinge on such nontransparent influences. Second, if we are aware of such influences, there are a number of control measures we can implement both individually and institutionally. For instance, we might have a university policy that when cuts must be made, the burdens will be distributed equally and not disproportionately on the basis of decisions few individuals have made. Individually we can make a commitment to reducing the influence of our implicit biases by forming various implementation intentions (cf. section 5.2.4). Of course, there is much more to say about this. However, my point is that fighting injustice is hard, but it is not impossible. Even if in setting back some legitimate human interests structural and institutional arrangements do not wear patriarchy, racial and ethnic dominance, heteronormativity, class elitism, and able-bodiedness on their sleeves, it is not impossible to undercover these shapes and contours of injustice and do something about them. In this way, the theory that I am offering can also meet the second and third adequacy conditions of EST: it facilitates our explanatory accounts of injustice, where these accounts can subsequently be employed to develop effective theories of resistance.

8.3. Feminist Social Theory and Dehumanization

A feminist social theory should (1) define different forms of injustice that individuals face due to their social identity designation (because they are designated as women, men, or trans*), (2) provide tools with which to explain those injustices and resultant harms suffered, (3) pave the way for ending the injustices identified, and (4) explicate why patriarchal injustices are not only harmful but also wrongful. I wish to elucidate next in more detail how my notion of *dehumanization* and the earlier proposed "gender" terminology and ontology (cf. chapter 5) help us meet these desiderata. In so doing, I will demonstrate how I avoid the pull of the gender controversy, which further clarifies the humanist feminist framework advanced here.

In short, this proposed framework has two interconnected parts: one normative, another social theoretical. These are needed in order to satisfy the above four adequacy conditions of a feminist EST. The normative part is comprised of the developed notion of *dehumanization*, which crucially hinges on the thin externalist understanding of humanity. The social theoretical part is comprised of the regimentation of injustice, which I have offered in this and the previous chapter. In short, the spelled-out forms and contours of injustice encompass this social theoretical part. Now, specifically with respect to feminist concerns, this regimentation hinges on a thin understanding of "gendered identities," in more traditional language—the thin understanding of the term 'woman'—and the trait/norm covariance relation that I argued for earlier (cf. chapter 5). This is because feminist social theory requires certain terminological and theoretical tools, and feminists must be able to talk about women. (As I noted earlier, I think that feminism is about more than "just women"; however, here I will discuss the issue with a more usual focus in order to demonstrate the point.) Contra those philosophers looked in chapters 2–4, I hold that the work of supporting feminist normative claims and political demands in the name of women (i.e., the normative aspects of feminist work) should not be undertaken by any conception of *woman*, but by my proposed conception of *dehumanization*. With this in mind, consider the following case: removing from *women* the opportunity to have reproductive control by cutting funding to abortion and sexual health clinics in some US states. This act of cutting the funding is a dehumanizing instance of *social injustice* iff it constitutes an *indefensible violation* of legitimate human welfare interests in a way that counts as *morally injurious*. Let me say more about the italicized expressions in order to illustrate how the story goes.

First, on my regimentation the act of cutting the funding would be oppressive. It places unjust constraints on women via certain material and psychological forces (e.g., in having to bear a child against one's will, in having one's economic opportunities and material well-being hampered). This instance is social: it hinges on some socially salient identifications, which elucidates the specific contour(s) that the injustice takes (more on this shortly). The funding cut is systematic, in being part of an interlocking system of social practices and institutions "throughout a society, [and] usually over a substantial period of time" (Clatterbaugh 1996, 290) that reinforce one another, thus creating and maintaining action-constraining oppressive social conditions. That is, the lack of some other social arrangements and practices (e.g., the nonexistence of support networks for mothers facing economic hardships) together with the funding cut make up precisely such an interlocking system that is self-reinforcing. And these constraints are made unjust in involving dehumanization (again, more shortly).

Second, those directly affected by the funding cut are particular women. In chapter 5, I argued that a thick *woman* concept is not needed to pick out the relevant social kind. Rather, we can rely on thin externalist intuitions that guide our deployment of terms commonly taken to denote gender. This enables us to use the term 'woman' (and other identity designators) as analytical tools in feminist explanatory accounts. In this case, the funding cut will not, of course, affect all individuals we call "women"—rather, it will affect those whose lives are changed by the cut and that our externalist intuitions in the relevant context track (namely, those designated as women in the state). So the term 'women' in our explanation will designate a contextually specific group of individuals picked out on the basis of features indicative of womanhood. We can avoid debilitating debates about the evaluative content of the concept *woman*. The thin understanding proposed in chapter 5, then, enables us to fix the relevant group without smuggling in worries about *woman*'s connotation and applicability conditions. In order to speak on behalf of the women affected, we need not take a stance on these issues, and feminists need not settle in which sense we ought to understand the concept *woman*. Rather, this justificatory task will be undertaken by my notion of *dehumanization*.

Third, with the help of this notion, we can single out the funding cut as problematic from a social justice perspective if the cut indefensibly violates some legitimate welfare interests of the women in question. Since women from economically nonprivileged backgrounds are disproportionately affected by such funding cuts in the United States, some of their legitimate welfare interests are surely set back by the cut (e.g., having their minimal means of subsistence threatened). The interest setback is made indefensible not only by the individual harms suffered (like subsequent economic/material deprivation or resultant psychological harms), but also by the setback's involving contours of injustice that specifically target those designated as women, that is, sexism or patriarchy (though de facto probably others too). Actual decisions to cut funding for abortion and sexual health clinics seem to involve these shapes. They involve individually sexist psychological states (e.g., beliefs about how the affected women ought not to have reproductive control, and that they are incapable of making the right decisions about reproduction) along with institutional patriarchal social arrangements (e.g., a male perspective on women's reproduction being taken as the norm). This example demonstrates how the different contours are also intertwined: the patriarchal arrangements are conceivably intertwined with heteronormative ones in that there is a presumption of heterosexual family arrangements informed by conservative religious views lurking in the background. And the sexism conceivably intertwines with racism ("Women ought not to have reproductive control and black women certainly ought not to!").

Finally, the interest violation must be morally injurious to count as dehumanizing: there must be a failure of recognition respect. In earlier chapters, I outlined how this failure may be due to insidious trait/norm pairings at work (a relation that I elucidated in chapter 5). For me, certain traits are paired with particular norms due to social agents' evaluative reactions pertaining to the traits. These pairings are bound together via quasi-essentialist covariance relations. Specific pairings are linked to women, and different modes of congealment explain the pairings' apparent essentialism and resistance to change. To explain the resiliency, I invoked acceptance dependence and implicit attitudes. Against this backdrop, I proposed the following way to think about the failure of recognition respect: one fails to appreciate some fact about another because of a problematic association of a norm with a trait that the other possesses. We have a problematic quasi-essentialist trait/norm pairing at work, which stands in the way of recognition respect (so to speak). The resiliency of the congealment and the lack of recognition respect are to be explained (in part, but to a significant degree) by public and widespread beliefs and implicit attitudes.

Relative to the example at hand, those cutting the abortion clinic funding are failing to respect some facts about the women adversely affected: that their welfare interests will be severely set back and violated, where this decision hinges on an insidious trait/norm pairing grounding the withholding of reproductive rights from women (who are typically poor or of color or both). That is, possessing physical traits having to do with femaleness is normatively viewed in a "feminine" way that renders the relinquishing of reproductive control to those with female bodies supposedly inappropriate. And this pairing is quasi-essentialist: given wider cultural and religious beliefs and attitudes, the physical traits are viewed *as if* their femininity inherently licenses withholding women reproductive rights. Rather than being seen for what they are (i.e., indefensible human-made constraints on women), the funding cuts are taken to track something agent independent (e.g., "the will of God"). These and other attitudes are responsible for the continuation and resiliency of the pairing, which hampers the attainment of recognition respect: the congealed trait/norm pairing stands in the way of respect, and wider institutional social arrangements further reinforce the acceptance of the congealed pairing.

The above meets the desiderata of a feminist social theory. Specifically, regarding the first and the second adequacy conditions: we have theoretical resources with which to identify the injustice in question and spell out its harms (i.e., the different forms of injustice, deflated "gender" terminology, the trait/norm covariance relation). We can also clarify how the injustice—in this case, oppression—targets those designated as women and hinges on sexist beliefs and patriarchal social arrangements (i.e., deflated "gender" terminology, my two-tier picture of the contours of injustice). Further, I offer resources to satisfy the fourth condition: we have a normative theory at our disposal that elucidates what makes the treatment unjust (i.e., my account of dehumanization). In the next and final chapter, I will say more about how the story so far can satisfy the third adequacy condition and pave the way for social justice. However, prior to this, let me consider a worry.

One might hold that the picture I put forward above looks too individualistic. One might worry that it relies too heavily on individual psychological states and fails to appreciate sufficiently the force of more diffuse and covert social arrangements and structures. It may appear that I am committed to some form of methodological individualism, where social structures and phenomena ultimately supervene on or are grounded in the psychological states of conscious human agents. This is not my view. Losing sight of the macroreality and focusing on psychological microphenomena alone would be seriously misguided. To illustrate, consider the following example. Bluntly put, social facts obtain (at least in part) in virtue of human agents' attitudes and actions in social contexts. A reductionist microtheory would aim to reduce social facts to some psychological antecedents (like the intentional mental states of social agents). But doing so plausibly loses sight of something important in our explanations. Take the claim that the rise of capitalism in modern Europe derives from a Protestant ethic (Jackson and Pettit 1992). Now, the Protestant ethic may explain the rise of capitalism in a number of more specific ways: perhaps it "condemned activities inimical to capitalism; . . . encouraged the relationships between people which capitalism requires; . . . gave people a goal which inspired capitalist activity as a means" (Jackson and Pettit 1992, 103). But the Protestant ethic is unlikely to involve a set of psychological antecedents that alone make good the explanandum. Or if we do find that the rise of capitalism reduces to some psychological antecedents and intentional mental states, we are nonetheless likely to miss something important along the way (e.g., that the Protestant ethic encouraged some forms of relationships conducive to capitalism).

Now, the explanation that I am offering is certainly not meant to provide such a blinkered reductionist story. As I see it, both individual intentions and more diffuse structural arrangements play a role. Therefore, I have offered my two-tier account of injustice's contours. On the institutional level, various policies and rules play a significant role. For instance, if university tenure rules make it de facto impossible for those with caretaking responsibilities to satisfy them and those picked out by the term 'woman' turn out to be the ones with most caretaking responsibilities, these rules are (in my terms) patriarchal. When the rules are "merely" patriarchal, the discrimination suffered is likely to be indirect (cf. section 7.3.1). If the university powers that be additionally hold that this is good since women are not really suited for academic careers anyway, implementing the rule will (in my terms) also involve sexism. These levels can and do function independently of one another, and the explanation offered certainly does not intend to ignore structuralist aspects. Nonetheless, I maintain that we should not lose sight of the fact that social structures and institutions are not self-sustaining and self-sufficient parts of our social ontology. Their existence and continuance do in complicated ways depend on us. How to cash this out is beyond what I can offer here. Accepting this claim, though, does not commit me to a substantive thesis like methodological individualism. Bluntly put, the moral of the story is that injustice involves both individual and institutional contours, which interact and intertwine in complex ways. This being the case, I submit, we should keep in mind both the structuralist and the individualist aspects in explanations, without privileging either.

8.4. The Argument So Far

Let me take stock of this book's two main arguments so far. In Part I, my goal was to motivate a move beyond the gender controversy. This involved a number of more detailed steps. For one, it involved showing that prior feminist positions aiming to resolve the ontological and semantic puzzles are unsatisfying and that the controversy looks intractable. Hence, I argued against the view that articulating a thick notion of *woman* should be a feminist philosophical desideratum. On the outlook that I reject, a conception of *woman* should be thick enough to support specific feminist normative demands and political claims, which include being able to elucidate how and why patriarchy damages women, to justify feminist critical claims about extant states of affairs, and to ground a vision of a feminist future. An analysis of *woman* should enable feminist theorists to conceptualize the social kind of women, and in so doing perhaps even allow us to ground feminist political solidarity. Therefore, (1) in order to secure the foundation for making emancipatory feminist claims on behalf of women, we ought to elucidate a social conception of womanhood (and gender) in some sufficiently substantive sense and in an inclusive manner; (2) in order to meet (1), it is up to feminist philosophers to settle how we ought to define womanhood; and (3) considerations relevant for deciding (2) usually hinge on feminist political considerations. That is, with a proper analysis of *woman*, feminists can make claims in the name and on behalf of women as a group, and they can conceptualize and critique gendered oppression as a systematic nonaccidental phenomenon.

By contrast, my view is that this outlook is bankrupt and perpetuates a theoretical impasse—the gender controversy—that we neither can nor should aim to settle. The semantic and ontological puzzles are intractable given certain theoretical underpinnings of extant feminist positions (discussed in chapter 5). I see little reason to suppose that these puzzles can be resolved in order to dispel the impasse. Of course, the lack of agreement does not entail that we should stop trying to reach a consensus. Still, I hold, the disagreement over gender concepts has become distracting, and it unnecessarily preserves debates about the "proper" understanding of gender—debates that (in my view) we need not continue in order to foster real progress in feminist political and social philosophy. Instead, feminist philosophers would do well to change the terms of the debate. Thus, the first part of the book aimed to motivate a feminist philosophical paradigm shift: the concepts of *gender* and *woman* should no longer be considered the theoretical focal points of emancipatory feminism; rather, we should articulate feminism's normative basis and point anew in a way that avoids the conceptual stalemate of the current debate.

Part II aims to do precisely that. For me, feminism should be "humanized" and feminist philosophers should theorize injustice without relying on thick gender concepts. This calls for (what I previously characterized as) theories of injustice that are freestanding from gender. As discussed in chapter 7, I am putatively not alone in offering such a theory—Frye, Young, and Cudd have also taken valuable steps toward this direction, and my overall position shares much with their views. For instance, Young provides a helpful descriptive formulation of domination, and Cudd does so with respect to oppression. Still, as I also argued earlier, I think that their explications of what makes injustice unjust leave something to be desired. Thus, I am suggesting here an alternative freestanding theory of injustice, whereby the theoretical and normative focal core of feminism ought to be the concept of *dehumanization* developed in chapter 6. This notion can help us support feminist normative demands and political claims noted above. The proposed humanist feminism has interconnected normative and social theoretical parts, which are needed in order to satisfy the four adequacy conditions of a feminist EST: (1) provide clear and coherent definitions of different forms of patriarchal injustice; (2) explain injustices women's face under patriarchy; (3) provide some way to account for the conditions of justice for women; and (4) articulate why patriarchy wrongs women. These conditions generalize and provide a way for us to conceive of emancipatory social theories more generally. In the previous and current chapters, I have proposed a regimentation of injustice by elucidating its wrongness-making feature (chapter 6), forms (chapter 7), and contours (the present chapter). This regimentation has enabled me to spell out the humanist feminism on offer. It has further allowed me to show that certain nonfeminist accounts of injustice leave something to be desired when viewed from a broadly feminist perspective. As I see it, then, dehumanization can help us grasp the wrongness-making feature of social injustice per se.

In the following (and final) chapter, I will address the third adequacy condition. My discussion will be partial and nonexhaustive since a thorough account of the conditions for justice requires a full theory of social justice. This is beyond the scope of the chapter to come and a task for another time. However, I wish to point out how my theory of injustice can contribute to such an endeavor by briefly looking at what overcoming dehumanization conceivably requires. On the face of it, there are three "emancipated" conditions that roughly correspond to the three forms of injustice outlined earlier. The injustices were

- Discrimination: unjust differential treatment that results in indefensible inequalities in the distribution of socially relevant goods
- Domination: unjust wielding of social power that forces the dominated to follow rules set by others and prevents them from determining the conditions of their own actions
- Oppression: systematic imposition of unjust constraints on social agents and their actions due to various material and psychological forces.

The three seemingly corresponding conditions are equality, human flourishing, and freedom respectively. Since discrimination is about unjust differential treatment, its correlate seems to be equality or equal treatment. The counterpart of oppression is commonly taken to be freedom. For instance, Jaggar writes that oppression is "the imposition of unjust constraints on the freedom of individuals or groups"; therefore, "Liberation is the correlate of oppression. It is release from oppressive constraints" (1983a, 6). This is a view that Cudd (2006) also shares. Finally, for some (Lovett 2010), domination hampers human flourishing. Which of these conditions (if any) best corresponds to overcoming dehumanization? Prima facie this requires that no form of injustice indefensibly set back our legitimate human welfare interests in morally injurious ways due to underlying (individual and/or institutional) prejudices or contours of injustice. With this in mind, I am unconvinced that freedom or human flourishing is the right correlate of social injustice, although they are certainly not unconnected to justice. As I see it, they are *outcomes* of overcoming dehumanization, but not constitutive of it. Instead, overcoming dehumanization requires something else. Ultimately, I will suggest that substantive equality of opportunity is the condition at the heart of nondehumanization.

Some preparatory remarks are in order, though. At the start of this book, I outlined a particular methodological commitment: that my examination of dehumanization (and injustice) would be nonideal. I noted that positions like Rawls's and Nussbaum's aim to elucidate an idealized theory of justice that we can use to measure actual social arrangements in order to demonstrate their shortcomings. That is, let's first fix what justice amounts to and then see whether and in which ways extant social relations and institutions fall short. Those that do are exemplary of social injustice. As should be clear, I am aiming to offer a different theory: one that starts by explicating what *injustice* amounts to without having first fixed an idealized theory of justice. This is because (I hold that) elucidations of justice and injustice are not just two aspects of the same theoretical undertaking. In order to understand injustice we should not theorize it through the lens of justice. It is one thing to diagnose the problem (injustice) and another to diagnose the solution (justice). This being the case, what is needed (and what I have developed here) is an interim theory of injustice that can subsequently be employed to develop a fully-fledged theory of social justice. The next chapter starts gesturing to the solution. As noted, I will suggest that at the heart of social justice should be substantive equality of opportunity. However, since I take the examinations of injustice and justice to come apart, it would be a mistake to infer from this that the *absence* of substantive equality of opportunity is at the heart of social injustice. Rather, there we will find dehumanization. And this (I submit) tells us something valuable about justice.

{ 9 }

Overcoming Dehumanization

9.1. Freedom

It might seem that overcoming dehumanization requires a particular form of freedom; namely, freedom from (interest) interference. Appealing to freedom as the correlate of social injustice is a rather popular strategy. However, it is also in my view misguided. Political and social philosophers traditionally understand *freedom* in two senses following Isaiah Berlin (1969): as negative (freedom *from* interference), or as positive (freedom *to* do something). Freedom is either the absence of some constraining conditions or a capacity that enables some actions. For instance, Cudd holds that "full freedom requires that all cases of oppression end" (2006, 222). Given her definition of *oppression* in terms of unjust constraints on action, it is easy to see how freedom in the negative sense provides the apparent correlate of oppression.

That said, Cudd's sense of freedom departs somewhat from Berlin's: she employs the terminology of internal and external freedom that correspond to indirect and direct forces of oppression, respectively. Internal freedom requires that indirect forces of oppression no longer constrain a person, whereas external freedom denotes the absence of direct forces of oppression (Cudd 2006, 225). These two are necessary, though not sufficient for full freedom. In addition, we must break the cycle of oppression so that we prevent it from reoccurring. Independence is additionally needed: that the material and psychological background conditions enable one to form one's own beliefs and desires free from oppressive constraints. We must be able to resist those moves that render the desires and beliefs of the oppressed dependent on those of the dominant—in short, we must be able to break the cycle of those indirect forces of oppression that Cudd calls "oppression by choice," where the oppressed are "made dependent on the desires of the dominant" (2006, 227). So freedom requires three steps. First, we must end direct forces of oppression. Second, we must have alternative social practices available to us "that would be attractive to a wide variety of persons (not just the oppressed), and yet would help to break the cycle of dependency on the dominant group" (2006, 228)—that is, attractive social incentives that foster independence must be available. Third, we must change individuals' social imaginaries of what is possible and desirable, so that the provision of social incentives will be effective. Bluntly put, we must create a social ethos of the kind that will make individuals desire freedom from oppression. This will be a sort of "indirect force of freedom enhancement" (2006, 230): we mold people's beliefs and preferences in ways that are freedom enhancing.

Cudd acknowledges that some might view such social engineering as coercive. However, she argues that it would not be. Social institutions are coercive only if they unfairly limit the choices of some group relative to another group. But (for Cudd) there is no coercion in her notion of freedom because social incentives will not *unfairly* limit choices. The fairness of the limitation will depend on a background moral theory, which Cudd explicitly admits not to have provided (2006, 231).[1] Nevertheless, she claims to have an independent rational argument for why everyone should find the freedom of all attractive. Humans are social beings who cooperate with one another in order to carry out and complete their individual projects. Our projects are in various ways intertwined with those of others, and their success often depends on the success of others' projects. Because humans form social unions (as Rawls put it), we come to find pleasure in others' achievements insofar as the successes of our own projects are integrally intertwined with others' projects. It is worth quoting Cudd in some length here to elucidate:

> In enjoying the achievements of others, we experience freedom from what Marx called the alienation of man from man. We gain valuable information about alternative ways of life that others pursue with interest and devotion. This in turn develops our own capacities, our imaginary domains, which allow each of us the psychic space to enhance our freedom and take pleasure in it. In learning the value of diversity and tolerance, we become motivated to end oppression and privilege, both our own and others. This transformation is not easy; it requires moral character to resist the enticements of privilege. . . .. But at least we can now see that it is rational to seek the freedom of others as well as ourselves. For, to be free is not merely to cast off one's chains, but to live in a way that respects and enhances the freedom of others. (2006, 237)

The idea is based on what Cudd calls (again, following Rawls) the "Aristotelian Principle": "individuals find pleasure in the achievements of their social unions, which also means that they find pleasure in the achievements of

---

[1] I already argued in chapter 7 that Cudd's normative considerations leave something to be desired. My discussion here further demonstrates the point.

others in those groups" (2006, 236). So it is rational to seek to enhance the freedom of others, which will foster the achievement of *our own* individual projects because those projects intertwine in complex and nuanced ways with others' projects. Thus, freedom for all will be good for each, and because freedom will enable us to achieve our individual projects, it is rational for us to desire everyone's freedom.

As eloquent as I find Cudd's case, I am unconvinced that this understanding of freedom provides the right counterpart to oppression. To begin with, I am unconvinced that the Aristotelian principle holds. Further, it seems to me that Cudd's sense of freedom depends on something prior: meaningful opportunities. Let's consider these in turn. First, finding pleasure in the achievements of my social union does not entail that I take pleasure in the achievements of those *in* my social union. Consider an easy example: imagine that the university "powers that be" subject my faculty to a review in order to determine how much funding should be allocated to the faculty. Imagine further that most faculty members work extremely hard on their publication and teaching records to ensure a good outcome for the faculty as a whole. Some, however, do not: they merely exploit their graduate students and steal their ideas in order to meet the required standards. (Imagine further that this can be done with impunity.) Now, let's say that my faculty receives a glowing report and as a social union we have achieved something remarkable. My pleasure in this achievement of the social union, nevertheless, is entirely compatible with my displeasure with—even deep resentment toward—those individuals in the union who merely used the hard work of others to contribute to our collective success. In fact, although the collective achievement in this case benefits me in particular and helps me pursue my own projects, this does not give me any reason to desire everyone's freedom in my collective. Rather, I would wish for some curbing of freedom: I would wish for some way to prevent my colleagues from acting in the ways that they did. More freedom and better incentives are not the appropriate means to remedy the situation.

Granted, much will depend here on what incentives amount to. And this brings me to my second point: that freedom is grounded in meaningful opportunities. Cudd briefly notes that although carrots make for better incentives, sticks can be incentives too. They would be warranted as punishment for oppressive behavior (2006, 229). So we might say that since my example involves exploitation and this is a prima facie indicator of injustice, the appropriate response would be incentives in the form of sticks rather than carrots. After all, the situation where faculty members are incentivized to do their own work by giving them extra research time would be an utterly wrongheaded way to respond to the problem. But now I am losing my grip on why we should focus on freedom. What Cudd's incentive-based freedom ultimately boils down to is that we have certain meaningful opportunities. To curb the freedoms of senior professors in my example requires that junior researchers have opportunities to challenge the exploitation. Other examples of incentives that Cudd offers support this. For instance, the situation for single and low-income parents will be greatly improved by offering affordable, good-quality child care facilities. And such child care will undercut oppression by developing in children capacities to resist internal oppression and enabling women to become economically independent (Cudd 2006, 228). That is, certain structural enabling conditions are responsible for freedom—they are the forces that (in Cudd's terms) fashion freedom. This, however, suggests to me that from the perspective of social justice it is the structural enabling conditions that we should focus on, instead of freedom. Freedom is rather an outcome of some more basic justice-enhancing conditions.

We might, of course, say that I have not yet shown that freedom per se is the incorrect correlate of social injustice. In fact, my example above about the junior researchers being able to resist exploitation might point to freedom in a different sense: freedom from domination. We might say then that freedom in the republican sense of nondomination (rather than Cudd's incentive-based freedom) is the correct correlate. Philip Pettit is probably the most prominent contemporary advocate of republican freedom. He outlines three ways in which political philosophers have theorized freedom (2011): as nonfrustration (Hobbes), noninterference (Berlin), and nondomination (Pettit). The key features of each are roughly the following. Freedom as nonfrustration is about being able to do that which one prefers or chooses to do without being externally hindered or frustrated in one's choice and action. Being externally prevented from doing something makes one unfree. Freedom as noninterference is about there not being obstacles to the fulfillment of one's preferences and the execution of one's chosen actions. The inference is not just about (say) facing coercive obstacles that prevent one from acting, but also about more subtle ways in which one might be manipulated to choose some course of action. Freedom as nondomination is about the following: so long as I have the power and resources to influence your decisions and make them dependent on my will, you are not free. This form is not about actually exercising power; rather, it is about "my having the power to interfere more or less without cost, should my will incline that way" (Pettit 2011, 707).

The open-doors metaphor is meant to illustrate the above three forms of freedom: imagine being in a room with a number of doors and deliberating which door to walk through. First, if all the doors are locked, you are obviously not free to walk through any of them. Even if only half are locked, your choice of which door to walk through is severely limited and your freedom will be frustrated. Second, imagine that the doors are open and that you can choose any of the doors. But someone manipulates your decision in a way that you walk through a particular door. In this case, you were not free from interference. Finally, imagine that the doors are unlocked and no one manipulates your decision. If there, nonetheless, were someone who *could* have stopped you from walking through some door had the person so wanted, you would not be free from domination. Drawing on Mary Wollstonecraft, Pettit puts this last idea thus:

> The woman who lives under the will of a husband may rely on mincing steps and beguiling smiles to keep her husband sweet and to get her way in a variety of choice. But she doesn't succeed thereby in getting out from under his will, escaping the constraint that it represents. . . . However kindly or gullible, however much he is a pushover, the husband remains a master. (2011, 709)

Now, I hold that freedom as nondomination also fails to provide the correct counterpart to oppression. First of all, it is not entirely obvious to me that those suffering contemporary social injustices are primarily looking for freedom as nondomination—oftentimes they are ultimately after meaningful social opportunities. This is an empirical point and cannot be settled just with philosophical reflection. However, there are ways to elucidate the point with philosophical means too. As I see it, meaningful opportunities are necessary requisites for freedom, rather than vice versa, which is something that the republican sense of freedom also fails to appreciate. I will say more about meaningful opportunities in section 9.3. Still, I wish to offer some preliminary remarks to motivate the view that freedom is not what we should first and foremost focus on.

Take the case of people of color being subject to stop-and-search policies. In a sense, there is a need to be free from arbitrary police harassment, and being free in this sense does fit the idea of freedom as nondomination: after all, those racialized as white are not subject to such policies because they have enough social power to escape the anterior domination. But this freedom from domination ultimately turns on having the possibility to go about one's business unharassed by the police, and those racialized as white have the necessary opportunities to do so. This suggests to me that what grounds our freedom (as noninterference and nondomination) is a form of substantive equality of opportunity. Let me be clear: it is not that I find freedom irrelevant for social justice. However, freedom seemingly turns on something prior without the achievement of which we cannot even hope to attain freedom in some sense. This is (I hold) to a large part due to the structural aspects of contemporary social injustices.

To put the point somewhat metaphorically: freedom-based accounts implicitly assume that on the first day there was freedom, but on the second day someone or something constrained us in a way that undermined that freedom. And thus, on the third day, we should seek to be liberated from these constraints in order to attain justice. But I think that this is the wrong picture. Freedom is not something that we would simply possess were it not for the unfortunate and unjust barriers that different forms and contours of injustice create. Rather, freedom is an achievement from the start: it is something that we come to possess provided that there are sufficient social and institutional arrangements that *enable* freedom. The case of stop-and-search policies should then be understood in the following manner. We should not think of those racialized as white having basic freedoms that everyone should enjoy were it not for some unfortunate social constraints. Rather, there are some structural conditions that enable those racialized as white to go about their business freely, but that prevent people of color from doing so. Social justice then demands that everyone has access to the same freedom-enabling conditions, which will crucially involve (in my view) substantive equality of opportunity.

Consider another example that demonstrates the problem with freedom. Take women who become stay-at-home mothers because there is no affordable child care, and because they face subsequent difficulties in combining work and family lives. Is this a problem of not being free? In one sense, yes: individuals are not free to pursue their chosen careers (for instance) as a result of structural constraints. But, in another sense, no: ultimately, what the women need is not freedom from constraining conditions, but opportunities to continue working and to do so in ways that make work arrangements compatible with caretaking responsibilities. Being free seems to follow from having some meaningful opportunities, not vice versa. This is poignantly demonstrated by an exchange that Joan Williams describes:

> I was sitting side by side with a woman I had just met at Plastercraft, chatting as our daughters painted. ... "I decided to quit my job and stay home," she told me. "But it was my choice; I have no regrets." I asked her whether she would not really prefer to continue working as a lawyer, with shorter hours of work. She replied wistfully: "Of course, that's what I really want." (2000, 271)

This example demonstrates that it is meaningful opportunities that first and foremost matter, rather than freedom. Furthermore, it shows that the former enable the latter. The interlocutors in the example are specific kinds of women: namely, ones in a partnership with a spouse who can financially support the whole family. The women in question have a specific socioeconomic position that enables them to stay at home, and many women from lower socioeconomic positions simply are not in a position to become stay-at-home mothers. The woman in this example already enjoys some freedoms that those who cannot afford to quit their jobs or who are not in partnerships simply do not have. Her freedom *not* to work is enabled by something else, which again undermines the picture that first came freedom and second came freedom-constraining structures.[2] Finally, the question arises again

---

[2] Thanks to Resa-Philip Lunau for helping me with this point.

about how fitting freedom as nondomination is when thinking about contemporary structural injustices. There is no obvious way in which the woman is dominated in Pettit's sense by some other social agent(s). But social justice surely does not characterize the above situation. We may possess freedom to do various things that mitigates at least some unjust structural conditions, but this may not render our situation just. Consequently, my contention is that focusing on freedom can obscure the situation in ways that prevent us from seeing what really is the problem.

9.2. Human Flourishing

In chapter 7, I discussed Lovett's arbitrary power conception of domination: domination is "a condition experienced by persons or groups to the extent that they are dependent on a social relationship in which some other person or group wields arbitrary power over them" (Lovett 2010, 2). I argued that this conception does not satisfy the first and second adequacy conditions of EST: it does not enable us to pick out and explain contemporary cases of social injustice. However, there is another reason to resist Lovett's account. Given what he thinks social justice involves, Lovett privileges domination as the form of injustice that should concern us from the perspective of social justice—something that I find misguided. For Lovett, domination is bad because it hampers human flourishing. And overcoming domination and attaining flourishing requires freedom in the republican sense discussed above. Lovett's view is not then entirely unlike Cudd's. Nevertheless, human flourishing for Lovett characterizes the "emancipated" condition, where freedom is the enabling factor. And this focus on flourishing justifies a particular take on social justice: *justice as minimizing domination* (JMD).

To begin with, Lovett aims to establish that not suffering from arbitrary domination is an important human good—it is a crucial ingredient of human flourishing. He stipulates the following understanding of flourishing: it is "success in achieving autonomously formulated, reasonable life plans, through fellowship or community with others, over a complete life" (2010, 131). Domination in his sense obstructs human flourishing in generating various material and psychological harms. Wielding arbitrary power results in direct material harms and injuries that result from the exploitation of the dominated so that "slave masters extract productive labor from their slaves, members of the class of nobles extract feudal dues from members of the peasant class, husbands extract household and/or sexual services from their wives" (Lovett 2010, 131). In addition, the dominated are likely to suffer from "harms of insecurity" that generate psychological hindrances to flourishing, like psychological anxiety and a "paralytic sense of helplessness" (2010, 132). Finally, domination diminishes self-respect and self-worth. Insofar as domination produces such harms that hinder human flourishing, it is bad, and nondomination will enable flourishing.

Lovett acknowledges that nondomination is not sufficient for human flourishing and that other conditions plausibly include health, education, some material goods, and cultural membership (2010, 135). But he does not spell out these conditions further. Rather, in order to achieve human flourishing, we must work toward reducing domination. This connects Lovett's position straightforwardly to the republication notion of political liberty. As already noted, freedom as noninterference will not do: a slave master may never interfere with the freedom of the slave, but this surely does not render the slave free, as the master can still wield power over the slave at will. Lovett's conception of domination is also meant to provide a more plausible account of what would increase political liberty. Increasing the level of noninterference would not make the slave freer. But if laws and institutions were created that regulated and diminished the slave master's power over the slave (i.e., that reduce domination), intuitively such laws and institutions would increase the slave's liberty. Therefore, the appropriate conception of freedom is the nondomination one.

Since nondomination is crucial for human flourishing and it constitutes the conception of freedom that we should endorse, social justice supposedly demands undermining domination whenever possible. This renders nondomination "the exclusive concern of a conception of social justice" (Lovett 2010, 170).[3] Social justice concerns itself with the basic structure of an "independent and ongoing" society—a structure that consists of the "complete set of political and social institutions and practices that constitute the relatively stable background conditions or expectations against which the members of that society live out their lives" (2010, 158). In particular, Lovett has in mind political institutions, modes of economic production, and public policies along with social norms and conventions. Our conception of social justice should provide an account of the best basic structure from the point of view of justice, which is to say that "in respecting and upholding its institutions and practices in the process of living out their lives, people would, in the traditional expression, be giving each their due" (2010, 158). Societies are just insofar as their basic structure and organization minimizes the expected sum total of domination their members' experience (2010, 159). This is Lovett's JMD conception of social justice.[4]

---

[3] It is worth noting that Lovett thinks we need not be committed to the republican conception of freedom for his argument for the JMD conception of social justice to get off the ground. We simply need to accept that nondomination is "an important condition of human flourishing," and that we have a prima facie obligation to reduce domination whenever possible (Lovett 2010, 156). Nevertheless, he clearly is committed to the republican conception.

[4] In fact, Lovett provides a second, more fleshed-out version of JMD. But nothing hangs on his specifications for my purposes here.

Why privilege nondomination as crucial for social justice over (say) meeting basic material needs? Lovett admits that nondomination is *a* human good, but clearly not the only one that matters, all things considered. His case for prioritizing nondomination over the distribution of primary goods like "basic rights and liberties, powers and prerogatives of office, income and wealth, and so on" (Lovett 2010, 171) is the following. To begin with, the JMD conception is not meant to be indifferent to the distribution of primary goods because their distribution will usually affect society's levels of domination. Thus, we have instrumental reasons to care about the distribution of primary goods, but their distribution is not the *direct* concern of social justice. Moreover, social and political philosophers should not merely care about justice—it is not the sole virtue of political and social institutions. These institutions and practices may also be more or less economically efficient and fair. Still, such virtues are not about social justice and "if two societies have done an equally good job in reducing domination, one would not be less just merely because it does not correct for as much unfairness as the other" (Lovett 2010, 172). Contra Rawls, Lovett takes our duties of fairness and justice to come apart. Finally, we have reason to believe that freedom from domination is the particular concern of social justice (rather than fair distribution of primary goods or basic material needs) because of past struggles for justice. Fights against feudal, colonial, and patriarchal domination were not about the fair distribution of primary goods. Those struggling to end such domination supposedly "almost certainly disagreed widely" about how goods should be distributed; instead, these struggles tap into something more fundamental: "our yearning to be free of domination" (Lovett 2010, 173). Satisfying this yearning will allegedly enable us to live flourishing lives.

Earlier I expressed skepticism about the contemporary applicability of Lovett's account precisely because his case depends so heavily on the above "core," historical examples. If we take these historical cases at face value, the struggles for justice do seem to be about a yearning for freedom. But the conception of freedom as nondomination ill fits cases of more covert structural injustices. For one thing, systematic and structural oppression often does not have clear actors who have power over others and can thereby constrain others' actions at will in ways that hamper flourishing. On the nondomination approach, a person is not free if someone else can at will interfere with the person's choices. The evil of domination is that there is a "form of subjection to the will of another" (Pettit 2011, 716). More often, though, our options are reduced in deeply covert ways that are detrimental to justice.

Consider the following example from Cudd that describes an instance of "oppression by choice" (2006, 148–9). Lisa and Larry decide to marry and have children. At the start of their relationship, they have equal power. Now, suppose that they do not hold prejudicial beliefs about gender-segregated work or alleged gendered capacities and believe that domestic household tasks should be equally divided. Nevertheless, they believe that one designated parent best executes childcaring and childrearing, although they hold no beliefs about whether this is best done by the mother or the father. If Larry and Lisa inhabit a society with a gendered wage gap and if they wish to maximize the family's income, it is rational for Lisa to specialize in child care and Larry in wage work. This (at least prima facie) rational decision may end up constraining Lisa's choices, prospects, and opportunities in severe ways, though. Her value as a worker will be reduced, which will make finding future meaningful work outside the home difficult. She will have less independent wealth, being dependent on Larry's wages. Lisa's prospects are much dimmer than Larry's if the relationship ends. She may have less bargaining power in the relationship, and Larry may end up having power over her in the long run. For Cudd, this case is first and foremost characterized by structural oppression, which subsequently gives rise to unequal power relations. But from the perspective of nondomination, only the final part of the story should concern us. *That's* where the evil lies. I am rather more convinced that we should focus on the conditions that make it possible for the domination relations that hamper flourishing to develop in the first place. Or, to put the point differently: if the structural enabling conditions also matter, why focus on nondomination as the exclusive concern of social justice?

Lovett provides two justifications. The first is a nonstarter for me, though. Lovett's case for focusing on political liberty as nondomination partly boils down to nothing more than a presumption about Americans:

> if we define political liberty or freedom as non-domination, civic republicanism can draw on a rich and powerful rhetorical tradition that resonates strongly with many people, and many Americans in particular. Such a doctrine captures our sense that freedom and justice must run together. (2010, 235)

I suspect that this conception of political liberty will not resonate with all Americans. Those who are poor, people of color, or both and who are *therefore* subject to many forms of structural constraints that prevent them from having equal access to social goods and opportunities may not find the rhetoric of freedom that compelling. Bluntly put: one may not care so much about one's opportunities being under "the will of another," but rather about having meaningful opportunities to begin with, given the structural and institutional constraints that deny one access to education, welfare, good housing, or safety on unjust grounds. Moreover, as a non-American I do not share the immediate pull of Lovett's claim, and it gives me no genuine reasons to privilege domination. I suspect that I am not alone.

The second (already noted) justification for privileging domination hinges on Lovett's notion of social justice. For him, the distribution of primary goods causally affects levels of domination (2010, 172), but arbitrary wielding of power is the "real evil" of domination. But Lovett's remarks about the relationship between primary good distribution and domination's structural enabling conditions suggest that domination on his view trades on something prior. After all, the JMD conception "demands the public provision of an unconditional basic income, policies of special toleration and accommodation to protect groups otherwise vulnerable to domination, and constitutionally constrained, democratic political and legal institutions" (2010, 234). This is presumably because they will indirectly contribute to nondomination. But now it seems that domination is (at least partly) grounded in the distribution of basic goods and other structural enabling conditions. It seems to supervene on something prior (like not having minimal means of subsistence or the right kinds of political and legal institutions). Another way of seeing this comes from the ways to reduce Lovett's domination: we can reduce it by reducing dependency, imbalances of power, or the arbitrariness of the wielded social power. Economic dependency usually trades on economic inequalities and poverty; these two are prior to resultant domination in being the constituent parts of economic dependency. This suggests to me that our efforts to bring about social justice by focusing on domination focuses on the symptoms rather than the underlying illness. We should rather focus on the more primary structural inequalities in the distribution of basic goods that give rise to relationships of domination in the first place. Again, take the Larry and Lisa case: we should focus on the underlying institutional arrangements and not just the resultant domination.[5]

The upshot is that Lovett's conception of social justice is implausible. For him, those societies that are organized in ways that fail to minimize the expected sum total of domination are less just than those that do. So two societies with the same sum total of domination because their basic structures have prevented (say) domination resulting from sexual slavery are both equally just. And these societies are equally just even if one has deeply unequal income distribution along racialized lines, whereas the other has reached income parity. The two are equally just, though not equally fair

---

[5] Of course, Lovett has a handy retort ready: given his conception of social justice, the forces underlying domination should not concern us from the perspective of justice. Curing the illness (so to speak) perhaps trades on our duties of fairness, but these come apart from those of justice. For a full moral theory, in Lovett's view, we need more than justice. But his theory of social justice is not meant to be a full moral theory. My contention is that this has not been satisfyingly established. Lovett holds that merging our duties of fairness and justice is possible only when "the set of persons affected by a community's institutions and practices [is] effectively coextensive with the members of that community" (2010, 172). This is no longer the case given global and transnational contexts; thus, justice and fairness are not equivalent, but about something else. However, much will depend on what fairness amounts to. Further, the available options are not that either justice and fairness are equivalent or they are utterly distinct from one another. We can conceive of the relationship between justice and fairness as integrally intertwined without having to merge the two and collapse the distinction altogether.

or good (morally speaking). Still, for Lovett, the income inequities should not concern us from the point of view of social justice because unfairness is about something *else*. I find this deeply uncompelling. Following Lovett, social and political philosophers have merely instrumental reasons to care about unjust income disparities. But if domination is grounded in some more fundamental patterns of unequal distribution of basic goods, does this not provide political and social philosophers more than instrumental reasons to care about the latter? I think that it does because domination (as Lovett understands it) ontologically depends on something else. Were we to understand social justice in Lovett's restricted sense, we would thereby lose sight of many other issues that should concern us from the perspective of social justice.

Finally, it is hard to see how Lovett's separation of justice and fairness squares with human flourishing, which is "success in achieving autonomously formulated, reasonable life plans, through fellowship or community with others, over a complete life" (Lovett 2010, 131). Even if two societies have equally reduced domination, stark income disparities conceivably will affect (and greatly so) these constituents of flourishing. And if achieving flourishing is the goal and this is within the purview of social justice, I do not see how we can dismiss and ignore considerations of fairness and the distribution of primary goods. Thinking that the achievement of autonomously formulated life plans simply hinges on being nondominated strikes me as woefully naive, and again ill fits cases of contemporary structural injustices. I am sure that full social justice hinges on some freedom from domination. But I see no good reasons to privilege domination over other forms of injustice in the manner that Lovett does.

9.3. Equality

9.3.1. THE BASIC PICTURE

Overcoming dehumanization, simply put, requires that our legitimate welfare interests *not* be indefensibly set back in morally injurious ways because of underlying forms of injustice that take (individual and/or institutional) contours. I argued above that freedom ill fits this idea. I also think that Lovett's case for human flourishing is unconvincing. There is a further reason to find human flourishing lacking as the right correlate. I have stressed time and again that well-being and human flourishing come apart (cf. chapter 6). The former provides the necessary foundation for the latter, and human flourishing is not what social justice should focus on. It is entirely possible that people's lives are not characterized by individual flourishing even though their social structures are characterized by social justice. This is because flourishing turns on subjective measures, like happiness. And one might simply live in a society that is socially characterized by justice, but culturally by "moodiness" and "brooding," perhaps because of the weather or geographical location (where winters are cold, long, and dark).[6] For me, overcoming dehumanization is not primarily about people being happy and flourishing; it is about guaranteeing the *possibility* for personal happiness and flourishing. Rather, what lies at the heart of social justice is that we all have the same or equal chances. The point is not that we treat everyone equally, but that we treat everyone *as* equals (R. Dworkin 1981a, 187). This has unmistakably egalitarian undertones, and I find egalitarianism pretheoretically an attractive position, although I do not here wish to commit myself to any such substantive doctrine. That said, my position does point to particular egalitarian considerations that I wish to sketch out next.

Start by considering Young's critique of (what she calls) "the distributive paradigm." For her, social justice means "the elimination of institutionalized domination and oppression" (1990, 15). This is in contrast to the "distributive paradigm" conception of social justice: roughly put, that justice amounts to the equal distribution of (usually) welfare or resources (Arneson 1989; R. Dworkin 1981a; 1981b). On this view, the concept of *distribution* is the starting point for our analyses of social justice; for instance, the norm of resource equality states that "to achieve equality the [relevant distributing] agency ought to give everybody a share of goods that is exactly identical to everyone else's and that exhausts all available resources to be distributed" (Arneson 1989, 77–78). Or, according the norm of welfare equality, goods ought to be "distributed equally among a group of persons to the degree that the distribution brings it about that each person enjoys the same welfare," where welfare is equivalent to preference satisfaction (1989, 82).

For Young, the distributive paradigm misses the point. Injustice does not amount to the misallocation of welfare or resources; rather, oppression and domination (in the senses already discussed) are those forces that hinder social justice (Young 1990, 16). This is at least partly supported by public calls for justice: they often have nothing to do with the distribution of some goods, but rather call for lifting some undue constraints. Further, the distributive paradigm focuses on results or end-based patterns (i.e., how goods are in the end distributed), instead of the social processes *in* the distribution of goods and benefits (1990, 25). For instance, thinking about whether individuals have many or few opportunities on the distributive model gets things wrong. Opportunity is not something one can possess. Rather, it denotes enablement: those who are less constrained by social structures and experience greater enabling conditions will have more opportunities (1990, 26). So it is not the distributive outcomes that matter for social justice, but whether one lives under

---

[6] As a native Finn, I find imagining such a society is extremely easy.

conditions that constrain or enable opportunities. And this is about whether one lives under oppressive conditions and suffers domination or not.

Young is surely right that equality is not just about the equal distribution of some relevant goods. But (I contend) which social goods we are distributing makes a difference. One immediate suggestion might be that my position is about welfare equality—after all, I hold that a key to social justice seems to be that our human welfare interests are not indefensibly set back. However, this would be a misconception. First, more usual positions that aim to distribute welfare equally turn on measuring welfare in terms of preference satisfaction (as the quote above attests to). But, for me, basic welfare interests are not about our subjective preferences. So whether our preferences are equally or unequally satisfied is neither here nor there. Second, justice for me should not be measured in an outcome-based manner. It is about our opportunities to achieve basic welfare, where these turn on how much our social structures and institutions enable such opportunities to arise. For me, it is a hallmark of justice that *no* subtle and covert structural forces exist that unjustly hamper our opportunities, whether we make use of them or not. Or, to put this somewhat differently: if we aimed to make use of some opportunities that others in our societies enjoy, we should not be prevented from doing so on unjust grounds. It is entirely possible that although we can equally achieve basic welfare, our individual "shares" of welfare might differ—we might have made some unwise or reckless choices that resulted in differential outcomes. For instance, my interest in basic means of subsistence might be hampered because as a teenager I did not want to study and therefore did not achieve some needed educational qualifications. Nevertheless, if our social and institutional arrangements are characterized by social justice, they should not prevent me from being able to alter my situation because of my age, parenting, or socioeconomic status. That is, if we cannot escape such interest hampering and this is because of some contour(s) of injustice, our social and institutional arrangements are not characterized by justice. This is because in such contexts, we are still missing *equality of opportunity*.

The key to me, then, is not that there is welfare equality per se, but that there is a kind of welfare equality of opportunity. How should we understand this idea? Equality of opportunity is a vexed philosophical notion. How we are to attain it is even more complicated and the stuff of policymaking. I cannot do justice to the rich literature on the topic here, and spelling out these issues fully is beyond the scope of the chapter. Nevertheless, let me briefly elucidate what I have in mind. What is it to have an opportunity? Arneson defines this as "a chance of getting a good if one seeks it" (1989, 85). One way to understand our chances of getting what we seek is in *formal* terms: equality of opportunity requires that available positions are open to all qualified applicants and that posts (along with subsequent advantages) be awarded on the grounds of merit. So all qualified candidates have the chance of getting (say) some job if they seek to, provided that our posts are allocated in a meritocratic manner.

Antidiscrimination laws most basically target precisely treatments that hamper such equality of opportunity: they aim to secure meritocratic post allocation by outlawing differential treatment of applicants on the grounds of sex/gender, race-ethnicity, sexual orientation, ability, class, or religion when these social identity vectors are irrelevant for the post in question. Feminists have already amply critiqued such apparently neutral antidiscrimination laws, and I will not rehearse their arguments here (MacKinnon 1989; Saul 2003, chap. 1; Williams 2000). A quick example suffices to show what goes wrong with formal equality of opportunity. Let's imagine that university places are open to all qualified candidates. But imagine further that the application process involves a face-to-face interview in order to determine who the most qualified ones are. Now, suppose further that only those who attend the most expensive schools are effectively coached for such interviews. In this case, even though we are choosing students by merit, there is de facto privileging of applicants from higher socioeconomic classes. Formal equality of opportunity yields suboptimal results. What we need is *substantive* equality of opportunity: our social and institutional arrangements must ensure that everyone can develop the required skills and that we level the playing field, so to speak. For instance, it requires making sure that university admissions criteria do not correlate with privileged socioeconomic groups. Most basically, we have achieved substantive equality of opportunity when

> all members of society are eligible to apply for [some desirable] position, applicants are fairly judged on their merits and the most meritorious are selected, and sufficient opportunity to develop the qualifications needed for successful application is available to all. (Arneson 2002)

An intuitively plausible idea (it seems to me) is that dehumanizing interest violations undermine precisely such opportunities to develop the required qualifications and skills in addition to preventing one from being fairly judged on one's merit. They lead us to being treated and socially positioned in ways that distort and misbalance our societal "playing fields." And so equality of opportunity seems to provide the appropriate counterpart to injustices characterized as dehumanizing in my sense.

Let me elucidate this idea further and make it more precise. For me, it is not how much we have that matters; rather, the underlying processes by which we gain what we have are of significance. Injustices do not pertain primarily to the differential distributions of some good, but to different social

and institutional arrangements and processes that either place some barriers to what it is possible for us to achieve or prevent those barriers from
being put into place, thus enabling certain courses of action. Specifically, I
am not thinking about substantive equality of opportunity just in terms of
some social goods (like education), although these are of crucial importance.
My thought is more along the following lines. Ronald Dworkin (1981a, 220)
considers the idea that equality of welfare is about equal amounts or degrees
of some conscious state, like enjoyment or happiness. Now, this view clearly
does not fit my position. First, basic welfare (again) is not about enjoyment
or happiness. Second, thinking about welfare in these terms faces problems
with adaptive preferences already discussed in chapter 6. However, there is
something attractive about the idea that equal opportunities pertain to *states
of affairs*, rather than to some specific goods. So we can make sense of what
I am after by saying that equality of welfare is about equal amounts or degrees of nondehumanizing states of affairs: social justice (at least partly) is
about equalizing opportunities for noninterference and for not having one's
interests set back.

This does not pertain just to available positions and educational opportunities, but to social states of affairs more broadly (like whether am I subject
to arbitrary stop-and-search policies because of my racialized social kind
membership). After all, what is underlying contemporary social injustices is
that different social agents have their human interests differentially set back
by structural and institutional arrangements; thus, some experience more
prejudicial interest hampering than others. And so for us to have substantive
equality of opportunity is for everyone to have the possibility and chance
equally to *avoid* indefensible interest violations that constitute moral injuries. Equality of opportunity is about removing barriers to opportunities. It
is less about what goods we are positively entitled to than about achieving
states of affairs, where we are not impaired and hampered in our daily lives.

Again, consider the example of being subject to arbitrary stop-and-search
policies because of one's racialized group membership. Some groups are subject to such interest violations through racist attitudes and racially dominant
social arrangements, while others are not. What I foresee equality of opportunity to deliver is the removal of those states of affairs, where social agents
encounter barriers to their opportunities (particularly I would foresee the
removal of those barriers that generate Cudd's psychological forces of oppression, like reduced self-worth). This is the nondehumanizing state that those
racialized as white already enjoy in contemporary Western contexts, and the
state that all (in my view) should enjoy. Of course, in a sense removing these
barriers corresponds to noninterference and negative freedom. But, I contend, the basic move that generates more justice is the removal of barriers
and not the increasing of negative freedoms—the latter is an outcome of the

former, but social justice requires first and foremost that our opportunities to be treated in nondehumanizing ways be enhanced and leveled out.[7]

This connects to my earlier claim that the moral injury underlying inde-fensible interest violations turns on the lack of recognition respect. I proposed a way to understand this lack in terms of trait/norm covariance relations out-lined in chapter 5. In short, insidious trait/norm pairings stand in the way of recognition respect, so to speak, and prevent us from appreciating some salient facts about others in our deliberation and conduct. My view of equal opportunities fits this idea of what dehumanization involves. What social justice and the removal of certain barriers would do (on my view) is prevent the insidious trait/norm pairings standing in the way of recognition respect, among other things: equal opportunities would create conditions that under-mine the possibility of recognition respect failures. They would do so by driv-ing a wedge between problematic quasi-essentialist pairings conceivably by creating institutional states of affairs that prevent such problematic pairings from having the appropriate force. The case of Swedish parental-leave legis-lation illustrates the idea: the legislation appears to achieve a state of affairs that removes barriers that block mothers opportunities to continue working. It further creates possibilities for men to undertake caretaking roles without this hampering their career prospects, and by normalizing a state of affairs where men undertake such roles. In facilitating these states, the legislation seemingly drives a wedge between caretaking and femininity. It not only alters the structural conditions underlying our personal decision-making, but also alters our cultural imaginaries about what we can do and undertake. Substantive equal opportunity for me, then, provides ways in which morally injurious interest violations can be undermined.

9.3.2. OBJECTIONS AND CLARIFICATIONS

Let me pause for a moment to consider some objections in order to clarify further the picture that I am putting forward. One might wonder how help-ful it is to focus on opportunities, and whether outcomes matter more than I have granted here. Focusing on opportunities, rather than outcomes and

---

[7] What if everyone were subject to random stop-and-search policies and police harassment? One might claim that such a situation goes against my appeal to equalizing our opportunities not to be harassed as a hallmark of social justice: in this case, the objection goes, no particular racialized group would disproportionately bear the burden of such harassment, but the situation is surely not characterized by social justice. I agree, but I do not think that this presents a counterexample to my view. It would be odd to conclude from my discussion that if everyone were equally badly off, this should not concern us from the perspective of social justice. My view is that everyone should have the opportunity equally to *avoid* dehumanizing modes of treatment. If no one can, this does not cancel out the injustice. It makes the prevalent states of affairs rather extremely unjust.

distributive patterns, may strike one as a rather conservative idea. After all, we may well have equality of opportunity in a society that nonetheless is divided into haves and have-nots. For conservatives, though, this is non-problematic: despite having opportunities, social agents might simply fail to utilize them through laziness or carelessness. Resultant distribution disparities should not concern us from the perspective of social justice since social agents chose those paths that generated the disparities. Progressive leftists, however, are likely to complain that caring just about equal opportunities is insufficient, and unequal distribution of wealth should also concern us from the perspective of justice. So my focus on equal opportunities may be unhelpful since outcomes prima facie also matter.

Now, neoliberal conservative thinking is certainly not what I have in mind when I talk about social justice. If our society is characterized by (say) gross income differentials, this should give us pause. However, the distinction between processes and outcomes is important when thinking about what constitutes social justice. As I see it, outcome disparities are surely indicators of some underlying social injustices. That is, if we think that our social processes are characterized by substantive equality of opportunity and nevertheless find ourselves in a society with gross income differentials, we would do well to investigate whether our society genuinely is characterized by justice-enhancing processes. I suspect that our findings will negate our earlier presumption. So the point is not that we can simply ignore differential outcomes; the point is that equal distributive outcomes are not at the heart of social justice. They rather follow from prior states of affairs that are characterized by social justice.

With this in mind, consider a second line of objection. One might wonder about comparative cases of prima facie unequal opportunities that do not trade on basic welfare interests. What if I am not disadvantaged in absolute terms and with respect to my basic welfare interests, but merely relative to some other social groupings in a manner that pertains to some less basic goods? For instance, imagine that my department distributes non-merit-based research leave only to full professors, and this happens to coincide with distributing such leave only to male professors (since my department has only male full professors). It looks like female junior faculty are worse off relative to male senior faculty, where this hinges on a comparative case: they are not worse off all things considered, but only relative to another group. Further, in this example being worse off does not seem to hamper any basic welfare interests in my sense, and it appears to be a case that should not concern us from a social justice perspective. Still, intuitively it looks like something has gone seriously wrong here, and the misallocation of leave plausibly would play a role in alienating the female faculty.[8]

---

[8] I am grateful to Sally Haslanger for this point.

Now, I think that there is something wrong with this case; but I also hold that my view can accommodate it (and similar cases). First, as noted above, unequal distribution outcomes do provide indications that something has gone wrong. So the distribution of leave only to male professors should act as an alarm bell to warn us that there is something worth investigating. In the case of philosophy, this alarm should alert us to a striking fact about the case: that only male philosophers happen to occupy full professorships. Second, this realization should lead us to ask why. For instance, it should move us to examine the university's hiring and promotion processes in order to see whether the decisions to hire and promote male philosophers were in fact characterized be substantive equality of opportunity. Now, I hesitate to guess that in many instances the answer will be no, and we can find covert and hard-to-detect instances of discrimination at work: differential treatments that result in unequal distribution of socially relevant goods (in this case, positions on merit).

Third, we must settle whether the discrimination was unjust—whether it involved some dehumanizing treatments that trade on some contour(s) of injustice. In order to determine this, we must ask some more specific questions.

- Does the case involve *sexism* or *patriarchy* (or perhaps both)? If not the former, it will probably involve the latter (given what we know about the situation in philosophy [cf. Hutchison and Jenkins 2013]). That is, the situation is likely to involve structural arrangements that take being a cis man as the norm and standard (e.g., work hours being arranged in a manner that fails to consider caretaking activities).
- Does the case involve a *setback* to legitimate human interests? In a sense yes, because it plausibly involves hampering female faculty's job prospects, which hampers financial security. The stress caused by this is likely to hamper emotional well-being and to produce anxiety and resultant physical manifestations of stress.
- Does the case involve an *indefensible* setback to our interests? Since indefensibility turns on an interest hampering's being inexcusable and/or unjustifiable *and* (in this example case) the setback involves patriarchy, the answer is yes. After all, it is this contour of injustice that makes the interest hampering inexcusable (roughly, in taking a cis man's perspective on academia as the standard against which everyone is measured); thus, the setback is indefensible.
- Does the case involve a *moral injury*, understood as a failure of recognition respect? I think that it does, and here we see the force of the comparative case. The example is an apparent case of certain comparative barriers being in place that hinge on problematic trait/norm pairings, which stand in the way of recognition respect. The pairings

pertain to dissociating femininity from philosophizing. Anecdotally at least, academic philosophical pursuits are not typically associated with those designated as women, but with those designated as men. So what stands in the way of recognition respect is an underlying normative reaction to academic philosophizing as being a masculine activity. And this plausibly renders female philosophers' contributions deviant and defective (cf. Beebee 2013).

This case is extremely subtle and complex but illustrates the point. In many cases, the injustice involved may not be immediately obvious, and we must engage in social theoretical investigation. Still, the lack of immediate welfare interest hampering and comparative cases like the above should not be taken at face value. Rather, the manifest inequalities and other such signals should prompt us to dig deeper in order to see what is ultimately doing the work.

Now, the approach that I am suggesting with respect to substantive equality of opportunity further avoids some common problems discussed in the literature on equality. First, consider the leveling-down problem: if we wish to achieve parity relative to some social good, one effective way to do so would be to bring everyone's welfare down to the level of the worst off. But this does not result in obviously just and fair societies. Recall the following example from chapter 6: in order to abolish the gendered wage gap, we simply cut men's wages so that everyone will be on an equal income level (relative to the job). This strategy is deeply worrisome if it pushes some men into relative poverty, even if it achieves income parity with women undertaking comparable jobs. Outcome equality does not always yield socially just arrangements. However, leveling down is not a problem for me, but rather something desirable. Leveling down everyone's interest *violations* would result in more people being treated in nondehumanizing ways. And thus, leveling down constraining barriers to achieve parity would result in more just societies. In fact, we should aim for the state of affairs where dehumanizing treatments are leveled down as much as possible. On my view, then, the leveling-down problem is not really a problem.

Second, let's discuss problems with choices (like expensive tastes), and circumstances (like being "disabled") that supposedly plague some welfare equality views (R. Dworkin 1981a, 228–240). What makes these situations allegedly problematic is that some social agents require more in order to achieve the necessary level of welfare. Some, for example, have more expensive tastes than others, and some have supposed "natural deficiencies" that we should compensate for in order to achieve equality. So equality of welfare seems to demand that those who have a taste for champagne should be afforded more of some good (like income) than someone with simple tastes in order to make sure that the two enjoy the same level of welfare. Similarly, those who require special mobility equipment should be given more resources in order to compensate for their "bad luck" and bring their level of welfare in line with those who do not suffer from such allegedly unfortunate circumstances. With this in mind, one might think that my proposal similarly requires some social correctives like affirmative action policies in order to undermine indefensible interest violations; and this blatantly goes against the idea of equal opportunities.

However, I think that my proposal avoids the first problem of expensive tastes and demonstrates that the second problem is misconceived. The key is that my position does not aim to maximize some desired states of affairs, but rather to minimize undesired ones. And the two are not equivalent. Furthermore, there are different ways to try to correct some problematic situations. The supposedly problematic solutions to both the expensive tastes and "disabilities" worries hinge on compensating people. But my strategy differs: I do not aim to offer a model for compensating people for "bad luck" or "natural" shortcomings. Rather, I am providing a way to conceptualize the removal of structural barriers that enable people to be oppressed, unjustly discriminated against, and dominated because of "bad luck." This tells us that the expensive tastes problem is not really a problem from a social justice point of view, and so there is no need to resolve it. Simply put: it does not involve a dehumanizing instance of social injustice (i.e., oppression, unjust discrimination, or domination).

Further, we can see that the "disabilities" problem is deeply misconceived. The standard formulation of the problem assumes a picture of "disability" that is highly problematic. It assumes an ableist view that having a nonnormal or "abnormal" bodily functioning impedes well-being. This buys into the idea that nonnormal, abnormal, or "disabled" bodily functionings are defective, imperfect, nonideal, and insufficient. Those with atypical bodily functioning supposedly lack some capacities, rendering them "impaired." I have already rejected this conception in chapter 6: it grossly misunderstands the experiences of people with atypical bodily functioning and helps to maintain the normative connection between ability and normalcy. Rather, social models of disability hold that what renders certain atypical bodily functionings disabling is "the exclusion of people with certain physical and mental characteristics from major domains of social life" (Wasserman et al. 2013). Well-being is not hampered by supposed physical or mental impairments, but by the stigma and discrimination that result from perceived and labeled impairments. This tells us that the "disabilities" problem is actually about oppression, discrimination, and domination—not about being "defective" because of accidents of life. The problem is falsely conceived to begin with, and therefore the remedy is unsatisfying too: compensation in Dworkin's sense is not the answer. Rather, to remedy the situation we should remove structures that take able-bodiedness as the norm and standard against which everyone is measured; it is these structures that result in hampering the interests of those with atypical bodily functioning. Of course, this probably will involve some special provisions for those with such bodily functioning, such as mobility assistance. But they should not (I contend) be understood as compensation. Rather, such provisions involve social and institutional processes that constitute the removal of barriers that indefensibly hamper the interests of some individuals. Such schemes are the *enabling* conditions demanded in the name of equal opportunities, rather than compensation for the ways in which some fall short of being "normal."

This relates my discussion back to freedom (cf. section 9.1). As already mentioned, what I outlined above appears similar to negative freedom. It matters less what we have; not being interfered with in our attempts to attain something is rather the central point. Again, these are not just two ways of saying the same thing. Consider the following as an illustration. We might construe an example of equality of educational opportunity in the following way (closely inspired by the landmark case of *Brown v. Board of Education*).

Take a society divided by Jim Crow laws that separates schools for black and white children. Now, imagine that black children can access good-quality education in the local black schools, and so have the opportunity to attain good education. The situation is not, for example, one where black children simply have no good educational opportunities. There are equally good, though segregated, schools. But suppose that a black neighborhood is significantly closer in proximity to a high-quality white school than to the black one. Further, in order to reach their school, black children must walk along busy roads that render their school journeys dangerous. Is this situation characterized by equality of opportunity, insofar as both groups of children can access equally good educational institutions and do not have their educational opportunities hampered? I think not. This is because the black children are prevented on prejudicial grounds from attending the closer white school, regardless of whether they are able to attend the more distant black school. And prima facie the children's interests are interfered with in a manner that is indefensible (due to racism or race-based dominance). The point of equal opportunities should not just be that one has the ability to attain some socially valuable goods, but also that one is not prevented on prejudicial grounds from having the possibility to attain some other goods. It is not only what we can get, but also what we are hampered from getting and why, that matters. This resonates with freedom, but I think demonstrates that freedom is not the right correlate of dehumanization. Being free from inference is what we attain once we have achieved something more fundamental: namely, substantive equality of opportunity. So even though freedom is not irrelevant to social justice and certainly characterizes a desirable state of affairs it is not, I submit, what constitutes justice.[9]

---

[9] That said, one might think that my idea of equal opportunities is actually positive freedom in disguise. After all, equal opportunities are about us being able to achieve something—they are about us having the freedom to do something. Be that as it may, I wish to resist calling my view freedom

9.3.3. DEMOCRATIC EQUALITY

Elizabeth Anderson has developed a rich idea of democratic equality that ties freedom and equality together in a slightly different manner. Considering briefly her position is instructive in clarifying my approach further. Anderson's conception of equality, first, aims to do away with socially generated oppression, rather than correct inequalities generated by "bad luck" or natural misfortunes. It further understands equality as a social relationship rather than a pattern of distribution; and so it "regards two people as equal when each accepts the obligation to justify their actions by principles acceptable to the other, and in which they take mutual consultation, reciprocation, and recognition for granted" (Anderson 1999, 313). Finally, Anderson aims to integrate considerations of equal distribution with demands of equal recognition. Her position is similar to Young's critique of the distributive paradigm and what I said above about equal opportunities: the actual distribution of some good is less important for social justice; rather, what matters are the social relationships within which distribution takes place. The distributive mechanism normatively trumps the outcome. Hence, to live in an egalitarian community is "to be free from oppression to participate in and enjoy the goods of society, and to participate in democratic self-government" (Anderson 1999, 315). More specifically, "egalitarians should seek equality for all in the space of capabilities" in order to secure the fulfillment of social conditions for freedom (1999, 316).

Anderson has Amartya Sen's (1992) work in mind. There are certain states that constitute individual well-being and autonomy (e.g., being healthy, literate, happy, an active member of society, self-determining). These states comprise "a set of interrelated 'functionings,' consisting of beings and doings. A person's achievement in this respect can be seen as the vector in his or her functionings" (Sen 1992, 39). The set of functionings we can achieve (given the available personal, material, and social resources) constitutes our *capabilities*. For Sen, what matters from the perspective of justice is our freedom in the "space of capabilities." Our social positions are not determined by our actual achievements, but by "the *real opportunity* that we have to accomplish what we value" (Sen 1992, 31). The main point is that achieved functionings constitute people's well-being, and the capability to achieve functionings constitutes our freedom (and our real opportunities) to have well-being (Sen 1992, 40).

---

in any sense. Ultimately, it is what we are able to do in the equal opportunities sense that matters. And, in my view, putting this in terms of positive freedom would obscure the point and render the rhetoric unhelpful. Further, I am not entirely convinced that such a thing as positive freedom exists to begin with. As I see it, it is simply substantive equality of opportunity in disguise. I see no reason, then, to frame my position in terms of positive freedom.

With this view in mind, Anderson holds that individuals are entitled to "whatever capabilities are necessary to enable them to avoid or escape entanglement in oppressive social relationships," where these capabilities are "necessary for functioning as an equal citizen in a democratic state" (1999, 316). First, we must be able to function as human beings, which requires access to the means needed to sustain one's biological existence and the basic conditions of human agency (e.g., means-ends reasoning, autonomy, self-confidence, and self-determination). Second, we must be capable of functioning as equal participants in systems of cooperative production, which requires access to education, free occupational choice, and fair remuneration for one's labor (among other things). Finally, functioning as a citizen demands that we have rights to political participation (e.g., right to free speech, action, and association) (Anderson 1999, 317–318). So to be capable of functioning as a citizen we must have the ability to function in a civil society and cooperative production; and our capabilities on these levels hinge on our capabilities to function as human beings. We need not in fact function equally in these respects (e.g., some people simply have more occupational choice than others); what matters is that our capabilities to function are characterized by freedom from constraints—the resources available to us do not take away or hamper our functioning, regardless of whether we choose to study, vote, relocate, or be active members of society. Bluntly put: we need guarantees that we would be capable of functioning were we so to choose.

Anderson's view that full social justice requires capabilities to function as a human being, social participant, and a citizen has pretheoretic appeal. And (relative to my view) indefensible interest violations seem precisely to hamper such capabilities. So there appears to be common ground, and one might wonder: isn't my appeal to equal opportunities just a variant of Anderson's view? Despite apparent agreement, I wish to resist thinking about social justice within "the space of capabilities." If we were after something like full freedom from injustice or human flourishing, focusing on the space of capabilities would be perfectly appropriate. But I am not here focusing on these goals, due to which Anderson's rich account is too rich for my purposes on two grounds.

First, I am here aiming to elucidate some minimal conditions of justice, or its most fundamental basic components. A full theory of justice requires more and conceivably includes something like freedom in our "space of capabilities." But for the most basic conditions, I think that this conception should be resisted. Again, this hinges on the difference between well-being and human flourishing. Anderson's rich list of functionings on the three different levels strikes me as being more about the latter. Elucidating flourishing may be relevant when we wish to explicate the good life; but from a social justice perspective we should (I contend) focus first and foremost on that which makes good life possible. Flourishing is too subjective a measure of justice and too vulnerable to adaptive preferences and individual tastes. I take a strength of my position precisely to be that since I am not aiming to elucidate some ideal state of affairs (like human flourishing), I need not posit a contentious threshold below which life is no longer properly human. Dehumanizing ways of treating others alert us to the fact that some conduct is illegitimate. My proposal thus functions like an alarm bell: it highlights those structural nodes, individual attitudes, and subsequent actions that are in need of remedying and intervention. But in so doing, I need not take a stance on how much needs to be remedied in order to prevent problematic social circumstances from rendering our lives "improperly" human. A nonideal approach can bypass these issues by starting and remaining grounded in nonideal states of affairs exemplary of unjust ways of treating others.

Second, a focus on human flourishing may bring in too socially and culturally specific values and so, such a focus ends up appealing to an internalist conception of humanity. In fact, Anderson's Sen-inspired conception of equality appears to depend precisely on such a conception. After all, the specific *human* functionings include

> effective access to the means of sustaining one's biological existence—food, shelter, clothing, medical care—and access to basic conditions of human agency—knowledge of one's circumstances and options, the ability to deliberate about means and ends, the psychological conditions of autonomy, including the self-confidence to think and judge for oneself, freedom of thought and movement. (Anderson 1999, 318)

I contend that we should avoid appealing to an internalist conception of humanity when fixing the basic tenets of a theory of injustice. The worry is that the picture of "our" functionings will be too rich, normatively speaking. For instance, one sort of capacity to function is possessing the psychological conditions of autonomy—but what are these conditions? And is this the correct way to think about autonomy to begin with? Many feminists in relational autonomy debates would dispute this and they would reject a picture of autonomy that hinges on fulfilling some internal psychological states (cf. MacKenzie and Stoljar 2000). Again, accepting autonomy as one of "our" human functionings will be acceptable only to those who antecedently are committed to Anderson's conception of autonomy. This highlights a methodological worry: we may end up offering a theory of a complicated and difficult notion—justice—in terms of other difficult and complex notions (e.g., autonomy). Instead, we should base our elucidations of justice on more readily acceptable basic commitments, like the externalist thin understanding of humanity that I endorse.

9.4. Humanist Feminism: Final Remarks

I have suggested that substantive equality of opportunity is at the heart of nondehumanizing states of affairs. This insight, I contend, not only can be used to frame positive emancipatory public policies more generally, but also contributes to supporting the specifically feminist normative demands. Feminist theorists must be able to articulate what is wrong with the status quo, what justifies their calls for change, and what would make for a gender-just future. I take my notion of *dehumanization* to provide ways to conceptualize the first two. It enables us to identify harmful ways in which women are treated and what underlies their wrongfulness. Further, dehumanization justifies feminist calls for change: what goes wrong with certain treatments is that they are dehumanizing, and this generates a prima facie moral prohibition of those treatments. Then again, equality of opportunity in the sense discussed here offers us a glimpse of the just future: it would be one where those designated as woman could avoid certain dehumanizing interest violations that trade on sexism and/or patriarchy.

We can see that a thick conception neither of *woman* nor of *gender* plays a pivotal role in meeting these demands. Injustice is not about what women qua gendered beings are prevented from achieving, but about what women qua human being are. The barriers that dehumanization sets up prevent us from achieving something qua human, and being picked out with the terms 'woman', 'man', and 'trans*' figures in the social explanations for those barriers and their particular shapes. Gender does not explicate the wrong of those barriers; rather it features in our social explanations. And so I am proposing that a conception of humanity, not gender, ultimately does the normative work for feminist (and other emancipatory) movements. Furthermore, for this task we need not rely on an internalist conception of humanity that trades on some contentious evaluative conditions, like being autonomous, practically rational, or having the capability to function as humans with dignity. Our broadly shared human embodiment and legitimate interests that arise from such embodiment underpin my externalist picture of humanity. This avoids Antony's critique of the internalist picture and makes my starting point less contentious than (say) Nussbaum's. That humans are members of the *homo sapiens sapiens* species and "featherless bipeds" with certain cognitive dispositions is not something one can easily dispute. That a proper conception of humanity trades on Anderson's functionings or Nussbaum's capabilities to function, however, is much more open to challenge.

I contend further that my picture is not assimilationist. As already noted (cf. section 6.2), Young takes humanist feminism to embody an ideal of assimilation: it is about "identifying sexual equality with gender blindness, with measuring women and men according to the same standards and treating them in the same way" (1990, 161). Humanist feminism supposedly posits an ideal of shared humanity that does not acknowledge group differences, and thus problematically creates a picture of neutral and universal humanity that is nonsituated and insensitive to diversity. The resulting picture of equality ends up being "gender/race blind," which Young rightly critiques.

Now, in a sense I am saying that at the heart of social justice we find a single standard for all: that of substantive equality of opportunity. But this standard is not applied in a strictly speaking identical manner, and thus it avoids Young's assimilationist critique. Removing barriers to equal opportunities will hinge on illegitimate ways in which social agents are treated by others, where this judgment can only be made context specifically. Subsequent judgments about which moves in our social environments would hinder or sustain dehumanizing treatments (thus either advancing or impeding equality) will differ from one case to another. The different contours of injustice demonstrate this in highlighting that we do not encounter social injustices simpliciter, but always in some specific form and on some particular grounds. Thus, humanist feminism need not disregard social identifications and subsequent differences arising from them. Equality for me is about leveling out our respective social playing fields; but of course this leveling out depends on which barriers constrain us and to what degree. Hence, it would be utterly wrongheaded to employ a single, identical standard to achieve social justice in the name of equality. The standard that I am advocating can accommodate difference because it is realizable in multiple ways: the details of the particular situations make a huge difference to what we can legitimately do in the name of equality and to overcome dehumanization.

Nonetheless, humanist feminism advanced here is committed to a sort of universalism—but to an unproblematic kind. As I see it, feminism is for everyone, not just for women. A just feminist future would be one where sexist and patriarchal barriers faced by those designated as woman have been removed. But a just future involves more: the removal of those barriers that prevent men, trans* people, and intersexes from having opportunities to avoid interest violations where these violations too are grounded in sexist and patriarchal contours of injustice. For instance, that men are prevented from having opportunities to engage in childrearing tasks also trades on sexist beliefs (e.g., that "real" men don't change diapers) and patriarchal social arrangements (e.g., "ideal worker" norms that do not accommodate caretaking responsibilities). In this sense, feminism is not just about women; it is about all individuals facing dehumanizing treatments due to sexist and/or patriarchal injustices. So the humanist feminism on offer does not reject the basic tenet of feminism that women as a group are subject to systematic and nonaccidental forms of injustice that are due to sexism and patriarchy. It simply highlights that women are not *alone* in having their lives so infringed. This being the case, humanist feminism tells us that sexist and patriarchal social injustices do not pose problems just for women—rather, they pose problems for humanity.

{ BIBLIOGRAPHY }

Alcoff, Linda. 2006. *Visible Identities*. Oxford: Oxford University Press.

Altman, Andrew. 2011. "Discrimination." *The Stanford Encyclopedia of Philosophy* (Spring 2011 ed.), edited by Edward N. Zalta. http://plato.stanford.edu/archives/spr2011/entries/discrimination/.

Amnesty International. 2005. "Rape as a Tool of War: A Fact Sheet." http://www.amnestyusa.org/get-activist-toolkit/about-amnesty/fact-sheet/page.do?id=1101301.

Anderson, Elizabeth. 1995. "Knowledge, Human Interests, and Objectivity in Feminist Epistemology." *Philosophical Topics* 23 (2): 27–58.

——. 1999. "What Is the Point of Equality?" *Ethics* 109: 287–337.

Antony, Louise. 1998. "'Human Nature' and Its Role in Feminist Theory." In *Philosophy in a Feminist Voice*, edited by Janet Kourany, 63–91. Princeton, NJ: Princeton University Press.

——. 2000. "Natures and Norms." *Ethics* 111: 8–36.

Archard, David. 2007. "The Wrong of Rape." *Philosophical Quarterly* 57: 374–393.

——. 2008. "Informed Consent: Autonomy and Self-Ownership." *Journal of Applied Philosophy* 25 (1): 19–34.

Armstrong, D. M. 1989. *Universals: An Opinionated Introduction*. Boulder, CO: Westview Press.

Arneson, R. J. 1989. "Equality and Equal Opportunity for Welfare." *Philosophical Studies* 56 (1): 77–93.

——. 2008. "Equality of Opportunity." *The Stanford Encyclopedia of Philosophy* (Fall 2008 ed.), edited by Edward N. Zalta. http://plato.stanford.edu/archives/fall2008/entries/equal-opportunity/.

Baber, H. E. 2002. "How Bad Is Rape?" In *The Philosophy of Sex*, edited by Alan Soble, 303–316. Lanham, MD: Rowman and Littlefield.

Bach, Theodore. 2012. "Gender Is a Natural Kind with a Historical Essence." *Ethics* 122: 231–272.

Bales, Kevin. 2012. *Disposable People: New Slavery in the Global Economy*. Berkeley: University of California Press.

BBC News. 2007. "Shock at Sex Crimes in DR Congo." July 30. http://news.bbc.co.uk/go/pr/fr/-/1/hi/world/africa/6922132.stm.

Beauvoir, Simone de. 1972. *The Second Sex*. Harmondsworth: Penguin.

Beebee, Helen. 2013. "Women and Deviance in Philosophy." In *Women in Philosophy: What Needs to Change?*, edited by Katrina Hutchinson and Fiona Jenkins, 61–80. Oxford: Oxford University Press.

Benhabib, Seyla. 1992. *Situating the Self*. New York: Routledge.

Berlin, Isaiah. 1969. *Four Essays on Liberty*. Oxford: Oxford University Press.

Bettcher, T. M. 2007. "Evil Deceivers and Make-Believers: On Transphobic Violence and the Politics of Illusion." *Hypatia* 22 (3): 43–65.

———. 2009. "Feminist Perspectives on Trans Issues." *The Stanford Encyclopedia of Philosophy* (Winter 2009 ed.), edited by Edward N. Zalta. http://plato.stanford.edu/archives/win2009/entries/feminism-trans/.

———. 2013. "Trans Women and the Meaning of 'Woman.'" In *Philosophy of Sex: Contemporary Readings*, 6th ed., edited by Alan Soble, Nicholas Power, and Raja Halwani, 233–250. Lanham, MD: Rowman and Littlefield.

Blackless, Melanie, Anthony Charuvastra, Amanda Derryck, Anne Fausto-Sterling, Karl Lauzanne, and Ellen Lee. 2000. "How Sexually Dimorphic Are We? Review and Synthesis." *American Journal of Human Biology* 12 (2): 151–166.

Brison, S. J. 2002. *Aftermath: Violence and the Remaking of a Self*. Princeton, NJ: Princeton University Press.

Burgess-Jackson, Keith. 1995. "Rape and Persuasive Definition." *Canadian Journal of Philosophy* 25 (3): 415–454.

———. 2000. "A Crime against *Women*: Calhoun on the Wrongness of Rape." *Journal of Social Philosophy* 31: 286–293.

Butler, Judith. 1990. "Performative Acts and Gender Constitution." In *Performing Feminisms*, edited by Sue-Ellen Case, 270–282. Baltimore: John Hopkins University Press.

———. 1991. "Contingent Foundations: Feminism and the Question of Postmodernism." *Praxis International* 11: 150–165.

———. 1993. *Bodies That Matter*. London: Routledge.

———. 1997. *The Psychic Life of Power*. Stanford, CA: Stanford University Press.

———. [1990] 1999. *Gender Trouble*. London: Routledge.

Cappelen, Herman. 2012. *Philosophy without Intuitions*. Oxford: Oxford University Press.

Card, Claudia. 1991. "Rape as a Terrorist Institution." In *Violence, Terrorism, and Justice*, edited by R. G. Frey and C. W. Morris, 296–319. Cambridge: Cambridge University Press.

Cherry, Christopher. 1973. "Regulative Rules and Constitutive Rules." *Philosophical Quarterly* 23: 301–315.

Chodorow, Nancy. 1978. *Reproducing Mothering*. Berkeley: University of California Press.

———. 1995. "Family Structure and Feminine Personality." In *Feminism and Philosophy*, edited by Nancy Tuana and Rosemarie Tong, 43–66. Boulder, CO: Westview Press.

Chudnoff, Elijah. 2011. "What Intuitions Are Like." *Philosophy and Phenomenological Research* 82: 625–654.

Clatterbaugh, Kenneth. 1996. "Are Men Oppressed?" In *Rethinking Masculinity: Philosophical Explorations in Light of Feminism*, edited by Larry May, Robert Strikwerda, and Patrick Hopkins, 298–306. Lanham, MD: Rowman & Littlefield.

Correia, Fabrice. 2008. "Ontological Dependence." *Philosophy Compass* 3 (5): 1013–1032.

Crenshaw, Kimberlé. 1989. "Demarginalizing the Intersection of Race and Sex: A Black Feminist Critique of Antidiscrimination Doctrine, Feminist Theory and Antiracist Politics." *University of Chicago Legal Forum* 1989: 139–167.

Cudd, Ann. 2006. *Analyzing Oppression*. New York: Oxford University Press.

Cudd, Ann, and Nancy Holmstrom. 2011. *Capitalism, for and against: A Feminist Debate*. Cambridge: Cambridge University Press.

Darwall, Stephen. 1977. "Two Kinds of Respect." *Ethics* 88: 36–49.

Deaux, Kay, and Brenda Major. 1990. "A Social-Psychological Model of Gender." In *Theoretical Perspectives on Sexual Difference*, edited by Deborah Rhode, 89–99. New Haven: Yale University Press.

Delaney, Janice, Mary Jane Lupton, and Emily Toth. 1988. *Curse: A Cultural History of Menstruation*. Urbana: University of Illinois Press.

Dworkin, Gerald. 1988. *The Theory and Practice of Autonomy*. Cambridge: Cambridge University Press.

Dworkin, Ronald. 1981a. "What Is Equality? Part 1: Equality of Welfare." *Philosophy & Public Affairs* 10 (3): 185–246.

———. 1981b. "What Is Equality? Part 2: Equality of Resources." *Philosophy & Public Affairs* 10 (4): 283–345.

European Commission. 2004. *EQUAL Guide on Gender Mainstreaming*. http://ec.europa. eu/employment_social/equal_consolidated/data/document/gendermain_en.pdf.

Fausto-Sterling, Anne. 1993a. *Myths of Gender: Biological Theories about Women and Men*. 2nd ed. New York: Basic Books.

———. 1993b. "The Five Sexes: Why Male and Female Are Not Enough." *Sciences* 33 (2): 20–24.

———. 2000a. "The Five Sexes, Revisited." *Sciences* 40 (4): 18–23.

———. 2000b. *Sexing the Body*. New York: Basic Books.

———. 2005. "The Bare Bones of Sex: Part 1—Sex and Gender." *Signs* 30: 1491–1527.

Feinberg, Joel. 1984. *Harm to Others*. Oxford: Oxford University Press.

Fine, Cordelia. 2010. *Delusions of Gender: How Our Minds, Society, and Neurosexism Create Difference*. New York: W.W. Norton.

Fine, Kit. 1994. "Essence and Modality." *Philosophical Perspectives* 8: 1–16.

Fricker, Miranda. 2007. *Epistemic Injustice*. Oxford: Oxford University Press.

Friedan, Betty. 1963. *The Feminine Mystique*. Harmondsworth: Penguin.

Frye, Marilyn. 1983. *The Politics of Reality: Essays in Feminist Theory*. Trumansburg, NY: Crossing Press.

———. 1996. "The Necessity of Differences: Constructing a Positive Category of Women." *Signs* 21: 991–1010.

———. 2011. "Metaphors of Being a φ." In *Feminist Metaphysics: Explorations in the Ontology of Sex, Gender and the Self*, edited by Charlotte Witt, 85–95. Dordrecht: Springer.

Garcia, J. L. A. 2001. "The Heart of Racism." In *Race and Racism*, edited by Bernard Boxill, 257–296. Oxford: Oxford University Press.

Gardner, John, and Stephen Shute. 2000. "The Wrongness of Rape." In *Oxford Essays in Jurisprudence*, edited by Jeremy Horder, 193–219. Oxford: Oxford University Press.

Gatens, Moira. 1996. *Imaginary Bodies*. London: Routledge.

Gauthier, David. 1986. *Morals by Agreement*. New York: Oxford University Press.

Gendler, T. S. 2008. "Alief and Belief." *Journal of Philosophy* 105: 634–663.

Gettleman, J. 2007. "Rape Epidemic Raises Trauma of Congo War." *New York Times*, October 7.

Gilbert, Margaret. 1989. *On Social Facts*. New York: Routledge.

Glasgow, Joshua. 2009. *A Theory of Race*. New York: Routledge.

Gorman, C. 1992. "Sizing up the Sexes." *Time*, January 20.

Grillo, Trina. 2006. "Anti-essentialism and Intersectionality." In *Theorizing Feminisms*, edited by Elizabeth Hackett and Sally Haslanger, 30–40. New York: Oxford University Press.

Grosz, Elizabeth. 1994. *Volatile Bodies: Toward a Corporeal Feminism*. Bloomington: Indiana University Press.

Hale, Jacob. 1996. "Are Lesbians Women?" *Hypatia* 11 (2): 94–121.

Hampton, Jean. 1999. "Defining Wrong and Defining Rape." In *The Most Detestable Crime: New Philosophical Essays on Rape*, edited by Keith Burgess-Jackson, 118–156. Oxford: Oxford University Press.

———. 2002. "Feminist Contractarianism." In *A Mind of One's Own*, edited by Louise Antony and Charlotte Witt, 337–368. Boulder, CO: Westview Press.

Harris, Angela. 1993. "Race and Essentialism in Feminist Legal Theory." In *Feminist Legal Theory: Foundations*, edited by D. Kelly Weisberg, 248–258. Philadelphia: Temple University Press.

Harvey, Jean. 1999. *Civilized Oppression*. Lanham, MD: Rowman & Littlefield.

———. 2010. "Victims, Resistance, and Civilized Oppression." *Journal of Social Philosophy* 41: 13–27.

Haslanger, Sally. 1995. "Ontology and Social Construction." *Philosophical Topics* 23 (2): 95–125.

———. 2000. "Gender and Race: (What) Are They? (What) Do We Want Them to Be?" *Noûs* 34: 31–55.

———. 2002. "On Being Objective and Being Objectified." In *A Mind of One's Own*, edited by Louise Antony and Charlotte Witt, 85–125. Boulder, CO: Westview Press.

———. 2003a. "Future Genders? Future Races?" *Philosophic Exchange* 34: 4–27.

———. 2003b. "Social Construction: The 'Debunking' Project." In *Socializing Metaphysics: The Nature of Social Reality*, edited by Frederick Schmitt, 301–325. Lanham: Rowman & Littlefield.

———. 2004. "Oppressions: Racial and Other." In *Racism, Philosophy and Mind*, edited by Michael Levine and Tamas Pataki, 97–123. Ithaca, NY: Cornell University Press.

———. 2005. "What Are We Talking About? The Semantics and Politics of Social Kinds." *Hypatia* 20 (4): 10–26.

———. 2006. "What Good Are Our Intuitions?" *Proceedings of the Aristotelian Society* Supplementary Volume 80: 89–118.

———. 2011. "Ideology, Generics and Common Ground." In *Feminist Metaphysics: Explorations in the Ontology of Sex, Gender and the Self*, edited by Charlotte Witt, 179–207. Dordrecht: Springer.

Haslanger, Sally, Nancy Tuana, and Peg O'Connor. 2015. "Topics in Feminism." *The Stanford Encyclopedia of Philosophy* (Fall 2015 ed.), edited by Edward N. Zalta. http://plato.stanford.edu/archives/fall2015/entries/feminism-topics/.

Hellman, Deborah. 2011. *When Is Discrimination Wrong?* Cambridge, MA: Harvard University Press.

Herbelot, Aurélie, Eva von Redecker, and Johanna Müller. 2012. "Distributional techniques for philosophical enquiry." *Proceedings of the 6th European Association for Computational Linguistics Workshop on Language Technology for Cultural Heritage, Social Sciences, and Humanities,* Avignon: 45–54.

Heyes, Cressida. 2000. *Line Drawings*. Ithaca & London: Cornell University Press.

———. 2012. "Identity Politics." *The Stanford Encyclopedia of Philosophy* (Spring 2012 ed.), edited by Edward N. Zalta. http://plato.stanford.edu/archives/spr2012/entries/identity-politics/.

Hindriks, F. A. 2006. "Acceptance-Dependence: A Social Kind Of Response Dependence." *Pacific Philosophical Quarterly* 87: 481–498.

Holroyd, Jules. 2012. "Responsibility for Implicit Bias." *Journal of Social Philosophy* 43: 274–306.

hooks, bell. 2000. *Feminist Theory: From Margins to Center.* 2nd ed. London: Pluto Press.

Human Rights Watch. 2002. "The War within the War." http://www.hrw.org/node/78573.

Hutchison, Katrina, and Fiona Jenkins, eds. 2013. *Women in Philosophy: What Needs to Change?* Oxford: Oxford University Press.

Irigaray, Luce. 1985. *Speculum of the Other Woman.* Ithaca, NY: Cornell University Press.

Jackson, F., and P. Pettit. 1992. "Structural Explanation in Social Theory." In *Reduction, Explanation, and Realism,* edited by D. Charles and K. Lennon, 97–131. Oxford: Clarendon.

Jaggar, Alison. 1983a. *Feminist Politics and Human Nature.* Lanham, MD: Rowman & Littlefield Publishers, Inc.

———. 1983b. "Human Biology in Feminist Theory: Sexual Equality Reconsidered." In *Beyond Domination: New Perspectives on Women and Philosophy,* edited by Carol Gould, 21–42. Lanham, MD: Rowman & Littlefield.

Jost, J. T., L. A. Rudman, I. V. Blair, D. R. Carney, N. Dasgupta, J. Glaser, and C. D. Hardin. 2009. "The Existence of Implicit Bias is Beyond Reasonable Doubt: A Refutation of Ideological and Methodological Objections and Executive Summary of Ten Studies that no Manager Should Ignore." *Research in Organizational Behavior* 29: 39–69.

Karkazis, Katrina, Rebecca Jordan-Young, Georgiann Davis, and Silvia Camporesi. 2012. "Out Of Bounds? A Critique Of The New Policies On Hyperandrogenism In Elite Female Athletes." *The American Journal of Bioethics* 12 (7): 3–16.

Kelly, Daniel, and Erica Roedder. 2008. "Racial Cognition and the Ethics of Implicit Bias." *Philosophy Compass* 3: 522–540.

Khader, Serena. 2011. *Adaptive Preferences and Women's Empowerment.* New York: Oxford University Press.

Kimmel, Michael. 2000. *The Gendered Society.* New York: Oxford University Press.

Langton, Rae. 1995. "Sexual Solipsism" *Philosophical Topics* 23 (2): 149–187.

———. 2009. *Sexual Solipsism.* Oxford: Oxford University Press.

Laqueur, Thomas. 1990. *Making Sex: Body and Gender from the Greeks to Freud.* Cambridge, MA: Harvard University Press.

Lippert-Rasmussen, Kasper. 2006. "The Badness of Discrimination." *Ethical Theory and Moral Practice* 9 (2): 167–185.

Lloyd, Genevieve. 1993. *The Man of Reason: 'Male' and 'Female' in Western Philosophy.* 2nd ed. London: Routledge.

Longino, H. E. 1990. *Science as Social Knowledge: Values and Objectivity in Scientific Inquiry.* Princeton, NJ: Princeton University Press.

Lovett, Frank. 2010. *A General Theory of Domination and Justice.* Oxford: Oxford University Press.

Ludwig, Kirk. 2010. "Intuitions and Relativity." *Philosophical Psychology* 23 (4): 427–445.

Mackenzie, Catriona, and Natalie Stoljar, eds. 2000. *Relational Autonomy.* Oxford: Oxford University Press.

MacKinnon, Catharine. 1987. *Feminism Unmodified.* Cambridge, MA: Harvard University Press.

———. 1989. *Toward a Feminist Theory of State*. Cambridge, MA: Harvard University Press.

Mallon, Ron. 2004. "Passing, Traveling and Reality: Social Constructionism and the Metaphysics of Race." *Noûs* 38 (4): 644–673.

Mandelbaum, Eric. 2013. "Against Alief." *Philosophical Studies* 165: 197–211.

Manne, K. 2014. "In Ferguson and Beyond: Punishing Humanity." *New York Times*, October 12. http://opinionator.blogs.nytimes.com/2014/10/12/in-ferguson-and-beyond-punishing-humanity/?_r=0.

Martin, J. R. 1994. "Methodological Essentialism, False Difference, and Other Dangerous Traps." *Signs* 19: 630–655.

Médecins Sans Frontières. 2004. "'I Have No Joy, No Peace of Mind.' Medical, Psychological, and Socio-economic Consequences of Sexual Violence in Eastern DRC." http://www.msf.org/sites/msf.org/files/old-cms/fms/article-images/2004-00/drcreport-nojoy.pdf.

Merricks, Trenton. 2001. *Objects and Persons*. Oxford: Clarendon.

Mikkola, Mari. 2006. "Elizabeth Spelman, Gender Realism, and Women." *Hypatia* 21 (4): 77–96.

———. 2007. "Gender Sceptics and Feminist Politics." *Res Publica* 13: 361–380.

———. 2012. "Feminist Perspectives on Sex and Gender." *The Stanford Encyclopedia of Philosophy* (Fall 2012 ed.), edited by Edward N. Zalta. http://plato.stanford.edu/archives/fall2012/entries/feminism-gender/.

———. Forthcoming 2016. "Gender Essentialism and Anti-essentialism." In *Routledge Companion to Feminist Philosophy*, edited by Ann Garry, Serene Khader and Alison Stone. New York: Routledge.

Mill, J. S. 1974. *On Liberty*. Harmondsworth: Penguin.

Millett, Kate. 1971. *Sexual Politics*. London: Granada.

Mills, C. W. 2005. "'Ideal Theory' as Ideology." *Hypatia* 20 (3): 165–183.

Moi, Toril. 1999. *What Is a Woman?* Oxford: Oxford University Press.

Moreau, Sophia. 2010. "What Is Discrimination?" *Philosophy & Public Affairs* 38: 143–179.

Nagl-Docekal, Herta. 1999. *Feministische Philosophie: Ergebnisse, Probleme, Perspektiven*. Frankfurt am Main: Fischer-Taschenbuch-Verlag.

Narayan, Uma. 1998. "Essence of Culture and a Sense of History: A Feminist Critique of Cultural Essentialism." *Hypatia* 13 (2): 86–106.

Nicholson, Linda. 1994. "Interpreting Gender." *Signs* 20: 79–105.

———. 1998. "Gender." In *A Companion to Feminist Philosophy*, edited by Alison Jaggar and Iris Marion Young, 289–297. Malden, MA: Blackwell.

Nolen, S. 2005. "'Not Women Anymore. . .' The Congo's Rape Survivors Face Pain, Shame and AIDS." *Ms. Magazine*, http://www.msmagazine.com/spring2005/congo.asp.

Nussbaum, Martha. 1995a. "Aristotle on Human Nature and the Foundations of Ethics." In *World, Mind, and Ethics*, edited by J.E.J. Altham and Ross Harrison, 86–131. Cambridge: Cambridge University Press.

———. 1995b. "Human Capabilities, Female Human Beings." In *Women, Culture and Development*, edited by Martha Nussbaum and Jonathan Glover, 61–104. Oxford: Clarendon Press.

———. 1995c. "Objectification." In *Philosophy and Public Affairs* 24: 249–291.

———. 2000. *Women and Human Development: The Capabilities Approach*. Cambridge: Cambridge University Press.

———. 2001. "Symposium on Amartya Sen's philosophy: 5 Adaptive Preferences and Women's Options." *Economics and Philosophy* 17: 67–88.

Okin, S. M. 1989. *Gender, Justice and the Family.* New York: Basic Books.

O'Neill, Onora. 1987. "Abstraction, Idealization and Ideology in Ethics." *Royal Institute of Philosophy Lecture Series.* Cambridge: Cambridge University Press.

Orange, Richard. 2012. "All Dads Together: My New Life Among Sweden's Latte Pappas." *The Guardian,* November 18. http://www.theguardian.com/money/2012/nov/18/ swedish-latte-pappa-shared-childcare.

Papadaki, Lina. 2012. "Feminist Perspectives on Objectification." *The Stanford Encyclopedia of Philosophy* (Winter 2012 ed.), edited by Edward N. Zalta. http://plato.stanford.edu/ archives/win2012/entries/feminism-objectification/.

Peterman, Amber, Tia Palermo, and Caryn Bredenkamp. 2011. "Estimates and Determinants of Sexual Violence Against Women in the Democratic Republic of Congo." *American Journal of Public Health* 101: 1060–1067.

Pettit, Philip. 2011. "The Instability of Freedom as Noninterference: The Case of Isaiah Berlin." *Ethics* 121: 693–716.

Price, H. H. 1953. *Thinking and Experience.* London: Hutchinson's University Library.

Prokhovnik, Raia. 1999. *Rational Woman.* London: Routledge.

Quine, W. V. O. 1953. *From a Logical Point of View.* Cambridge, MA: Harvard University Press.

Rapaport, Elizabeth. 2002. "Generalizing Gender: Reason and Essence in the Legal Thought of Catharine MacKinnon." In *A Mind of One's Own,* edited by Louise Antony and Charlotte Witt, 254–272. Boulder, CO: Westview Press.

Rawls, John. 1971. *A Theory of Justice.* Cambridge, MA: Harvard University Press.

Reitan, Eric. 2001. "Rape as an Essentially Contested Concept." *Hypatia* 16 (2): 43–66.

Renzetti, Claire, and Daniel Curran. 1992. "Sex-Role Socialization." In *Feminist Philosophies,* edited by Janet Kourany, James Sterba, and Rosemarie Tong, 31–47. New Jersey: Prentice Hall.

Rodriguez-Pereyra, Gonzalo. 2002. *Resemblance Nominalism.* Oxford: Oxford University Press.

Rogers, Lesley. 1999. *Sexing the Brain.* London: Phoenix.

Rubin, Gayle. 1975. "The Traffic in Women: Notes on the 'Political Economy' of Sex." In *Toward an Anthropology of Women,* edited by Rayna Reiter, 157–210. New York: Monthly Review Press.

Rudman, L. A., and R. D. Ashmore. 2007. "Discrimination and the Implicit Association Test." *Group Processes & Intergroup Relations* 10: 359–372.

Russell, Bertrand. 1967. *The Problems of Philosophy.* Oxford: Oxford University Press.

Salih, Sara. 2002. *Judith Butler.* London: Routledge.

Sartre, Jean-Paul. 1976. *Critique of Dialectical Reason.* London: New Left Books.

Saul, Jennifer. 2003. *Feminism: Issues and Arguments.* Oxford: Oxford University Press.

———. 2006. "Gender and Race." *Proceedings of the Aristotelian Society* Supplementary volume 80: 119–143.

———. 2012a. "Politically Significant Terms and Philosophy of Language." In *Out from the Shadows: Analytical Feminist Contributions to Traditional Philosophy,* edited by Sharon Crasnow and Anita Superson, 195–216. New York: Oxford University Press.

——. 2012b. "Ranking Exercises in Philosophy and Implicit Bias." *Journal of Social Philosophy* 43: 256–273.

Schaffer, Jonathan. 2009. "On What Grounds What." In *Metametaphysics: New Essays on the Foundations of Ontology*, edited by David Chalmers, David Manley, and Ryan Wasserman, 347–383. Oxford: Oxford University Press.

Schroeter, Laura. 2004. "The Limits of Conceptual Analysis." *Pacific Philosophical Quarterly* 85: 425–453.

Searle, John. 1969. *Speech Acts: An Essay in the Philosophy of Language*. Cambridge: Cambridge University Press.

——. 1993. "Rationality and Realism: What Is At stake?" *Daedalus* 122: 55–83.

——. 1995. *The Construction of Social Reality*. London: Penguin.

Sen, Amartya. 1992. *Inequality Reexamined*. Cambridge, MA: Harvard University Press.

Shafer, Carolyn, and Marilyn Frye. 1981. "Rape and Respect." In *Feminism and Philosophy*, edited by Mary Vetterling-Braggin, Frederick A. Elliston, and Jane English, 333–346. Totowa, NJ: Rowman and Littlefield.

Shelby, Tommie. 2002. "Is Racism in the 'Heart'?" *Journal of Social Philosophy* 33: 411–420.

Silvers, Anita. 2012. "Feminist Perspectives on Disability." *The Stanford Encyclopedia of Philosophy* (Summer 2012 ed.), edited by Edward N. Zalta. http://plato.stanford.edu/archives/sum2012/entries/feminism-disability/.

Slegh, H., G. Barker, B. Ruratotoye, and T. Shand. 2012. "Gender Relations, Sexual Violence and the Effects of Conflict on Women and Men in North Kivu, Eastern Democratic Republic of Congo: Preliminary Results of the International Men and Gender Equality Survey (IMAGES)." *Sonke Gender Justice Network* and *Promundo-US*. http://www.promundo.org.br/en/reports/.

Smith, D. L. 2013. "Indexically Yours: Why Being Human Is More Like Being Here Than It Is Like Being Water." In *The Politics of Species*, edited by Raymond Corbey and Annette Lanjouw, 40–52. Cambridge: Cambridge University Press.

Spelke, Elizabeth. 2005. "Sex Differences in Intrinsic Aptitude for Mathematics and Science?" *American Psychologist* 60: 950–958.

Spelman, Elizabeth. [1988] 1990. *Inessential Woman: Problems of Exclusion in Feminist Thought*. Boston: Beacon Press.

Stoljar, Natalie. 1995. "Essence, Identity and the Concept of Woman." *Philosophical Topics* 23 (2): 261–293.

——. 2000. "The Politics of Identity and the Metaphysics of Diversity." In *Proceedings of the 20th World Congress of Philosophy*, edited by Daniel Dahlstrom, 21–30. Bowling Green, OH: Bowling Green State University.

——. 2011. "Different Women: Gender and the Realism-Nominalism Debate." In *Feminist Metaphysics: Explorations in the Ontology of Sex, Gender and the Self*, edited by Charlotte Witt, 27–46. Dordrecht: Springer.

Stone, Alison. 2004. "Essentialism and Anti-essentialism in Feminist Philosophy." *Journal of Moral Philosophy* 1: 135–153.

——. 2007. *An Introduction to Feminist Philosophy*. Cambridge: Polity Press.

Sundelin, Jenny. 2008. "Paradise for families?" *The Guardian*, February 18. http://www.theguardian.com/society/2008/feb/18/children.parents.

Sussman, David. 2005. "What Is Wrong with Torture?" *Philosophy and Public Affairs* 33: 1–33.

Sveinsdóttir, A. K. 2011. "The Metaphysics of Sex and Gender." In *Feminist Metaphysics: Explorations in the Ontology of Sex, Gender and the Self*, edited by Charlotte Witt, 47–65. Dordrecht: Springer.

Swoyer, Chris, and Francesco Orilia. 2011. "Properties." *The Stanford Encyclopedia of Philosophy* (Winter 2011 ed.), edited by Edward N. Zalta. http://plato.stanford.edu/archives/win2011/entries/properties/.

Tanesini, Alessandra. 1996. "Whose Language?" In *Women, Knowledge, and Reality*, edited by Ann Garry and Marilyn Pearsall, 353–365. London: Routledge.

Tessman, Lisa, ed. 2009. *Feminist Ethics and Social and Political Philosophy: Theorizing the Non-ideal*. Dordrecht: Springer.

van Inwagen, Peter. 1990. *Material Beings*. Ithaca, NY: Cornell University Press.

Walby, Sylvia. 2002. "Feminism in a Global Era." *Economy and Society* 31: 533–557.

Ward, Lucy. 2007. "Baby-Time Initiative Fails Most New Fathers." *Guardian*, June 2. http://www.guardian.co.uk/society/2007/jun/02/childrensservices.workandcareer.

Warren, M. A. 1977. "Secondary Sexism and Quota Hiring." *Philosophy & Public Affairs* 6: 240–261.

Wasserman, D., A. Asch, J. Blustein, and D. Putnam. 2013. "Disability: Definitions, Models, Experience." *The Stanford Encyclopedia of Philosophy* (Fall 2013 ed.), edited by Edward N. Zalta. http://plato.stanford.edu/archives/fall2013/entries/disability/.

Webster, Hutton. 1942. *Taboo: A Sociological Study*. Stanford, CA: Stanford University Press.

Whisnant, Rebecca. 2013. "Feminist Perspectives on Rape." *The Stanford Encyclopedia of Philosophy* (Fall 2013 ed.), edited by Edward N. Zalta. http://plato.stanford.edu/archives/fall2013/entries/feminism-rape/.

Williams, Joan. 2000. *Unbending Gender*. Oxford: Oxford University Press.

Witt, Charlotte. 1995. "Anti-essentialism in Feminist Theory." *Philosophical Topics* 23 (2): 321–344.

———. 2011a. *The Metaphysics of Gender*. Oxford: Oxford University Press.

———. 2011b. "What Is Gender Essentialism?" In *Feminist Metaphysics: Explorations in the Ontology of Sex, Gender and the Self*, edited by Charlotte Witt, 11–25. Dordrecht: Springer.

Wittgenstein, Ludwig. 1997. *Philosophical Investigations*. Oxford: Blackwell.

Young, Iris Marion. 1990. *Justice and the Politics of Difference*. Princeton, NJ: Princeton University Press.

———. 1997. "Gender as Seriality: Thinking about Women as a Social Collective." In Iris Marion Young, *Intersecting Voices*, 12–37. Princeton, NJ: Princeton University Press.

Zack, Naomi. 2005. *Inclusive Feminism*. Lanham, MD: Rowman & Littlefield.

{ INDEX }